Teen Titans

A KID'S GAME

Dan DiDio VP-Editorial
Eddie Berganza & Ivan Cohen
Editors-original series
Tom Palmer, Jr.
Associate Editor-original series
Bob Greenberger
Senior Editor-collected edition
Robbin Brosterman Senior Art Director
Paul Levitz President & Publisher
Georg Brewer VP-Design & Retail
Product Development
Richard Bruning
Senior VP-Creative Director
Patrick Caldon
Senior VP-Finance & Operations
Chris Caramalis VP-Finance
Terri Cunningham VP-Managing Editor
Alison Gill VP-Manufacturing
Rich Johnson VP-Book Trade Sales
Hank Kanalz
VP-General Manager-WildStorm
Lillian Laserson
Senior VP & General Counsel
Jim Lee VP-Editorial Director-WildStorm
David McKillips
VP-Advertising & Custom Publishing
John Nee VP-Business Development
Gregory Noveck
Senior VP-Creative Affairs
Cheryl Rubin
Senior VP-Brand Management
Bob Wayne VP-Sales & Marketing

TEEN TITANS: A KID'S GAME
Published by DC Comics. Cover,
introduction, and compilation copyright
© 2004 DC Comics. All Rights Reserved.
Originally published in single magazine
form in TEEN TITANS 1-7, TEEN
TITANS/OUTSIDERS SECRET FILES
2003. Copyright © 2003 DC Comics.
All Rights Reserved. All characters,
their distinctive likenesses and related
elements featured in this publication
are trademarks of DC Comics.
The stories, characters and incidents
featured in this publication are entirely
fictional. DC Comics does not read or
accept unsolicited submissions of
ideas, stories or artwork.

DC Comics, 1700 Broadway, New
York, NY 10019. A Warner Bros.
Entertainment Company. Printed in
Canada. Second Printing.
ISBN: 1-4012-0308-6.
Cover illustration by Michael Turner.

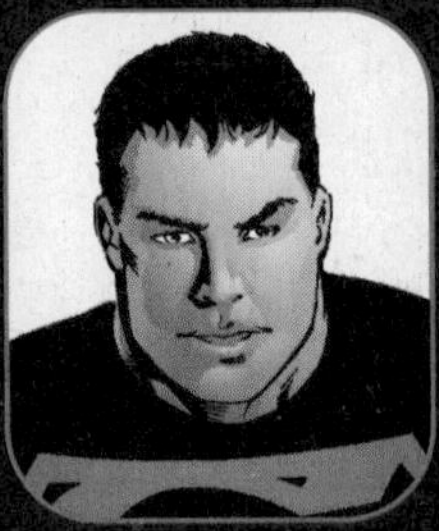

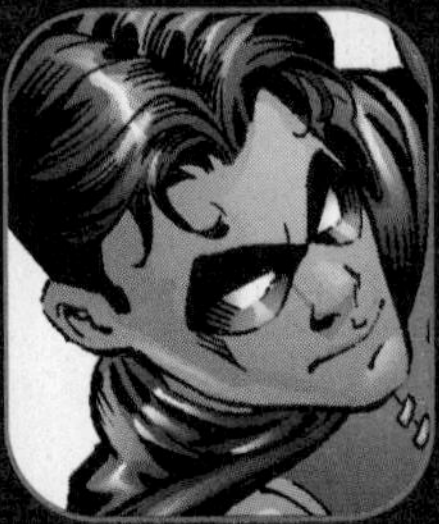

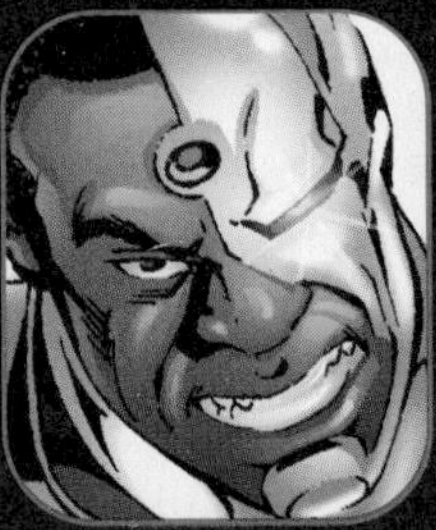

Teen Titans

A KID'S GAME

Geoff Johns Writer

Mike McKone & Tom Grummett Pencillers

Marlo Alquiza & Nelson Inkers

Jeromy Cox Colorist

Comicraft Letterer

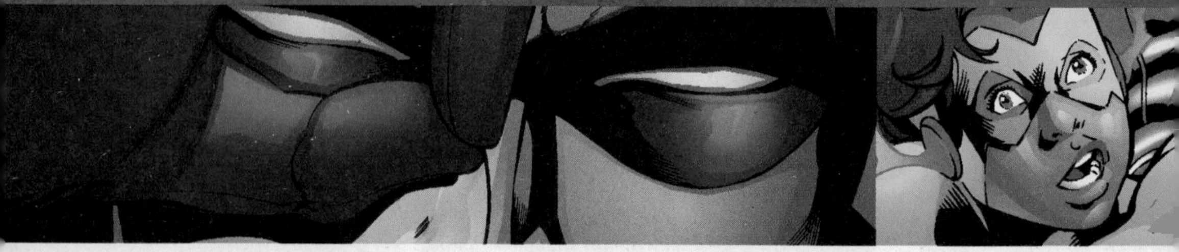

I N T R O D U C T I O N

Teenage super-heroes rule.

And hanging out together, they rule even more.

Way back in 1940, DC introduced the first teenaged sidekick, Robin the Boy Wonder, in DETECTIVE COMICS #38. Bob Kane and Bill Finger created the character, in an attempt to create someone the kids in the audience could relate to. Sales not only went up, they almost doubled.

See, there's a reason sidekicks sprung up throughout the land of comic books. Everyone had one. Aquaman had Aqualad, Green Arrow had Speedy, the Flash had Kid Flash. And with the success of the Justice League of America, DC decided to introduce the teenage equivalent. In 1964, under the guidance of editors Murray Boltinoff and George Kashdan, writer Bob Haney and artist Bruno Premiani gave us THE BRAVE AND THE BOLD #54. It featured Robin, Aqualad and Kid Flash joining together to stop a Pied Piper-like criminal named Mr. Twister. It wasn't until a year later in THE BRAVE AND THE BOLD #60 that the team officially gained the name TEEN TITANS and added Wonder Girl to their roster.

Proving a successful feature, the TEEN TITANS soon got their own magazine because the readers really did demand it. Throughout the early years, the Teen Titans picked up new members like Speedy, telepath Lilith, and caveboy Gnarrk. The first series of TEEN TITANS ended with issue #43 in 1973.

TEEN TITANS was briefly revived in 1976 with issue #44 and new members Joker's Daughter, Mal Duncan (a.k.a.

Hornblower), Bumblebee and, my personal favorite, the Golden Eagle. A second group of Titans, Teen Titans West, formed as well, including members Bat-Girl, Hawk & Dove and Beast Boy. This time it lasted until #53, ending in 1978.

It's amazing to think that the monumental NEW TEEN TITANS debuted only two years later when editor Len Wein, writer Marv Wolfman and super-star artist George Pérez created one of DC Comics' most successful monthly titles of all time. Robin, Kid Flash and Wonder Girl were joined by Changeling, former junior member of a team of "super-freaks" called the Doom Patrol, and new characters Cyborg, Starfire and the mysterious Raven. And, to me, the most impressive thing with these three new Titans was the thought and energy that went into creating them. Len, Marv and George didn't just come up with super-powers or gimmicks for these new Titans, they had incredibly deep histories and personalities. And each of them acted as a doorway to a different type of adventure. Starfire was an extraterrestrial, Raven the daughter of a dimensional demon, Cyborg the incredibly powerful hi-tech former jock, and Changeling a youth whose long lost original team was still missing in action. These creators not only crafted modern iconic DC characters, they also opened themselves up to worlds of storytelling.

For years, the Titans dominated the sales charts, and though George eventually moved on, he returned from time to time. Marv scripted the series, and its direct sales-only Baxter series, which debuted in 1984, for sixteen years. Sixteen years. And during those record-setting years, characters like Deathstroke the Terminator, Brother Blood, Jericho, Trigon, Kole, the Fearsome Five and the Ravager were all introduced. NEW TITANS, as it was then called, ended with issue #130 in 1996.

By then, most of the "teen" Titans had grown up. Robin had become Nightwing, Speedy changed his identity to Arsenal, Aqualad was transformed into Tempest, Kid Flash took over the mantle of the Flash, and Wonder Girl had gone through several different identities before finally settling on simply Donna Troy.

At the same time, the "growing up" of the original Teen Titans allowed for a new generation of teenaged heroes to enter into the DC Universe. Superboy, the clone of Superman, appeared in Metropolis after the world believed Superman had died. A third Robin, Tim Drake, was leaping through the streets of Gotham City. The Flash's grandson, Bart Allen, journeyed to the present from the future to learn how to be a hero as Impulse. And Cassie Sandsmark became the new Wonder Girl in the pages of WONDER WOMAN after she borrowed ancient artifacts that bestowed upon her the powers of flight and strength.

The face of the DC Universe was changing.

It was the series by Marv and George and the great crop of new young heroes exploding in the DC Universe that inspired everything that has become this volume of TEEN TITANS. Without them, without their creations and inspiration, this book simply would not exist.

Which leads up to one of my first meetings with Dan DiDio. It was at a convention in 2001, and Dan was just stepping into his new role as editor-in-chief of the DC Universe. I had been working for DC for about three years, and was having an absolute blast with all of the characters. As Dan and I walked through the rows of comics around us, he said to me, "I hear you like the Teen Titans. Do you want to relaunch the book?" There was no hesitation. I said, "Yes." I immediately pitched Dan the ending of the first issue, which will be the first chapter in this collection, and we were off and running.

The book was being edited by Eddie Berganza (with assists by Titans neophyte Tom Palmer, Jr.), whose passion for the Titans is overwhelming. Eddie mentioned the artist they wanted to team me up with. Mr. Michael McKone. I was floored. I've loved Mike's work for ages, and he was ready to jump aboard. It was so funny. I remember reading a story about when George Pérez told Marvel he was going to DC to do TEEN TITANS. They thought he was crazy. When Mike told Marvel he was going to DC to do TEEN TITANS, guess what? They thought he was crazy. We all wanted this new relaunch to be a success, but no one, I think, was prepared for just how big a success this volume of TEEN TITANS would be. With the TEEN TITANS series on Cartoon Network and the excitement around these characters among comics readers, it's a great time to be a Titans fan.

I couldn't be prouder of the stories you're about to read. Mike McKone, Marlo Alquiza, Tom Grummett, Nelson, Jeromy Cox and Richard Starkings all did a beautiful job. Enjoy it. And come back for more.

Geoff Johns
November, 2003

Geoff Johns currently writes TEEN TITANS, JSA, and THE FLASH for DC Comics. He lives with his wife, Anissa – whose favorite Teen Titan is Raven – and their dog, Beau in, Sherman Oaks, California.

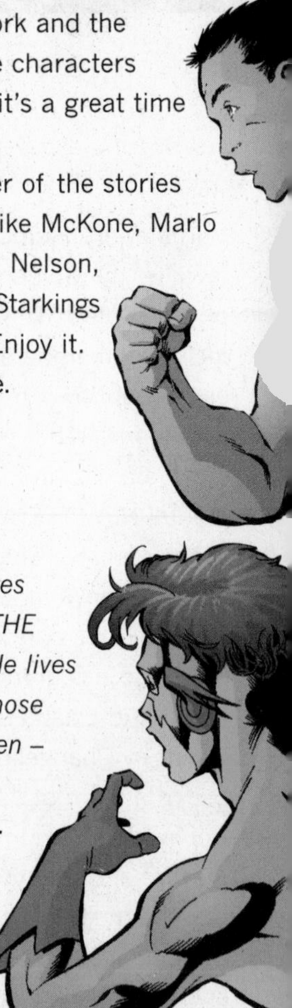

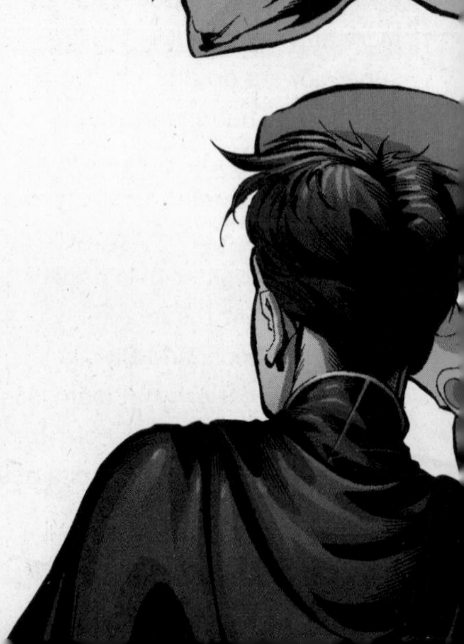

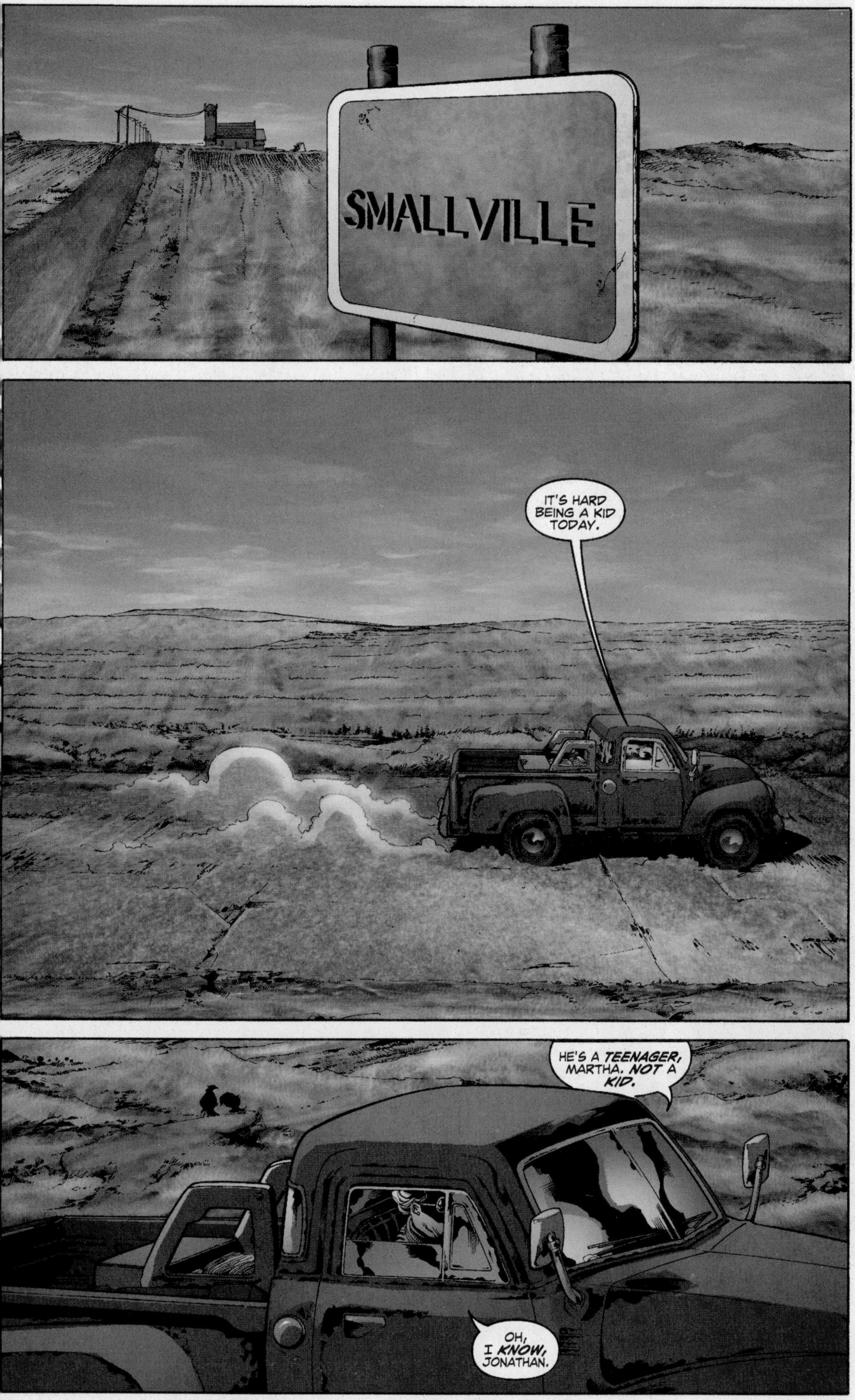
SMALLVILLE
IT'S HARD BEING A KID TODAY.
HE'S A TEENAGER, MARTHA. NOT A KID.
OH, I KNOW, JONATHAN.

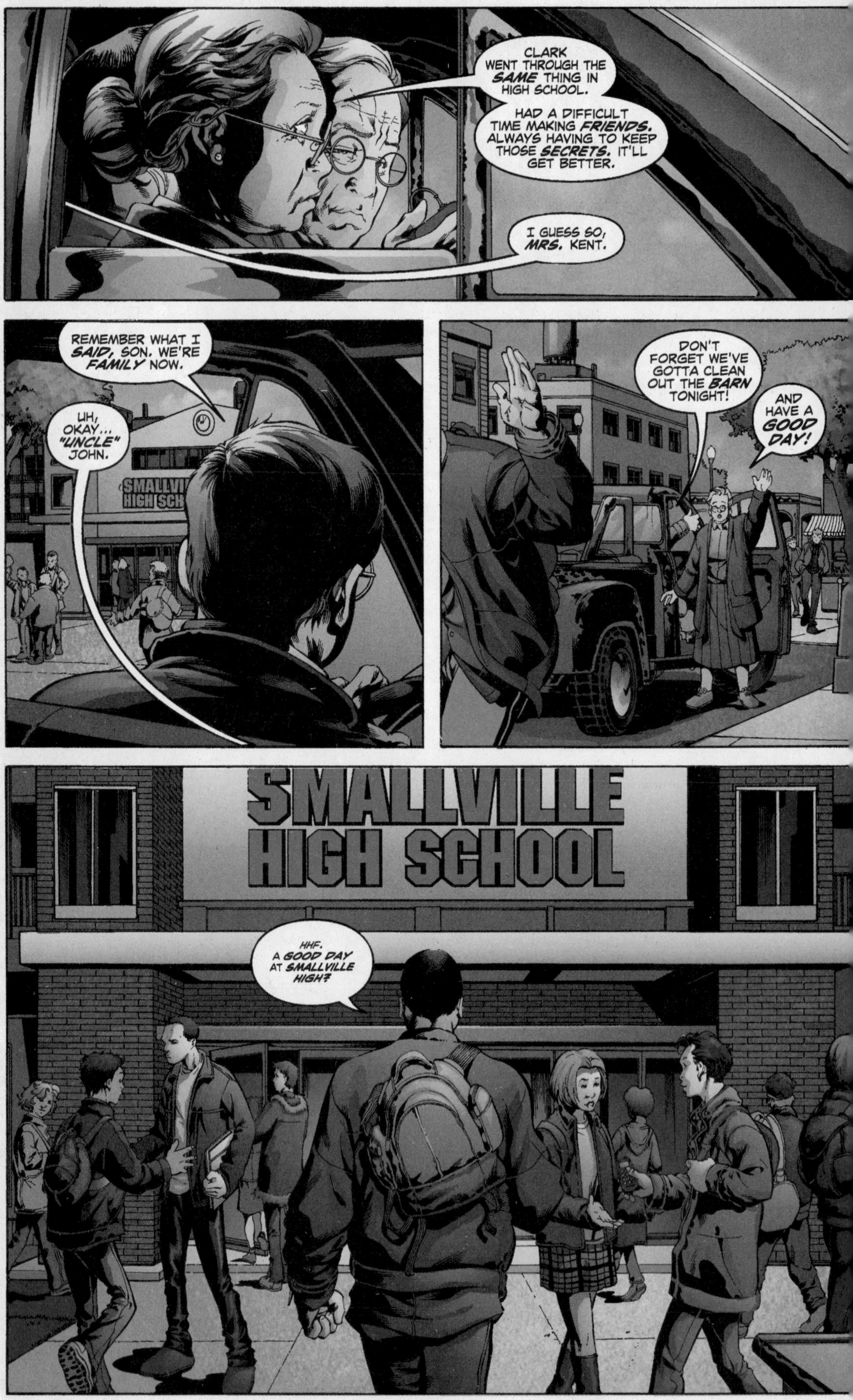
CLARK WENT THROUGH THE SAME THING IN HIGH SCHOOL.
HAD A DIFFICULT TIME MAKING FRIENDS. ALWAYS HAVING TO KEEP THOSE SECRETS. IT'LL GET BETTER.
I GUESS SO, MRS. KENT.
REMEMBER WHAT I SAID, SON. WE'RE FAMILY NOW.
UH, OKAY... "UNCLE" JOHN.
DON'T FORGET WE'VE GOTTA CLEAN OUT THE BARN TONIGHT!
AND HAVE A GOOD DAY!
SMALLVILLE HIGH SCHOOL
HHF. A GOOD DAY AT SMALLVILLE HIGH?

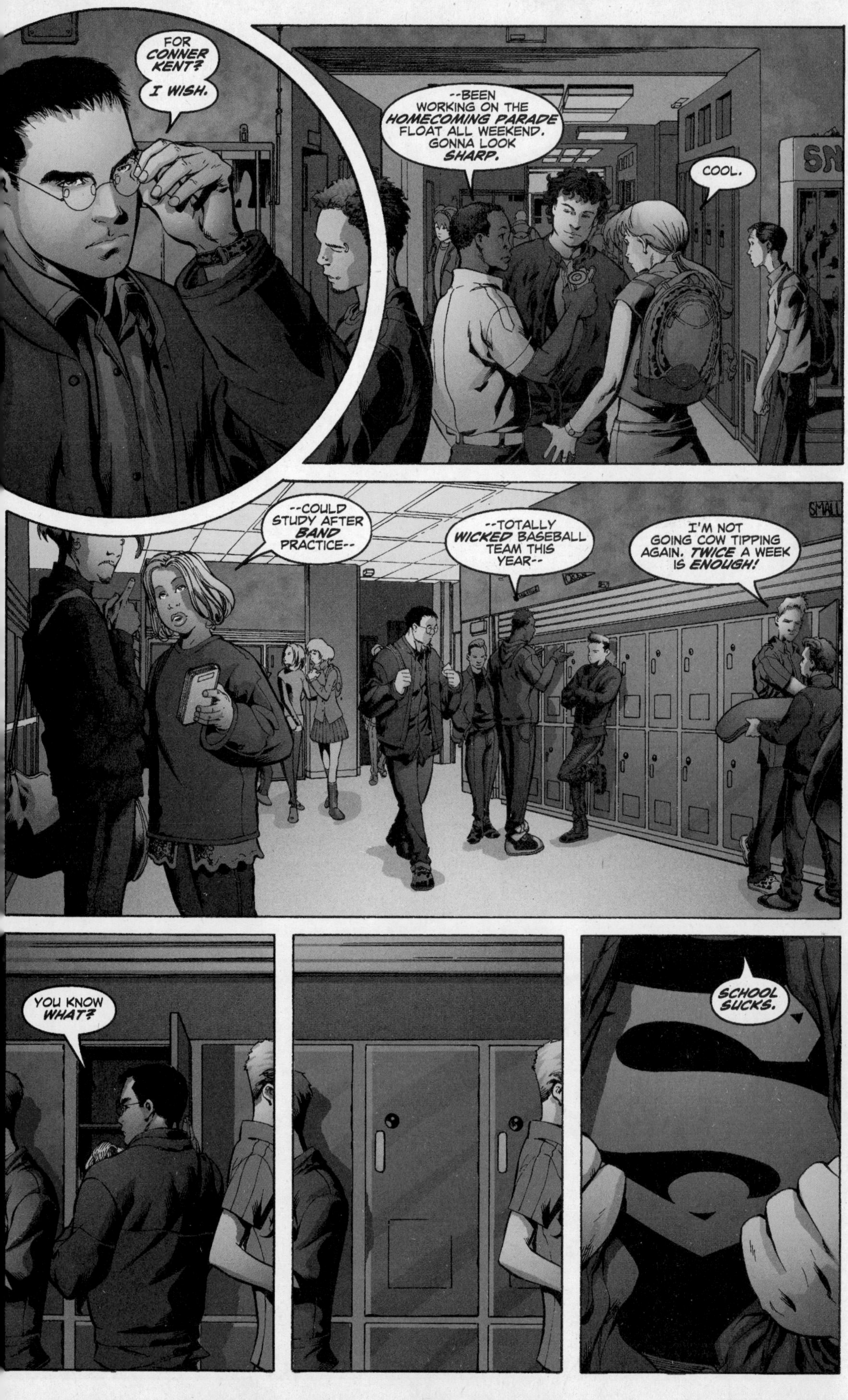
FOR CONNER KENT? I WISH.
--BEEN WORKING ON THE HOMECOMING PARADE FLOAT ALL WEEKEND. GONNA LOOK SHARP.
COOL.
--COULD STUDY AFTER BAND PRACTICE--
--TOTALLY WICKED BASEBALL TEAM THIS YEAR--
I'M NOT GOING COW TIPPING AGAIN. TWICE A WEEK IS ENOUGH!
YOU KNOW WHAT?
SCHOOL SUCKS.

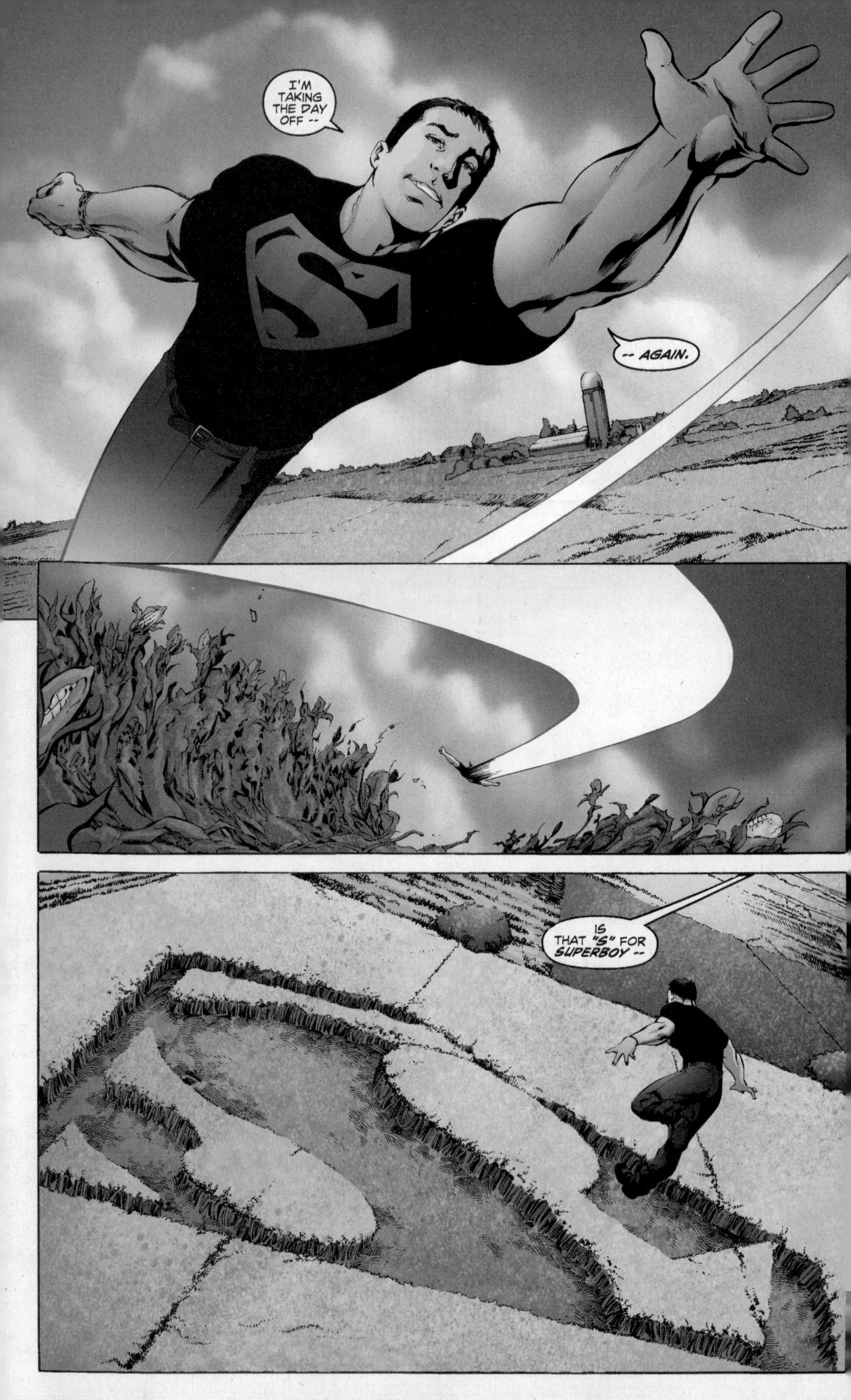
I'M TAKING THE DAY OFF --
-- AGAIN.
IS THAT "S" FOR SUPERBOY --

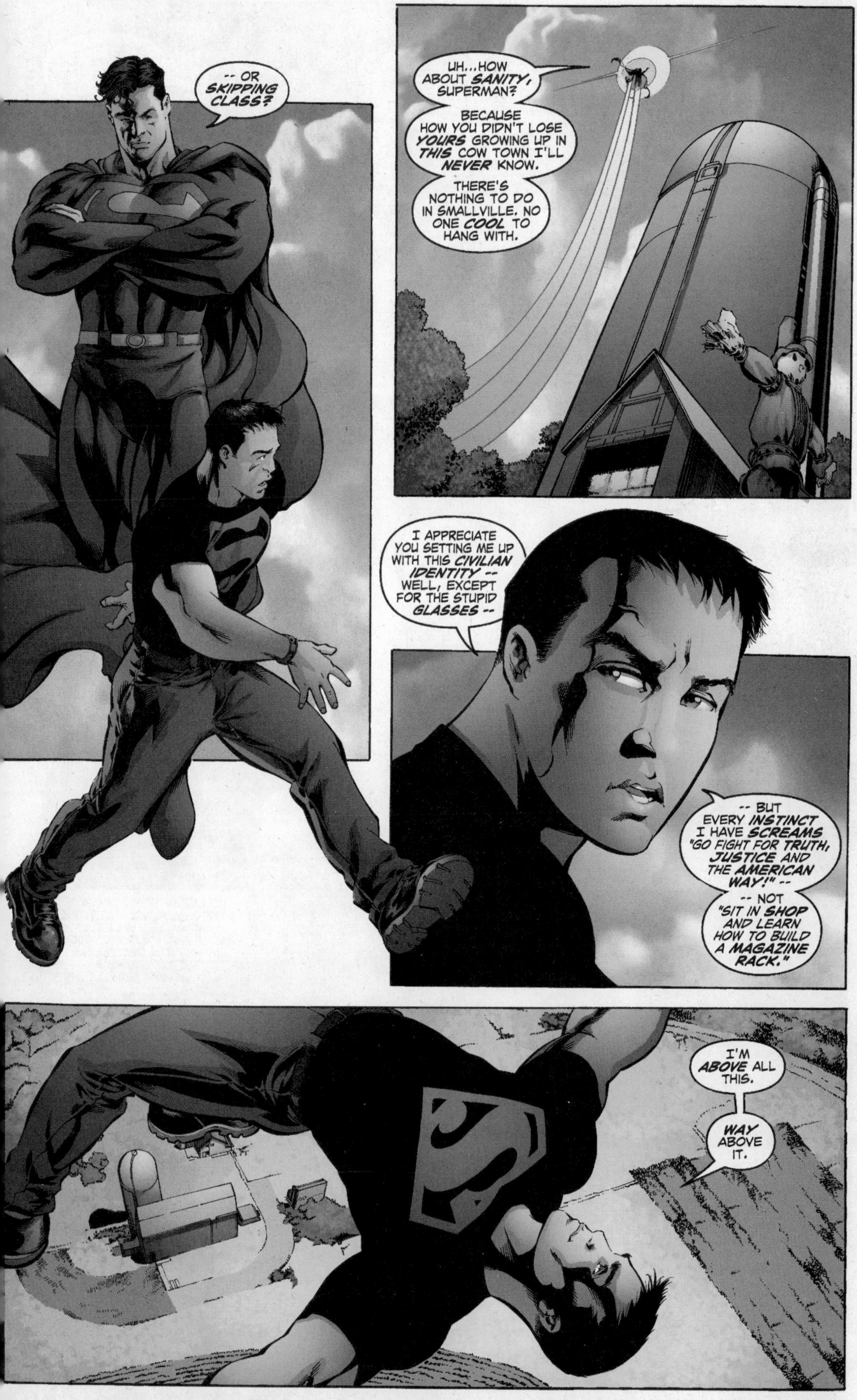
-- OR SKIPPING CLASS?
UH...HOW ABOUT SANITY, SUPERMAN?
BECAUSE HOW YOU DIDN'T LOSE YOURS GROWING UP IN THIS COW TOWN I'LL NEVER KNOW.
THERE'S NOTHING TO DO IN SMALLVILLE. NO ONE COOL TO HANG WITH.
I APPRECIATE YOU SETTING ME UP WITH THIS CIVILIAN IDENTITY -- WELL, EXCEPT FOR THE STUPID GLASSES --
-- BUT EVERY INSTINCT I HAVE SCREAMS "GO FIGHT FOR TRUTH, JUSTICE AND THE AMERICAN WAY!" --
-- NOT "SIT IN SHOP AND LEARN HOW TO BUILD A MAGAZINE RACK."
I'M ABOVE ALL THIS.
WAY ABOVE IT.

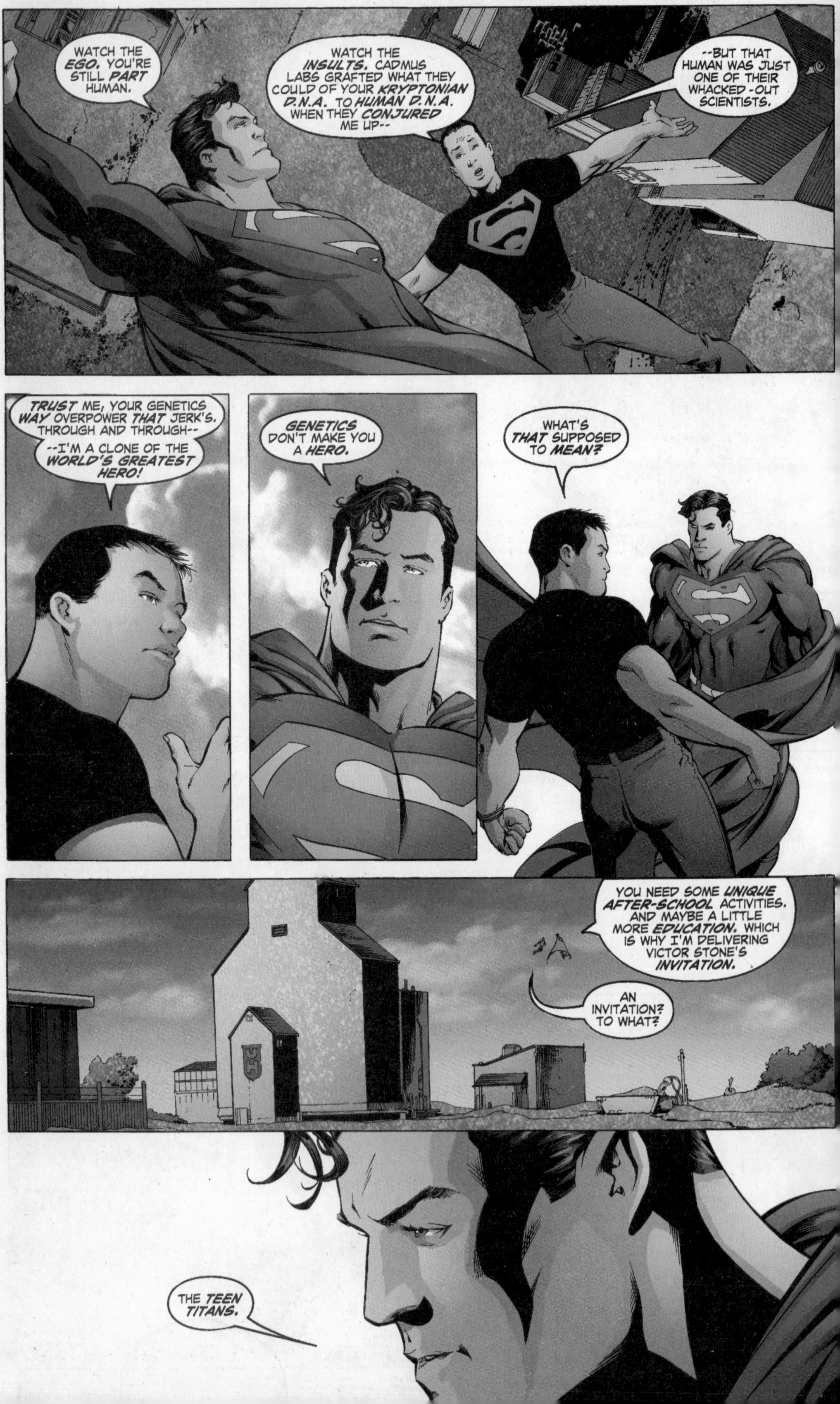

WATCH THE EGO. YOU'RE STILL PART HUMAN.
WATCH THE INSULTS. CADMUS LABS GRAFTED WHAT THEY COULD OF YOUR KRYPTONIAN D.N.A. TO HUMAN D.N.A. WHEN THEY CONJURED ME UP--
--BUT THAT HUMAN WAS JUST ONE OF THEIR WHACKED-OUT SCIENTISTS.
TRUST ME, YOUR GENETICS WAY OVERPOWER THAT JERK'S. THROUGH AND THROUGH--
--I'M A CLONE OF THE WORLD'S GREATEST HERO!
GENETICS DON'T MAKE YOU A HERO.
WHAT'S THAT SUPPOSED TO MEAN?
YOU NEED SOME UNIQUE AFTER-SCHOOL ACTIVITIES. AND MAYBE A LITTLE MORE EDUCATION. WHICH IS WHY I'M DELIVERING VICTOR STONE'S INVITATION.
AN INVITATION? TO WHAT?
THE TEEN TITANS.

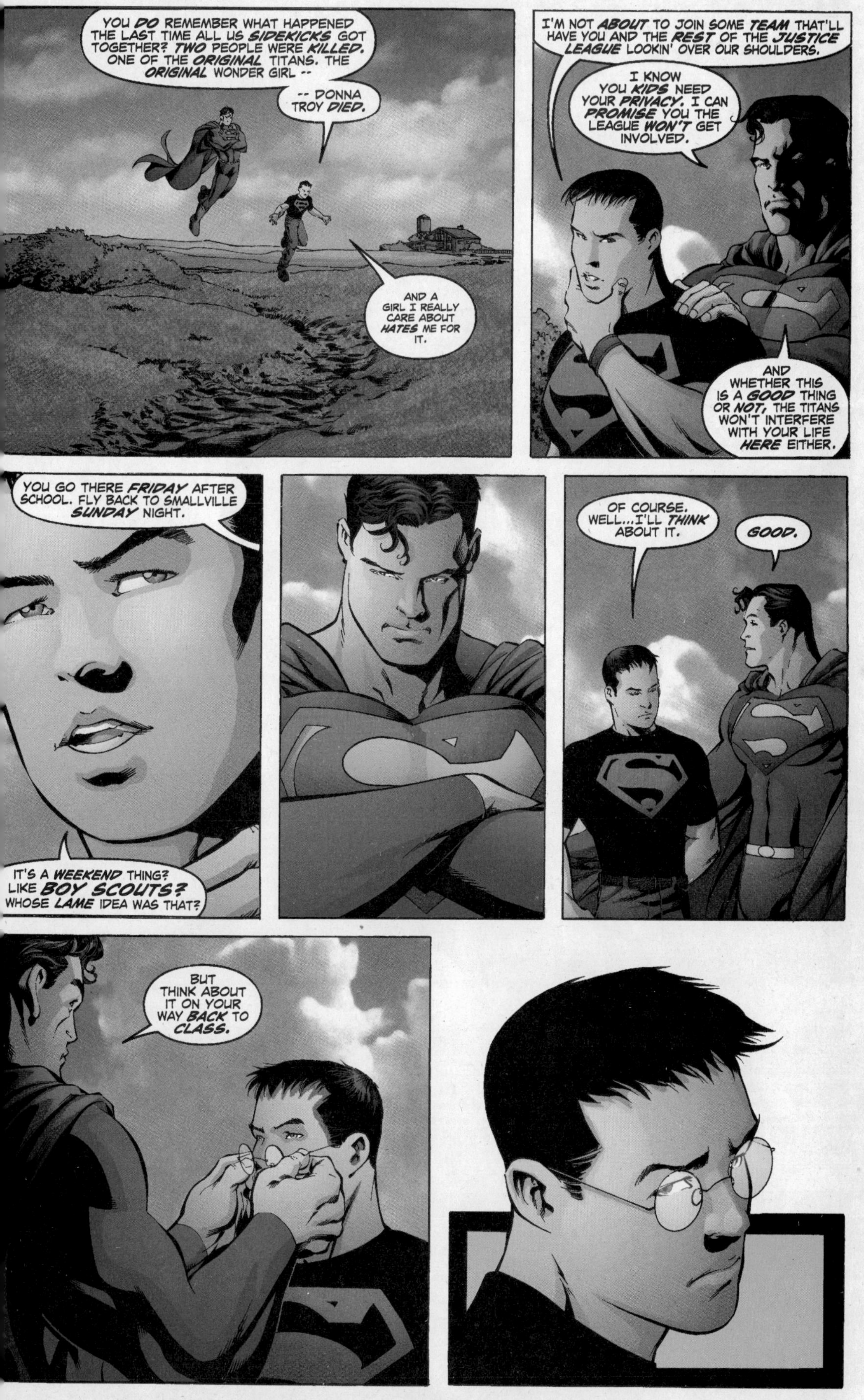
YOU DO REMEMBER WHAT HAPPENED THE LAST TIME ALL US SIDEKICKS GOT TOGETHER? TWO PEOPLE WERE KILLED. ONE OF THE ORIGINAL TITANS. THE ORIGINAL WONDER GIRL --
-- DONNA TROY DIED.
AND A GIRL I REALLY CARE ABOUT HATES ME FOR IT.
I'M NOT ABOUT TO JOIN SOME TEAM THAT'LL HAVE YOU AND THE REST OF THE JUSTICE LEAGUE LOOKIN' OVER OUR SHOULDERS.
I KNOW YOU KIDS NEED YOUR PRIVACY. I CAN PROMISE YOU THE LEAGUE WON'T GET INVOLVED.
AND WHETHER THIS IS A GOOD THING OR NOT, THE TITANS WON'T INTERFERE WITH YOUR LIFE HERE EITHER.
YOU GO THERE FRIDAY AFTER SCHOOL. FLY BACK TO SMALLVILLE SUNDAY NIGHT.
IT'S A WEEKEND THING? LIKE BOY SCOUTS? WHOSE LAME IDEA WAS THAT?
OF COURSE. WELL...I'LL THINK ABOUT IT.
GOOD.
BUT THINK ABOUT IT ON YOUR WAY BACK TO CLASS.

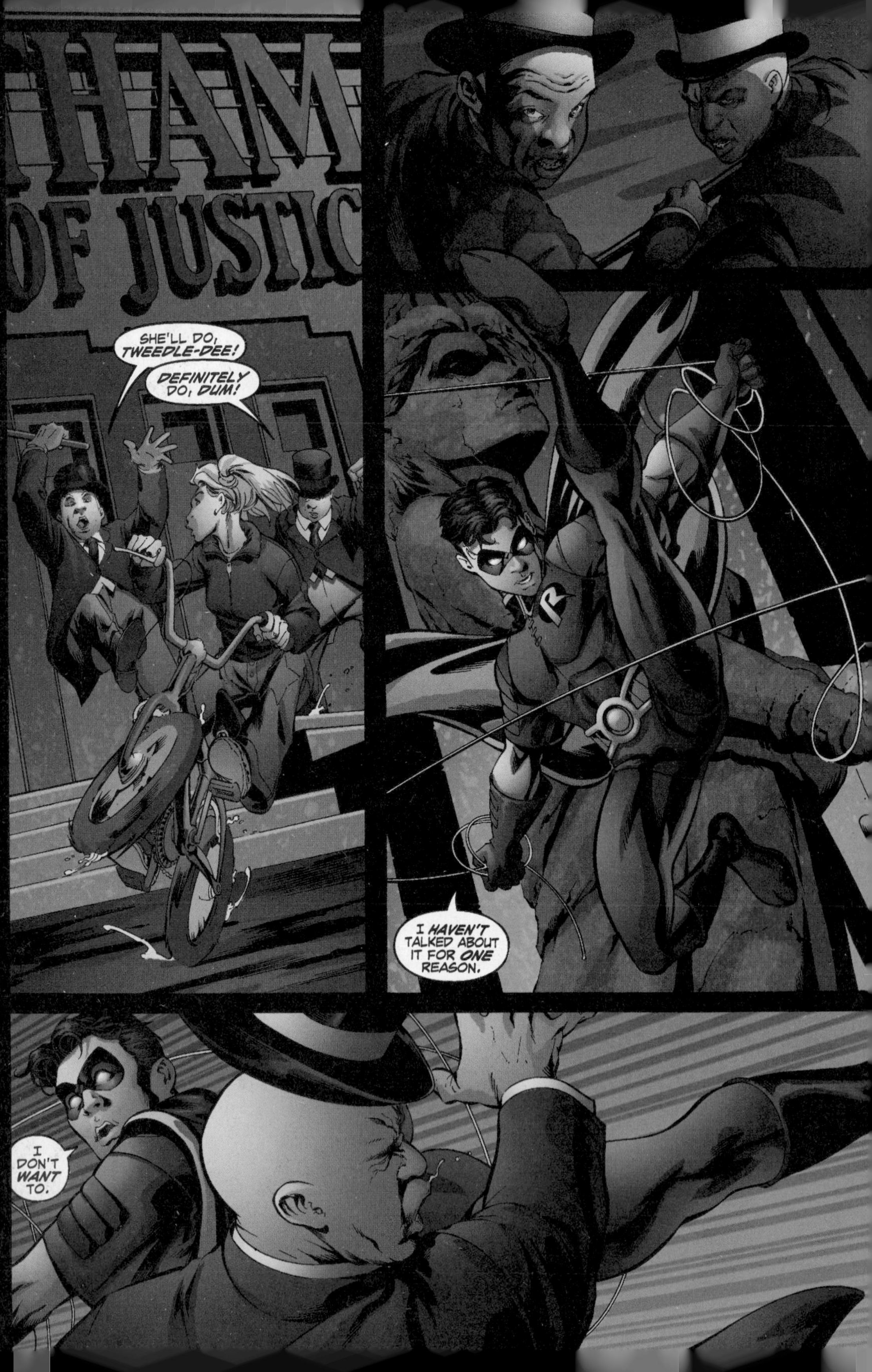
HAM
OF JUSTIC
SHE'LL DO, TWEEDLE-DEE!
DEFINITELY DO, DUM!
I HAVEN'T TALKED ABOUT IT FOR ONE REASON.
I DON'T WANT TO.

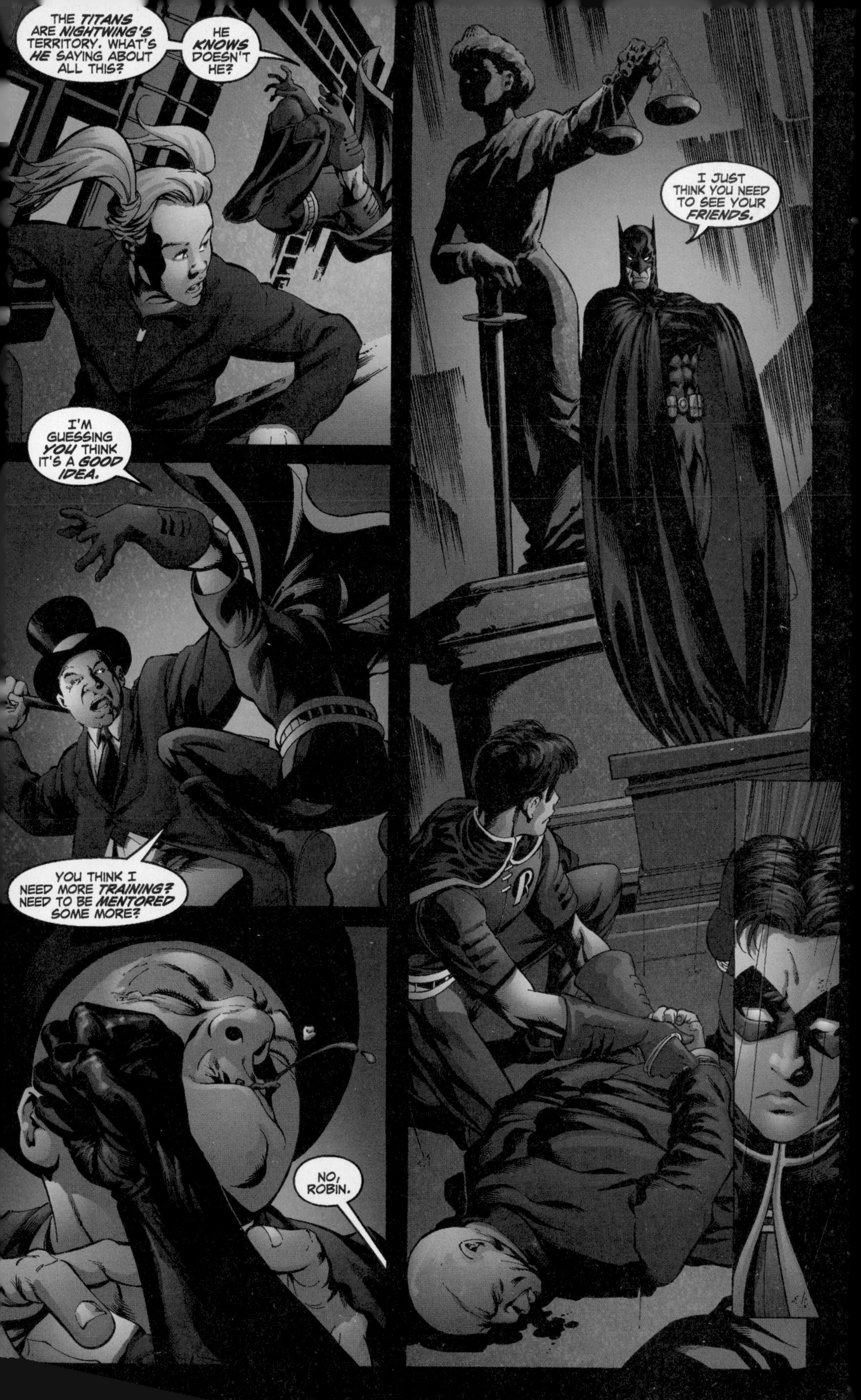
THE *TITANS* ARE *NIGHTWING'S* TERRITORY. WHAT'S *HE* SAYING ABOUT ALL THIS?
HE *KNOWS* DOESN'T HE?
I JUST THINK YOU NEED TO SEE YOUR *FRIENDS.*
I'M GUESSING *YOU* THINK IT'S A *GOOD IDEA.*
YOU THINK I NEED MORE *TRAINING?* NEED TO BE *MENTORED* SOME MORE?
NO, ROBIN.

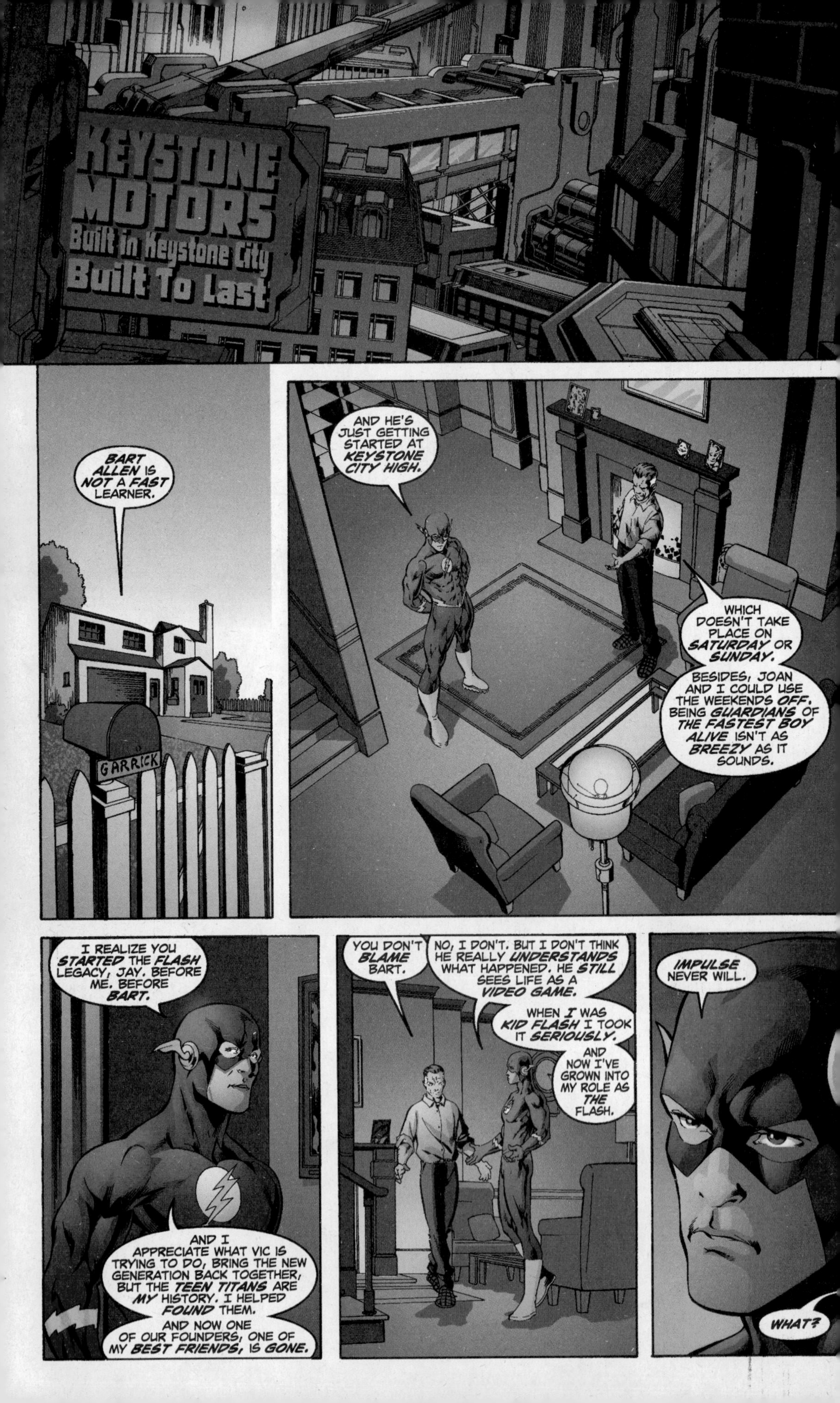
KEYSTONE MOTORS
Built in Keystone City
Built To Last
BART ALLEN IS NOT A FAST LEARNER.
GARRICK
AND HE'S JUST GETTING STARTED AT KEYSTONE CITY HIGH.
WHICH DOESN'T TAKE PLACE ON SATURDAY OR SUNDAY.
BESIDES, JOAN AND I COULD USE THE WEEKENDS OFF. BEING GUARDIANS OF THE FASTEST BOY ALIVE ISN'T AS BREEZY AS IT SOUNDS.
I REALIZE YOU STARTED THE FLASH LEGACY, JAY. BEFORE ME. BEFORE BART.
AND I APPRECIATE WHAT VIC IS TRYING TO DO, BRING THE NEW GENERATION BACK TOGETHER, BUT THE TEEN TITANS ARE MY HISTORY. I HELPED FOUND THEM.
AND NOW ONE OF OUR FOUNDERS, ONE OF MY BEST FRIENDS, IS GONE.
YOU DON'T BLAME BART.
NO, I DON'T. BUT I DON'T THINK HE REALLY UNDERSTANDS WHAT HAPPENED. HE STILL SEES LIFE AS A VIDEO GAME.
WHEN I WAS KID FLASH I TOOK IT SERIOUSLY.
AND NOW I'VE GROWN INTO MY ROLE AS THE FLASH.
IMPULSE NEVER WILL.
WHAT?

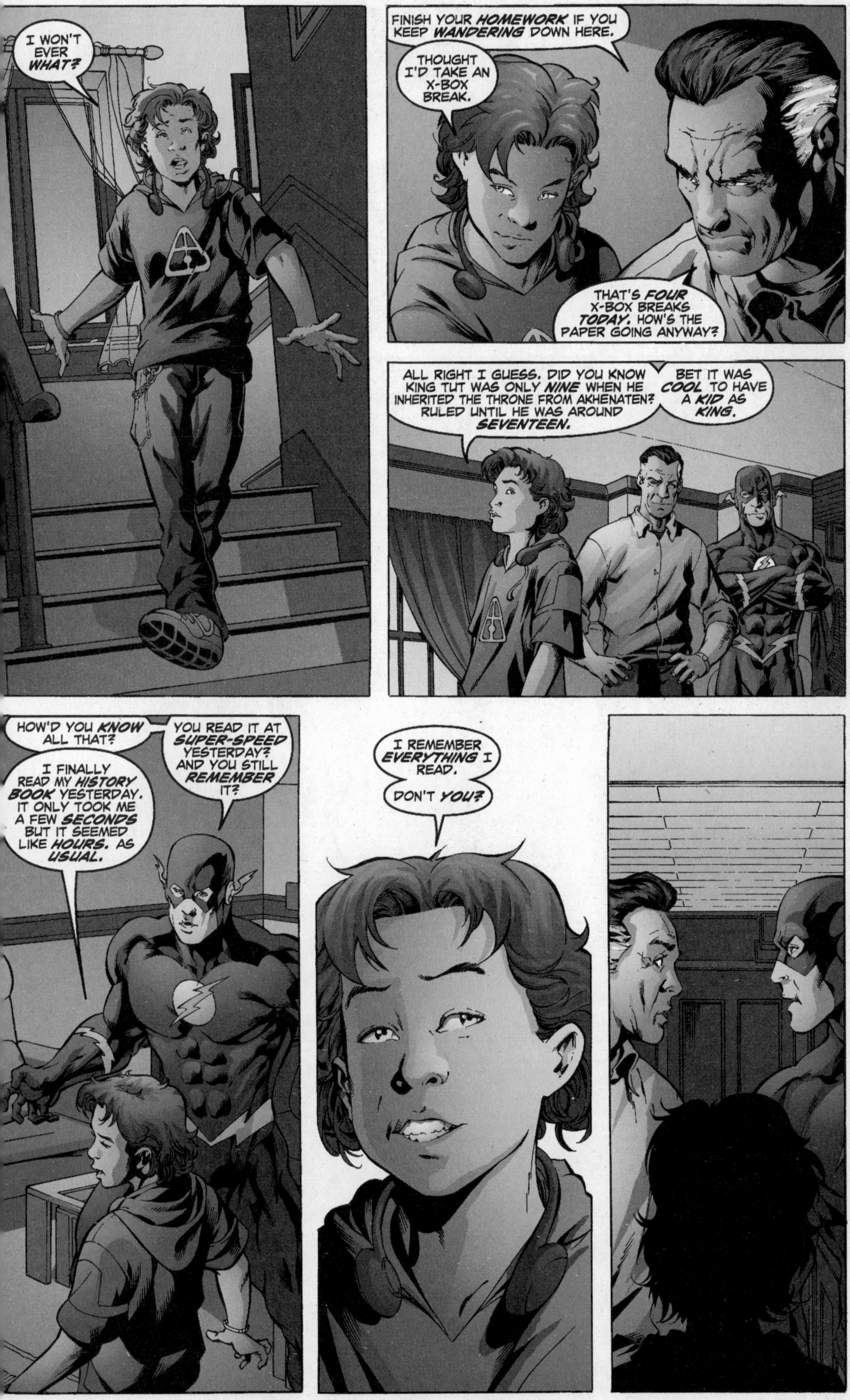
I WON'T EVER WHAT?
FINISH YOUR HOMEWORK IF YOU KEEP WANDERING DOWN HERE.
THOUGHT I'D TAKE AN X-BOX BREAK.
THAT'S FOUR X-BOX BREAKS TODAY. HOW'S THE PAPER GOING ANYWAY?
ALL RIGHT I GUESS. DID YOU KNOW KING TUT WAS ONLY NINE WHEN HE INHERITED THE THRONE FROM AKHENATEN? RULED UNTIL HE WAS AROUND SEVENTEEN.
BET IT WAS COOL TO HAVE A KID AS KING.
HOW'D YOU KNOW ALL THAT?
I FINALLY READ MY HISTORY BOOK YESTERDAY. IT ONLY TOOK ME A FEW SECONDS BUT IT SEEMED LIKE HOURS. AS USUAL.
YOU READ IT AT SUPER-SPEED YESTERDAY? AND YOU STILL REMEMBER IT?
I REMEMBER EVERYTHING I READ.
DON'T YOU?

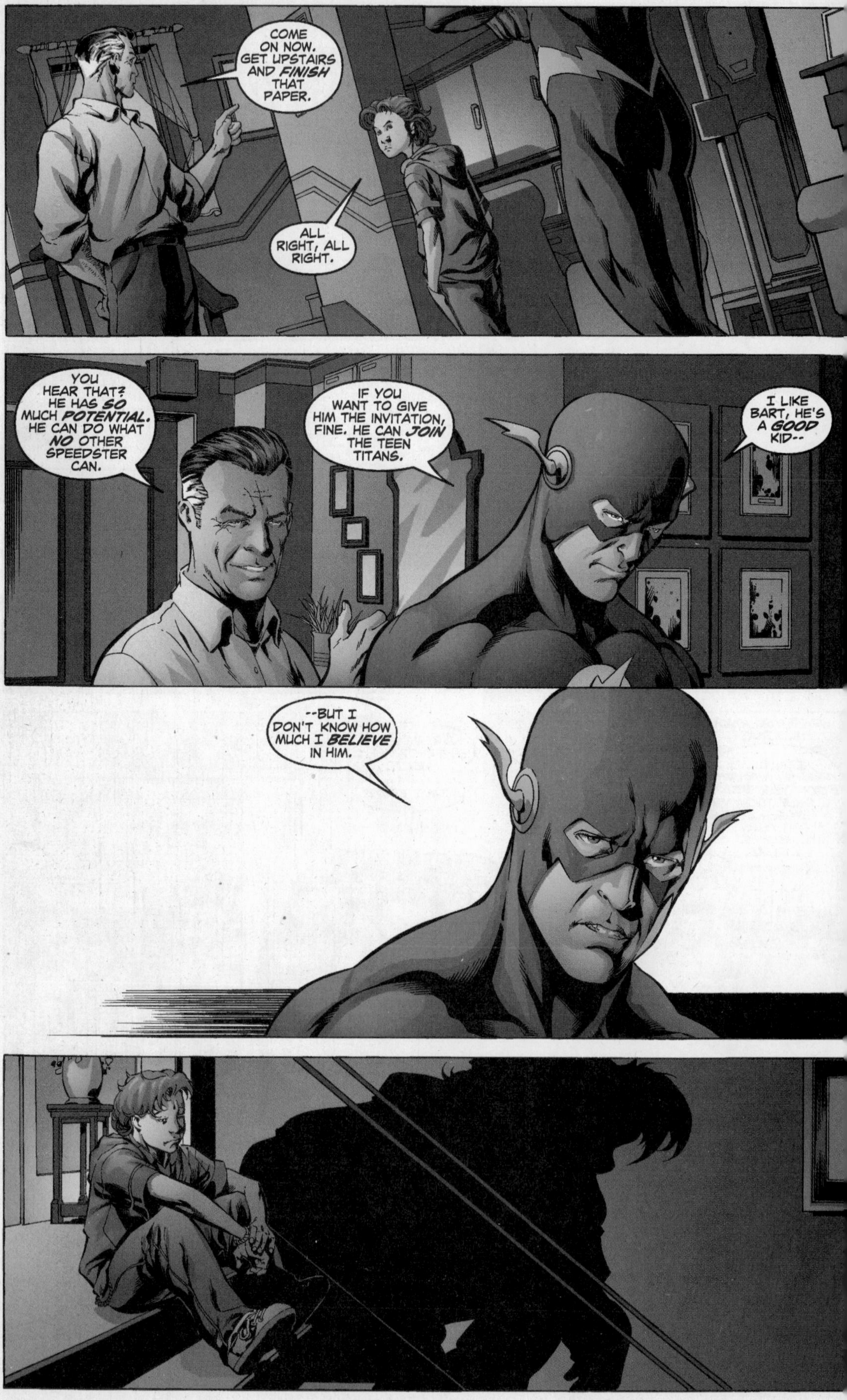
COME ON NOW. GET UPSTAIRS AND FINISH THAT PAPER.
ALL RIGHT, ALL RIGHT.
YOU HEAR THAT? HE HAS SO MUCH POTENTIAL. HE CAN DO WHAT NO OTHER SPEEDSTER CAN.
IF YOU WANT TO GIVE HIM THE INVITATION, FINE. HE CAN JOIN THE TEEN TITANS.
I LIKE BART, HE'S A GOOD KID--
--BUT I DON'T KNOW HOW MUCH I BELIEVE IN HIM.

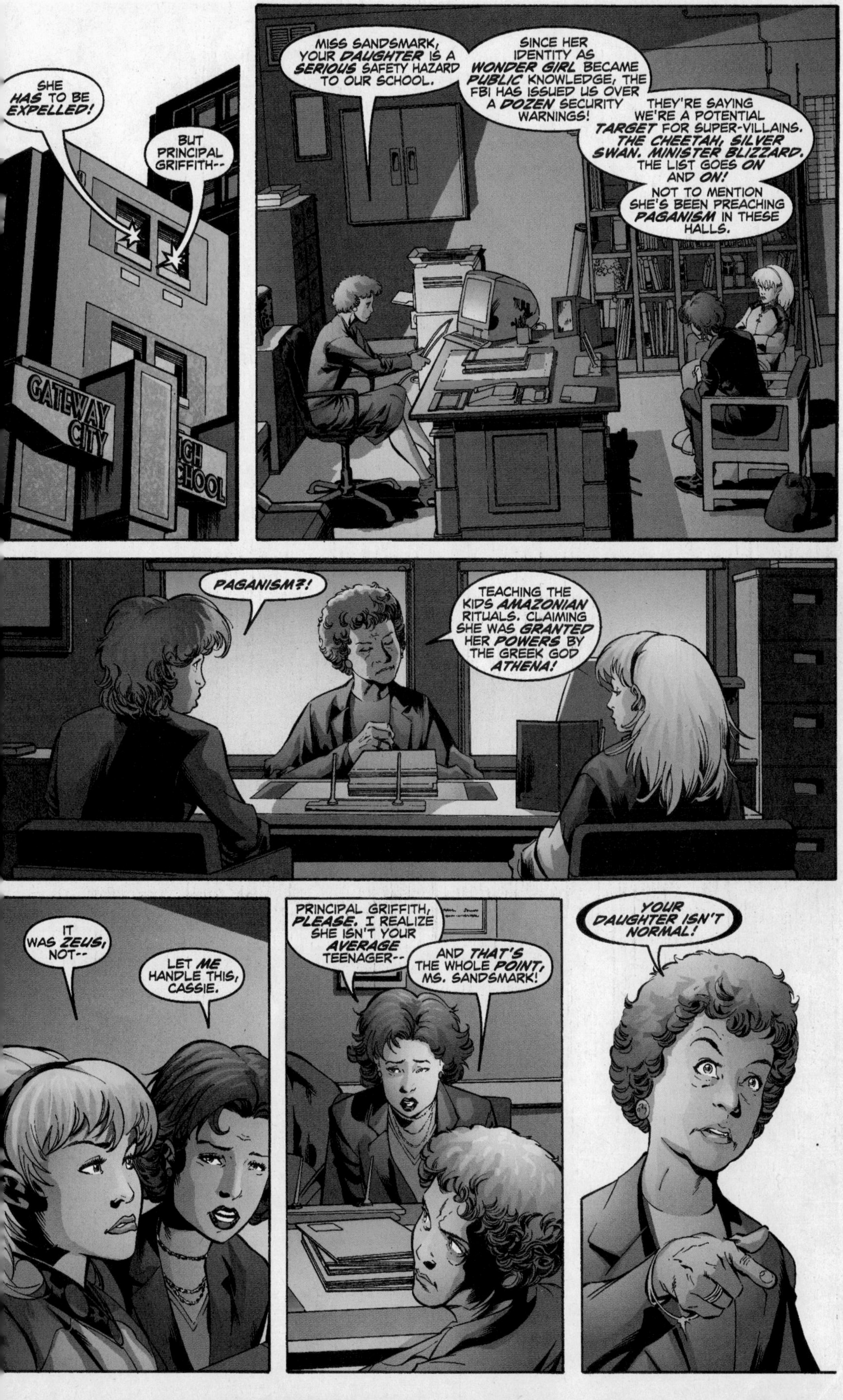

SHE HAS TO BE EXPELLED!
BUT PRINCIPAL GRIFFITH--
GATEWAY CITY HIGH SCHOOL
MISS SANDSMARK, YOUR DAUGHTER IS A SERIOUS SAFETY HAZARD TO OUR SCHOOL.
SINCE HER IDENTITY AS WONDER GIRL BECAME PUBLIC KNOWLEDGE, THE FBI HAS ISSUED US OVER A DOZEN SECURITY WARNINGS!
THEY'RE SAYING WE'RE A POTENTIAL TARGET FOR SUPER-VILLAINS. THE CHEETAH, SILVER SWAN. MINISTER BLIZZARD. THE LIST GOES ON AND ON!
NOT TO MENTION SHE'S BEEN PREACHING PAGANISM IN THESE HALLS.
PAGANISM?!
TEACHING THE KIDS AMAZONIAN RITUALS. CLAIMING SHE WAS GRANTED HER POWERS BY THE GREEK GOD ATHENA!
IT WAS ZEUS, NOT--
LET ME HANDLE THIS, CASSIE.
PRINCIPAL GRIFFITH, PLEASE. I REALIZE SHE ISN'T YOUR AVERAGE TEENAGER--
AND THAT'S THE WHOLE POINT, MS. SANDSMARK!
YOUR DAUGHTER ISN'T NORMAL!

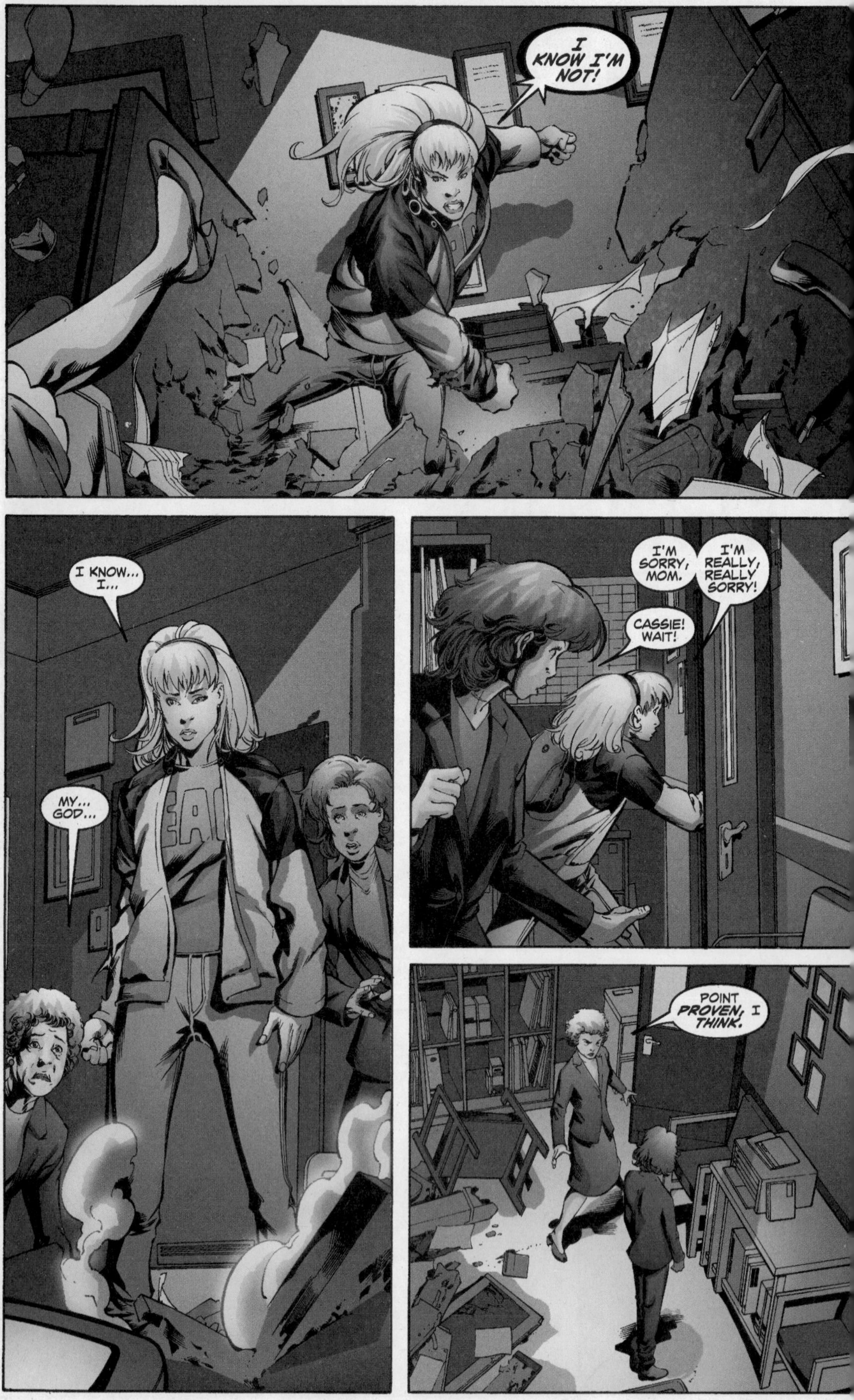
I KNOW I'M NOT!
I KNOW... I...
MY... GOD...
I'M SORRY, MOM.
I'M REALLY, REALLY SORRY!
CASSIE! WAIT!
POINT PROVEN, I THINK.

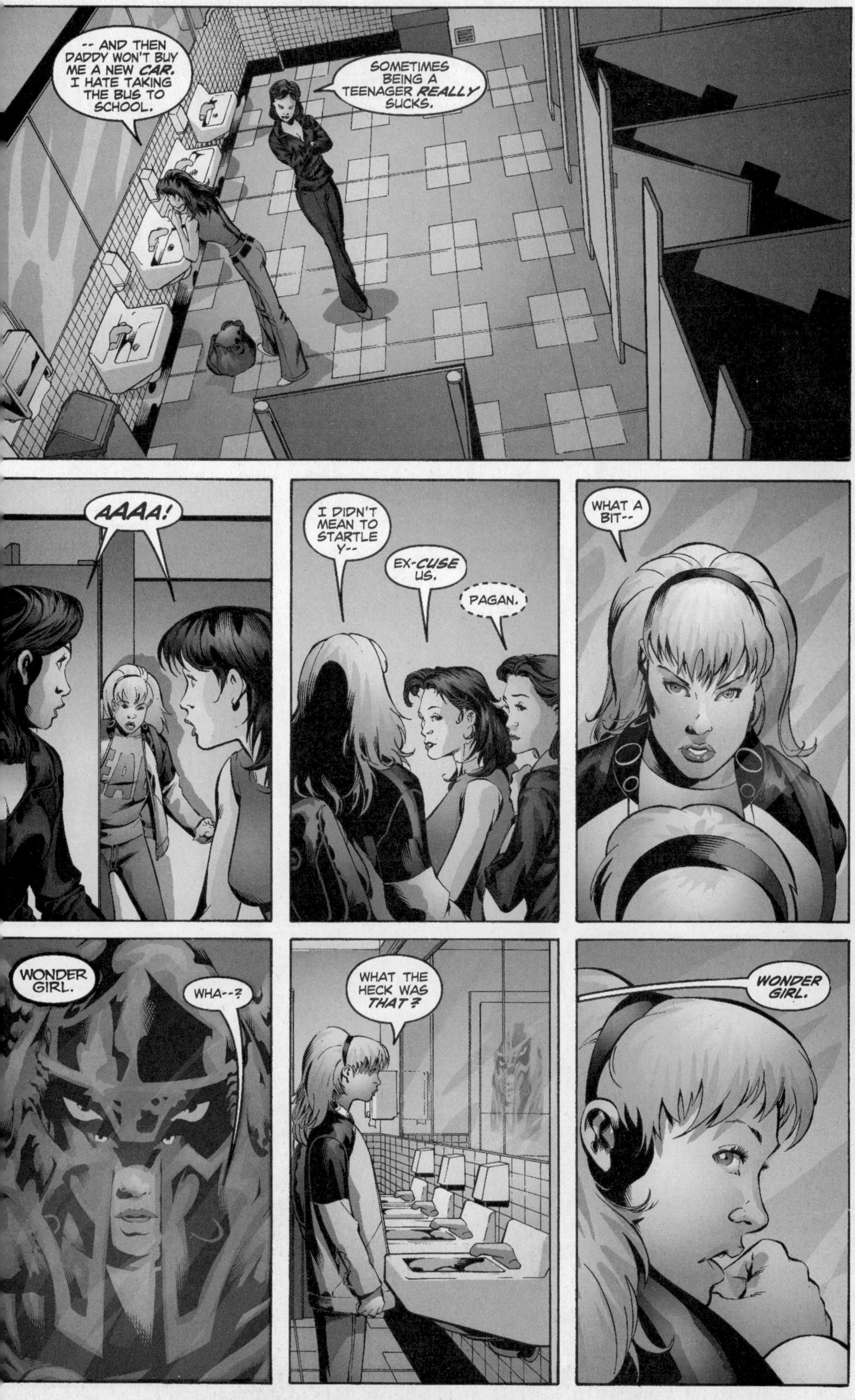
-- AND THEN DADDY WON'T BUY ME A NEW CAR. I HATE TAKING THE BUS TO SCHOOL.
SOMETIMES BEING A TEENAGER REALLY SUCKS.
AAAA!
I DIDN'T MEAN TO STARTLE Y--
EX-CUSE US.
PAGAN.
WHAT A BIT--
WONDER GIRL.
WHA--?
WHAT THE HECK WAS THAT?
WONDER GIRL.

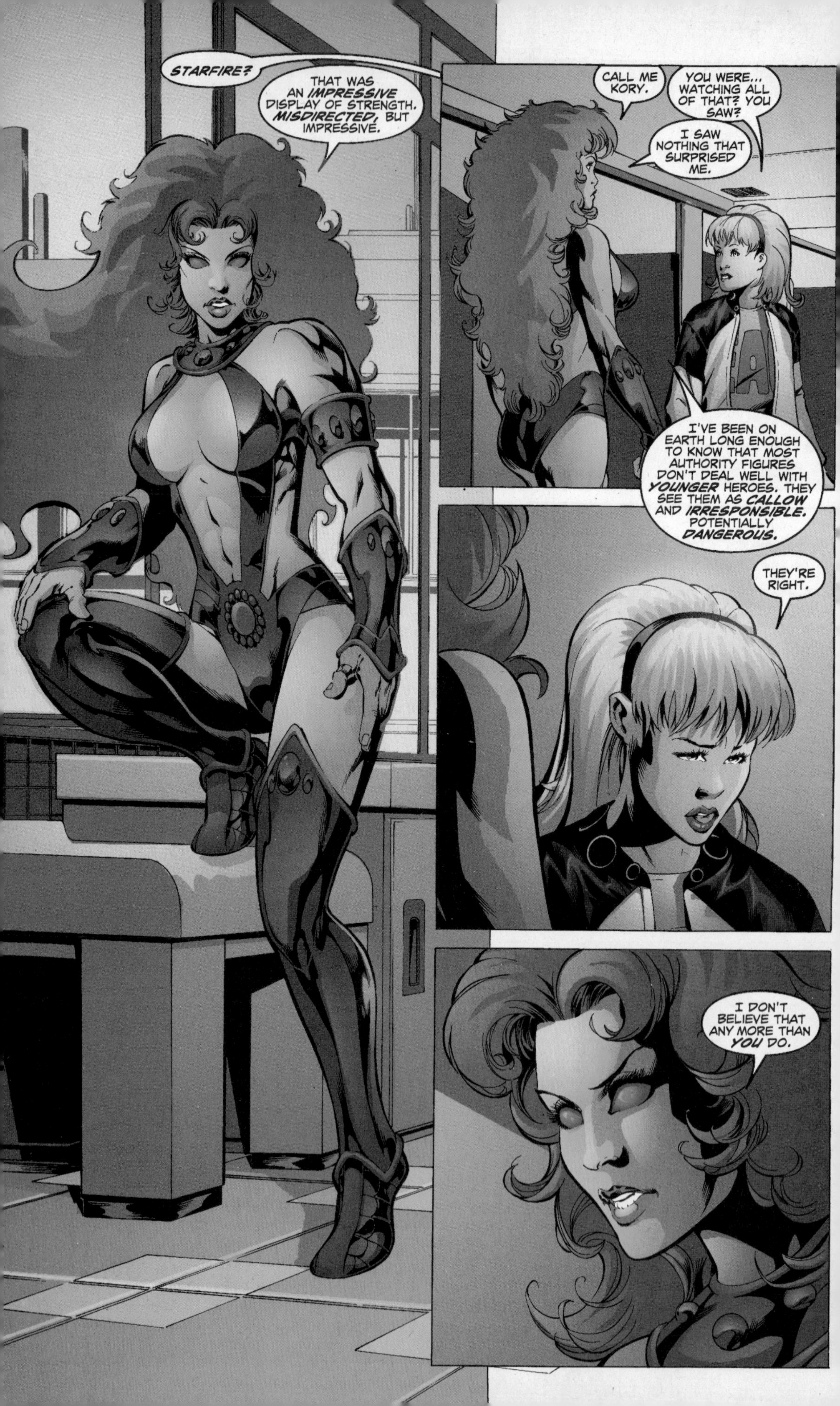
STARFIRE?
THAT WAS AN IMPRESSIVE DISPLAY OF STRENGTH. MISDIRECTED, BUT IMPRESSIVE.
CALL ME KORY.
YOU WERE... WATCHING ALL OF THAT? YOU SAW?
I SAW NOTHING THAT SURPRISED ME.
I'VE BEEN ON EARTH LONG ENOUGH TO KNOW THAT MOST AUTHORITY FIGURES DON'T DEAL WELL WITH YOUNGER HEROES. THEY SEE THEM AS CALLOW AND IRRESPONSIBLE. POTENTIALLY DANGEROUS.
THEY'RE RIGHT.
I DON'T BELIEVE THAT ANY MORE THAN YOU DO.

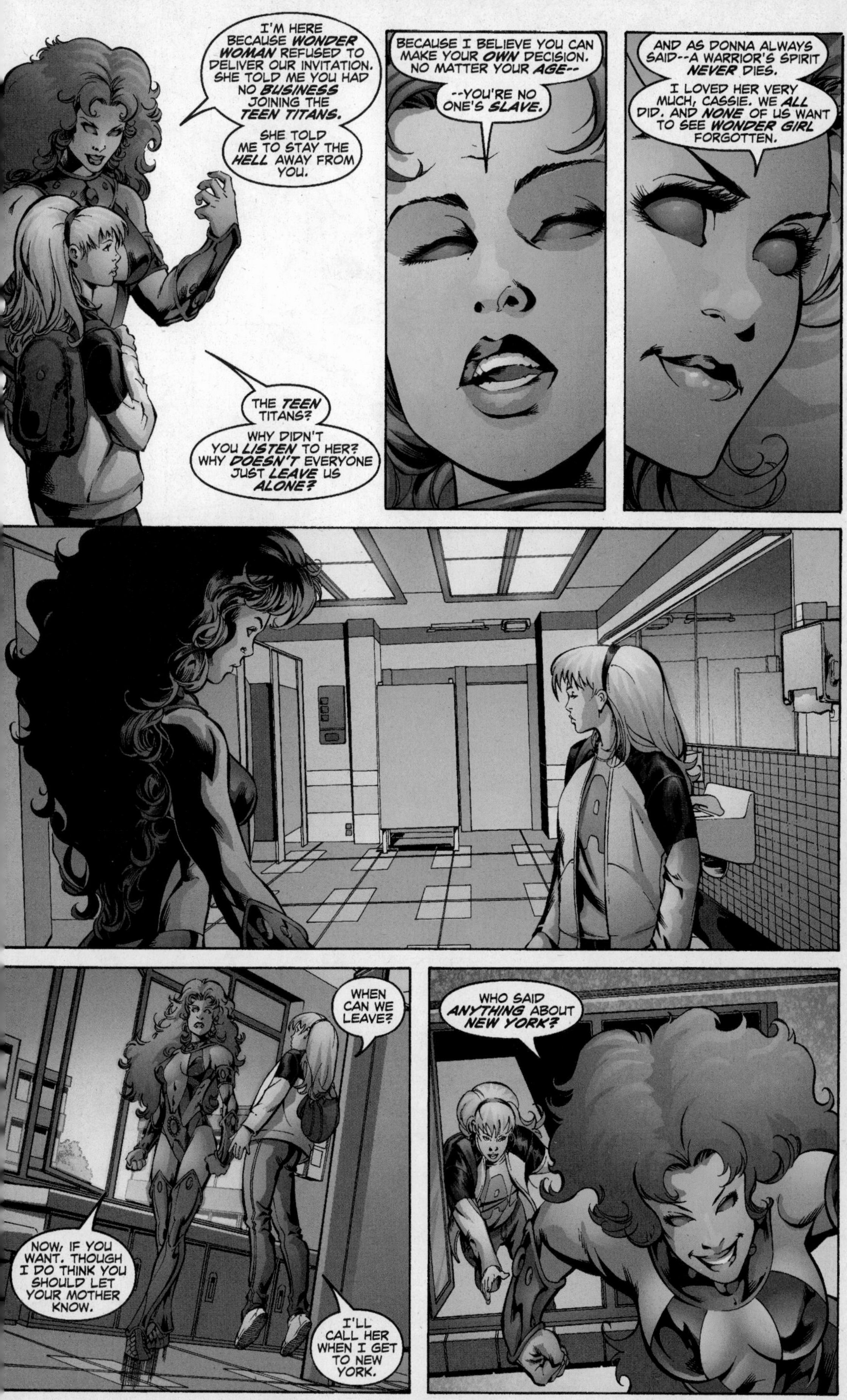

I'M HERE BECAUSE WONDER WOMAN REFUSED TO DELIVER OUR INVITATION. SHE TOLD ME YOU HAD NO BUSINESS JOINING THE TEEN TITANS.
SHE TOLD ME TO STAY THE HELL AWAY FROM YOU.
THE TEEN TITANS?
WHY DIDN'T YOU LISTEN TO HER? WHY DOESN'T EVERYONE JUST LEAVE US ALONE?
BECAUSE I BELIEVE YOU CAN MAKE YOUR OWN DECISION. NO MATTER YOUR AGE--
--YOU'RE NO ONE'S SLAVE.
AND AS DONNA ALWAYS SAID--A WARRIOR'S SPIRIT NEVER DIES.
I LOVED HER VERY MUCH, CASSIE. WE ALL DID. AND NONE OF US WANT TO SEE WONDER GIRL FORGOTTEN.
WHEN CAN WE LEAVE?
NOW, IF YOU WANT. THOUGH I DO THINK YOU SHOULD LET YOUR MOTHER KNOW.
I'LL CALL HER WHEN I GET TO NEW YORK.
WHO SAID ANYTHING ABOUT NEW YORK?

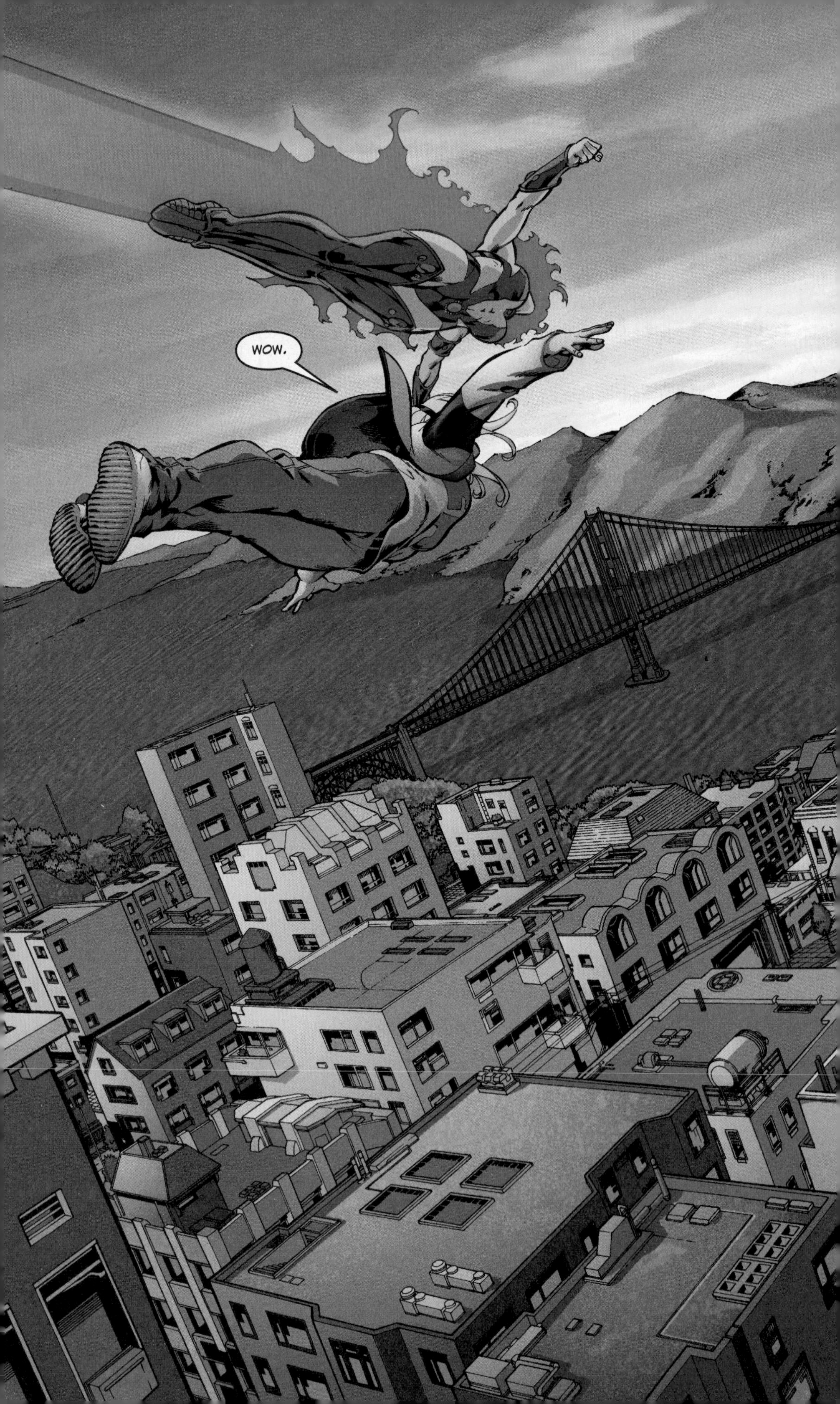
WOW.

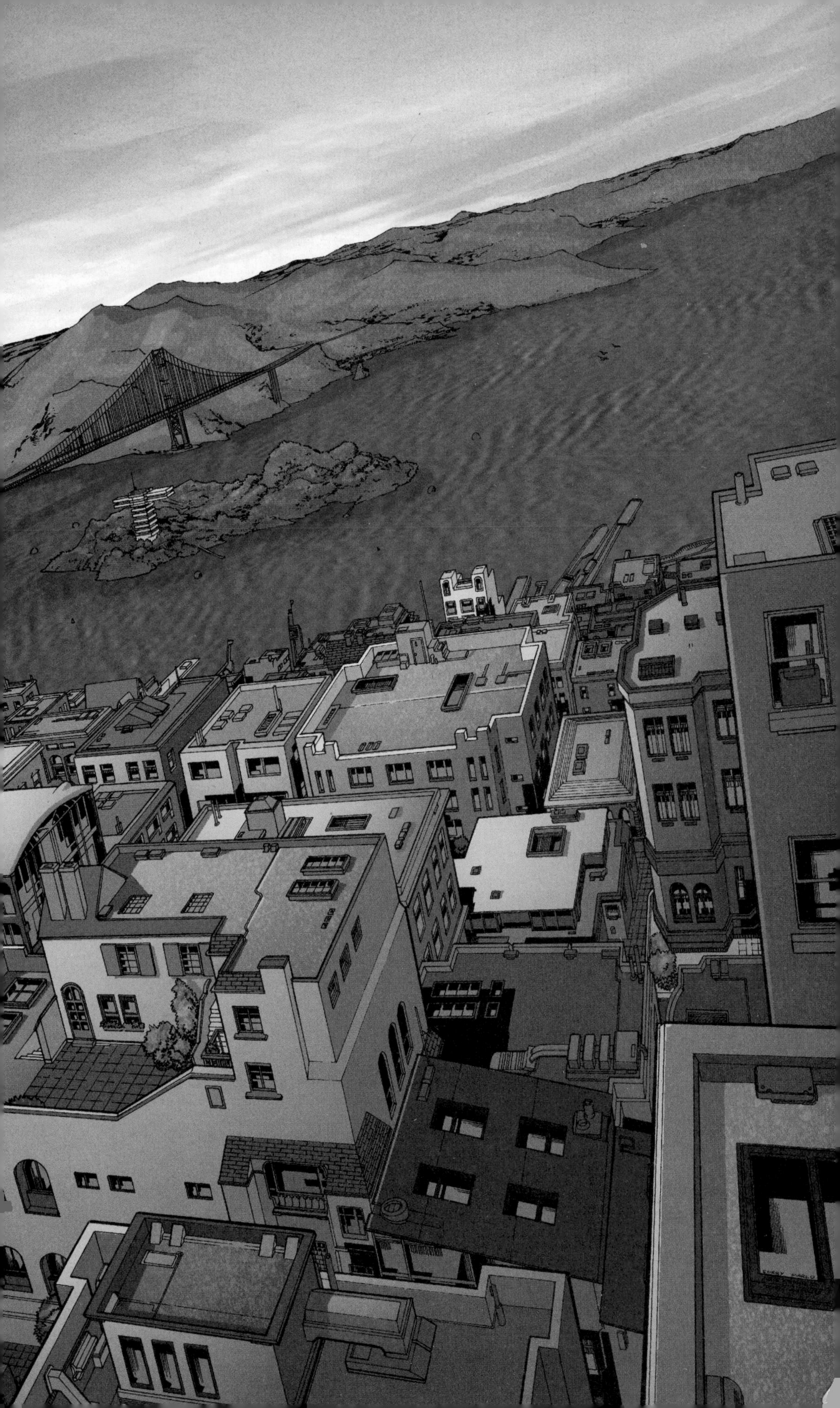

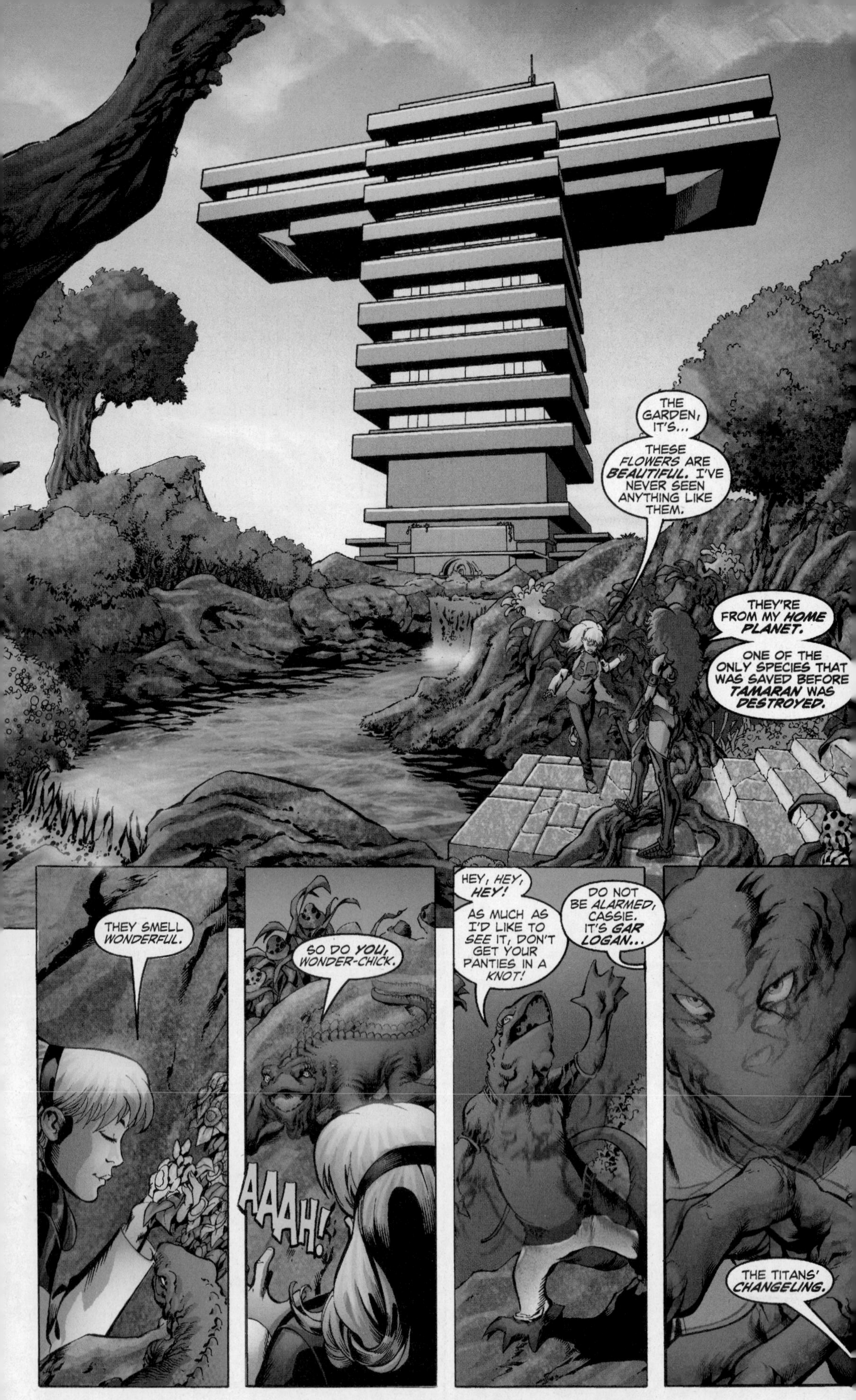
THE GARDEN, IT'S...
THESE *FLOWERS* ARE ***BEAUTIFUL.*** I'VE NEVER SEEN ANYTHING LIKE THEM.
THEY'RE FROM MY ***HOME PLANET.***
ONE OF THE ONLY SPECIES THAT WAS SAVED BEFORE ***TAMARAN*** WAS ***DESTROYED.***
THEY SMELL *WONDERFUL.*
SO DO ***YOU,*** WONDER-CHICK.
AAAH!
HEY, HEY, ***HEY!***
AS MUCH AS I'D LIKE TO *SEE* IT, DON'T GET YOUR PANTIES IN A *KNOT!*
DO NOT BE *ALARMED,* CASSIE. IT'S ***GAR LOGAN...***
THE TITANS' ***CHANGELING.***

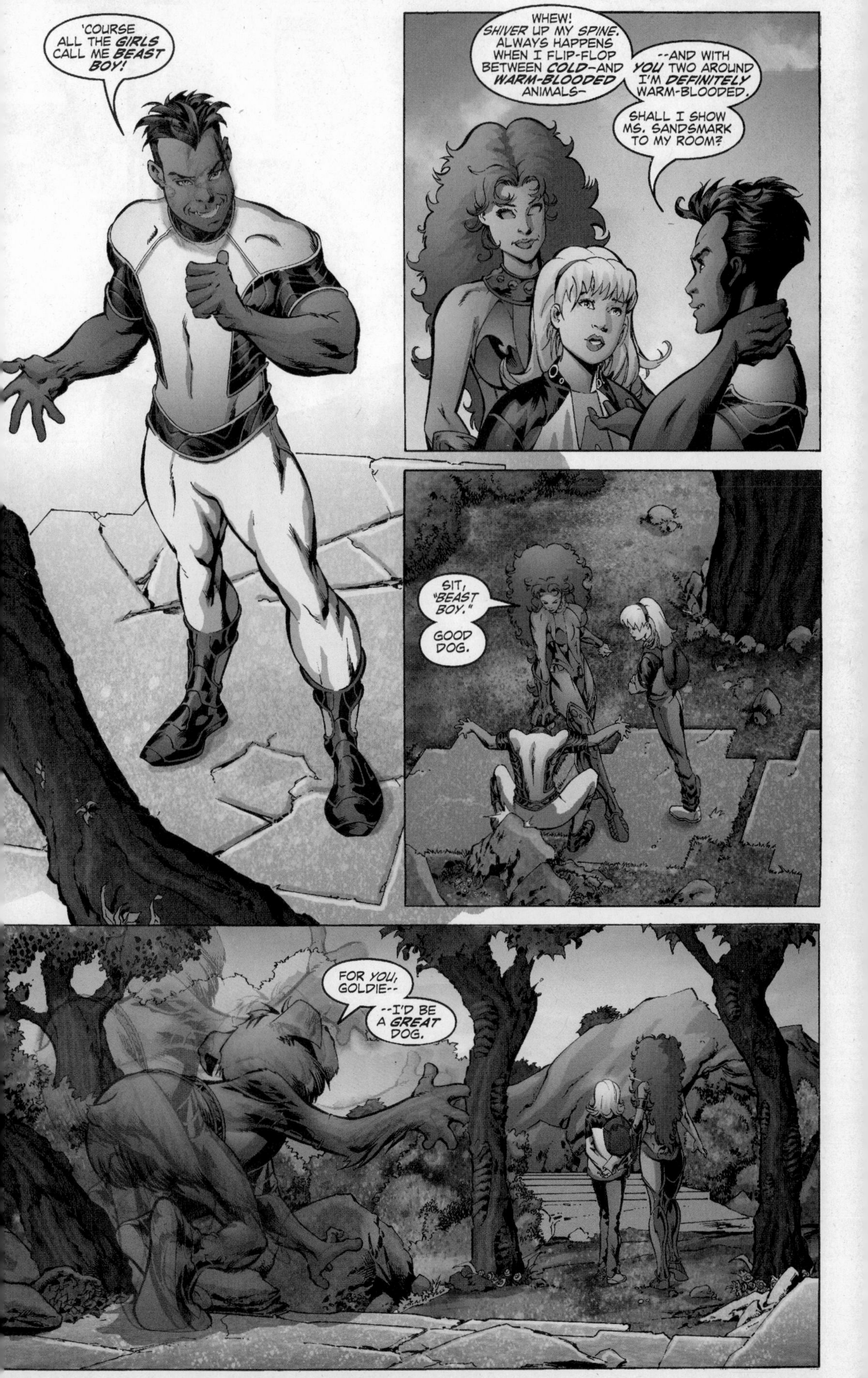
'COURSE ALL THE GIRLS CALL ME BEAST BOY!
WHEW! SHIVER UP MY SPINE. ALWAYS HAPPENS WHEN I FLIP-FLOP BETWEEN COLD--AND WARM-BLOODED ANIMALS-
--AND WITH YOU TWO AROUND I'M DEFINITELY WARM-BLOODED.
SHALL I SHOW MS. SANDSMARK TO MY ROOM?
SIT, "BEAST BOY."
GOOD DOG.
FOR YOU, GOLDIE--
--I'D BE A GREAT DOG.

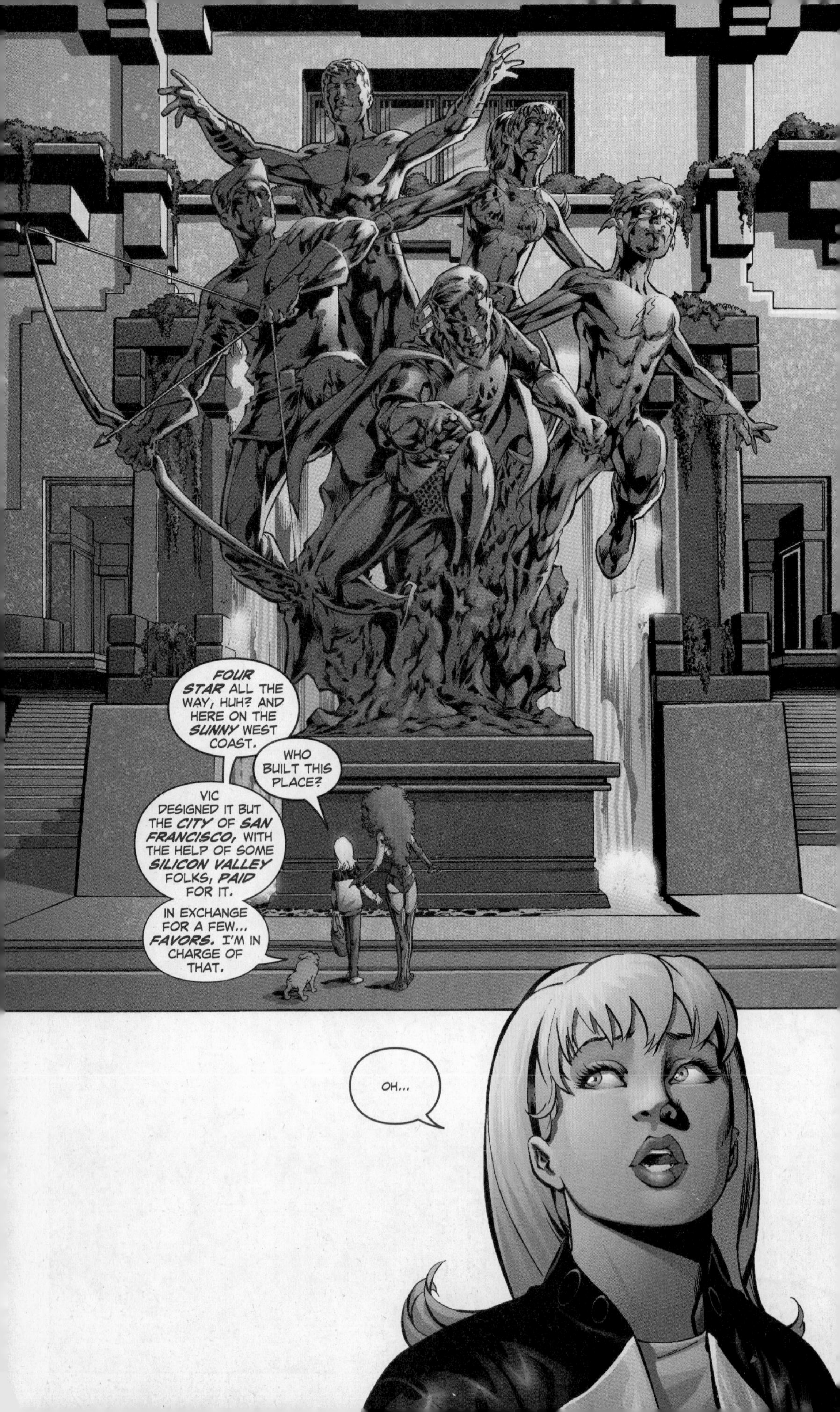
FOUR STAR ALL THE WAY, HUH? AND HERE ON THE SUNNY WEST COAST.
WHO BUILT THIS PLACE?
VIC DESIGNED IT BUT THE CITY OF SAN FRANCISCO, WITH THE HELP OF SOME SILICON VALLEY FOLKS, PAID FOR IT.
IN EXCHANGE FOR A FEW... FAVORS. I'M IN CHARGE OF THAT.
OH...

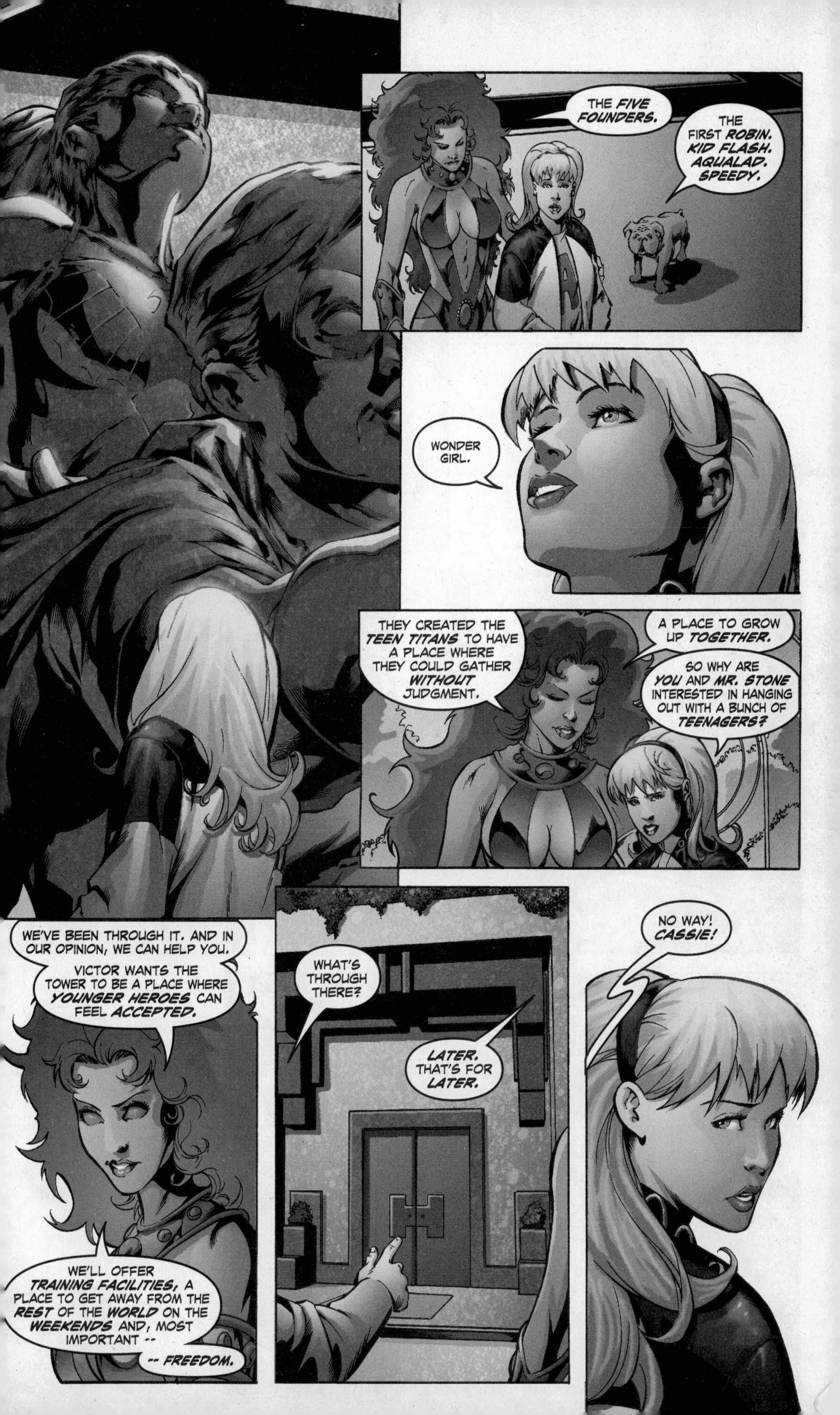
THE FIVE FOUNDERS.
THE FIRST ROBIN. KID FLASH. AQUALAD. SPEEDY.
WONDER GIRL.
THEY CREATED THE TEEN TITANS TO HAVE A PLACE WHERE THEY COULD GATHER WITHOUT JUDGMENT.
A PLACE TO GROW UP TOGETHER.
SO WHY ARE YOU AND MR. STONE INTERESTED IN HANGING OUT WITH A BUNCH OF TEENAGERS?
WE'VE BEEN THROUGH IT. AND IN OUR OPINION, WE CAN HELP YOU.
VICTOR WANTS THE TOWER TO BE A PLACE WHERE YOUNGER HEROES CAN FEEL ACCEPTED.
WE'LL OFFER TRAINING FACILITIES, A PLACE TO GET AWAY FROM THE REST OF THE WORLD ON THE WEEKENDS AND, MOST IMPORTANT --
-- FREEDOM.
WHAT'S THROUGH THERE?
LATER. THAT'S FOR LATER.
NO WAY! CASSIE!

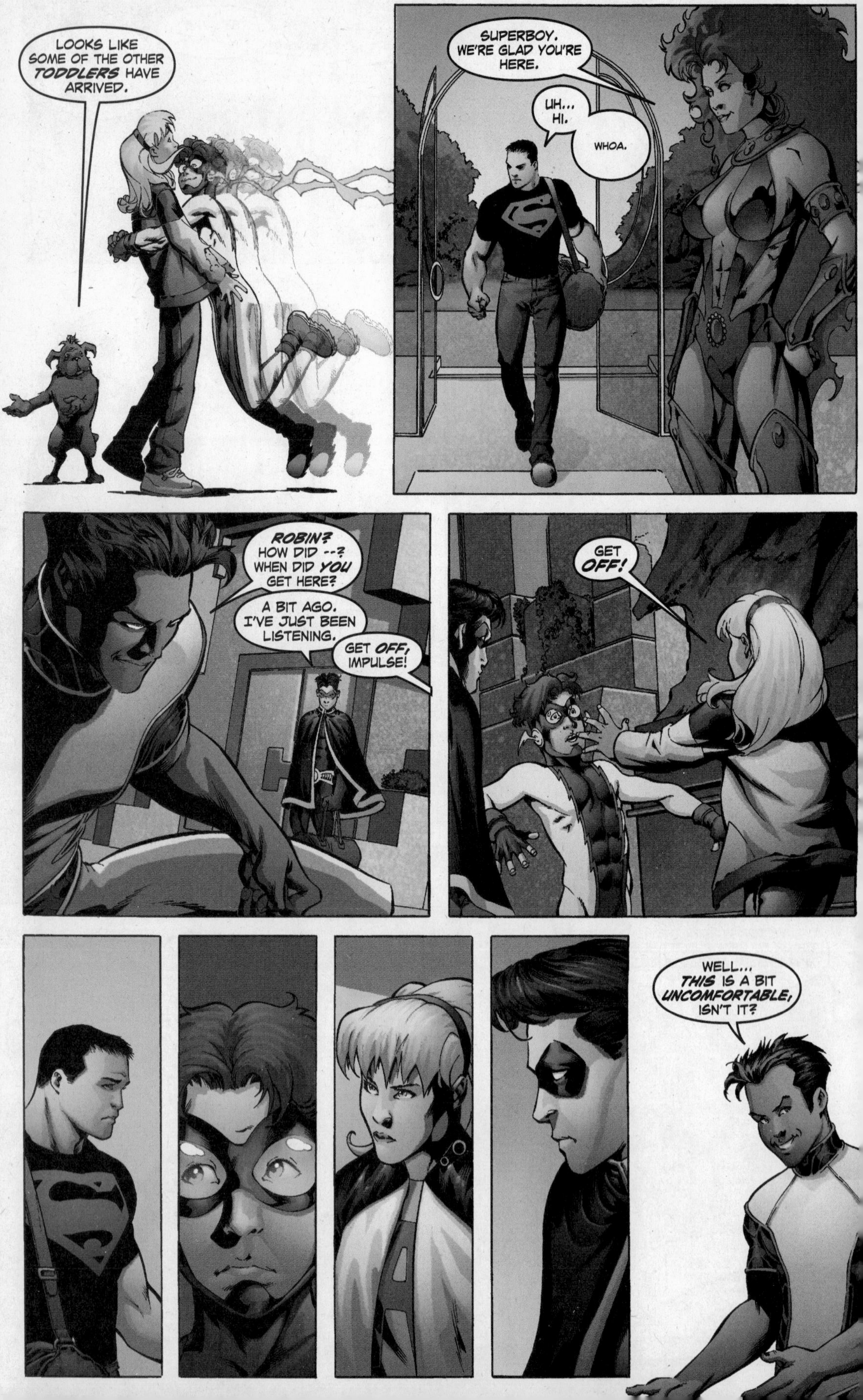
LOOKS LIKE SOME OF THE OTHER TODDLERS HAVE ARRIVED.
SUPERBOY. WE'RE GLAD YOU'RE HERE.
UH... HI.
WHOA.
ROBIN? HOW DID --? WHEN DID YOU GET HERE?
A BIT AGO. I'VE JUST BEEN LISTENING.
GET OFF, IMPULSE!
GET OFF!
WELL... THIS IS A BIT UNCOMFORTABLE, ISN'T IT?

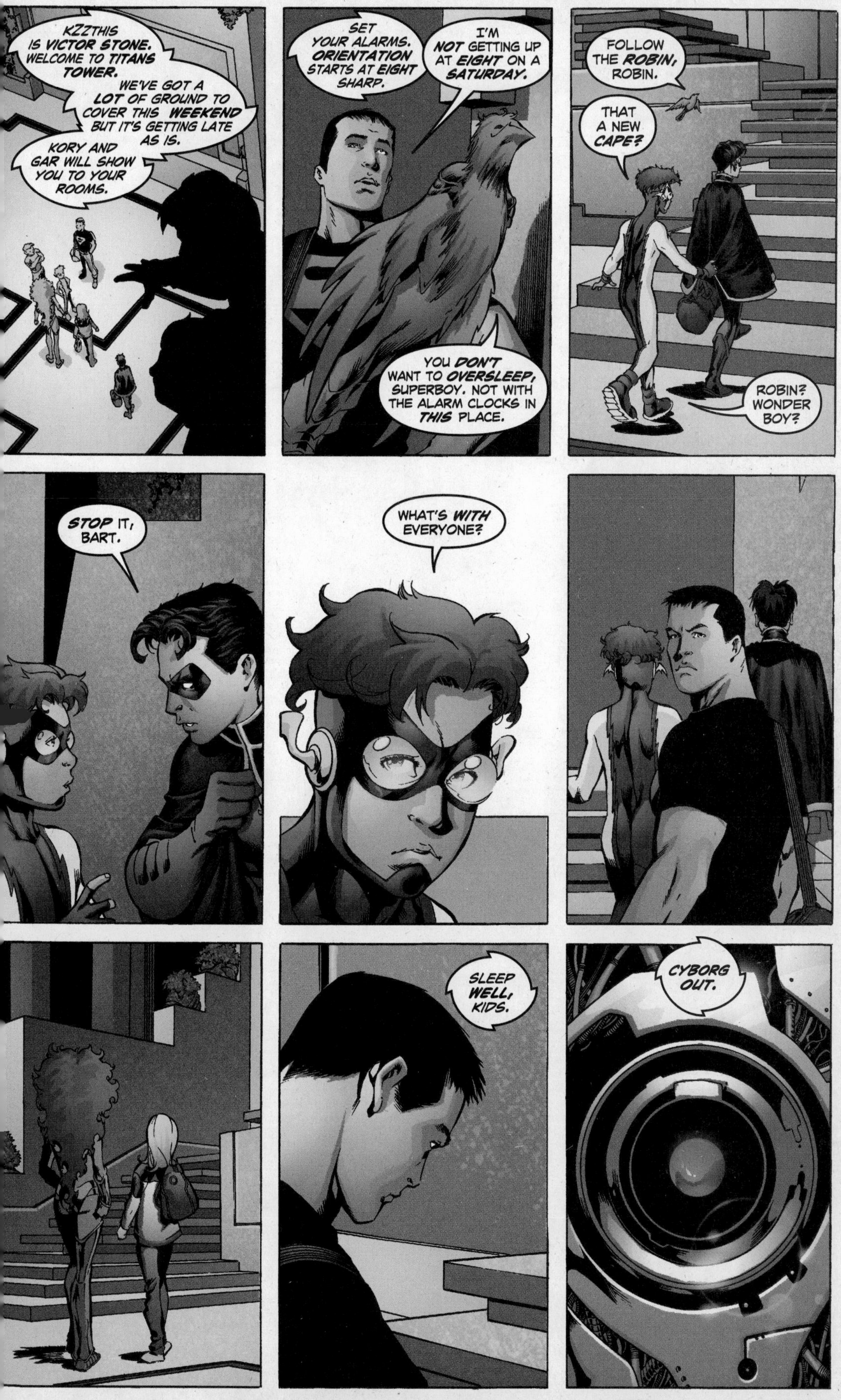
KZZTHIS IS VICTOR STONE. WELCOME TO TITANS TOWER.
WE'VE GOT A LOT OF GROUND TO COVER THIS WEEKEND BUT IT'S GETTING LATE AS IS.
KORY AND GAR WILL SHOW YOU TO YOUR ROOMS.
SET YOUR ALARMS. ORIENTATION STARTS AT EIGHT SHARP.
I'M NOT GETTING UP AT EIGHT ON A SATURDAY.
YOU DON'T WANT TO OVERSLEEP, SUPERBOY. NOT WITH THE ALARM CLOCKS IN THIS PLACE.
FOLLOW THE ROBIN, ROBIN.
THAT A NEW CAPE?
ROBIN? WONDER BOY?
STOP IT, BART.
WHAT'S WITH EVERYONE?
SLEEP WELL, KIDS.
CYBORG OUT.

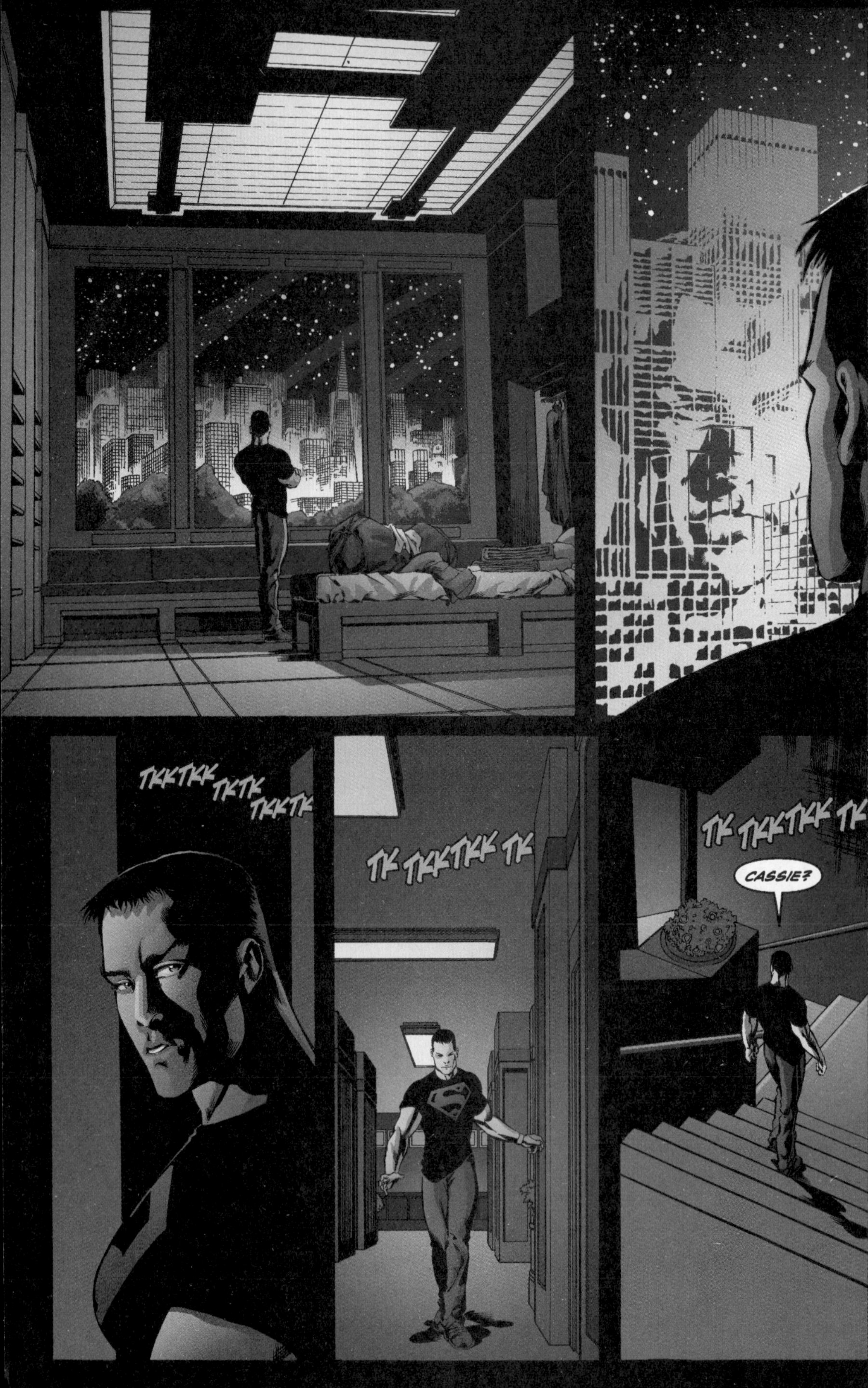
TKKTKK TKTK TKKTK
TK TKKTKK TK
TK TKKTKK TK
CASSIE?

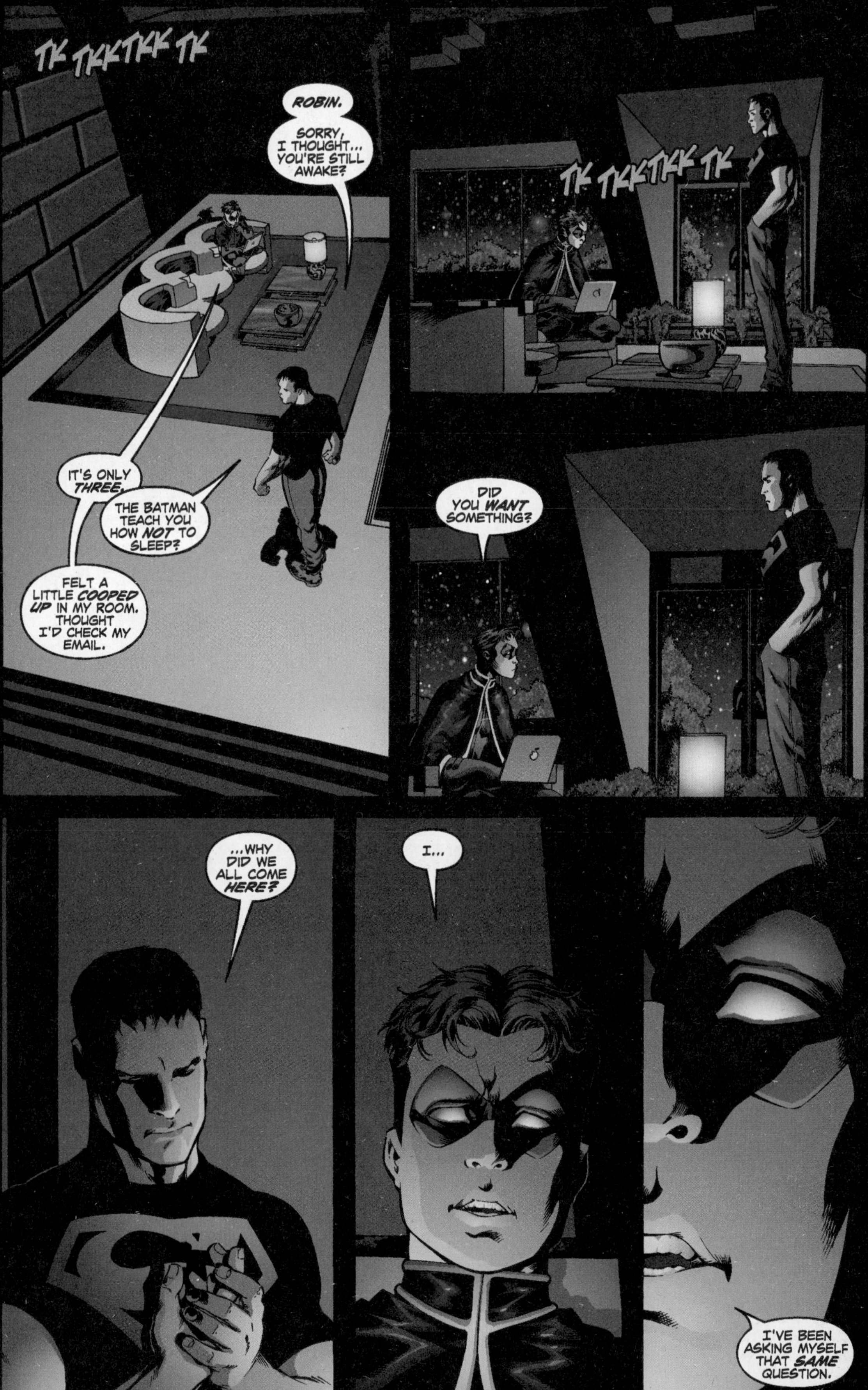

TK TKKTKK TK
ROBIN.
SORRY, I THOUGHT... YOU'RE STILL AWAKE?
IT'S ONLY THREE.
THE BATMAN TEACH YOU HOW NOT TO SLEEP?
FELT A LITTLE COOPED UP IN MY ROOM. THOUGHT I'D CHECK MY EMAIL.
TK TKKTKK TK
DID YOU WANT SOMETHING?
...WHY DID WE ALL COME HERE?
I...
I'VE BEEN ASKING MYSELF THAT SAME QUESTION.

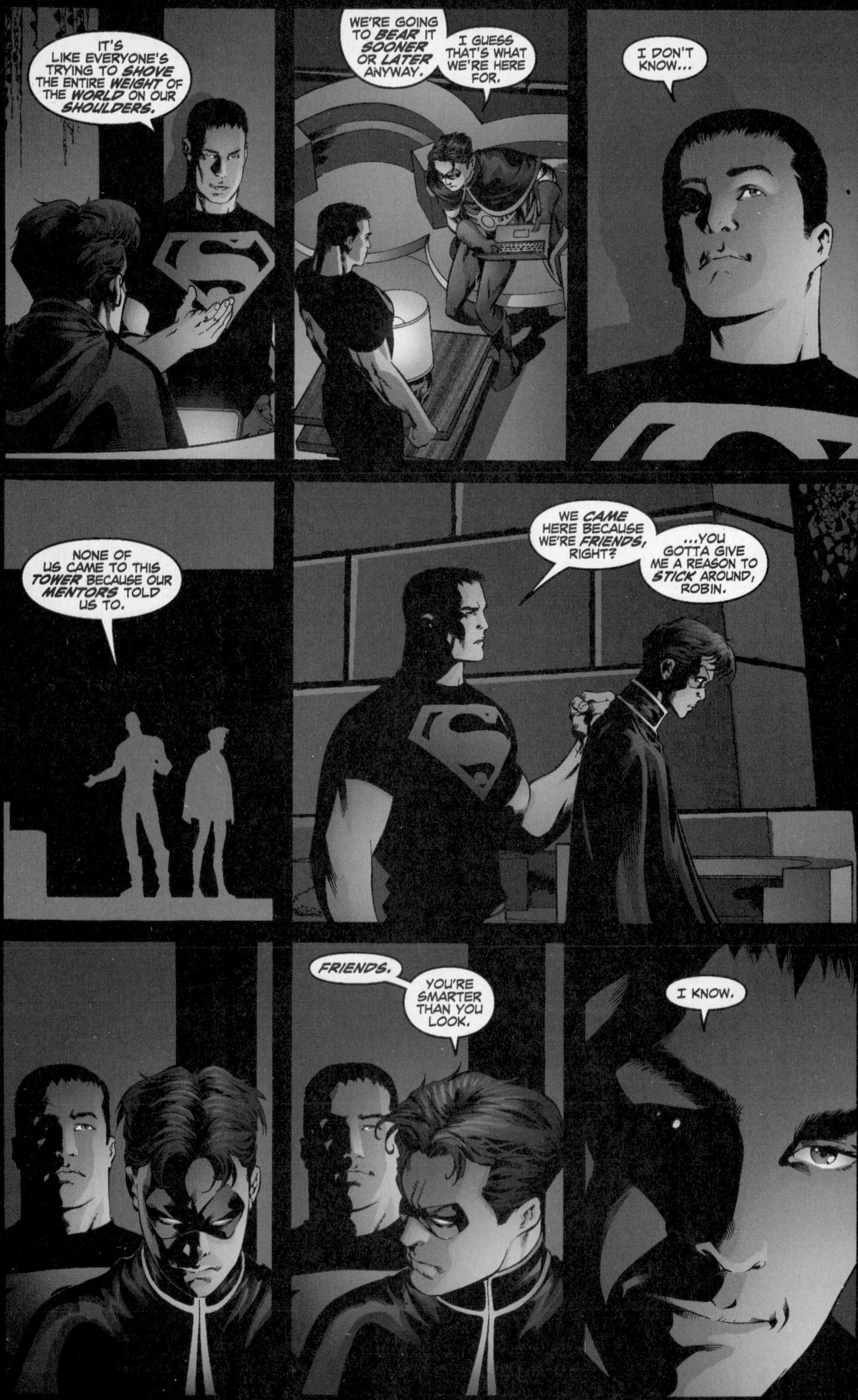
IT'S LIKE EVERYONE'S TRYING TO SHOVE THE ENTIRE WEIGHT OF THE WORLD ON OUR SHOULDERS.
WE'RE GOING TO BEAR IT SOONER OR LATER ANYWAY.
I GUESS THAT'S WHAT WE'RE HERE FOR.
I DON'T KNOW...
NONE OF US CAME TO THIS TOWER BECAUSE OUR MENTORS TOLD US TO.
WE CAME HERE BECAUSE WE'RE FRIENDS, RIGHT?
...YOU GOTTA GIVE ME A REASON TO STICK AROUND, ROBIN.
FRIENDS.
YOU'RE SMARTER THAN YOU LOOK.
I KNOW.

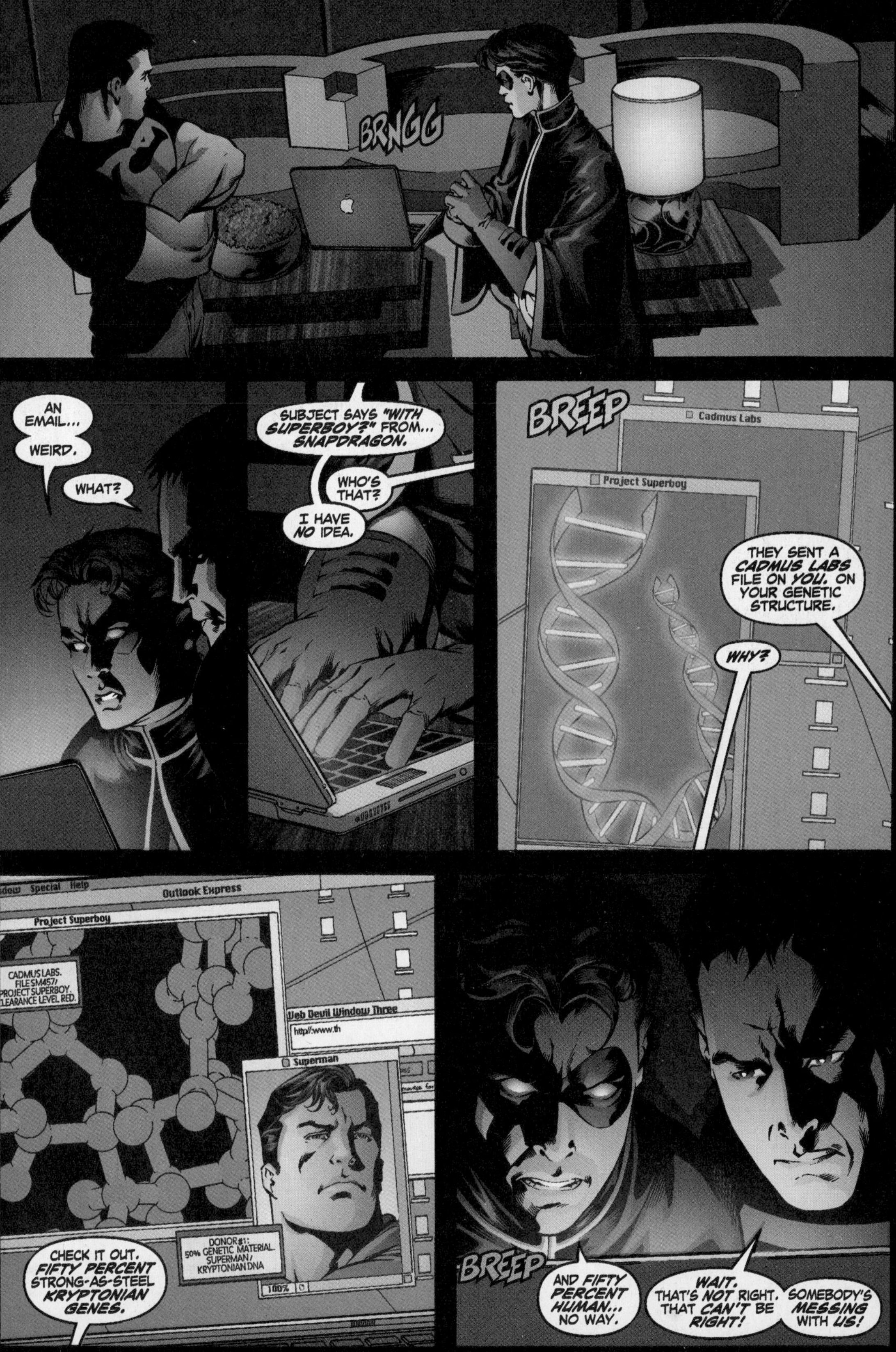
BRNGG
AN EMAIL...
WEIRD.
WHAT?
SUBJECT SAYS "WITH SUPERBOY?" FROM... SNAPDRAGON.
WHO'S THAT?
I HAVE NO IDEA.
BREEP
Cadmus Labs
Project Superboy
THEY SENT A CADMUS LABS FILE ON YOU. ON YOUR GENETIC STRUCTURE.
WHY?
Special Help
Outlook Express
Project Superboy
CADMUS LABS. FILE SM457/ PROJECT SUPERBOY.
Web Devil Window Three
Superman
DONOR#1: 50% GENETIC MATERIAL. SUPERMAN/ KRYPTONIAN DNA
100%
CHECK IT OUT. FIFTY PERCENT STRONG-AS-STEEL KRYPTONIAN GENES.
BREEP
AND FIFTY PERCENT HUMAN... NO WAY.
WAIT. THAT'S NOT RIGHT. THAT CAN'T BE RIGHT!
SOMEBODY'S MESSING WITH US!

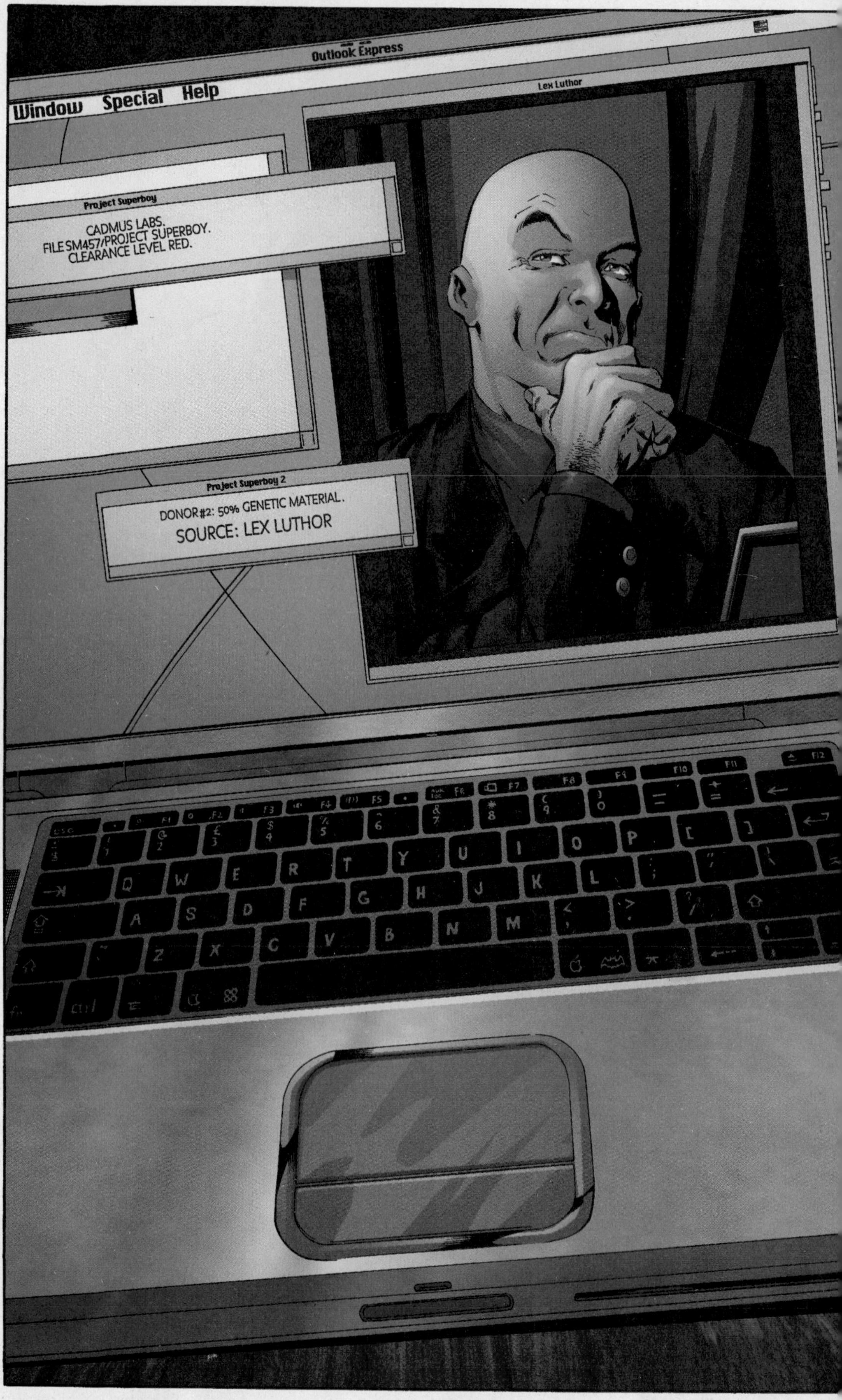
Outlook Express
Window Special Help
Lex Luthor
Project Superboy
CADMUS LABS.
FILE SM457/PROJECT SUPERBOY.
CLEARANCE LEVEL RED.
Project Superboy 2
DONOR#2: 50% GENETIC MATERIAL.
SOURCE: LEX LUTHOR

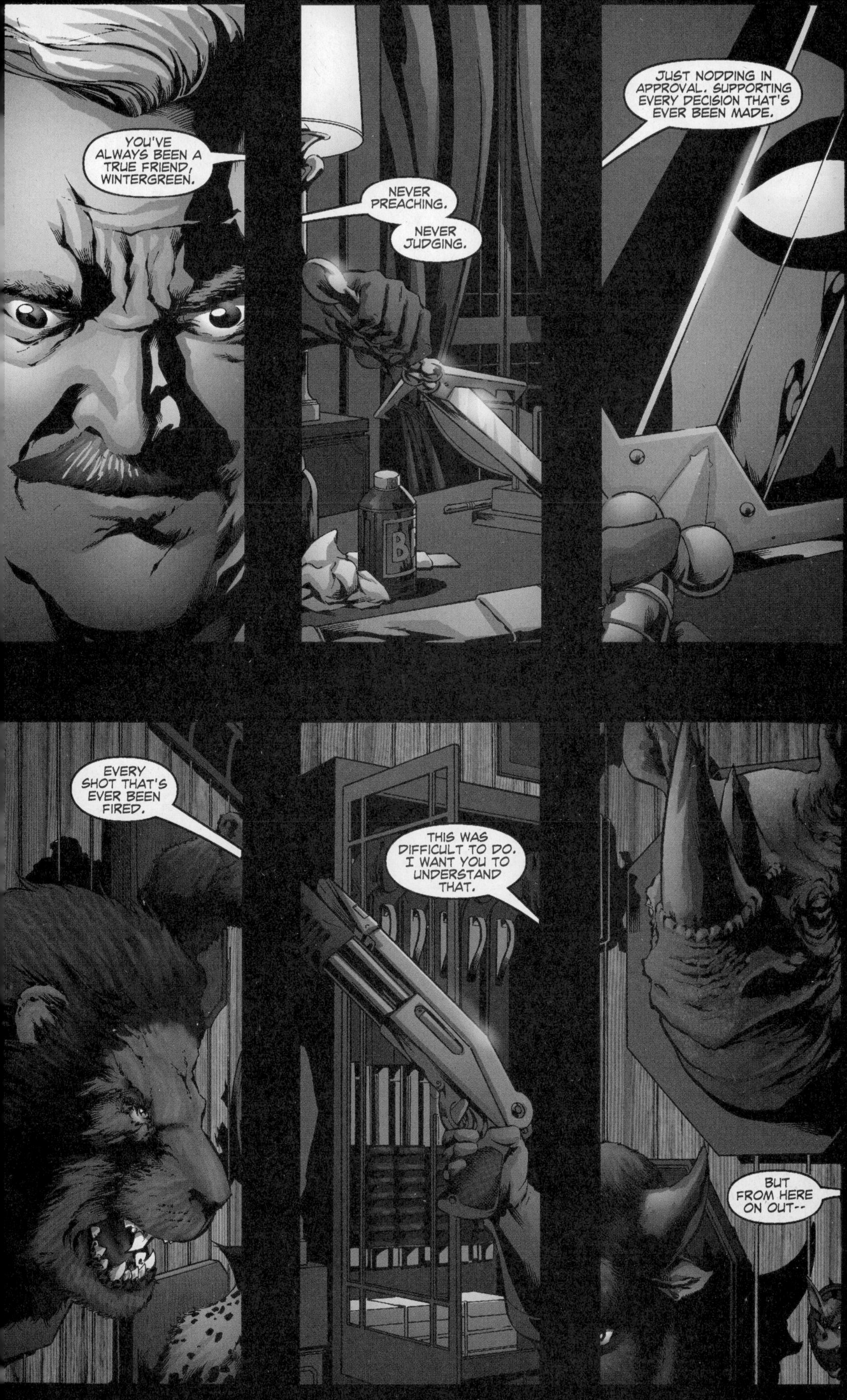
YOU'VE ALWAYS BEEN A TRUE FRIEND, WINTERGREEN.
NEVER PREACHING.
NEVER JUDGING.
JUST NODDING IN APPROVAL. SUPPORTING EVERY DECISION THAT'S EVER BEEN MADE.
EVERY SHOT THAT'S EVER BEEN FIRED.
THIS WAS DIFFICULT TO DO. I WANT YOU TO UNDERSTAND THAT.
BUT FROM HERE ON OUT--

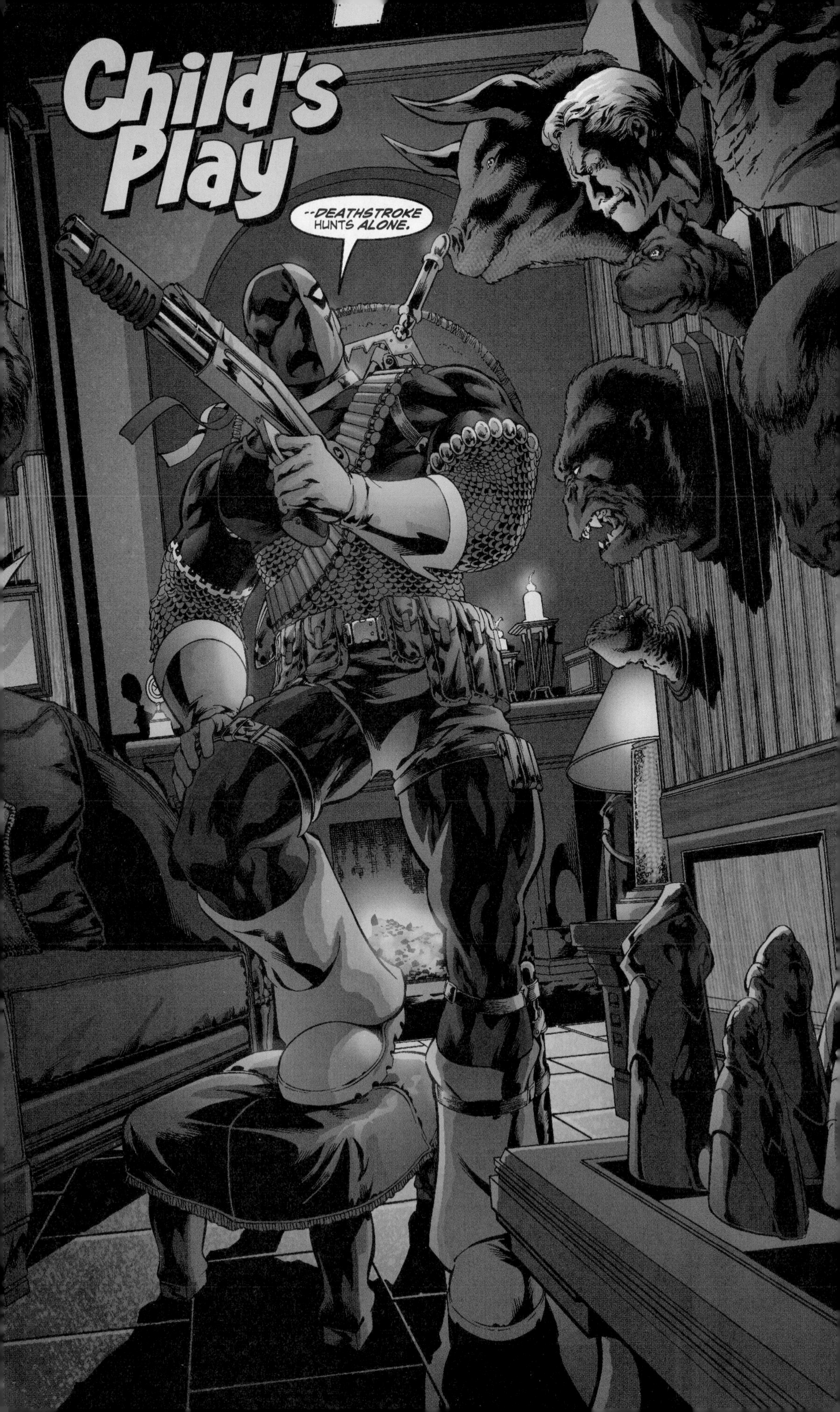
Child's Play
--DEATHSTROKE HUNTS ALONE.

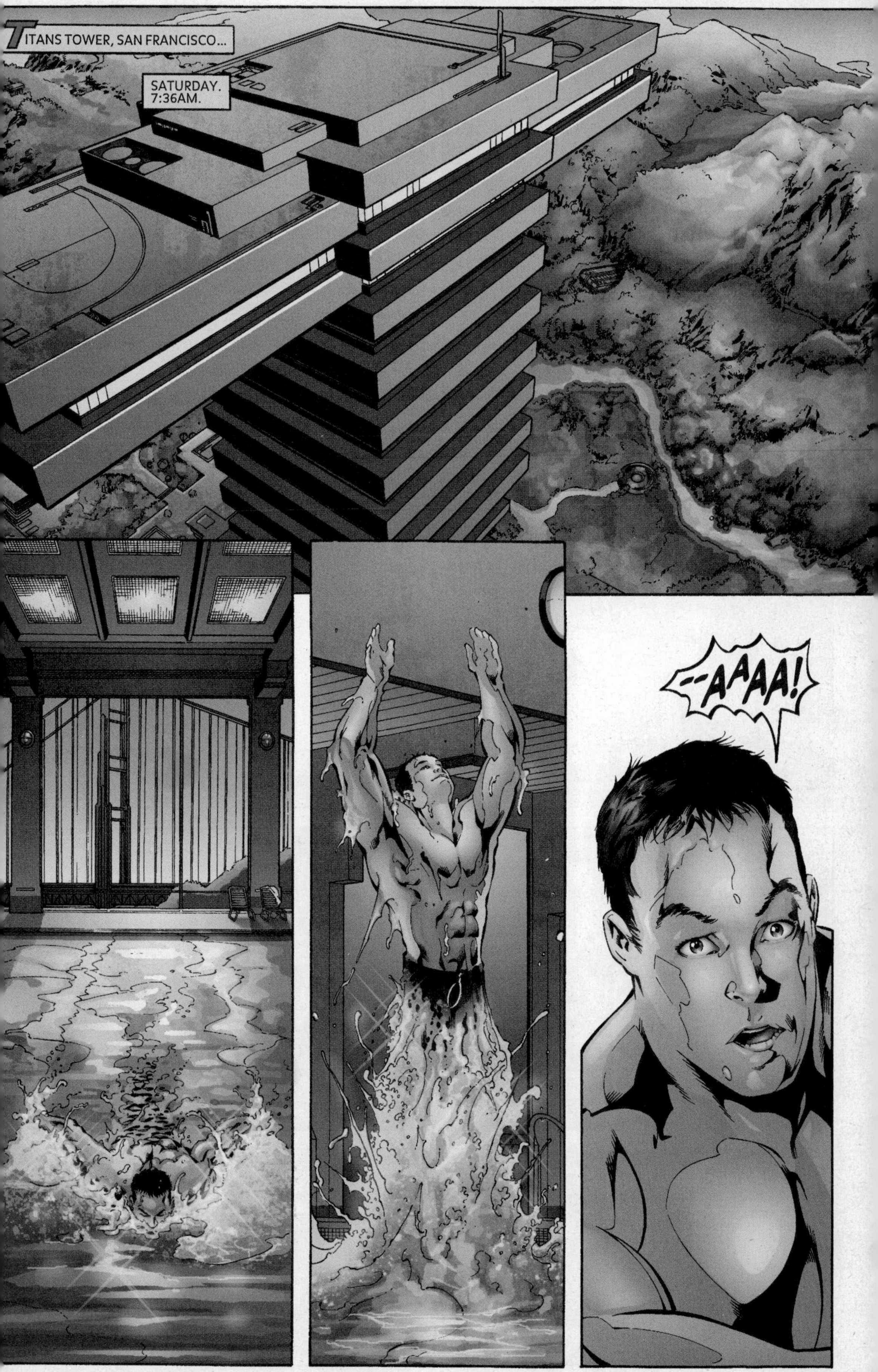

TITANS TOWER, SAN FRANCISCO...
SATURDAY. 7:36AM.
--AAAA!

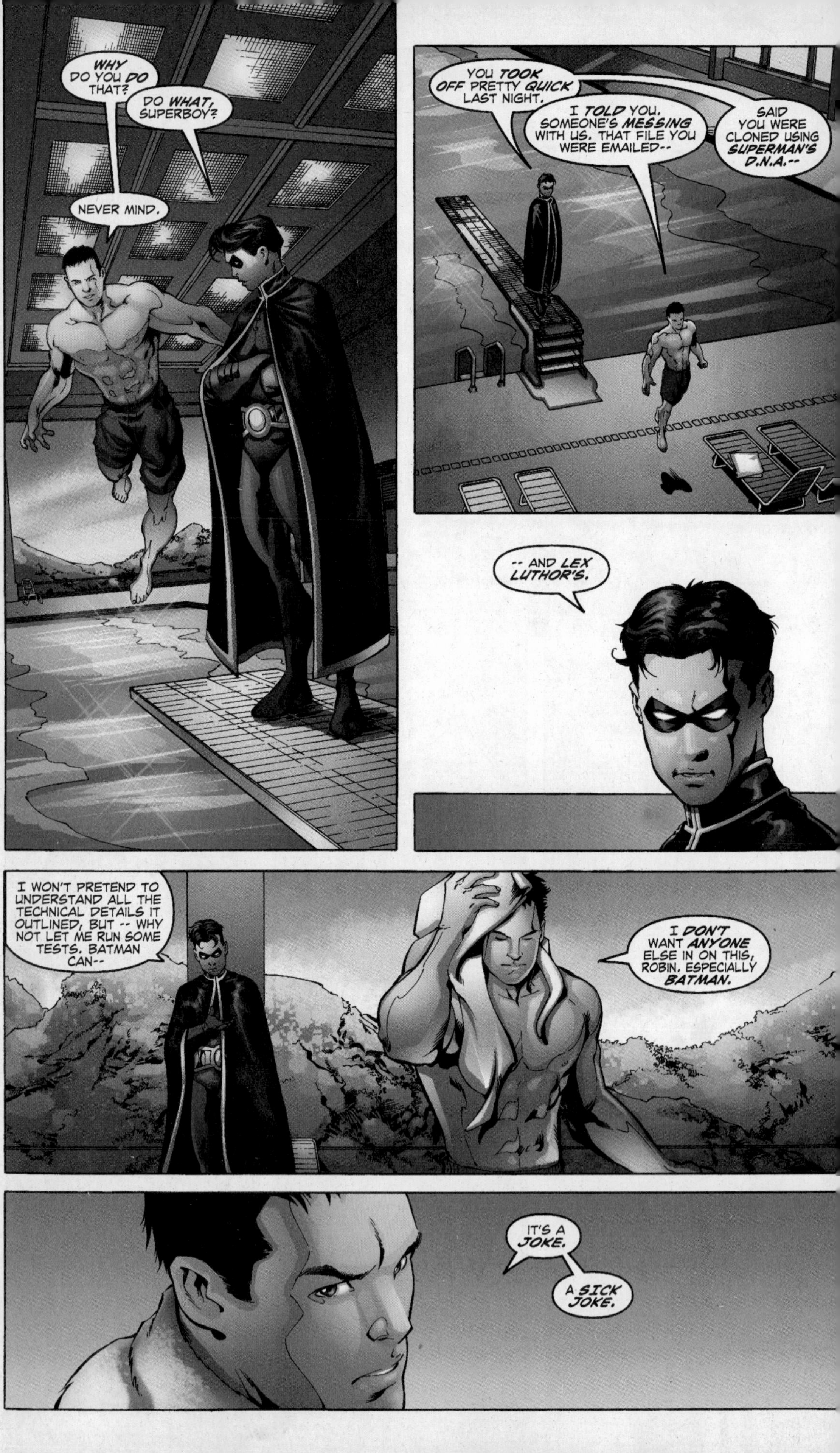
WHY DO YOU DO THAT?
DO WHAT, SUPERBOY?
NEVER MIND.
YOU TOOK OFF PRETTY QUICK LAST NIGHT.
I TOLD YOU. SOMEONE'S MESSING WITH US. THAT FILE YOU WERE EMAILED--
SAID YOU WERE CLONED USING SUPERMAN'S D.N.A.--
-- AND LEX LUTHOR'S.
I WON'T PRETEND TO UNDERSTAND ALL THE TECHNICAL DETAILS IT OUTLINED, BUT -- WHY NOT LET ME RUN SOME TESTS. BATMAN CAN--
I DON'T WANT ANYONE ELSE IN ON THIS, ROBIN. ESPECIALLY BATMAN.
IT'S A JOKE.
A SICK JOKE.

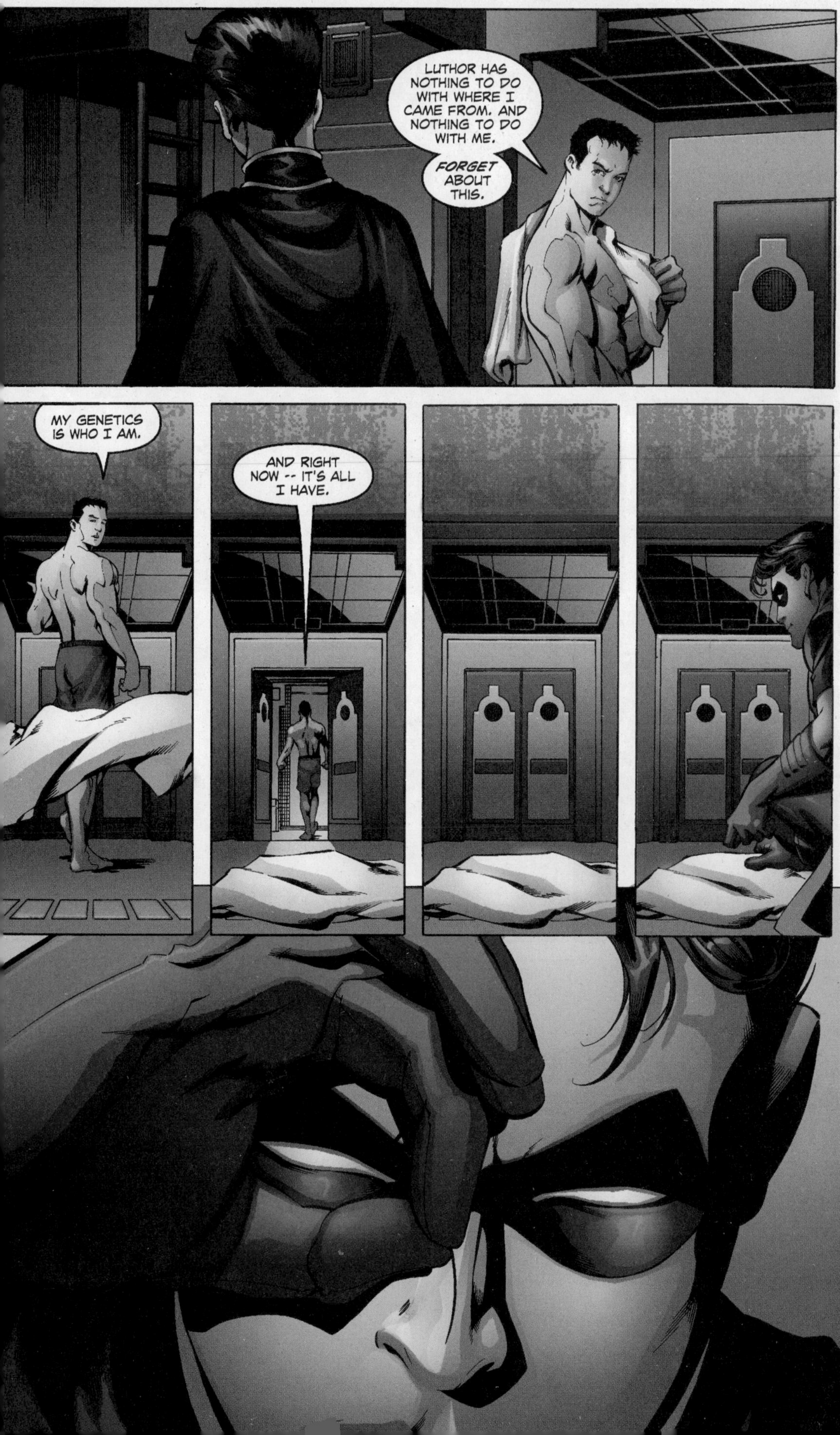
LUTHOR HAS NOTHING TO DO WITH WHERE I CAME FROM. AND NOTHING TO DO WITH ME.
FORGET ABOUT THIS.
MY GENETICS IS WHO I AM.
AND RIGHT NOW -- IT'S ALL I HAVE.

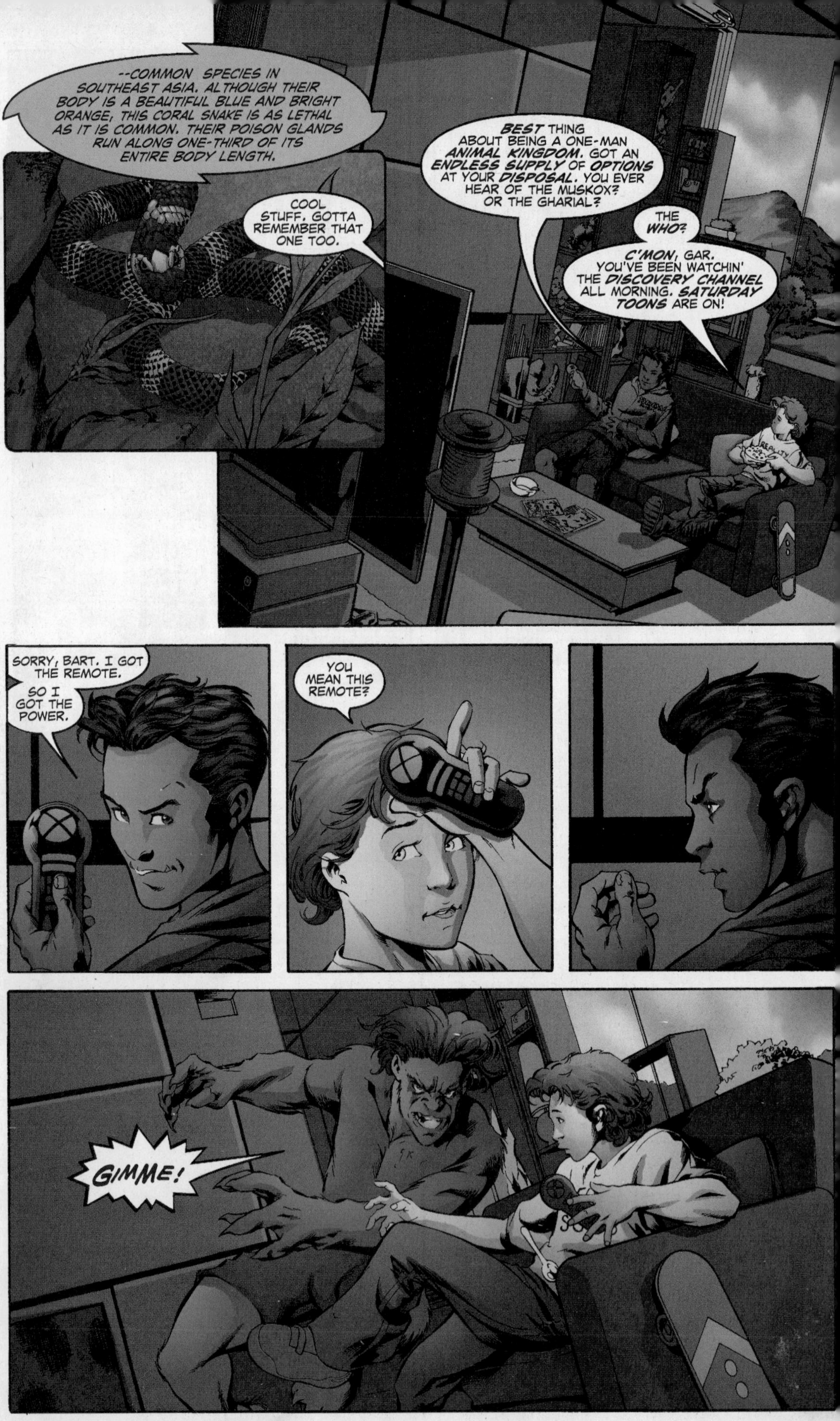
--COMMON SPECIES IN SOUTHEAST ASIA. ALTHOUGH THEIR BODY IS A BEAUTIFUL BLUE AND BRIGHT ORANGE, THIS CORAL SNAKE IS AS LETHAL AS IT IS COMMON. THEIR POISON GLANDS RUN ALONG ONE-THIRD OF ITS ENTIRE BODY LENGTH.
COOL STUFF. GOTTA REMEMBER THAT ONE TOO.
BEST THING ABOUT BEING A ONE-MAN ANIMAL KINGDOM. GOT AN ENDLESS SUPPLY OF OPTIONS AT YOUR DISPOSAL. YOU EVER HEAR OF THE MUSKOX? OR THE GHARIAL?
THE WHO?
C'MON, GAR. YOU'VE BEEN WATCHIN' THE DISCOVERY CHANNEL ALL MORNING. SATURDAY TOONS ARE ON!
SORRY, BART. I GOT THE REMOTE.
SO I GOT THE POWER.
YOU MEAN THIS REMOTE?
GIMME!

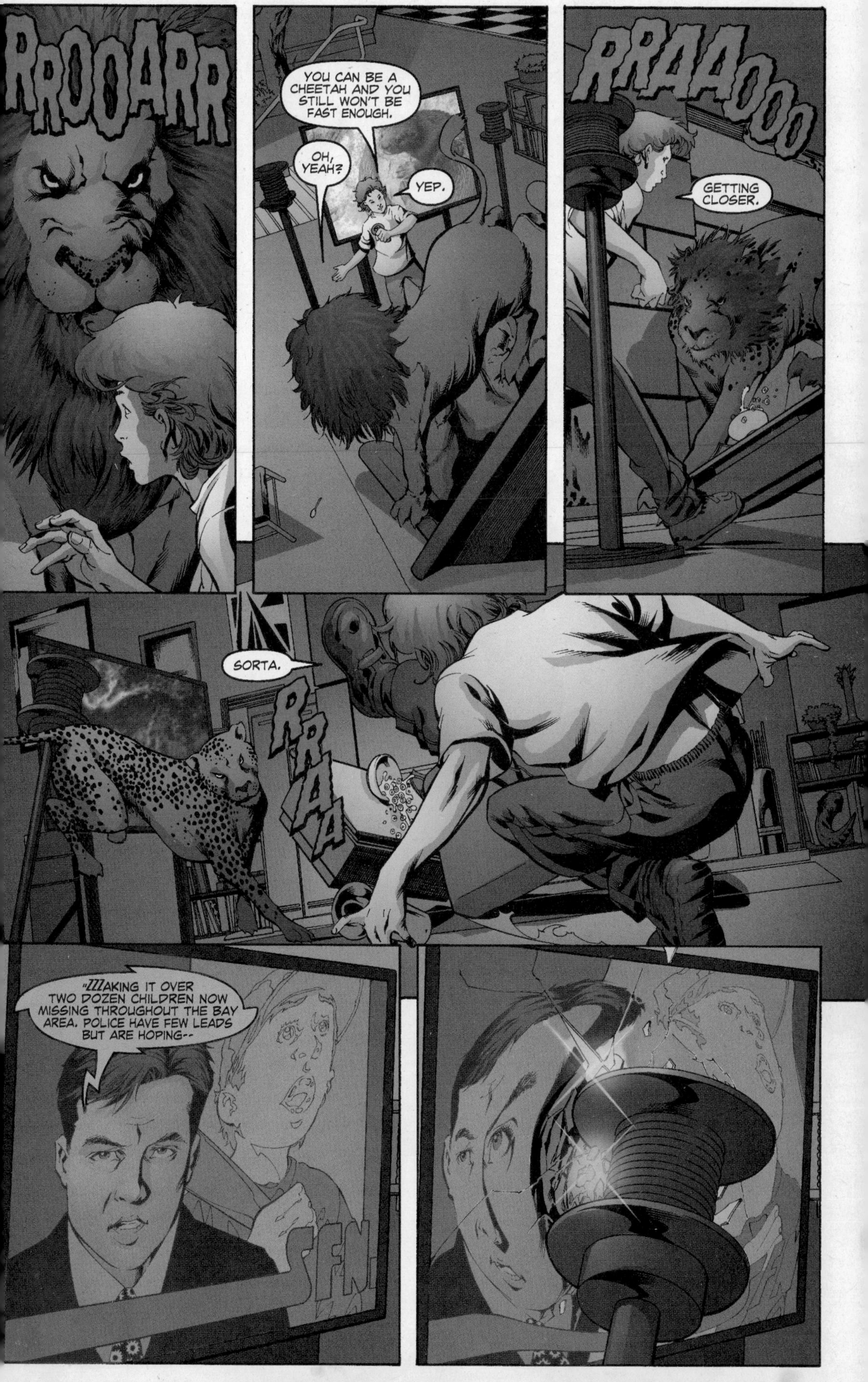
RROOARR
YOU CAN BE A CHEETAH AND YOU STILL WON'T BE FAST ENOUGH.
OH, YEAH?
YEP.
RRAAOOO
GETTING CLOSER.
SORTA.
RRAA
"ZZZAKING IT OVER TWO DOZEN CHILDREN NOW MISSING THROUGHOUT THE BAY AREA. POLICE HAVE FEW LEADS BUT ARE HOPING--
SFN

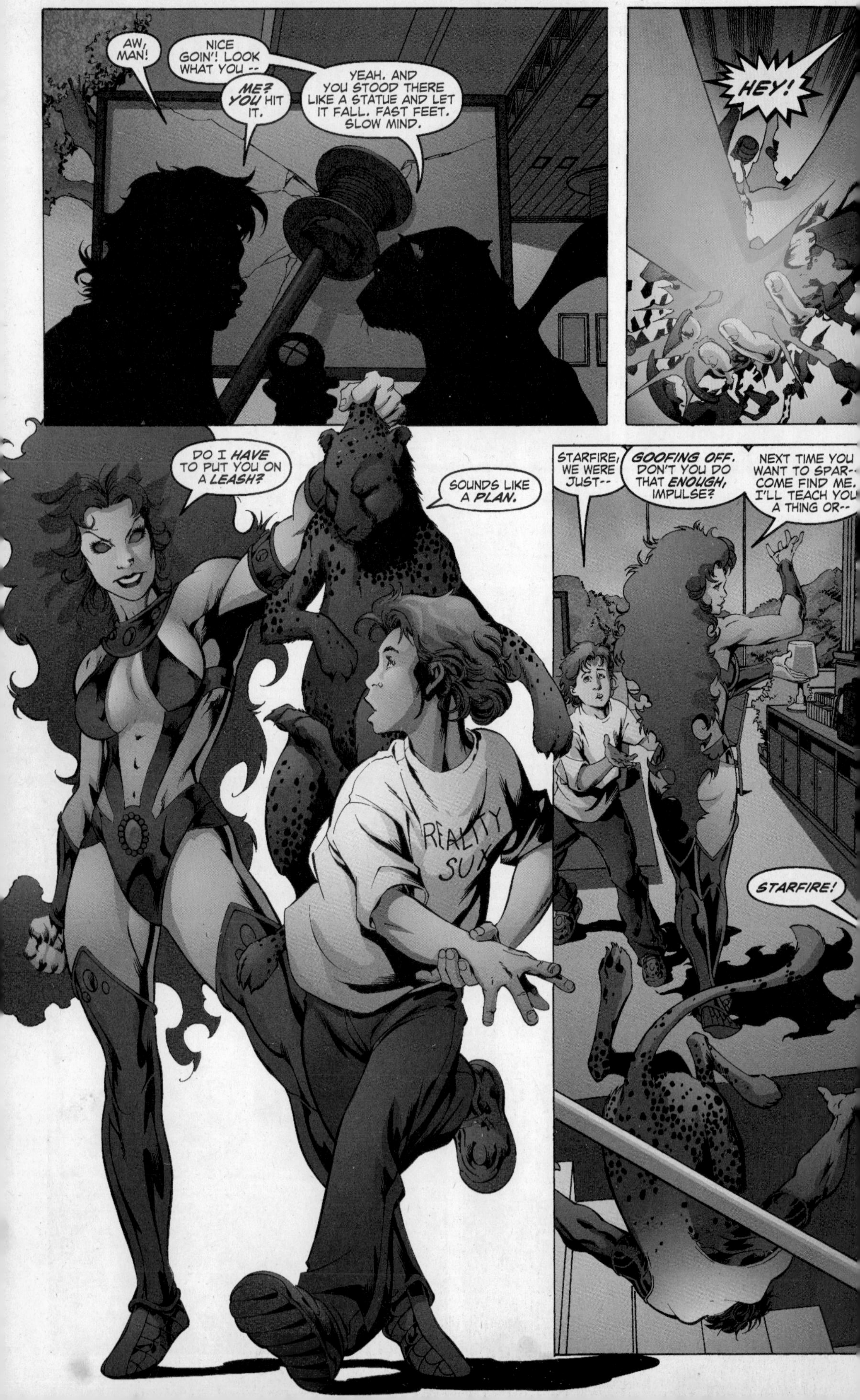
AW, MAN!
NICE GOIN'! LOOK WHAT YOU --
ME? YOU HIT IT.
YEAH. AND YOU STOOD THERE LIKE A STATUE AND LET IT FALL. FAST FEET. SLOW MIND.
HEY!
DO I HAVE TO PUT YOU ON A LEASH?
SOUNDS LIKE A PLAN.
REALITY SUX
STARFIRE, WE WERE JUST--
GOOFING OFF. DON'T YOU DO THAT ENOUGH, IMPULSE?
NEXT TIME YOU WANT TO SPAR-- COME FIND ME. I'LL TEACH YOU A THING OR--
STARFIRE!

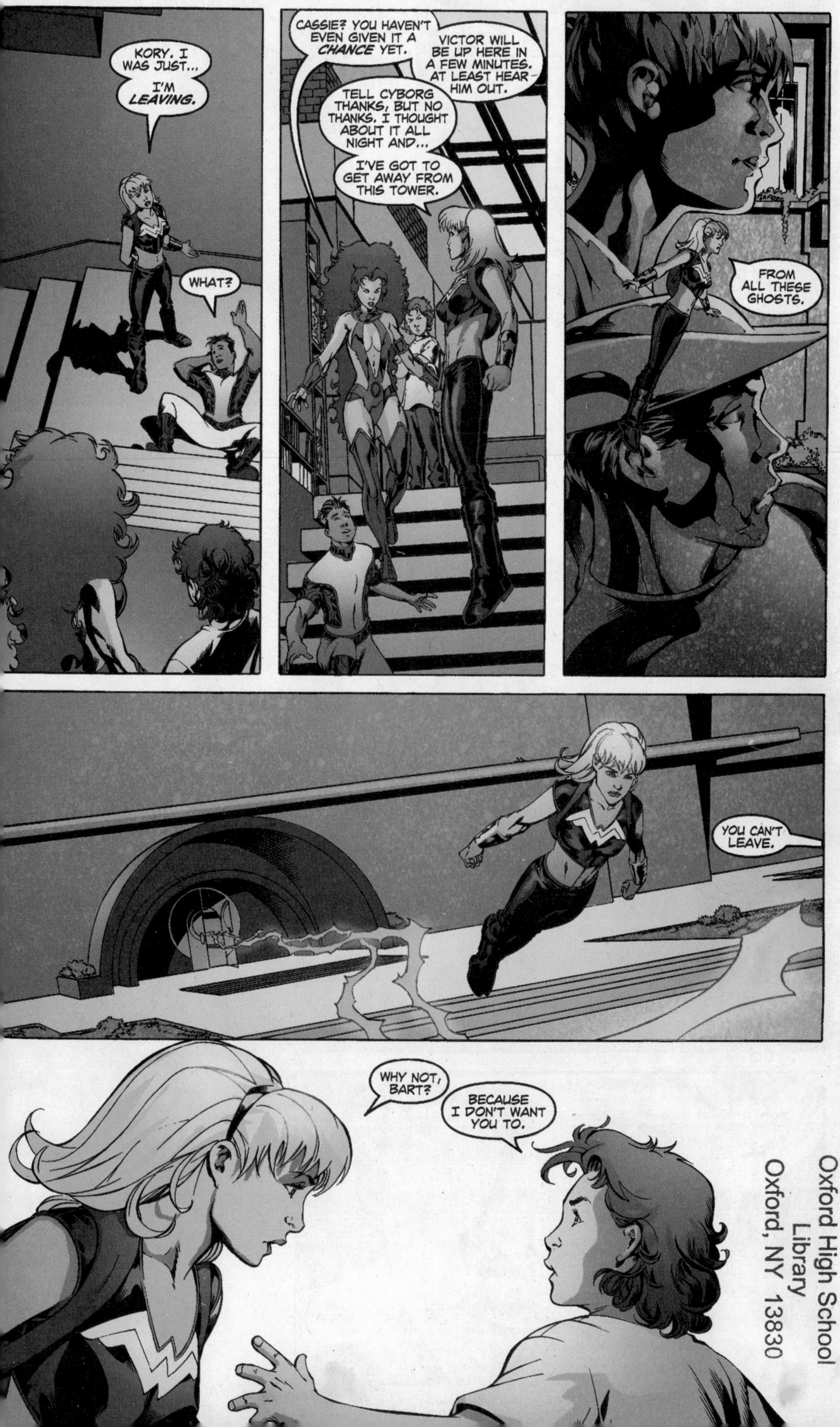
KORY. I WAS JUST... I'M LEAVING.
WHAT?
CASSIE? YOU HAVEN'T EVEN GIVEN IT A CHANCE YET.
VICTOR WILL BE UP HERE IN A FEW MINUTES. AT LEAST HEAR HIM OUT.
TELL CYBORG THANKS, BUT NO THANKS. I THOUGHT ABOUT IT ALL NIGHT AND...
I'VE GOT TO GET AWAY FROM THIS TOWER.
FROM ALL THESE GHOSTS.
YOU CAN'T LEAVE.
WHY NOT, BART?
BECAUSE I DON'T WANT YOU TO.

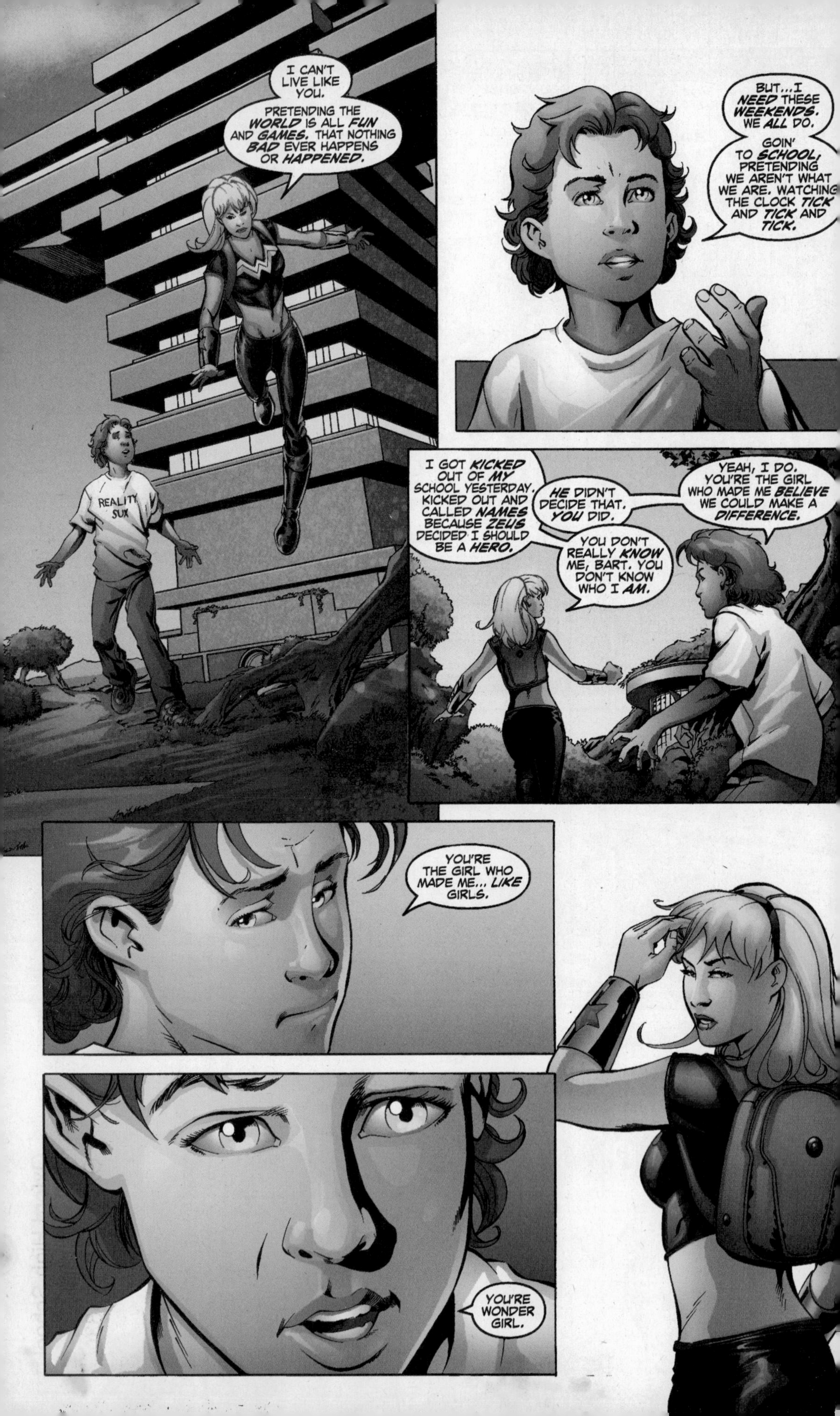
I CAN'T LIVE LIKE YOU.
PRETENDING THE WORLD IS ALL FUN AND GAMES. THAT NOTHING BAD EVER HAPPENS OR HAPPENED.
REALITY SUX
BUT...I NEED THESE WEEKENDS. WE ALL DO.
GOIN' TO SCHOOL, PRETENDING WE AREN'T WHAT WE ARE. WATCHING THE CLOCK TICK AND TICK AND TICK.
I GOT KICKED OUT OF MY SCHOOL YESTERDAY. KICKED OUT AND CALLED NAMES BECAUSE ZEUS DECIDED I SHOULD BE A HERO.
HE DIDN'T DECIDE THAT. YOU DID.
YOU DON'T REALLY KNOW ME, BART. YOU DON'T KNOW WHO I AM.
YEAH, I DO. YOU'RE THE GIRL WHO MADE ME BELIEVE WE COULD MAKE A DIFFERENCE.
YOU'RE THE GIRL WHO MADE ME... LIKE GIRLS.
YOU'RE WONDER GIRL.

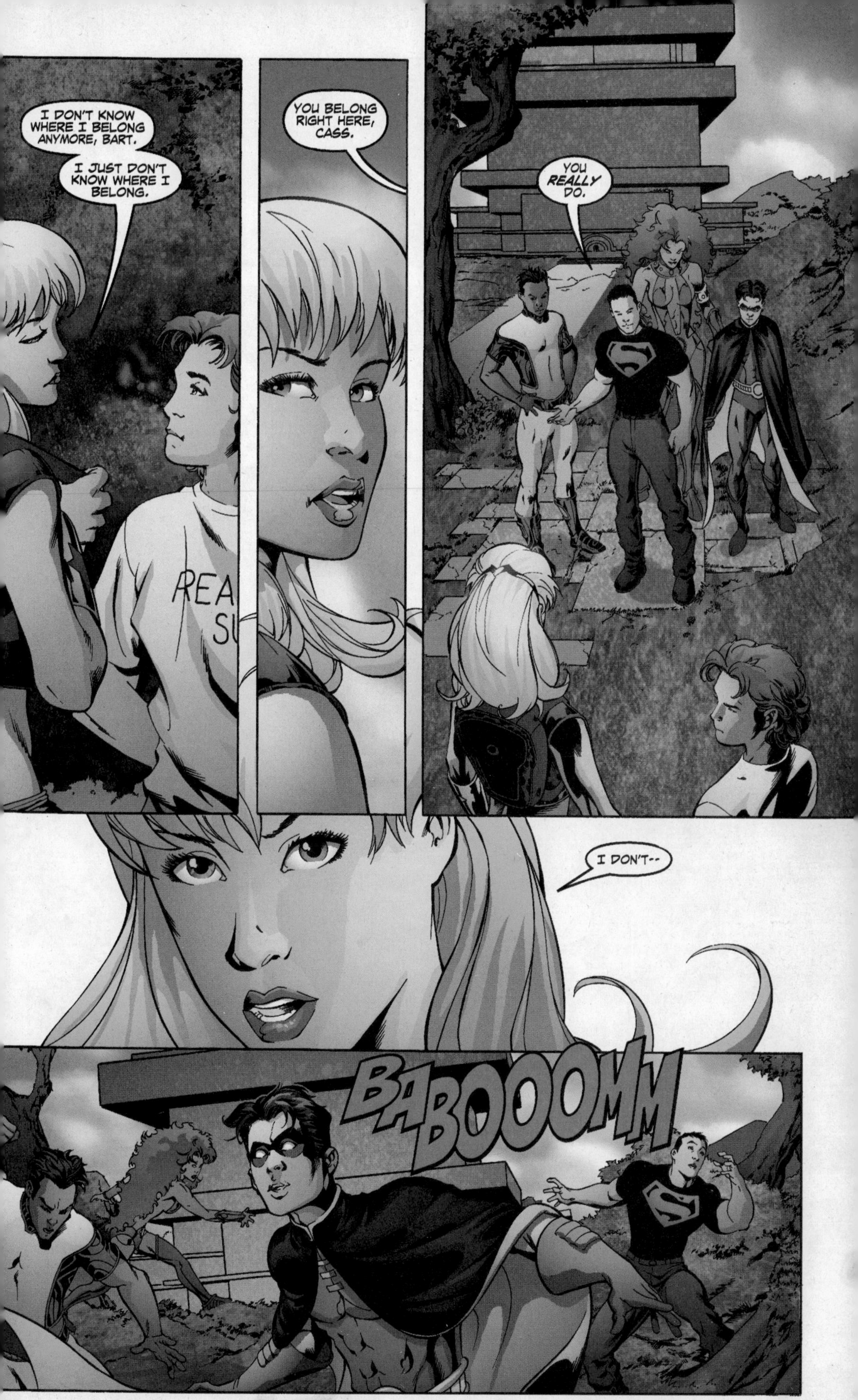
I DON'T KNOW WHERE I BELONG ANYMORE, BART.
I JUST DON'T KNOW WHERE I BELONG.
YOU BELONG RIGHT HERE, CASS.
YOU REALLY DO.
I DON'T--
BABOOOMM

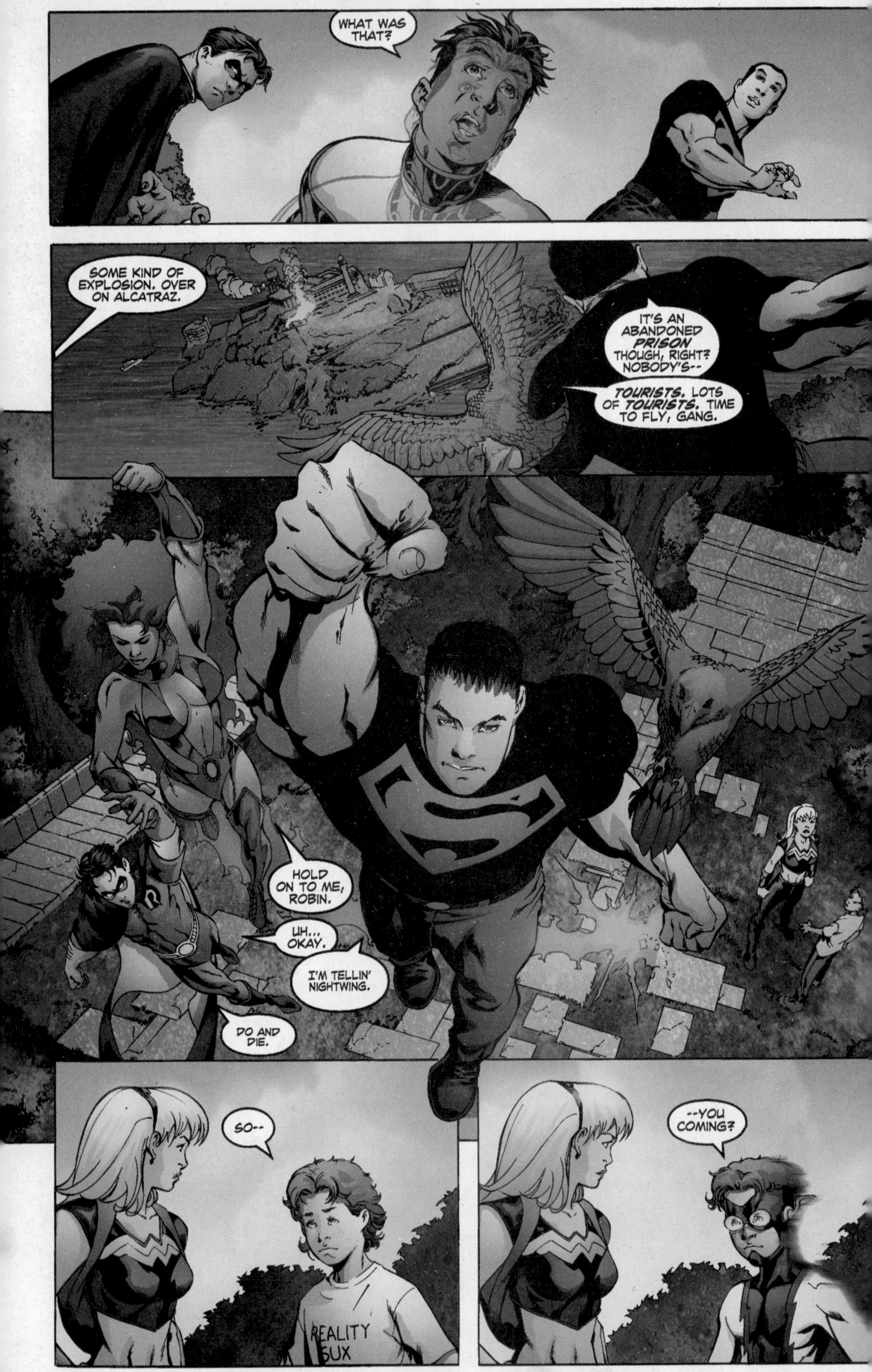

WHAT WAS THAT?
SOME KIND OF EXPLOSION. OVER ON ALCATRAZ.
IT'S AN ABANDONED PRISON THOUGH, RIGHT? NOBODY'S--
TOURISTS. LOTS OF TOURISTS. TIME TO FLY, GANG.
HOLD ON TO ME, ROBIN.
UH... OKAY.
I'M TELLIN' NIGHTWING.
DO AND DIE.
SO--
REALITY SUX
--YOU COMING?

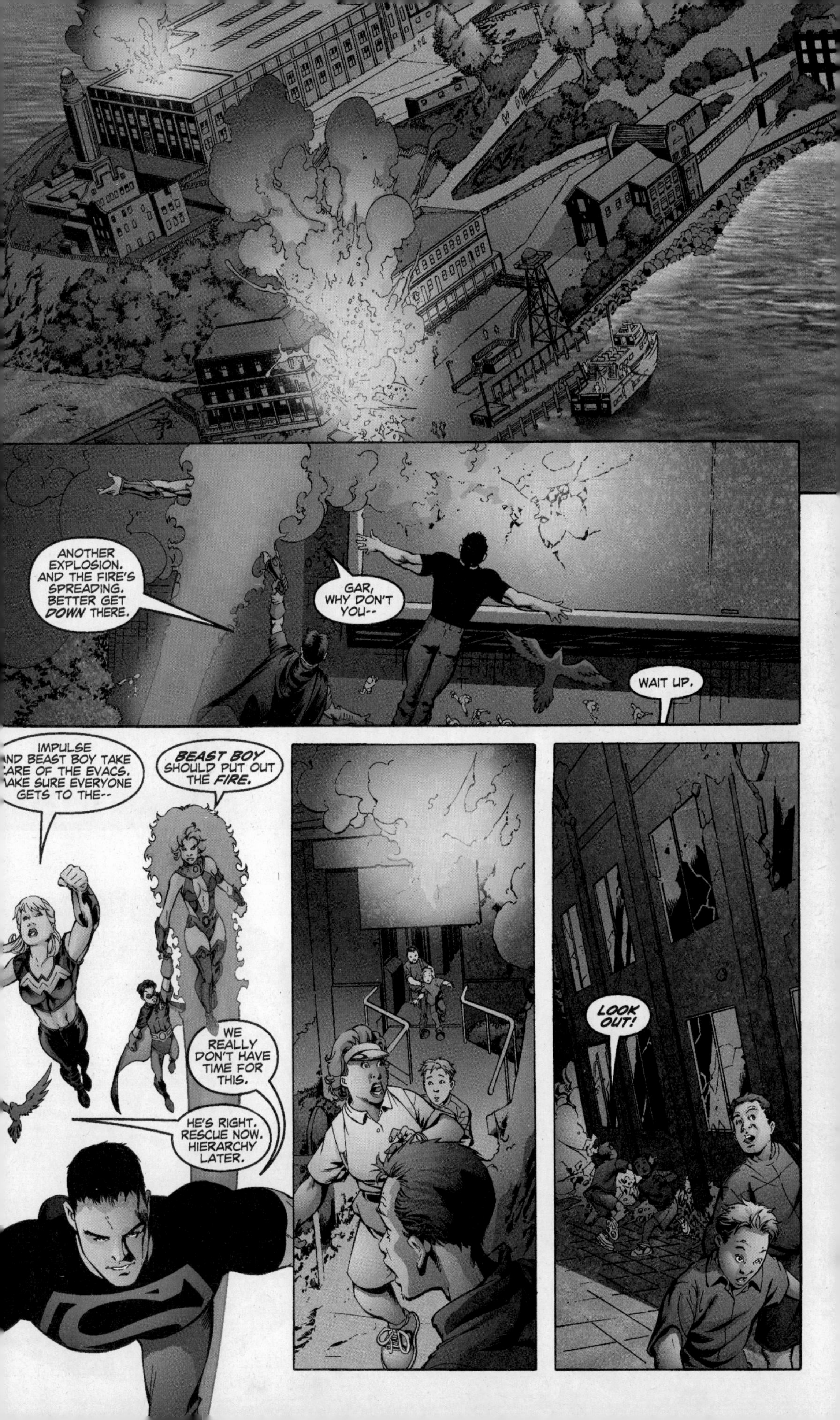

ANOTHER EXPLOSION. AND THE FIRE'S SPREADING. BETTER GET *DOWN* THERE.
GAR, WHY DON'T YOU--
WAIT UP.
IMPULSE AND BEAST BOY TAKE CARE OF THE EVACS. MAKE SURE EVERYONE GETS TO THE--
BEAST BOY SHOULD PUT OUT THE *FIRE.*
WE REALLY DON'T HAVE TIME FOR THIS.
HE'S RIGHT. RESCUE NOW. HIERARCHY LATER.
LOOK OUT!

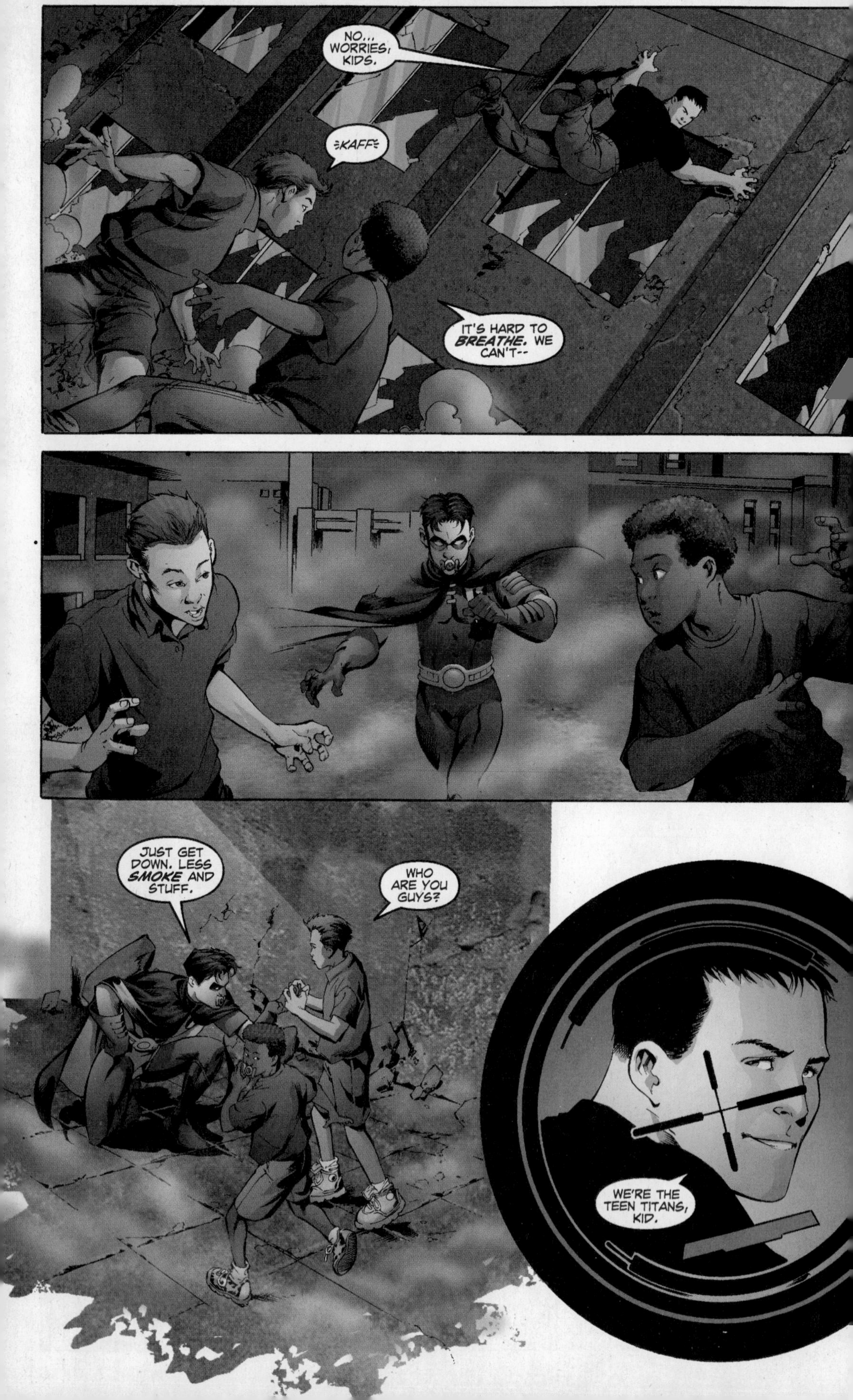
NO... WORRIES, KIDS.
≈KAFF≈
IT'S HARD TO BREATHE. WE CAN'T--
JUST GET DOWN. LESS SMOKE AND STUFF.
WHO ARE YOU GUYS?
WE'RE THE TEEN TITANS, KID.

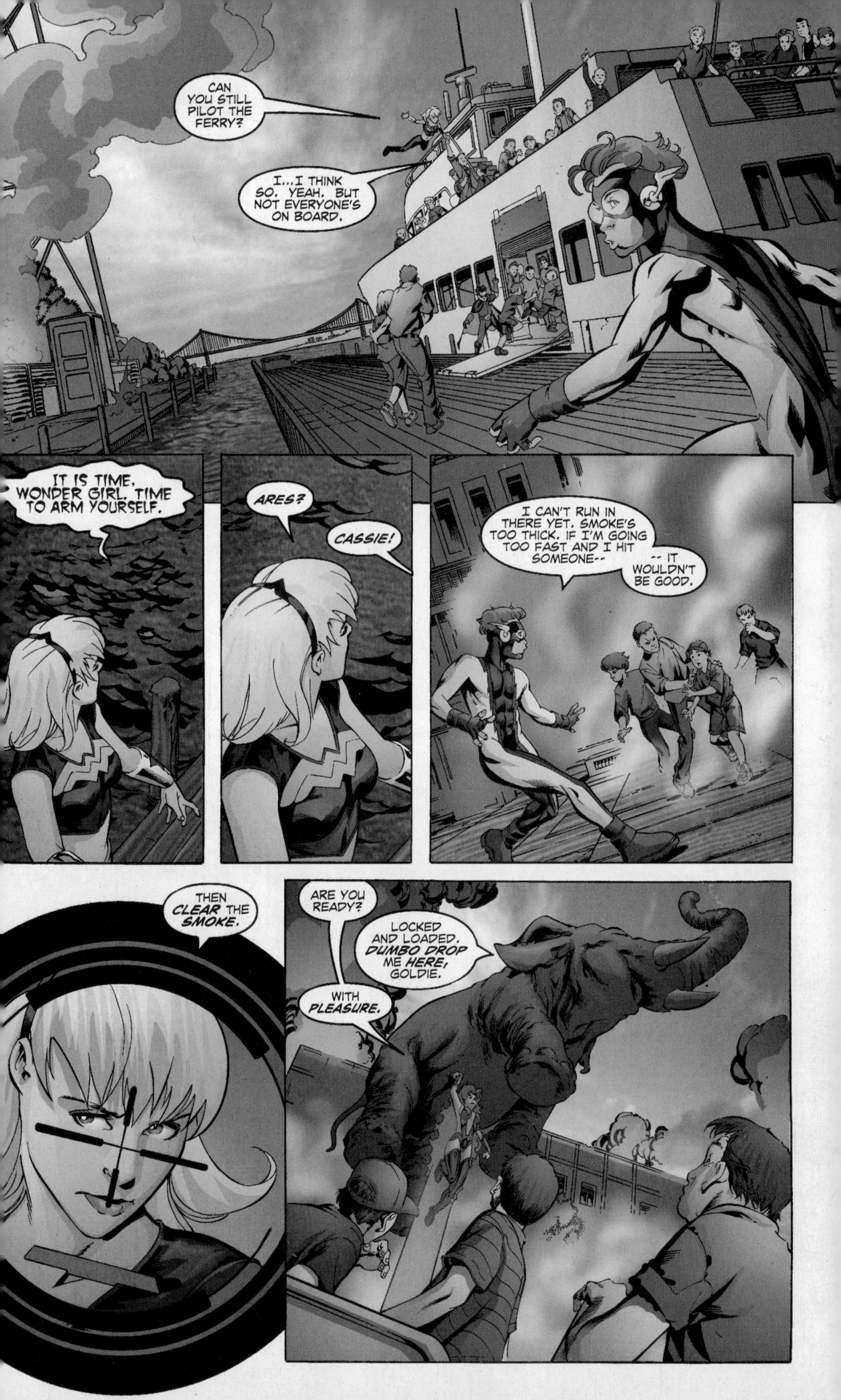
CAN YOU STILL PILOT THE FERRY?
I...I THINK SO. YEAH. BUT NOT EVERYONE'S ON BOARD.
IT IS TIME, WONDER GIRL. TIME TO ARM YOURSELF.
ARES?
CASSIE!
I CAN'T RUN IN THERE YET. SMOKE'S TOO THICK. IF I'M GOING TOO FAST AND I HIT SOMEONE--
-- IT WOULDN'T BE GOOD.
THEN CLEAR THE SMOKE.
ARE YOU READY?
LOCKED AND LOADED. DUMBO DROP ME HERE, GOLDIE.
WITH PLEASURE.

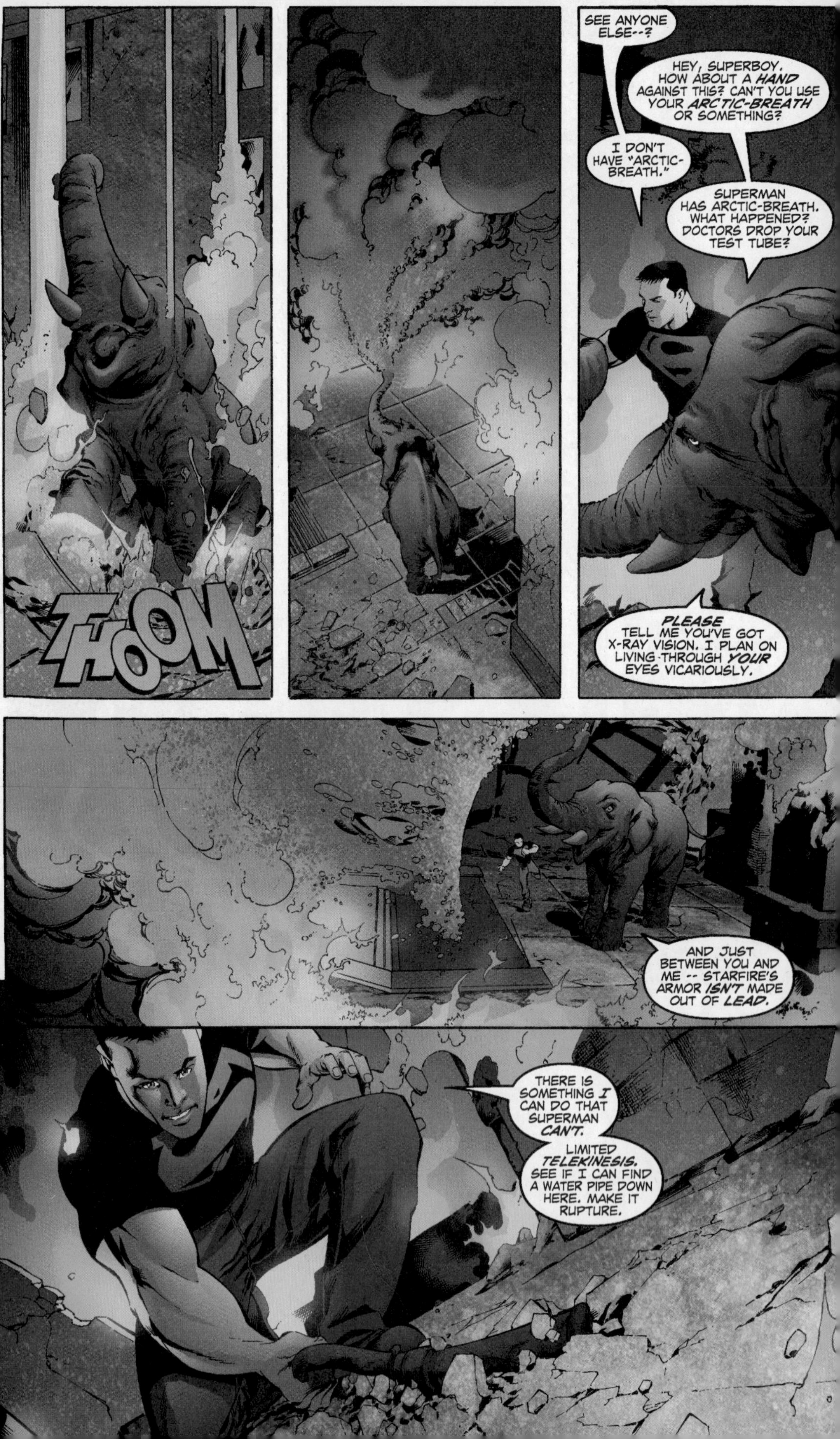
THOOM
SEE ANYONE ELSE--?
HEY, SUPERBOY. HOW ABOUT A HAND AGAINST THIS? CAN'T YOU USE YOUR ARCTIC-BREATH OR SOMETHING?
I DON'T HAVE "ARCTIC-BREATH."
SUPERMAN HAS ARCTIC-BREATH. WHAT HAPPENED? DOCTORS DROP YOUR TEST TUBE?
PLEASE TELL ME YOU'VE GOT X-RAY VISION. I PLAN ON LIVING-THROUGH YOUR EYES VICARIOUSLY.
AND JUST BETWEEN YOU AND ME -- STARFIRE'S ARMOR ISN'T MADE OUT OF LEAD.
THERE IS SOMETHING I CAN DO THAT SUPERMAN CAN'T.
LIMITED TELEKINESIS. SEE IF I CAN FIND A WATER PIPE DOWN HERE. MAKE IT RUPTURE.

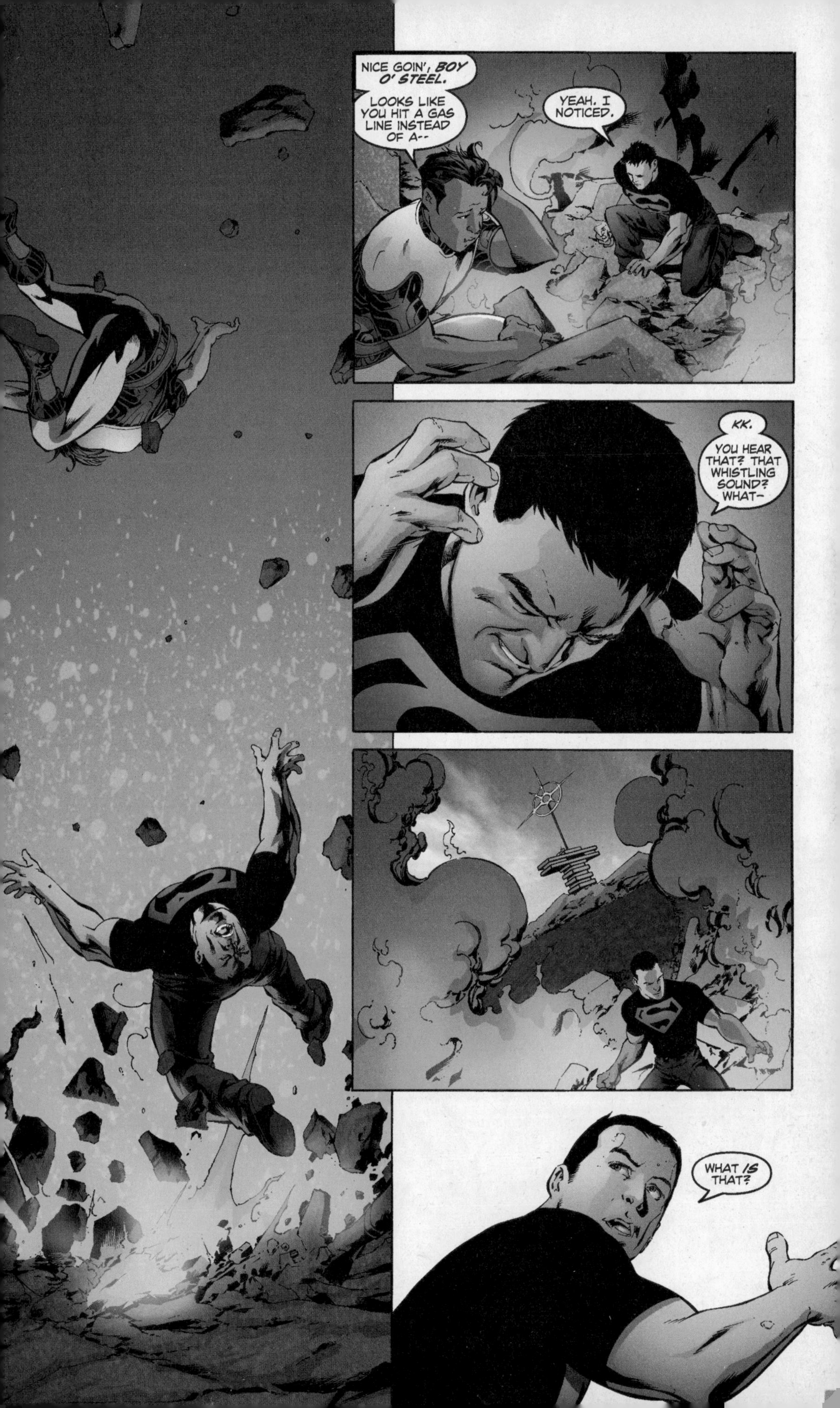
NICE GOIN', BOY O' STEEL.
LOOKS LIKE YOU HIT A GAS LINE INSTEAD OF A--
YEAH. I NOTICED.
KK.
YOU HEAR THAT? THAT WHISTLING SOUND? WHAT-
WHAT IS THAT?

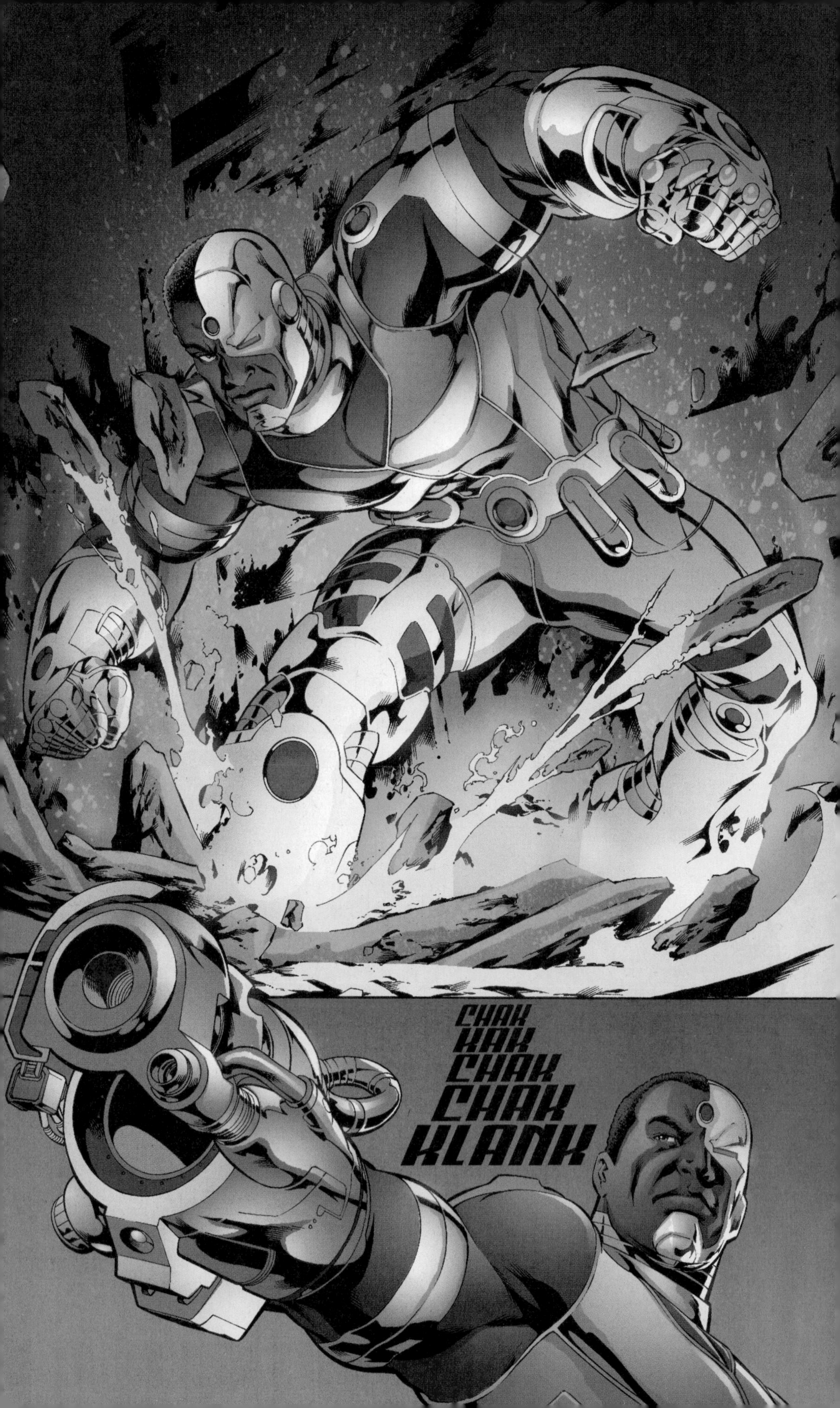
CHAK
KAK
CHAK
CHAK
KLANK

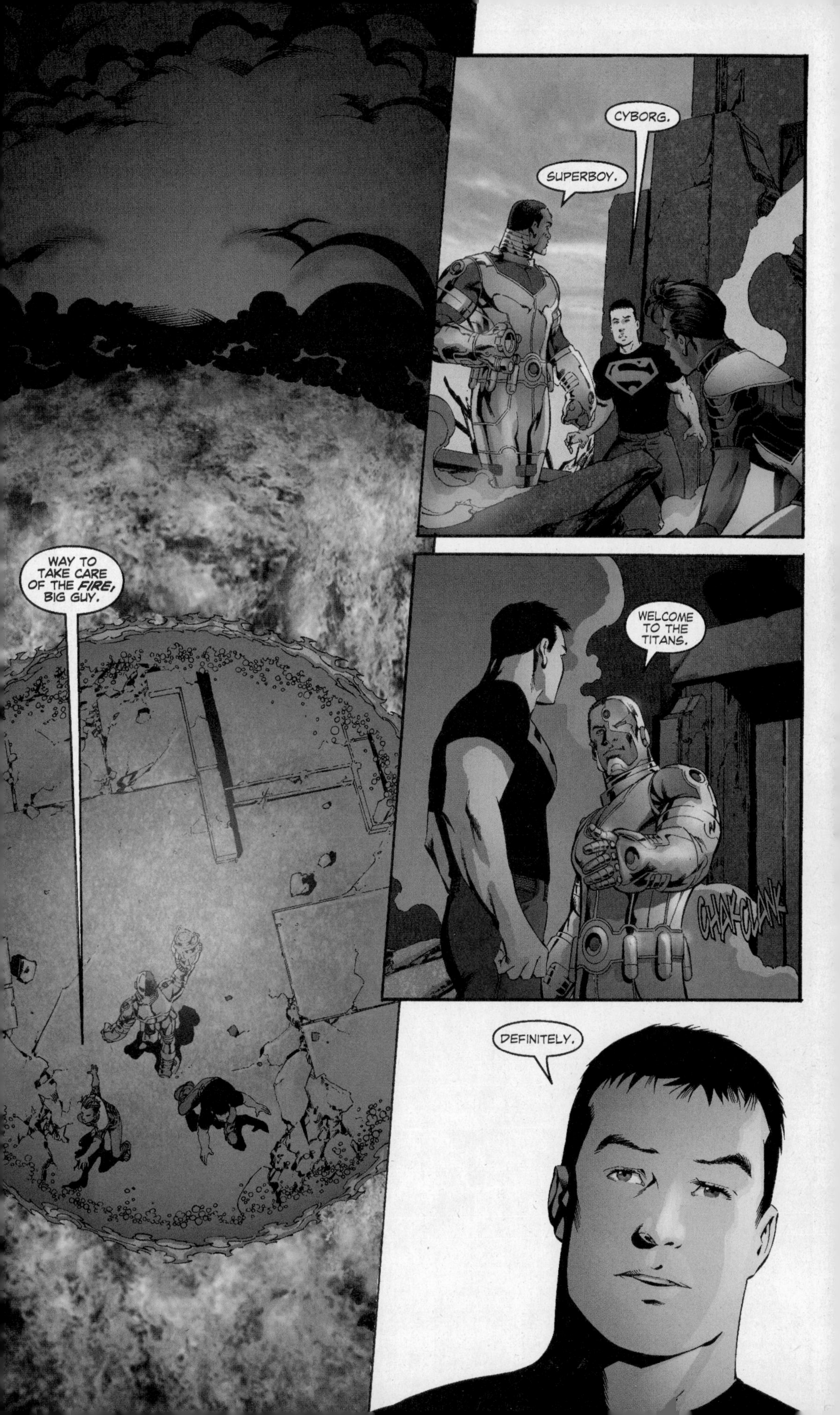
WAY TO TAKE CARE OF THE *FIRE*, BIG GUY.
CYBORG.
SUPERBOY.
WELCOME TO THE TITANS.
CHAK-CLANK
DEFINITELY.

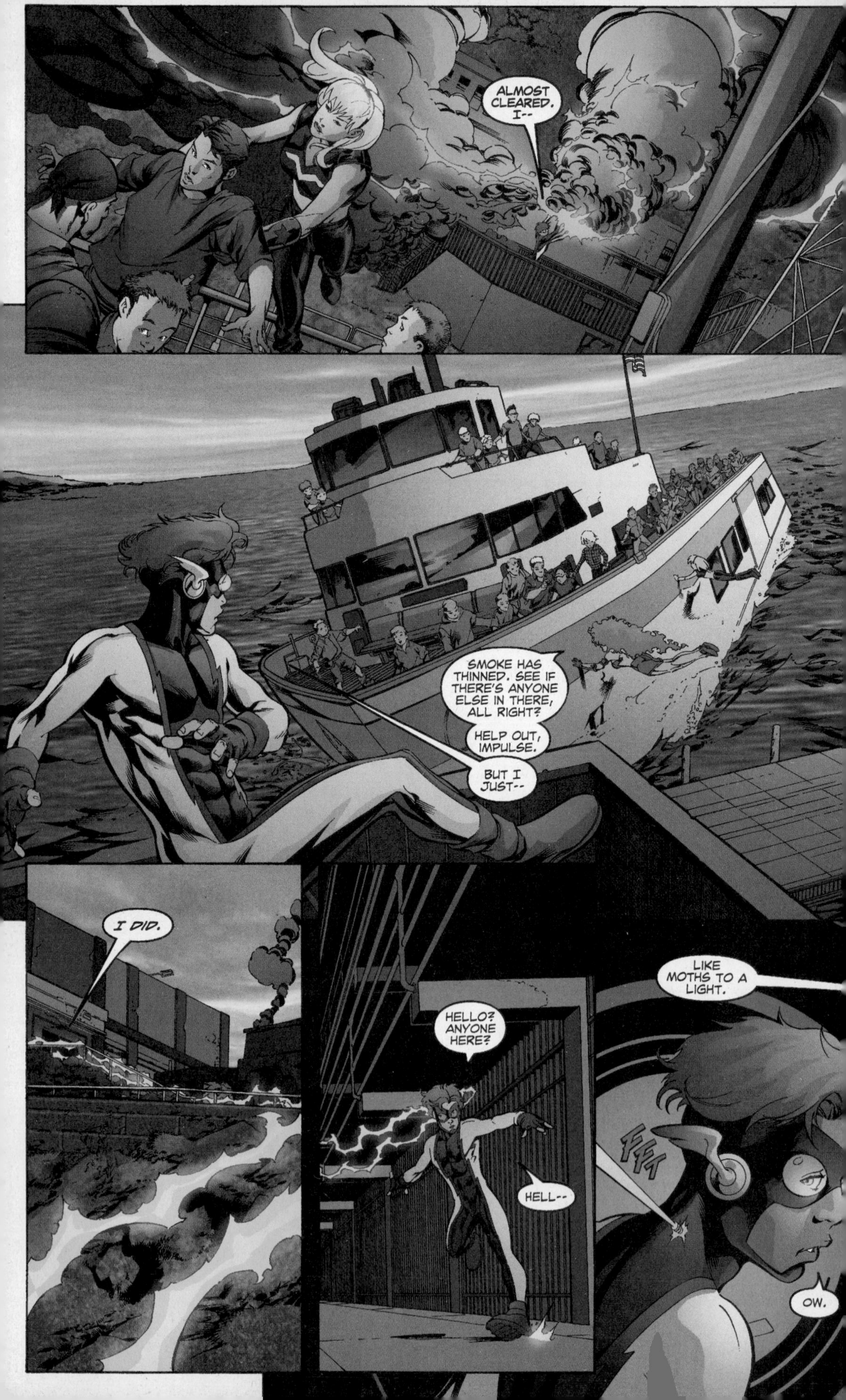
ALMOST CLEARED. I--
SMOKE HAS THINNED. SEE IF THERE'S ANYONE ELSE IN THERE, ALL RIGHT?
HELP OUT, IMPULSE.
BUT I JUST--
I DID.
HELLO? ANYONE HERE?
HELL--
LIKE MOTHS TO A LIGHT.
FFT
OW.

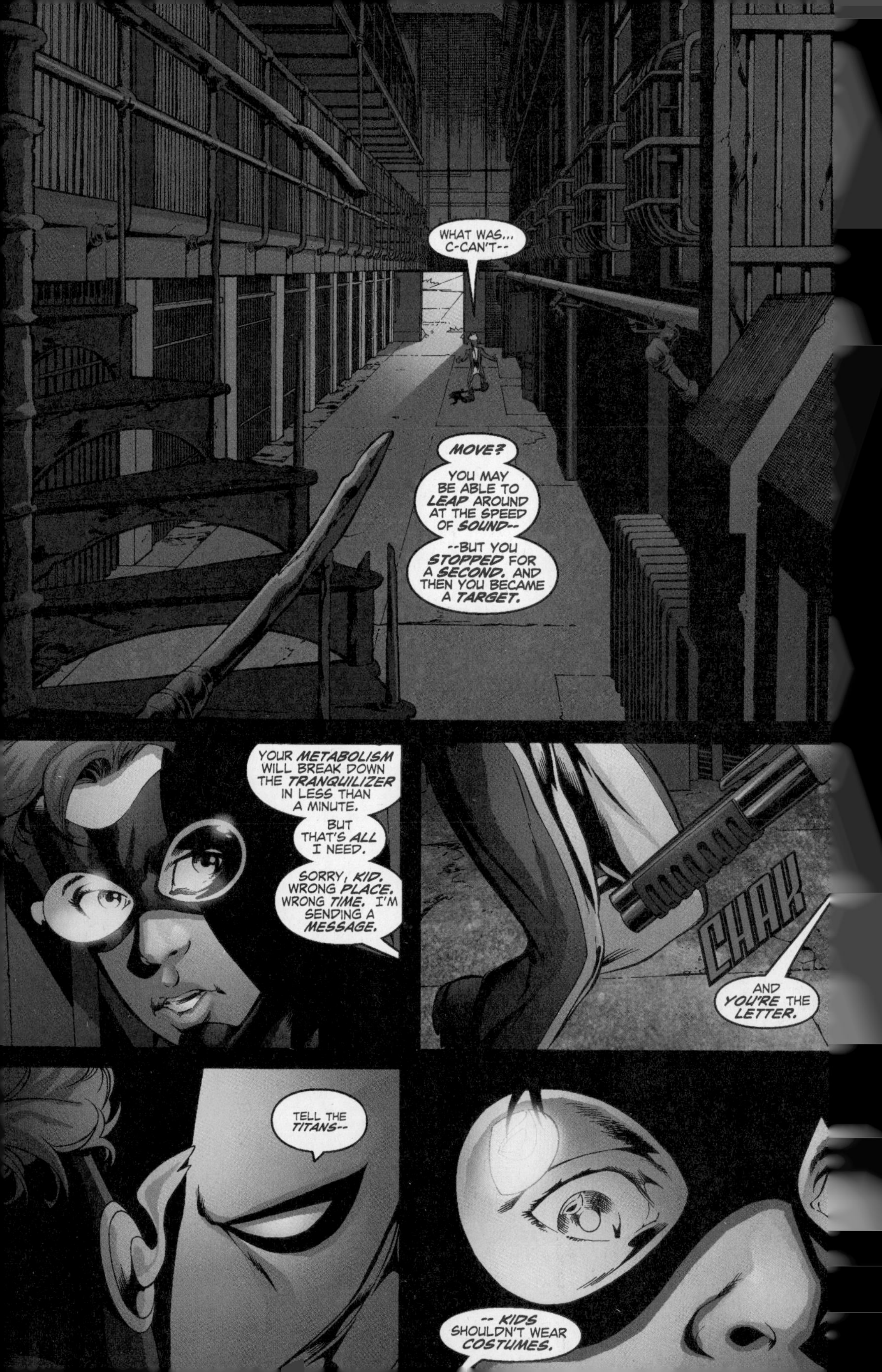
WHAT WAS... C-CAN'T--
MOVE?
YOU MAY BE ABLE TO LEAP AROUND AT THE SPEED OF SOUND--
--BUT YOU STOPPED FOR A SECOND. AND THEN YOU BECAME A TARGET.
YOUR METABOLISM WILL BREAK DOWN THE TRANQUILIZER IN LESS THAN A MINUTE.
BUT THAT'S ALL I NEED.
SORRY, KID. WRONG PLACE. WRONG TIME. I'M SENDING A MESSAGE.
CHAK
AND YOU'RE THE LETTER.
TELL THE TITANS--
-- KIDS SHOULDN'T WEAR COSTUMES.

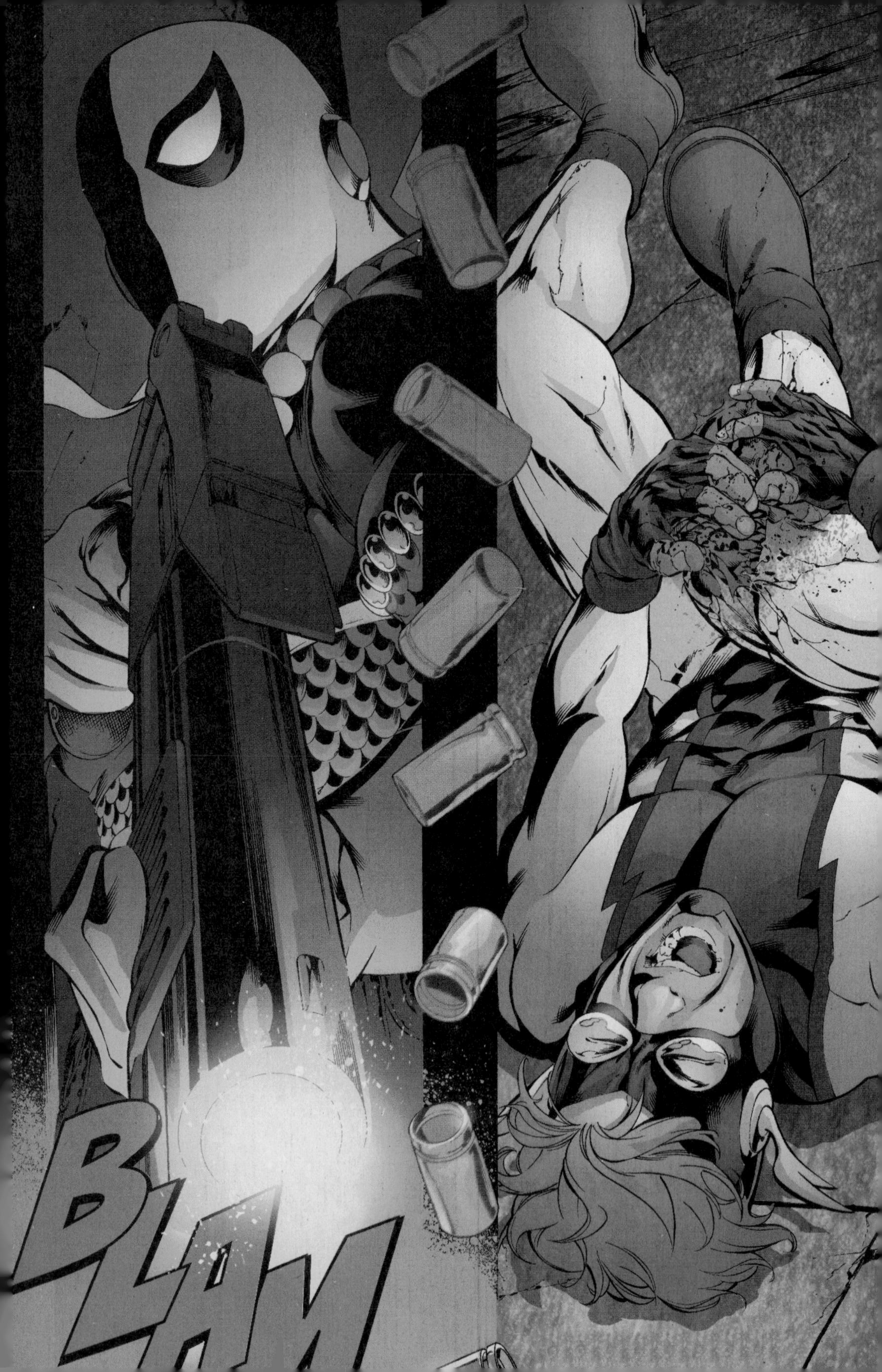
BLAM

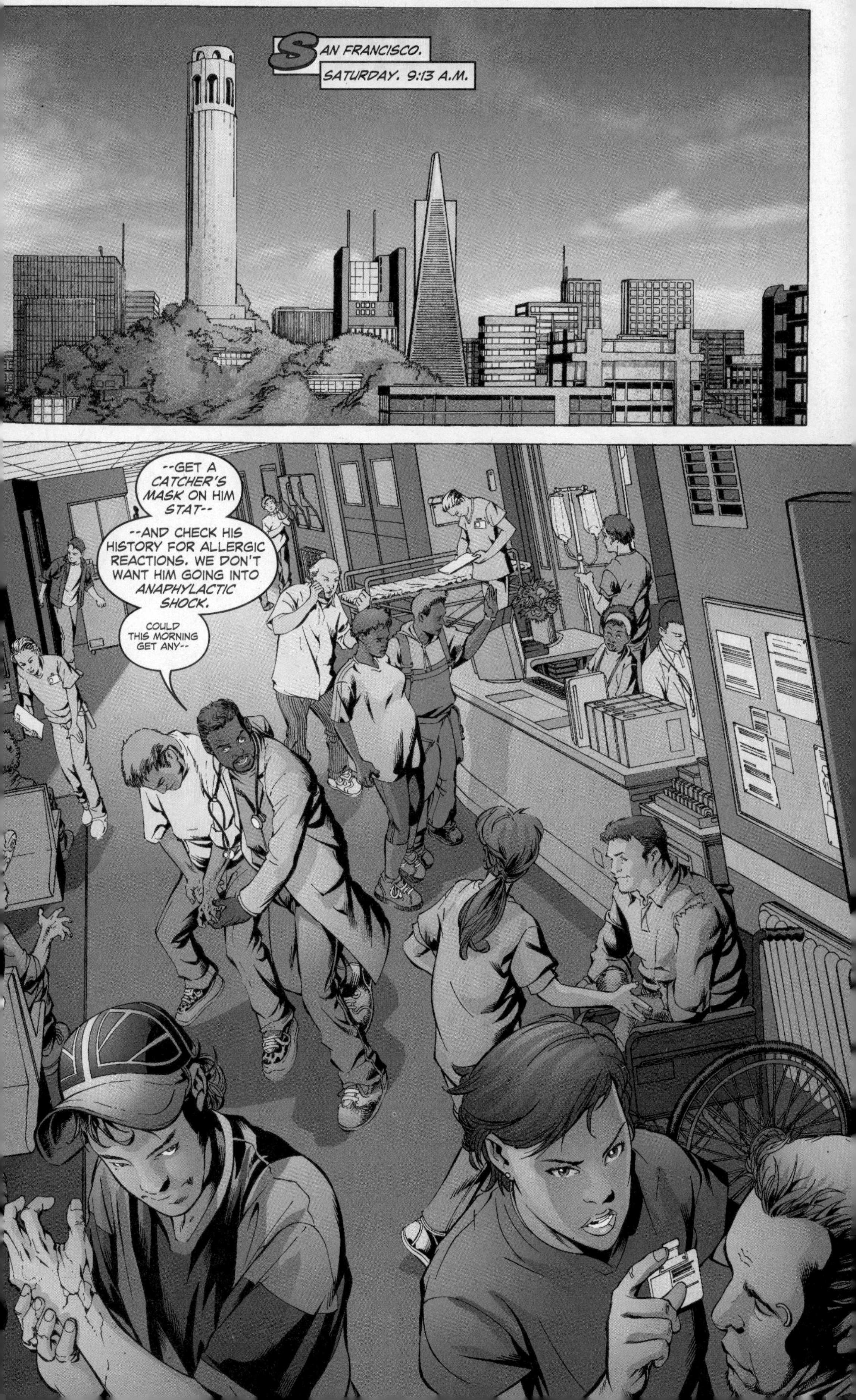
SAN FRANCISCO.
SATURDAY. 9:13 A.M.
--GET A CATCHER'S MASK ON HIM STAT--
--AND CHECK HIS HISTORY FOR ALLERGIC REACTIONS. WE DON'T WANT HIM GOING INTO ANAPHYLACTIC SHOCK.
COULD THIS MORNING GET ANY--

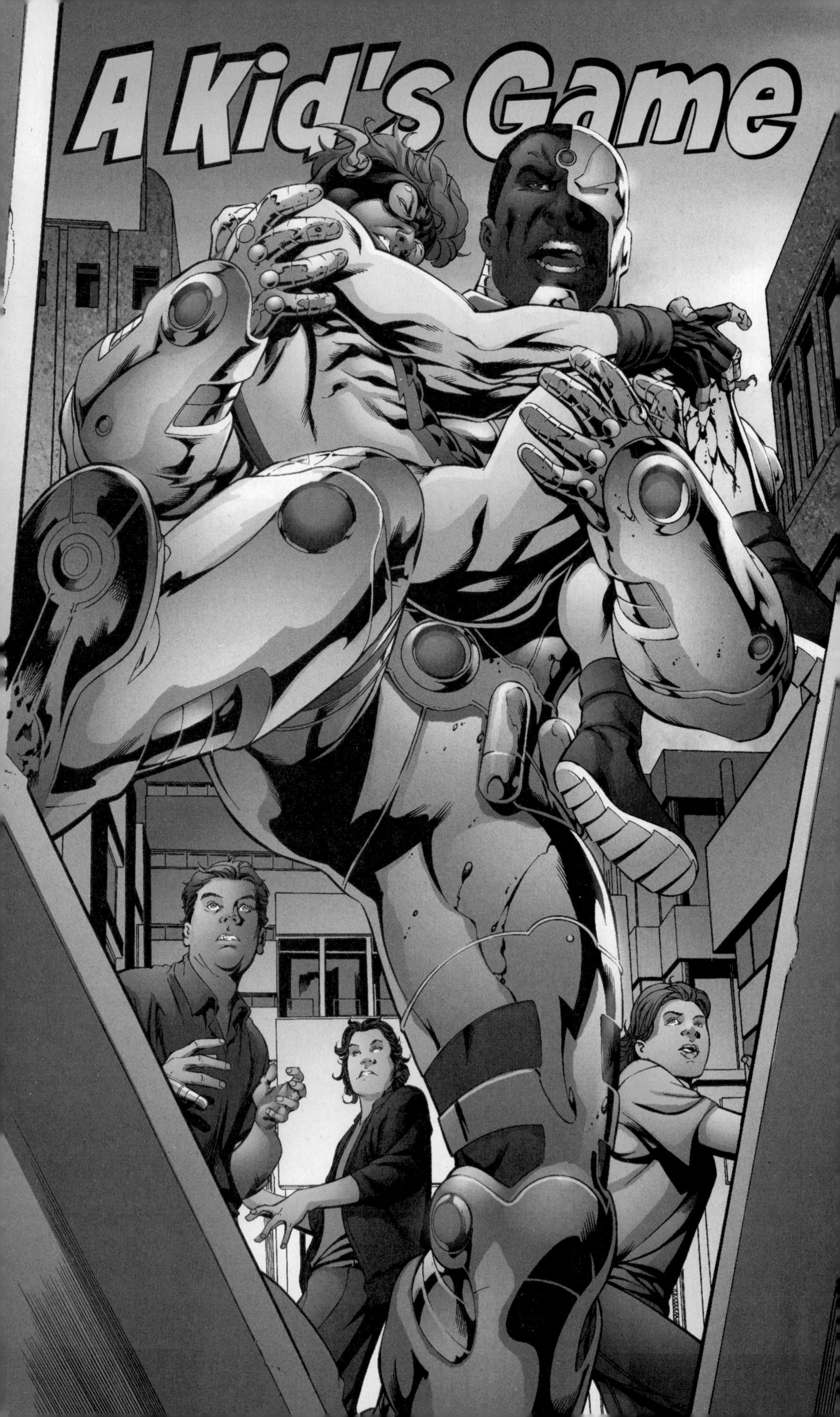
A Kid's Game

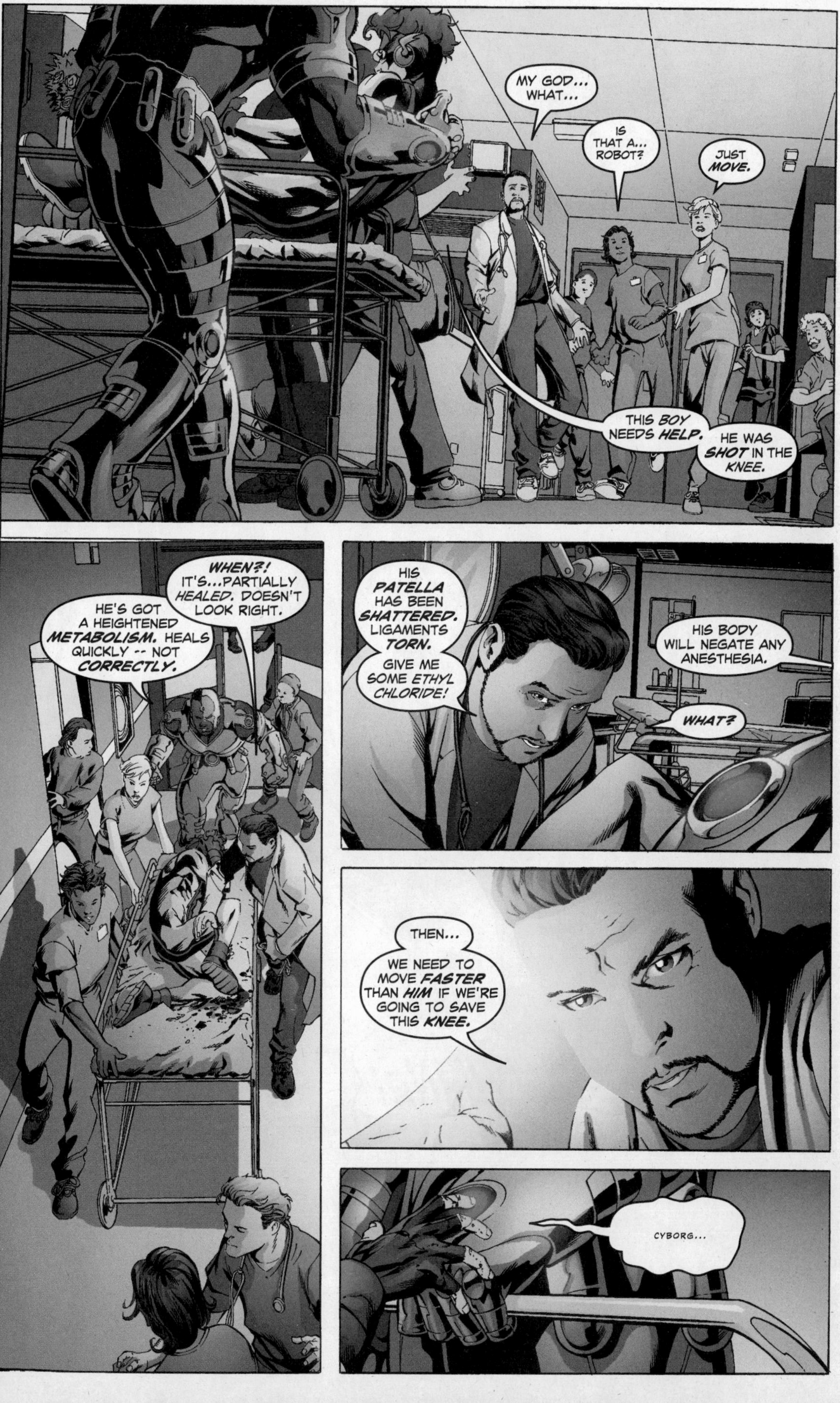
MY GOD... WHAT...
IS THAT A... ROBOT?
JUST MOVE.
THIS BOY NEEDS HELP.
HE WAS SHOT IN THE KNEE.
HE'S GOT A HEIGHTENED METABOLISM. HEALS QUICKLY -- NOT CORRECTLY.
WHEN?! IT'S...PARTIALLY HEALED. DOESN'T LOOK RIGHT.
HIS PATELLA HAS BEEN SHATTERED. LIGAMENTS TORN.
GIVE ME SOME ETHYL CHLORIDE!
HIS BODY WILL NEGATE ANY ANESTHESIA.
WHAT?
THEN...
WE NEED TO MOVE FASTER THAN HIM IF WE'RE GOING TO SAVE THIS KNEE.
CYBORG...

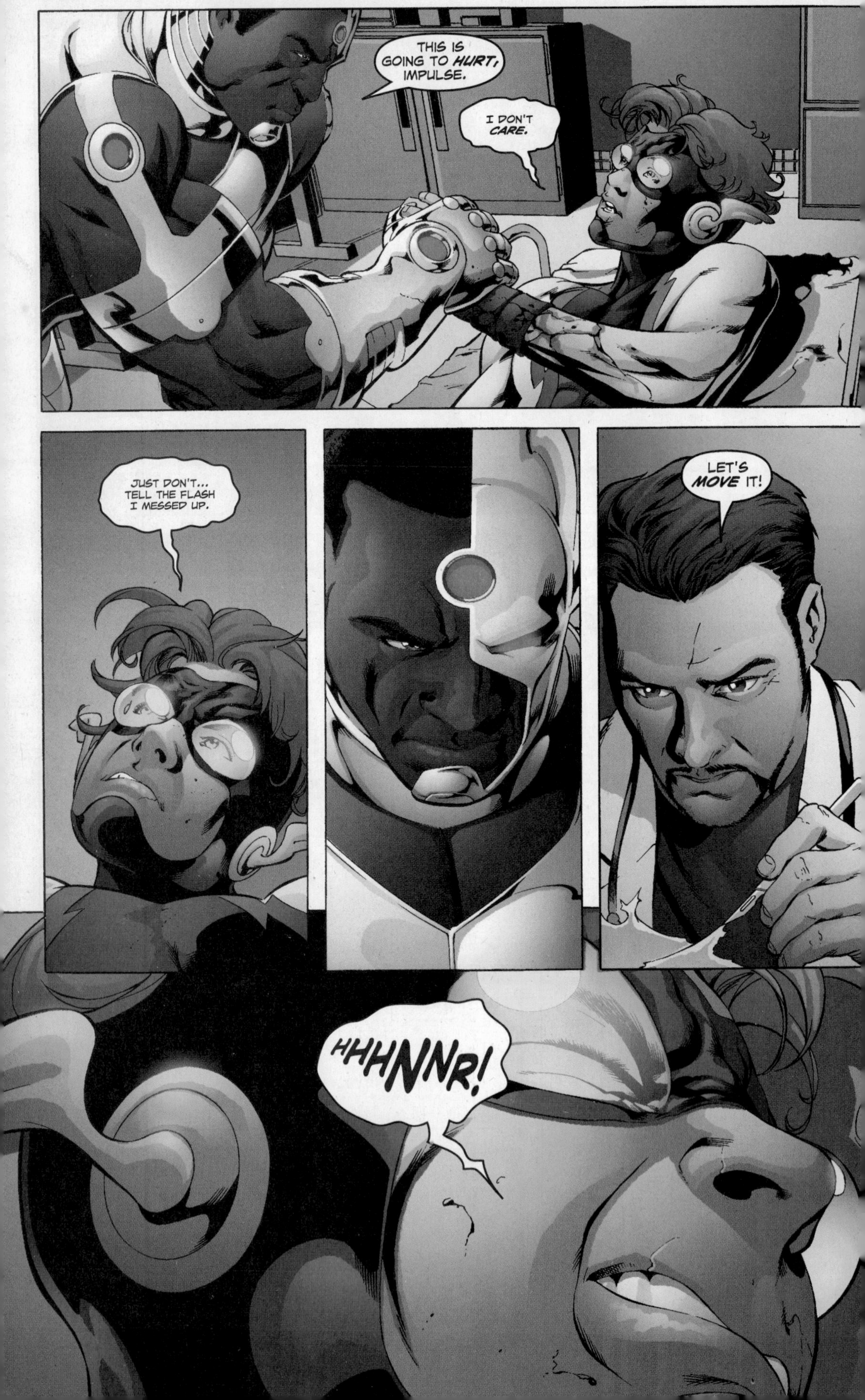
THIS IS GOING TO HURT, IMPULSE.
I DON'T CARE.
JUST DON'T... TELL THE FLASH I MESSED UP.
LET'S MOVE IT!
HHHNNR!

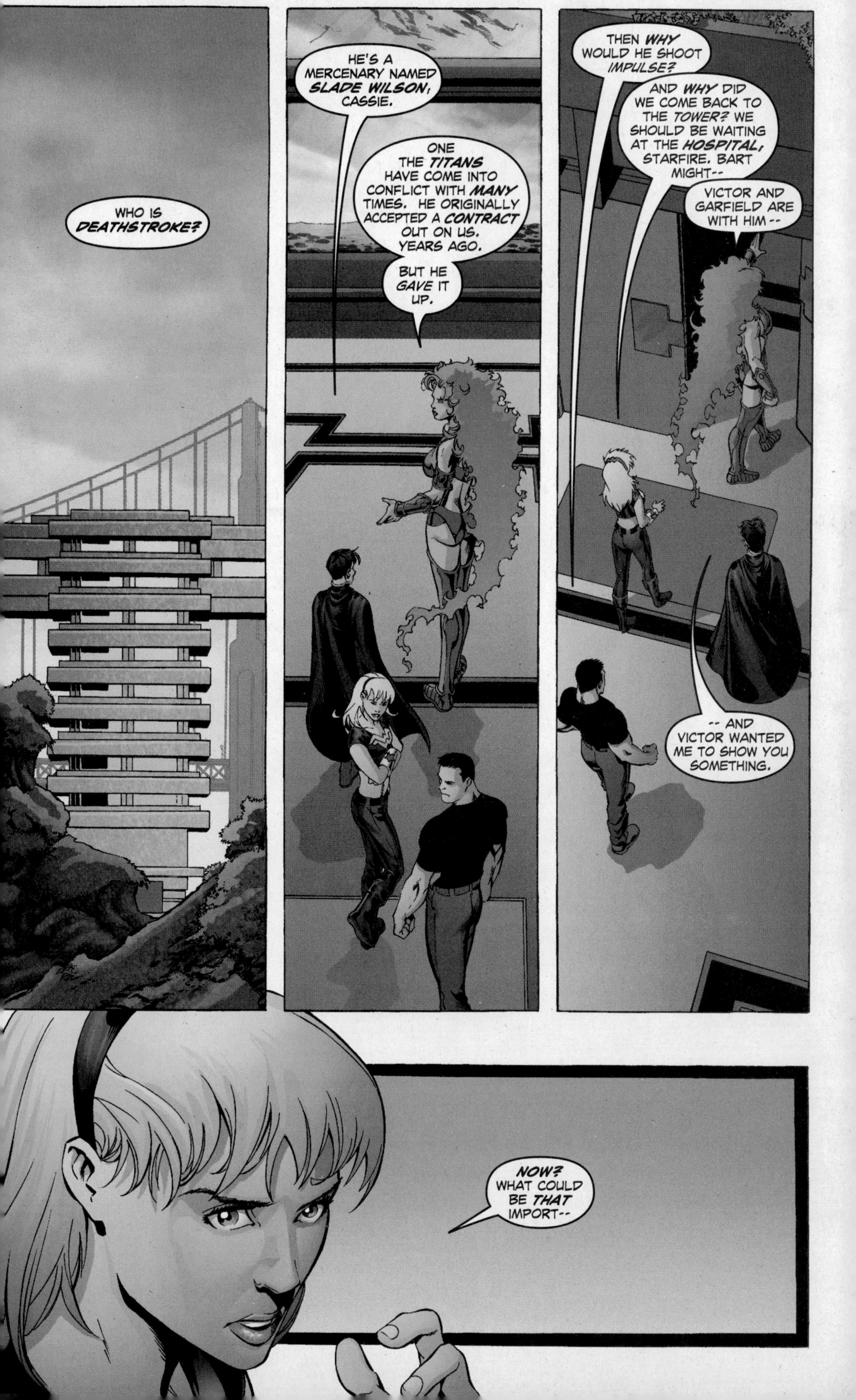
WHO IS *DEATHSTROKE?*
HE'S A MERCENARY NAMED *SLADE WILSON*, CASSIE.
ONE THE *TITANS* HAVE COME INTO CONFLICT WITH *MANY* TIMES. HE ORIGINALLY ACCEPTED A *CONTRACT* OUT ON US. YEARS AGO.
BUT HE *GAVE* IT UP.
THEN *WHY* WOULD HE SHOOT *IMPULSE?*
AND *WHY* DID WE COME BACK TO THE *TOWER?* WE SHOULD BE WAITING AT THE *HOSPITAL*, STARFIRE. BART MIGHT--
VICTOR AND GARFIELD ARE WITH HIM --
-- AND VICTOR WANTED ME TO SHOW YOU SOMETHING.
NOW? WHAT COULD BE *THAT* IMPORT--

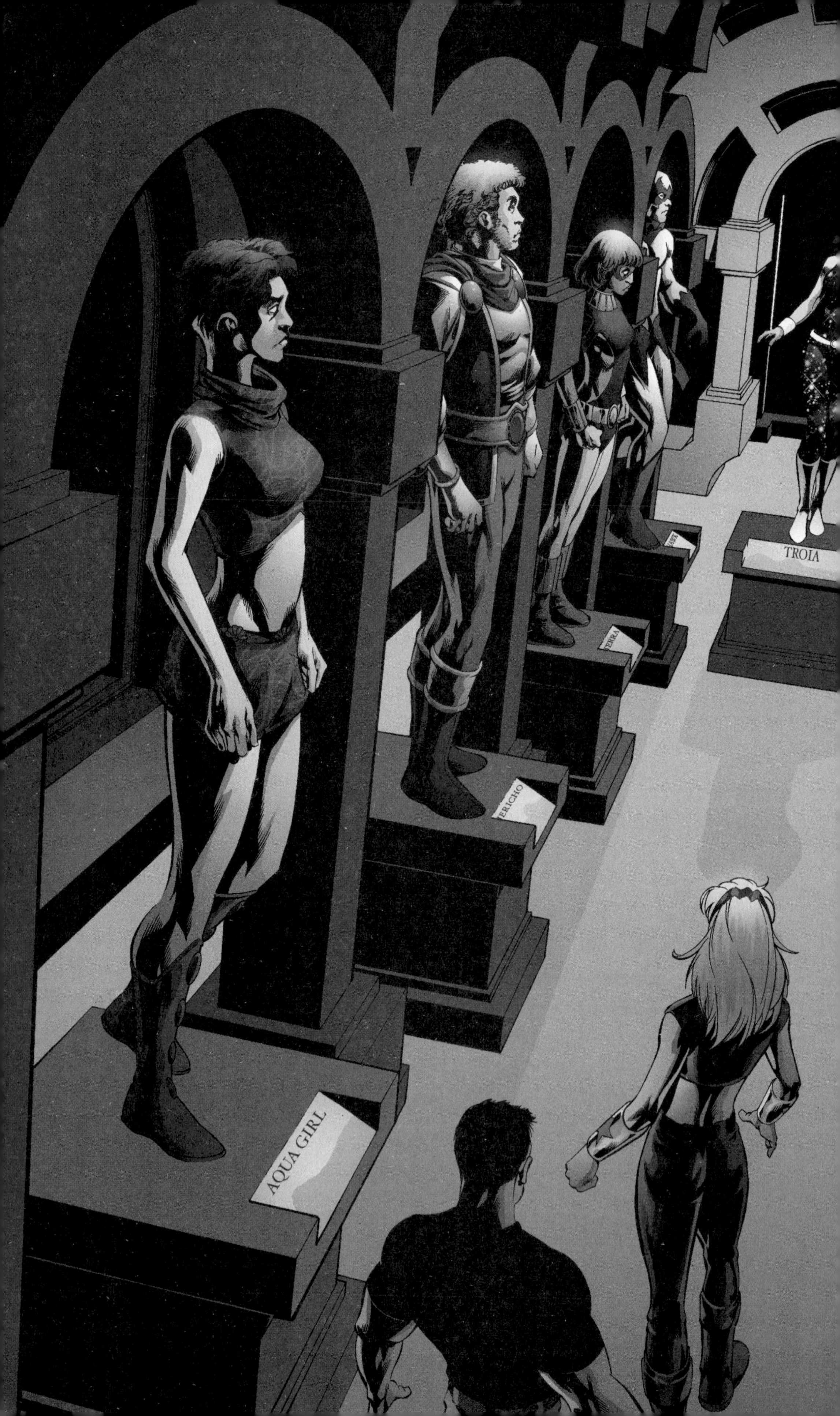
AQUA GIRL
TROIA

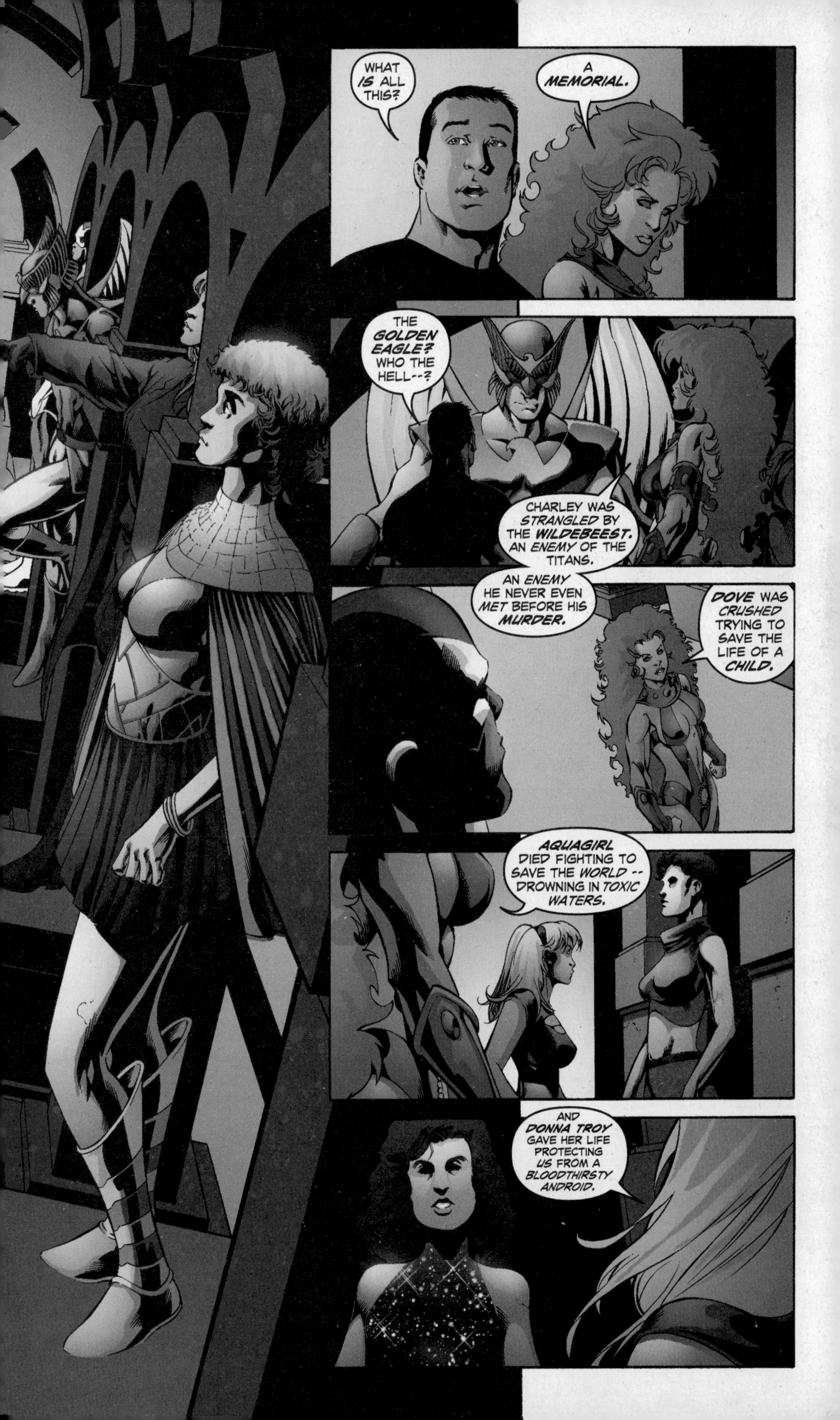

WHAT *IS* ALL THIS?
A *MEMORIAL.*
THE *GOLDEN EAGLE?* WHO THE HELL--?
CHARLEY WAS *STRANGLED* BY THE *WILDEBEEST.* AN *ENEMY* OF THE TITANS.
AN *ENEMY* HE NEVER EVEN *MET* BEFORE HIS *MURDER.*
DOVE WAS *CRUSHED* TRYING TO SAVE THE LIFE OF A *CHILD.*
AQUAGIRL DIED FIGHTING TO SAVE THE *WORLD* -- DROWNING IN *TOXIC WATERS.*
AND *DONNA TROY* GAVE HER LIFE PROTECTING *US* FROM A *BLOODTHIRSTY ANDROID.*

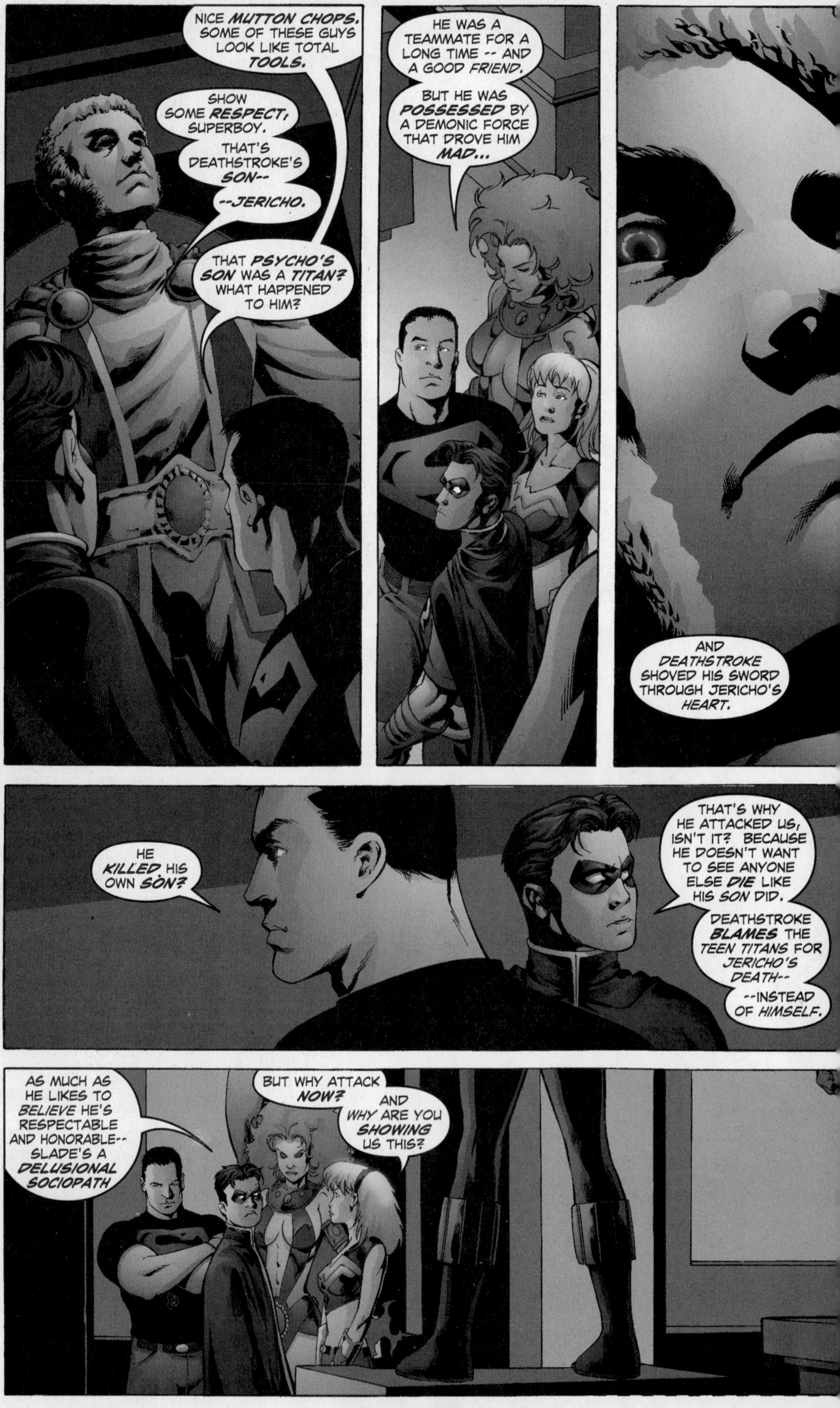
NICE MUTTON CHOPS. SOME OF THESE GUYS LOOK LIKE TOTAL TOOLS.
SHOW SOME RESPECT, SUPERBOY.
THAT'S DEATHSTROKE'S SON--
--JERICHO.
THAT PSYCHO'S SON WAS A TITAN? WHAT HAPPENED TO HIM?
HE WAS A TEAMMATE FOR A LONG TIME -- AND A GOOD FRIEND.
BUT HE WAS POSSESSED BY A DEMONIC FORCE THAT DROVE HIM MAD...
AND DEATHSTROKE SHOVED HIS SWORD THROUGH JERICHO'S HEART.
HE KILLED HIS OWN SON?
THAT'S WHY HE ATTACKED US, ISN'T IT? BECAUSE HE DOESN'T WANT TO SEE ANYONE ELSE DIE LIKE HIS SON DID.
DEATHSTROKE BLAMES THE TEEN TITANS FOR JERICHO'S DEATH--
--INSTEAD OF HIMSELF.
AS MUCH AS HE LIKES TO BELIEVE HE'S RESPECTABLE AND HONORABLE-- SLADE'S A DELUSIONAL SOCIOPATH
BUT WHY ATTACK NOW?
AND WHY ARE YOU SHOWING US THIS?

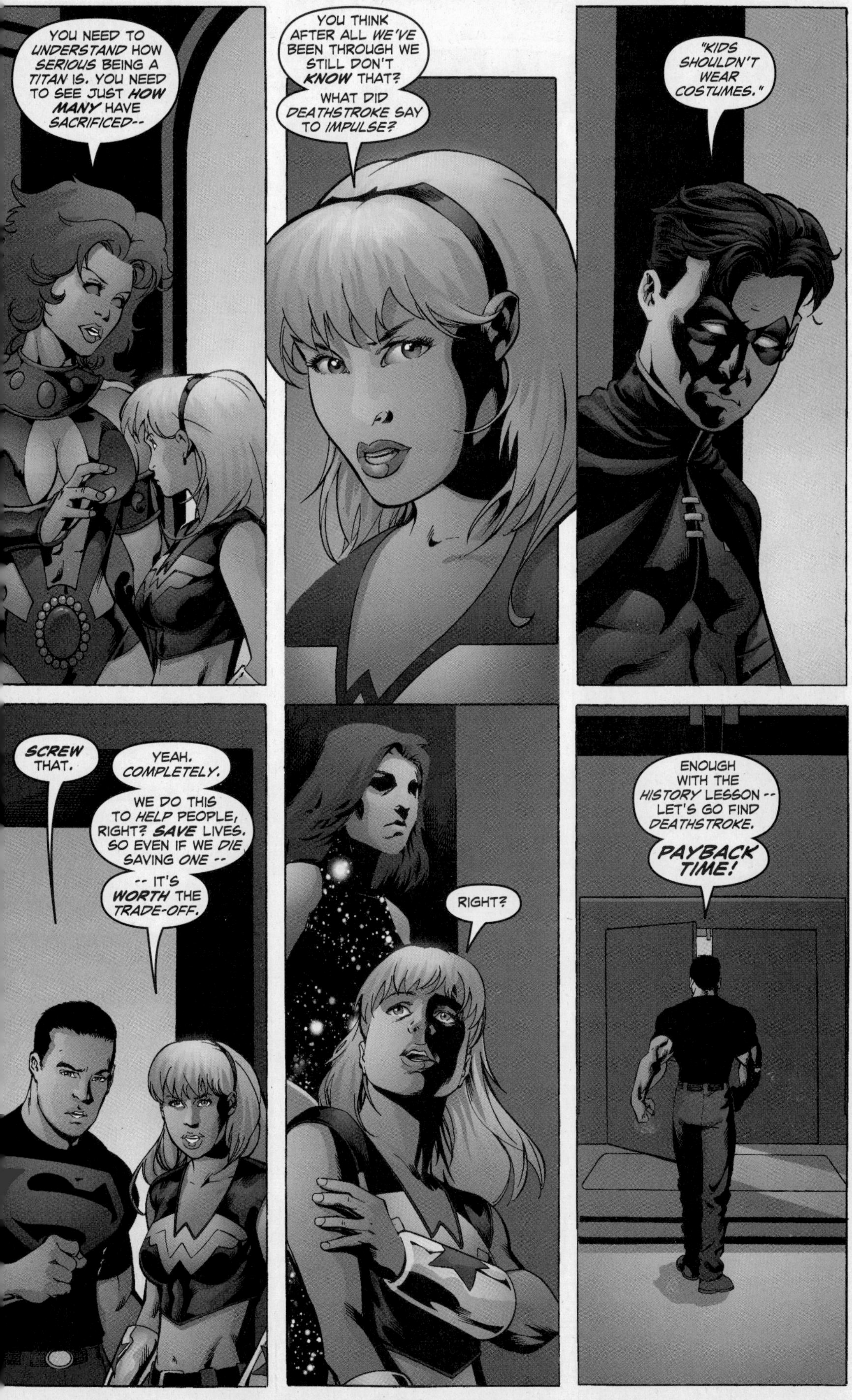
YOU NEED TO UNDERSTAND HOW SERIOUS BEING A TITAN IS. YOU NEED TO SEE JUST HOW MANY HAVE SACRIFICED--
YOU THINK AFTER ALL WE'VE BEEN THROUGH WE STILL DON'T KNOW THAT?
WHAT DID DEATHSTROKE SAY TO IMPULSE?
"KIDS SHOULDN'T WEAR COSTUMES."
SCREW THAT.
YEAH. COMPLETELY.
WE DO THIS TO HELP PEOPLE, RIGHT? SAVE LIVES. SO EVEN IF WE DIE SAVING ONE --
-- IT'S WORTH THE TRADE-OFF.
RIGHT?
ENOUGH WITH THE HISTORY LESSON -- LET'S GO FIND DEATHSTROKE.
PAYBACK TIME!

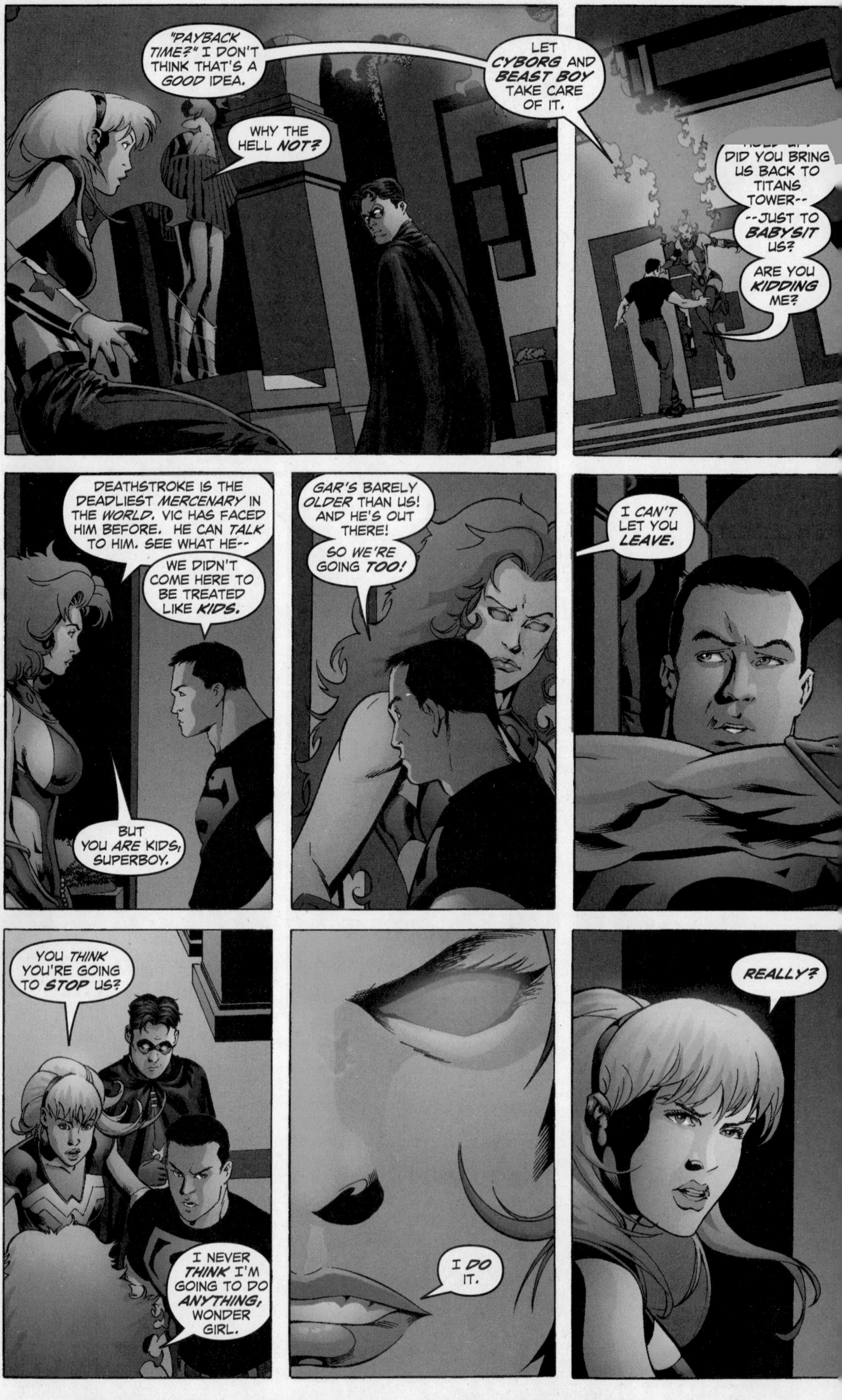
"PAYBACK TIME?" I DON'T THINK THAT'S A GOOD IDEA.
LET CYBORG AND BEAST BOY TAKE CARE OF IT.
WHY THE HELL NOT?
DID YOU BRING US BACK TO TITANS TOWER--
--JUST TO BABYSIT US?
ARE YOU KIDDING ME?
DEATHSTROKE IS THE DEADLIEST MERCENARY IN THE WORLD. VIC HAS FACED HIM BEFORE. HE CAN TALK TO HIM. SEE WHAT HE--
WE DIDN'T COME HERE TO BE TREATED LIKE KIDS.
BUT YOU ARE KIDS, SUPERBOY.
GAR'S BARELY OLDER THAN US! AND HE'S OUT THERE!
SO WE'RE GOING TOO!
I CAN'T LET YOU LEAVE.
YOU THINK YOU'RE GOING TO STOP US?
I NEVER THINK I'M GOING TO DO ANYTHING, WONDER GIRL.
I DO IT.
REALLY?

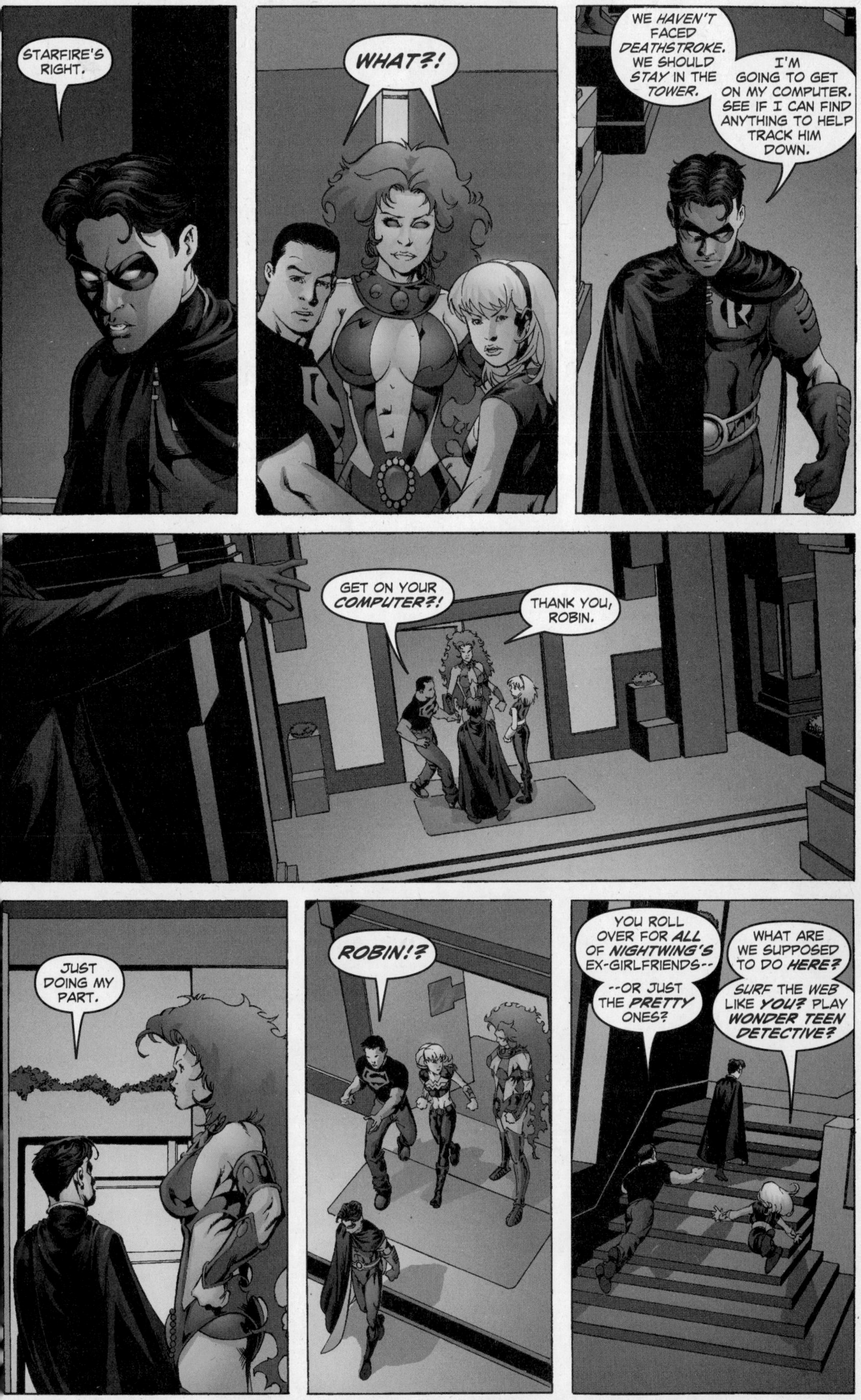

STARFIRE'S RIGHT.
WHAT?!
WE HAVEN'T FACED DEATHSTROKE. WE SHOULD STAY IN THE TOWER.
I'M GOING TO GET ON MY COMPUTER. SEE IF I CAN FIND ANYTHING TO HELP TRACK HIM DOWN.
GET ON YOUR COMPUTER?!
THANK YOU, ROBIN.
JUST DOING MY PART.
ROBIN!?
YOU ROLL OVER FOR ALL OF NIGHTWING'S EX-GIRLFRIENDS--
--OR JUST THE PRETTY ONES?
WHAT ARE WE SUPPOSED TO DO HERE?
SURF THE WEB LIKE YOU? PLAY WONDER TEEN DETECTIVE?

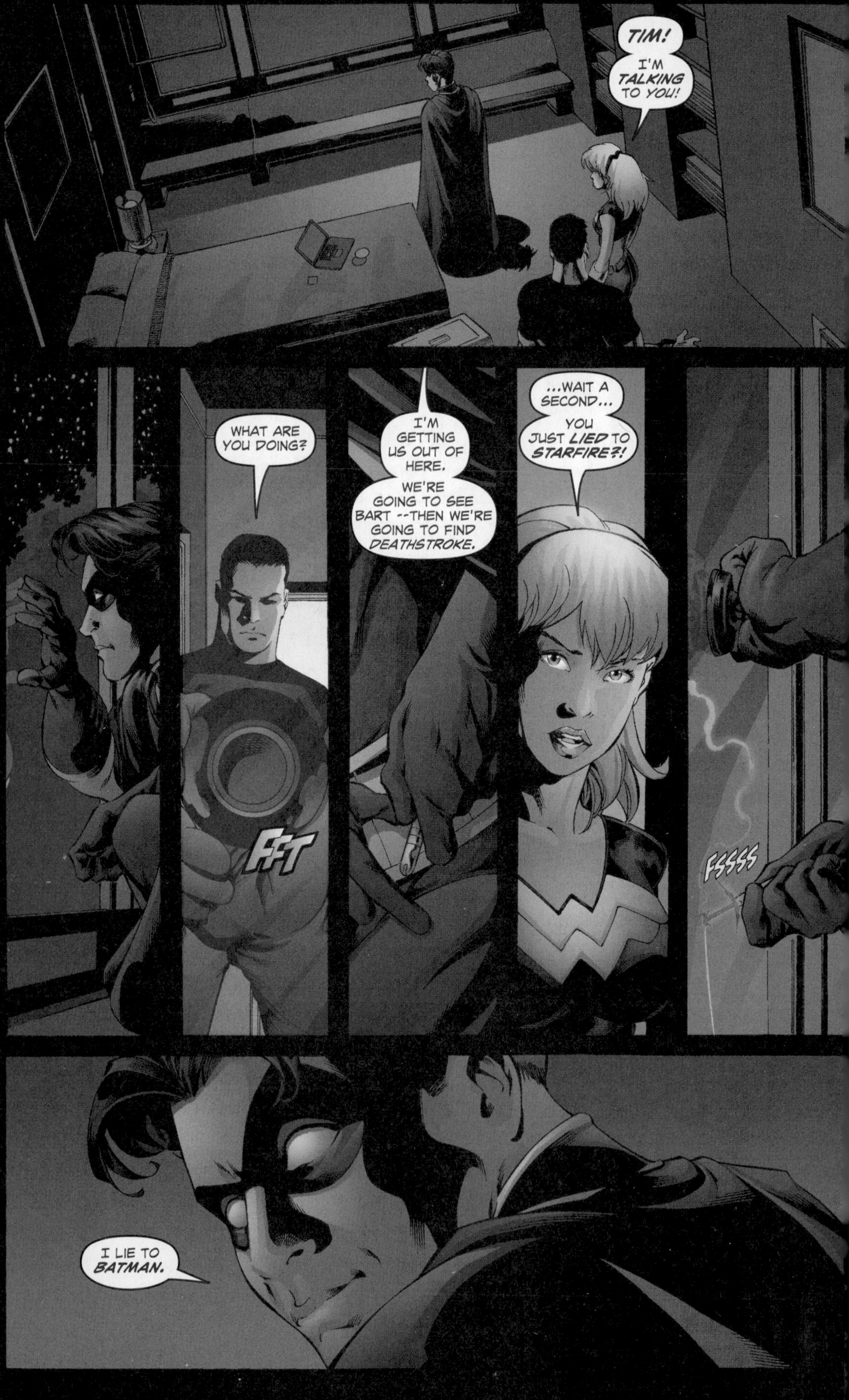
TIM! I'M TALKING TO YOU!
WHAT ARE YOU DOING?
FFT
I'M GETTING US OUT OF HERE.
WE'RE GOING TO SEE BART --THEN WE'RE GOING TO FIND DEATHSTROKE.
...WAIT A SECOND...
YOU JUST LIED TO STARFIRE?!
FSSSS
I LIE TO BATMAN.

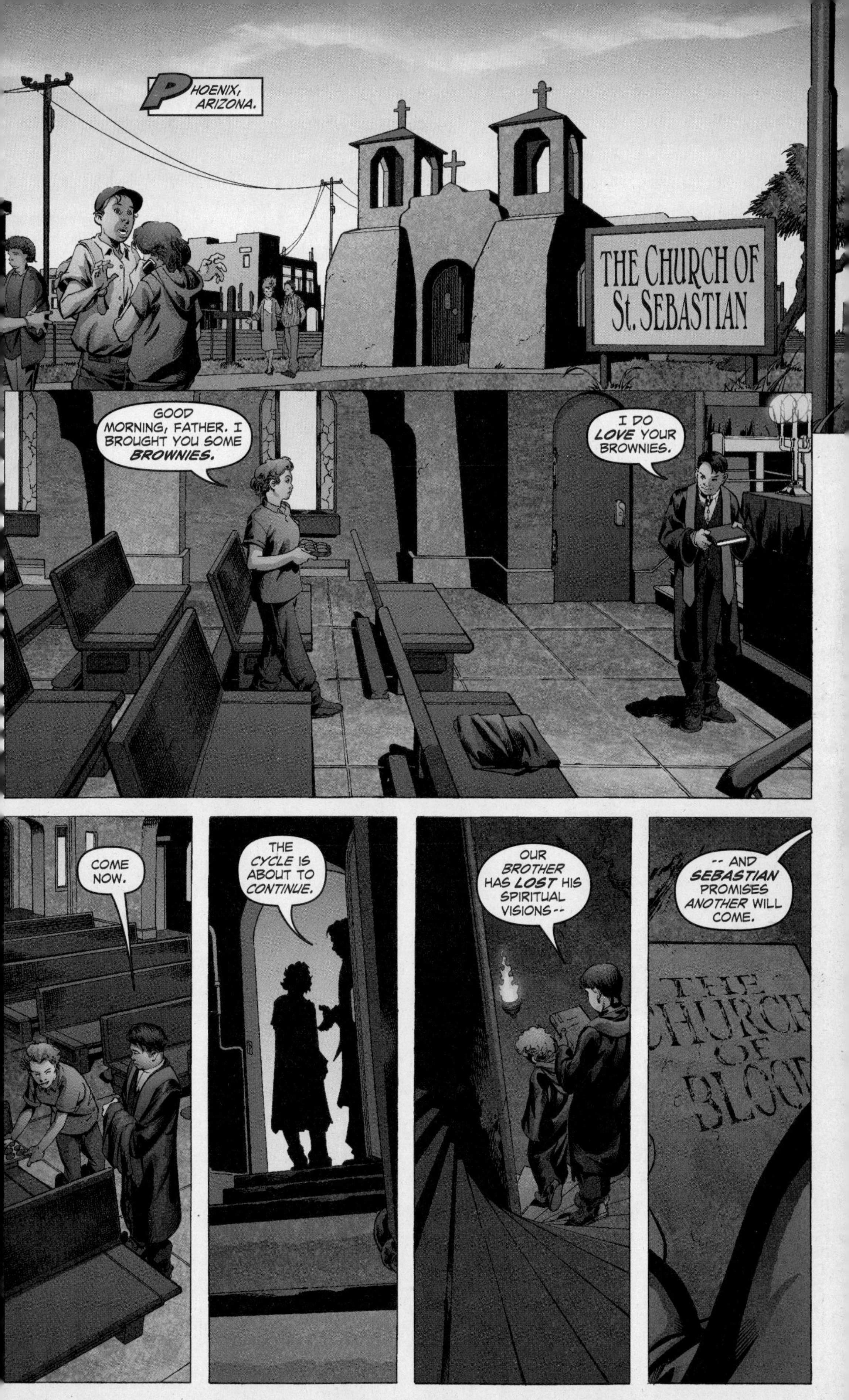
PHOENIX, ARIZONA.
THE CHURCH OF St. SEBASTIAN
GOOD MORNING, FATHER. I BROUGHT YOU SOME BROWNIES.
I DO LOVE YOUR BROWNIES.
COME NOW.
THE CYCLE IS ABOUT TO CONTINUE.
OUR BROTHER HAS LOST HIS SPIRITUAL VISIONS --
-- AND SEBASTIAN PROMISES ANOTHER WILL COME.

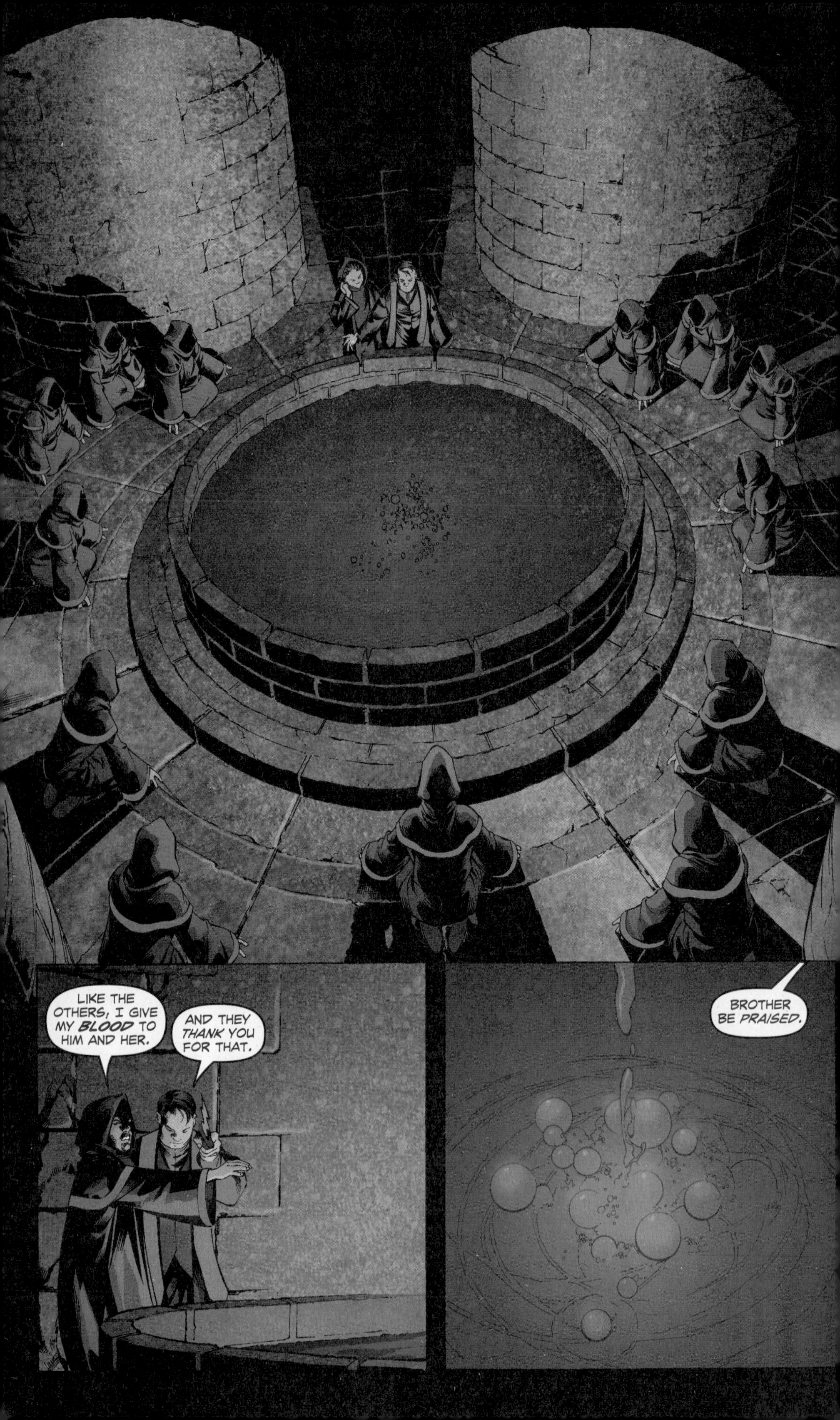
LIKE THE OTHERS, I GIVE MY BLOOD TO HIM AND HER.
AND THEY THANK YOU FOR THAT.
BROTHER BE PRAISED.

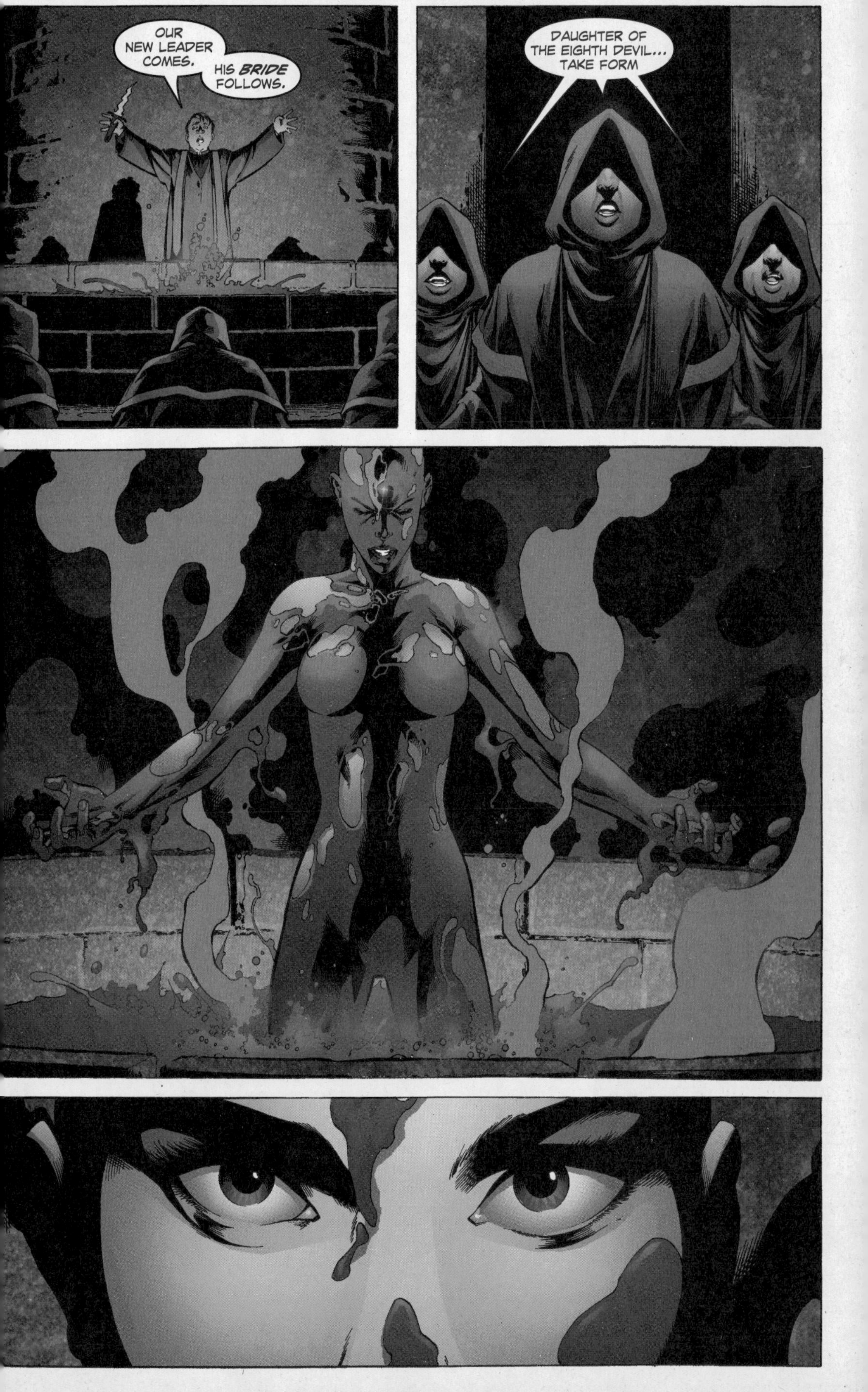
OUR NEW LEADER COMES.
HIS *BRIDE* FOLLOWS.
DAUGHTER OF THE EIGHTH DEVIL... TAKE FORM

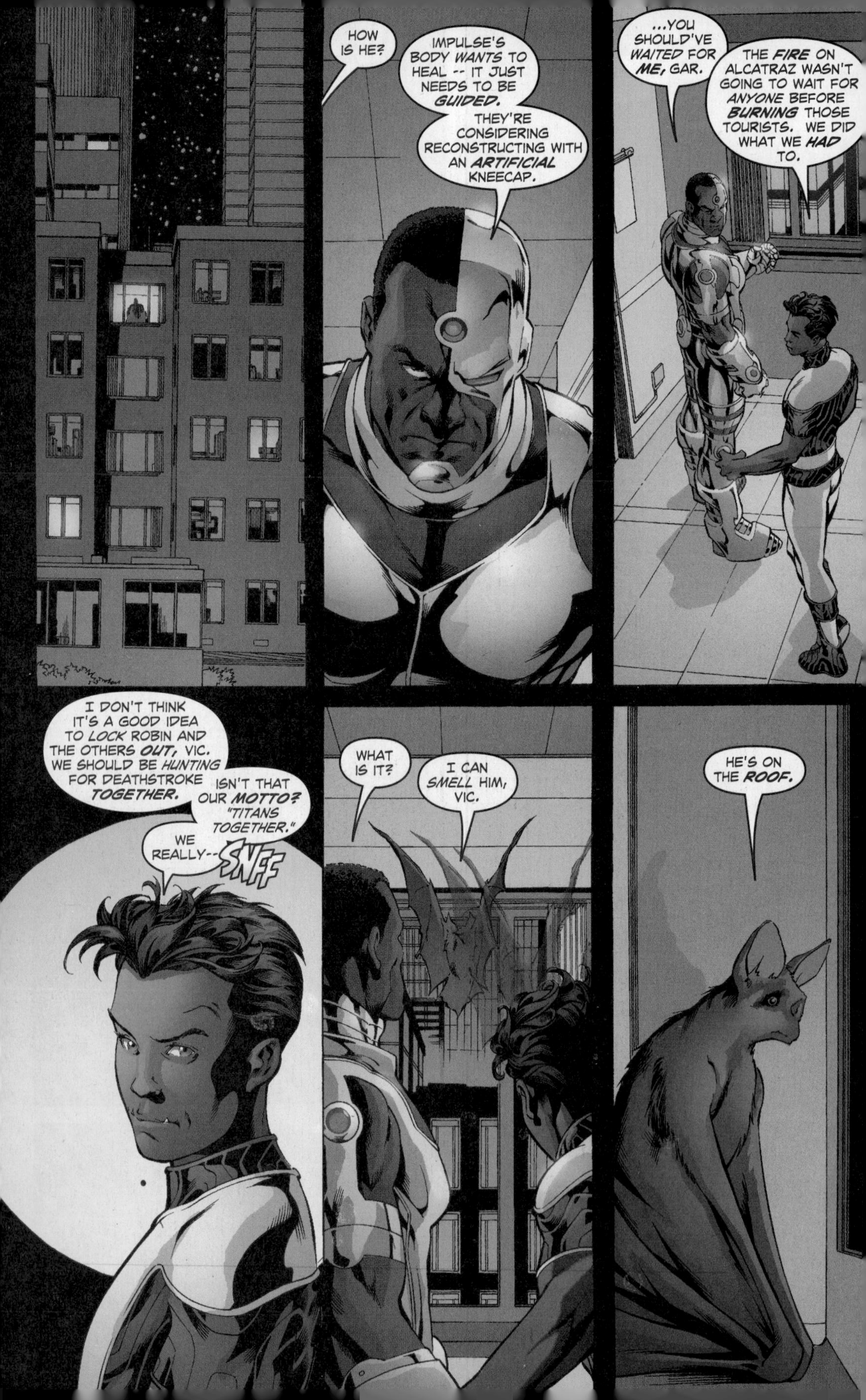
HOW IS HE?
IMPULSE'S BODY *WANTS* TO HEAL -- IT JUST NEEDS TO BE *GUIDED.*
THEY'RE CONSIDERING RECONSTRUCTING WITH AN *ARTIFICIAL* KNEECAP.
...YOU SHOULD'VE *WAITED* FOR *ME,* GAR.
THE *FIRE* ON ALCATRAZ WASN'T GOING TO WAIT FOR *ANYONE* BEFORE *BURNING* THOSE TOURISTS. WE DID WHAT WE *HAD* TO.
I DON'T THINK IT'S A GOOD IDEA TO *LOCK* ROBIN AND THE OTHERS *OUT,* VIC. WE SHOULD BE *HUNTING* FOR DEATHSTROKE *TOGETHER.*
ISN'T THAT OUR *MOTTO?* "TITANS TOGETHER."
WE REALLY--
SNFF
WHAT IS IT?
I CAN *SMELL* HIM, VIC.
HE'S ON THE *ROOF.*

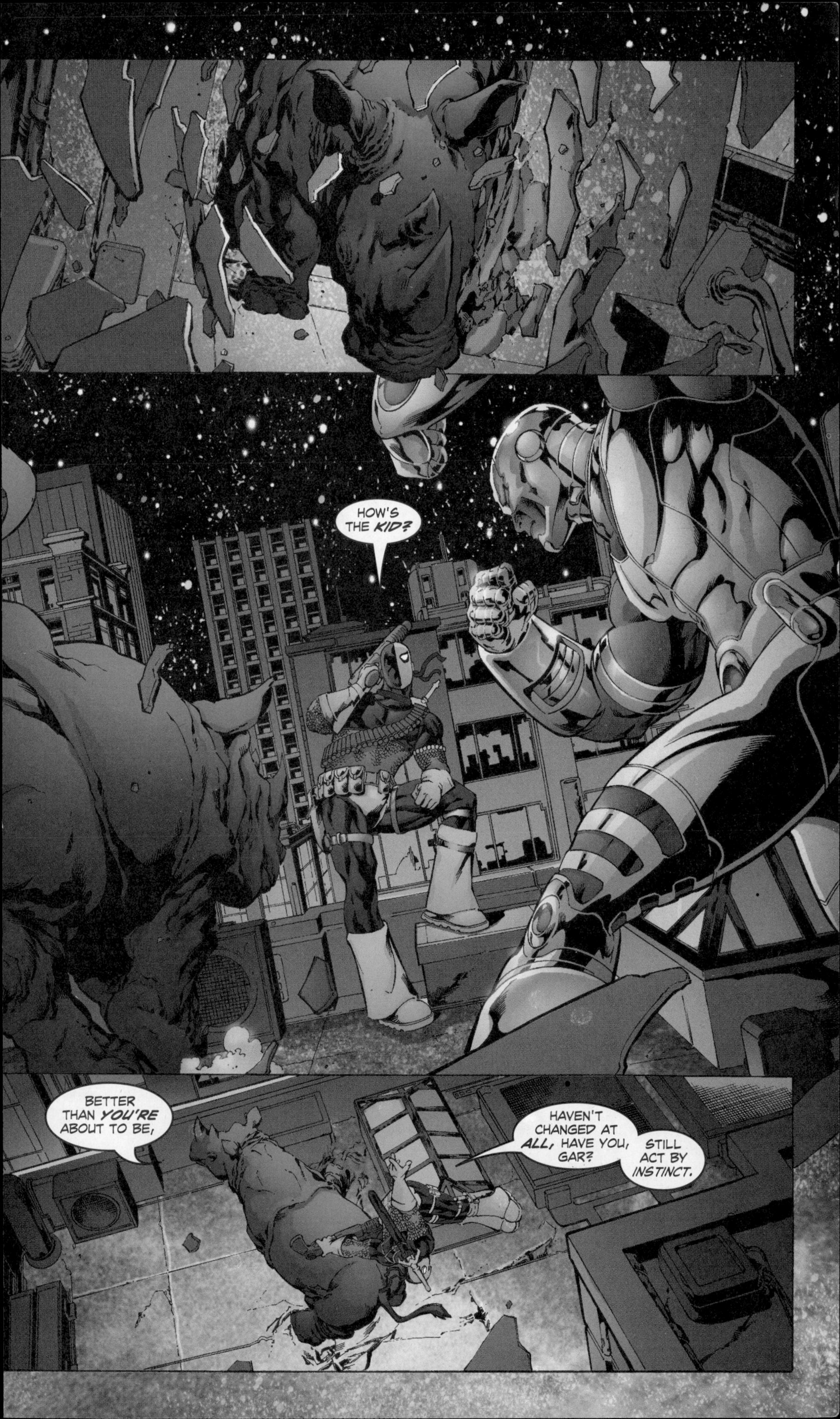
HOW'S THE KID?
BETTER THAN YOU'RE ABOUT TO BE,
HAVEN'T CHANGED AT ALL, HAVE YOU, GAR?
STILL ACT BY INSTINCT.

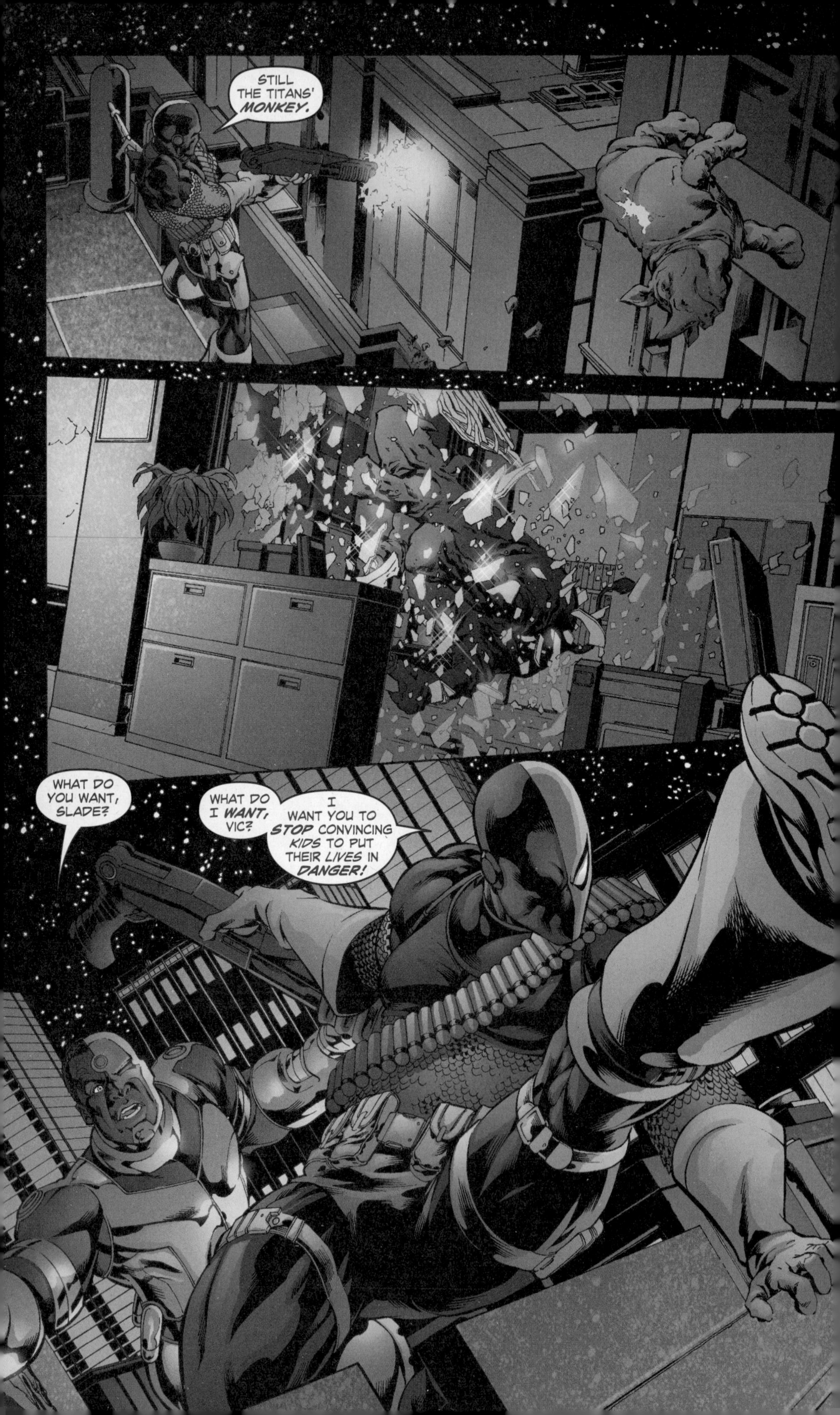
STILL THE TITANS' MONKEY.
WHAT DO YOU WANT, SLADE?
WHAT DO I WANT, VIC?
I WANT YOU TO STOP CONVINCING KIDS TO PUT THEIR LIVES IN DANGER!

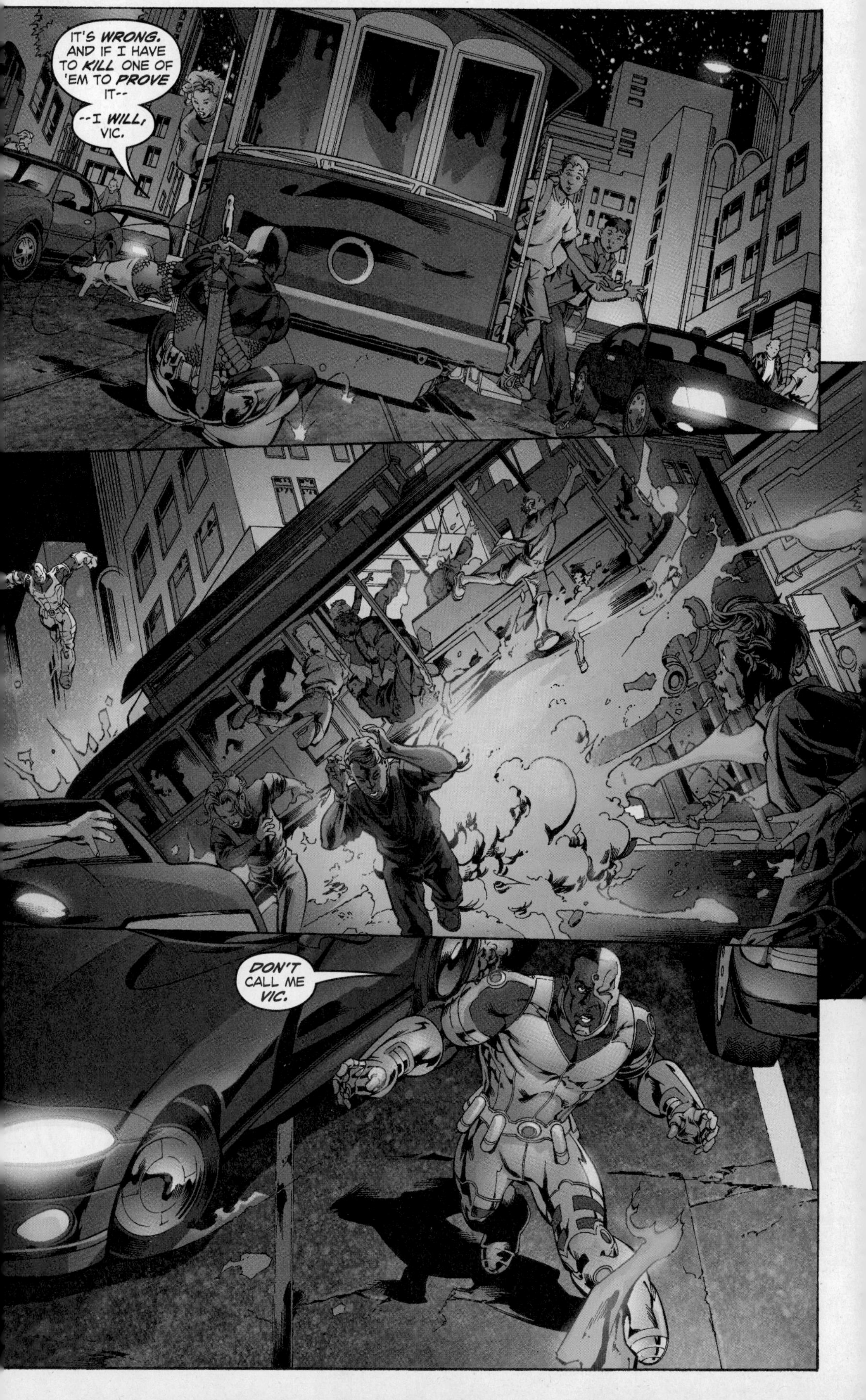
IT'S WRONG. AND IF I HAVE TO KILL ONE OF 'EM TO PROVE IT--
--I WILL, VIC.
DON'T CALL ME VIC.

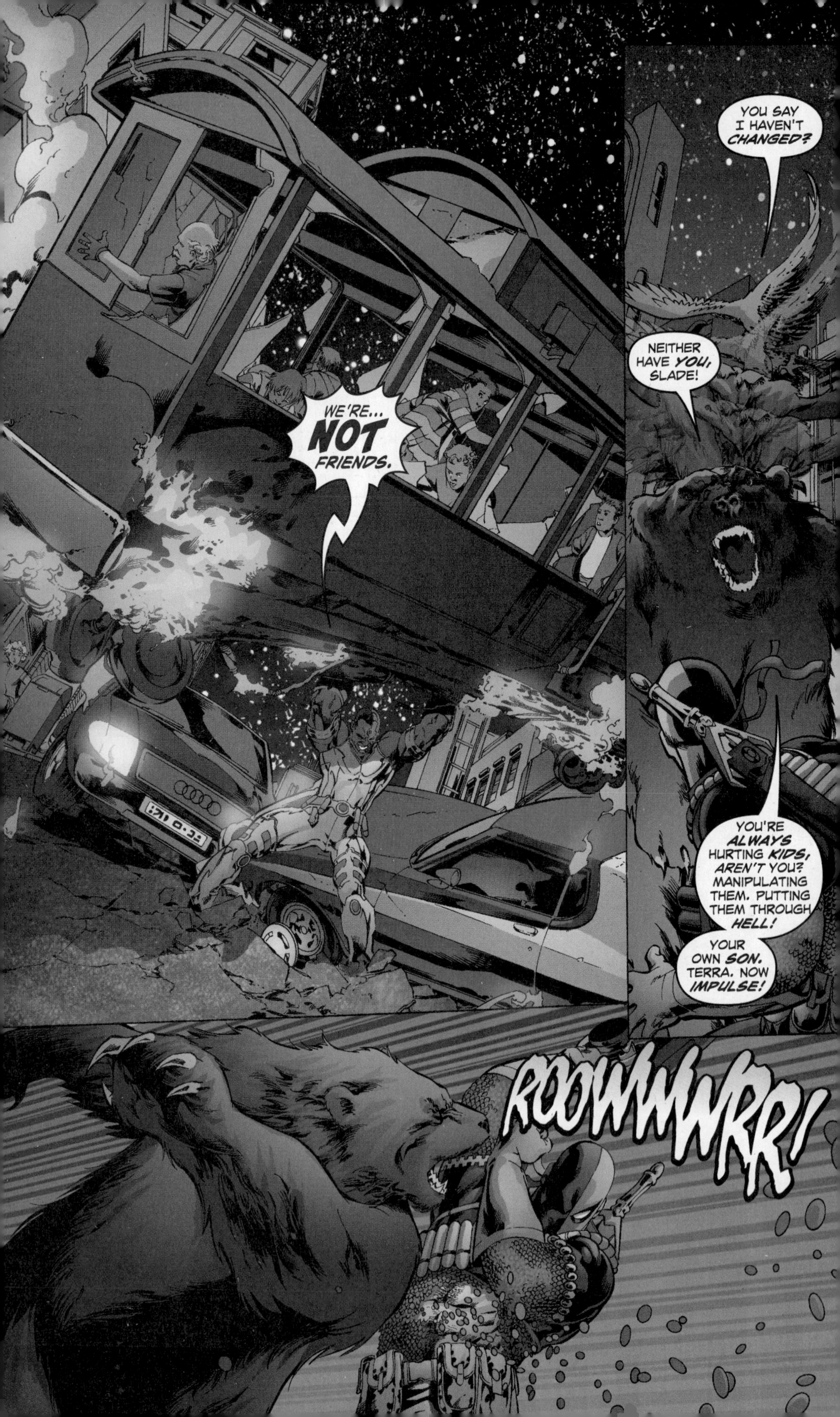
WE'RE... NOT FRIENDS.
YOU SAY I HAVEN'T CHANGED?
NEITHER HAVE YOU, SLADE!
YOU'RE ALWAYS HURTING KIDS, AREN'T YOU? MANIPULATING THEM. PUTTING THEM THROUGH HELL!
YOUR OWN SON. TERRA. NOW IMPULSE!
ROOWWWRR!

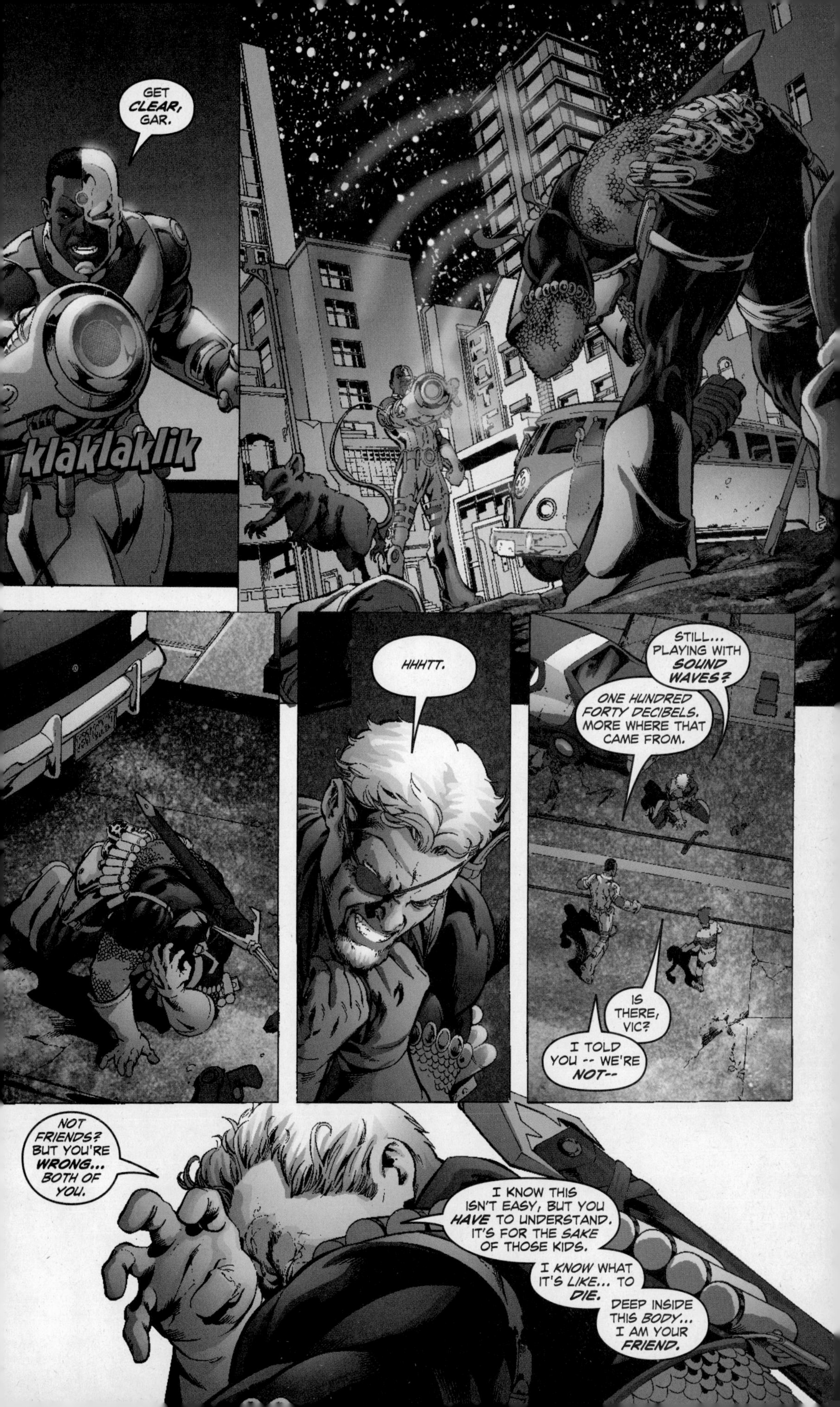
GET CLEAR, GAR.
klaklaklik
HHHTT.
STILL... PLAYING WITH SOUND WAVES?
ONE HUNDRED FORTY DECIBELS. MORE WHERE THAT CAME FROM.
IS THERE, VIC?
I TOLD YOU -- WE'RE NOT--
NOT FRIENDS? BUT YOU'RE WRONG... BOTH OF YOU.
I KNOW THIS ISN'T EASY, BUT YOU HAVE TO UNDERSTAND. IT'S FOR THE SAKE OF THOSE KIDS.
I KNOW WHAT IT'S LIKE... TO DIE.
DEEP INSIDE THIS BODY... I AM YOUR FRIEND.

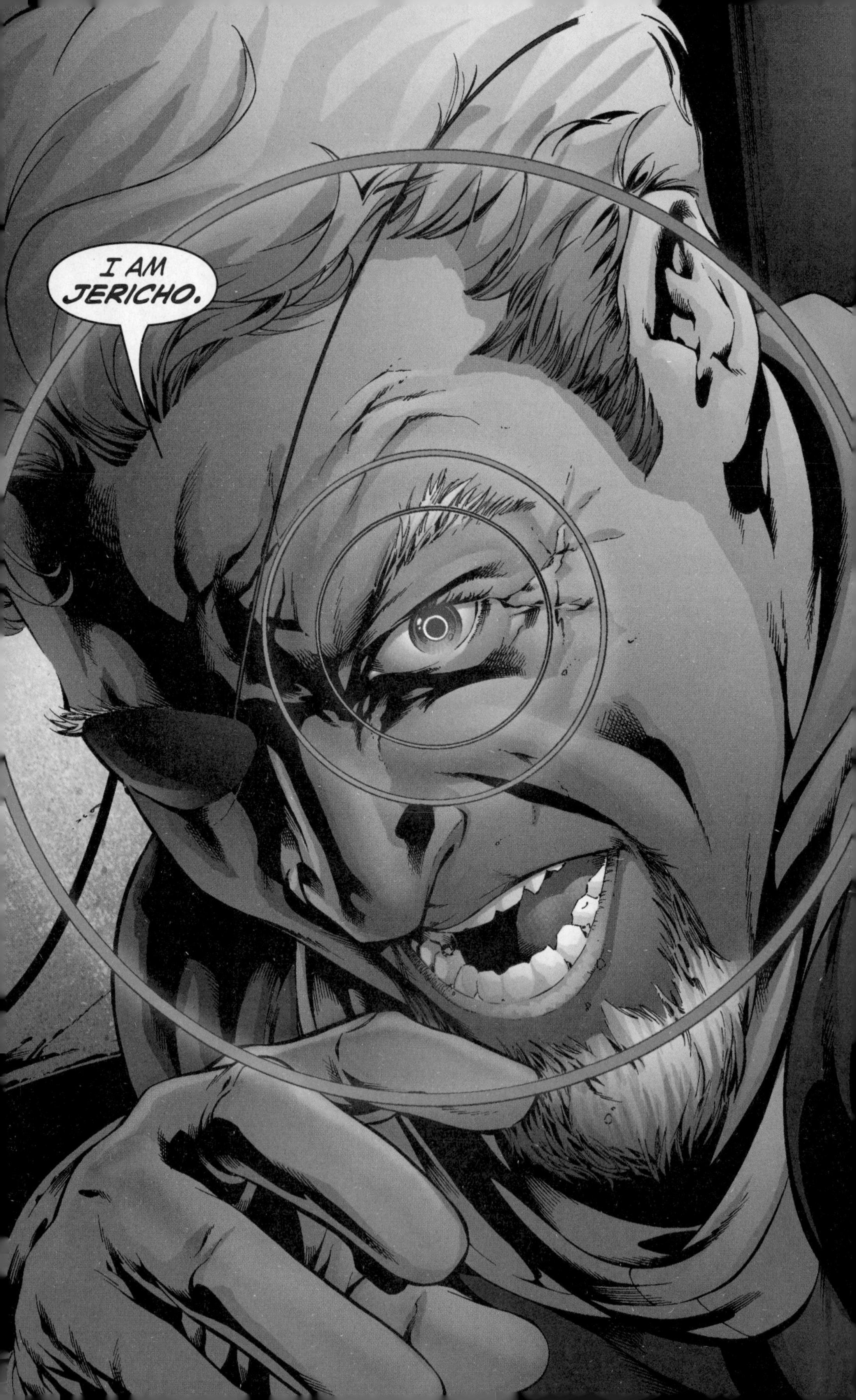
I AM JERICHO.

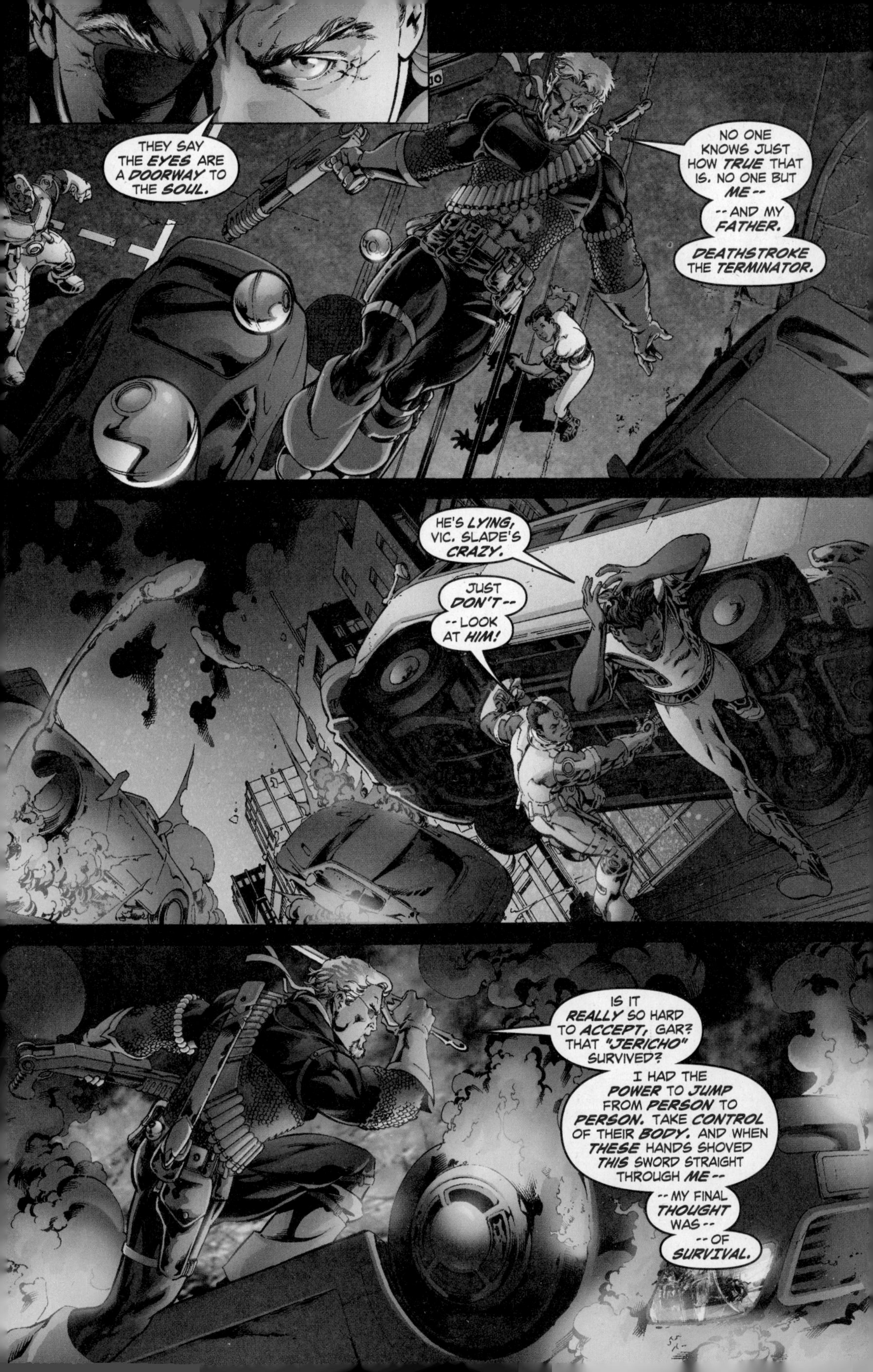
THEY SAY THE EYES ARE A DOORWAY TO THE SOUL.
NO ONE KNOWS JUST HOW TRUE THAT IS. NO ONE BUT ME --
-- AND MY FATHER.
DEATHSTROKE THE TERMINATOR.
HE'S LYING, VIC. SLADE'S CRAZY.
JUST DON'T --
-- LOOK AT HIM!
IS IT REALLY SO HARD TO ACCEPT, GAR? THAT "JERICHO" SURVIVED?
I HAD THE POWER TO JUMP FROM PERSON TO PERSON. TAKE CONTROL OF THEIR BODY. AND WHEN THESE HANDS SHOVED THIS SWORD STRAIGHT THROUGH ME --
-- MY FINAL THOUGHT WAS --
-- OF SURVIVAL.

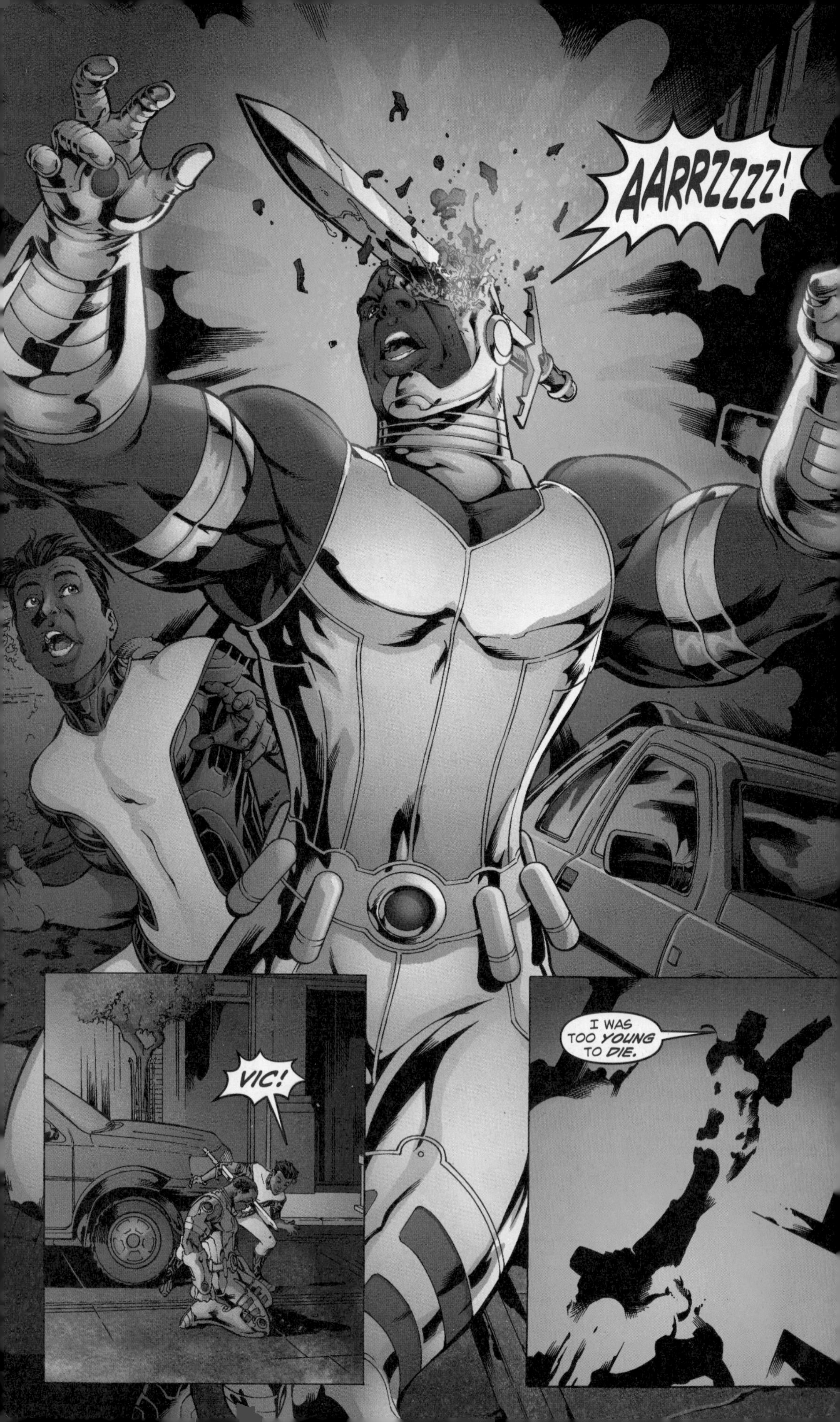
AARRZZZZZ!
VIC!
I WAS TOO YOUNG TO DIE.

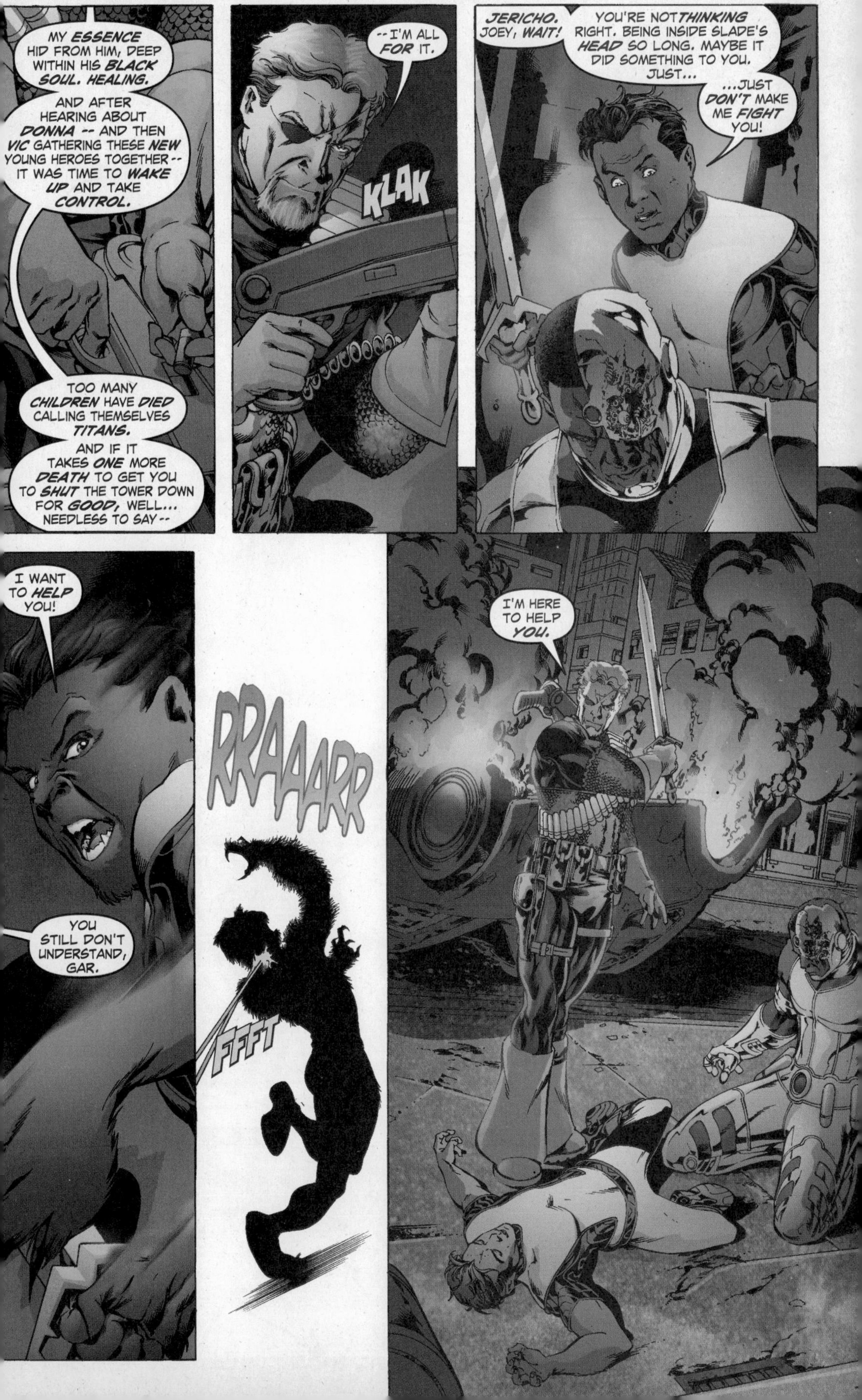
MY ESSENCE HID FROM HIM, DEEP WITHIN HIS BLACK SOUL. HEALING.
AND AFTER HEARING ABOUT DONNA -- AND THEN VIC GATHERING THESE NEW YOUNG HEROES TOGETHER -- IT WAS TIME TO WAKE UP AND TAKE CONTROL.
TOO MANY CHILDREN HAVE DIED CALLING THEMSELVES TITANS.
AND IF IT TAKES ONE MORE DEATH TO GET YOU TO SHUT THE TOWER DOWN FOR GOOD, WELL... NEEDLESS TO SAY --
-- I'M ALL FOR IT.
KLAK
JERICHO. JOEY, WAIT!
YOU'RE NOT THINKING RIGHT. BEING INSIDE SLADE'S HEAD SO LONG. MAYBE IT DID SOMETHING TO YOU. JUST...
...JUST DON'T MAKE ME FIGHT YOU!
I WANT TO HELP YOU!
YOU STILL DON'T UNDERSTAND, GAR.
RRAAARR
FFFT
I'M HERE TO HELP YOU.

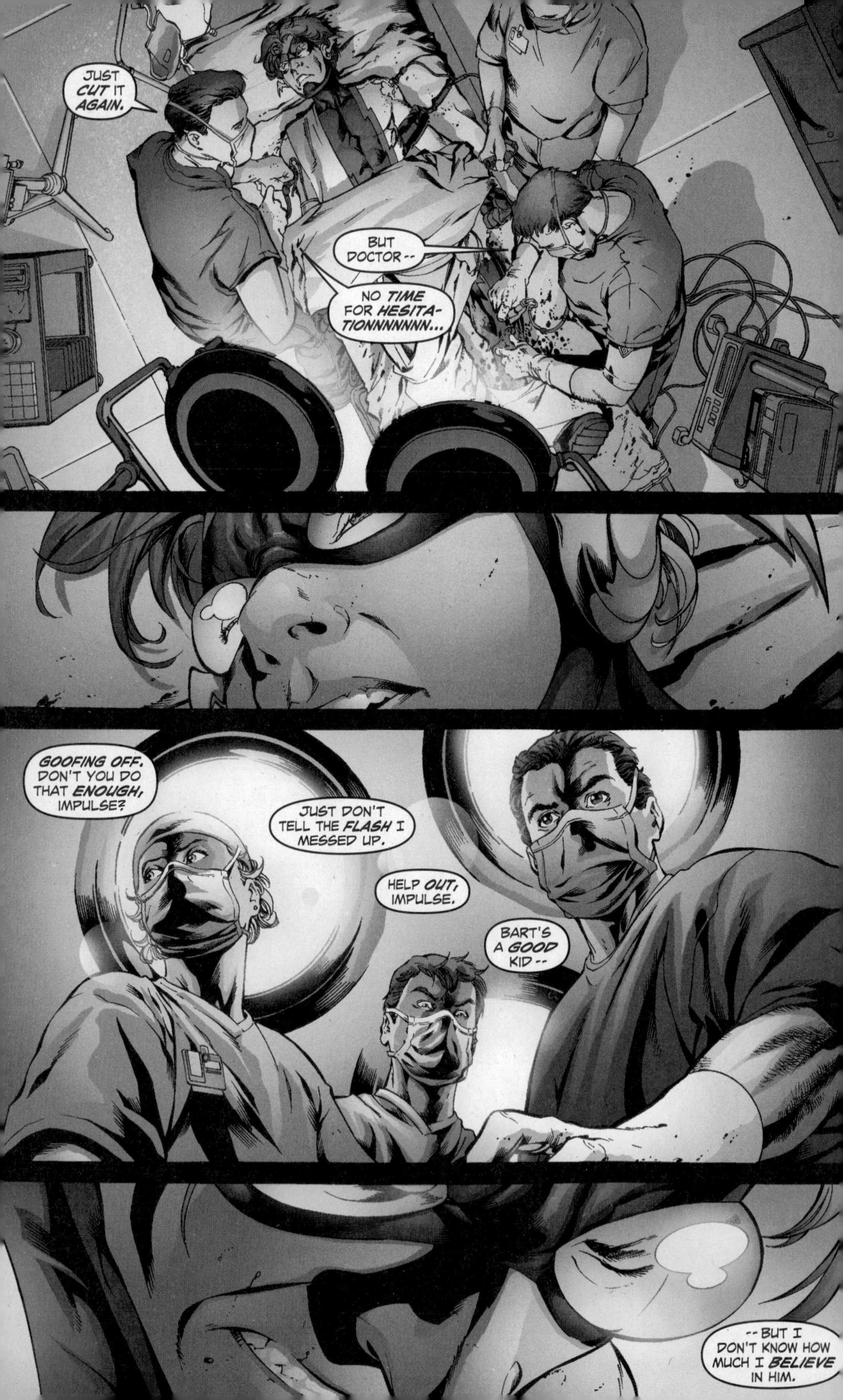

JUST CUT IT AGAIN.
BUT DOCTOR --
NO TIME FOR HESITA-TIONNNNNNN...
GOOFING OFF. DON'T YOU DO THAT ENOUGH, IMPULSE?
JUST DON'T TELL THE FLASH I MESSED UP.
HELP OUT, IMPULSE.
BART'S A GOOD KID --
-- BUT I DON'T KNOW HOW MUCH I BELIEVE IN HIM.

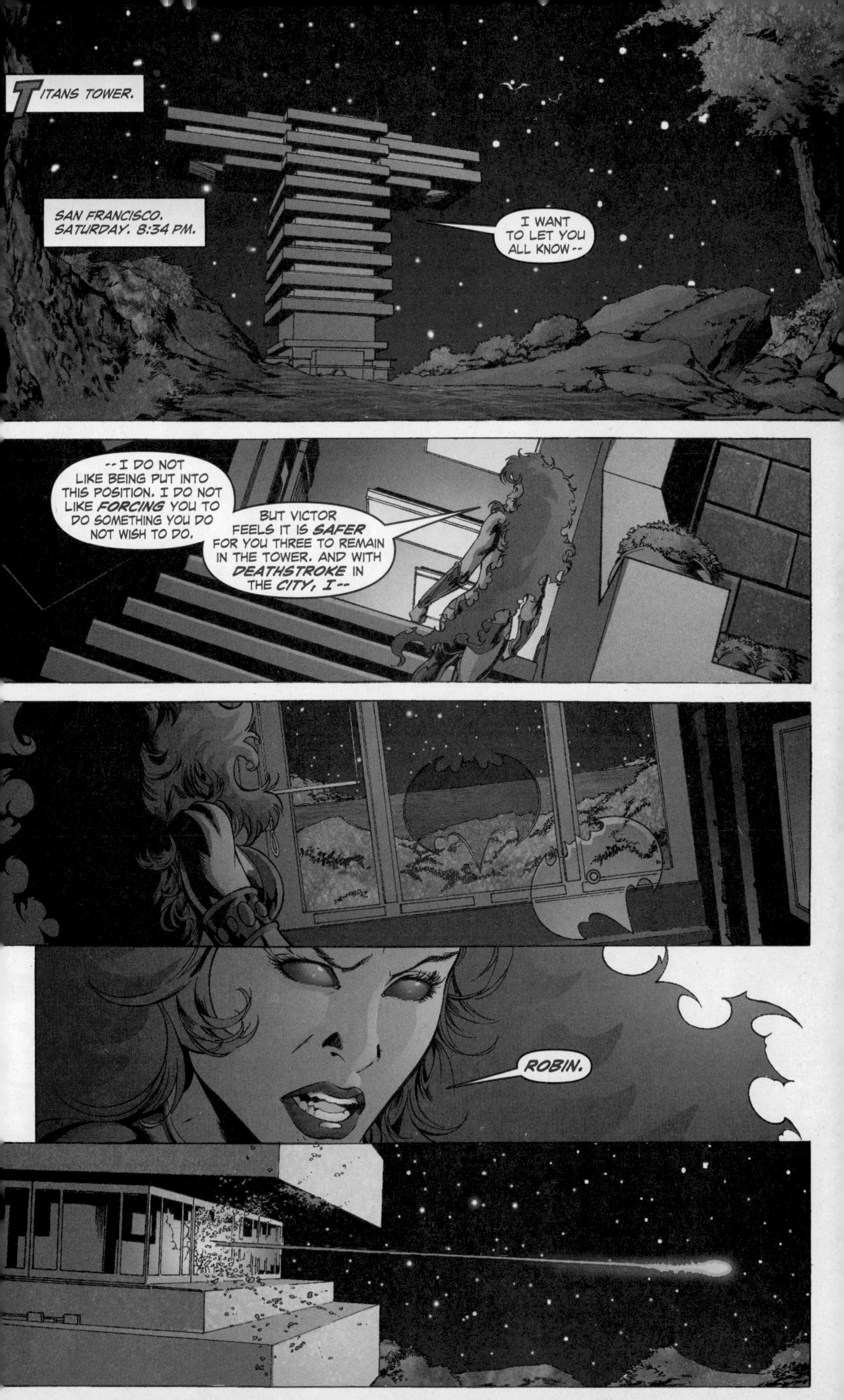
TITANS TOWER.
SAN FRANCISCO. SATURDAY. 8:34 PM.
I WANT TO LET YOU ALL KNOW--
--I DO NOT LIKE BEING PUT INTO THIS POSITION. I DO NOT LIKE FORCING YOU TO DO SOMETHING YOU DO NOT WISH TO DO.
BUT VICTOR FEELS IT IS SAFER FOR YOU THREE TO REMAIN IN THE TOWER. AND WITH DEATHSTROKE IN THE CITY, I--
ROBIN.

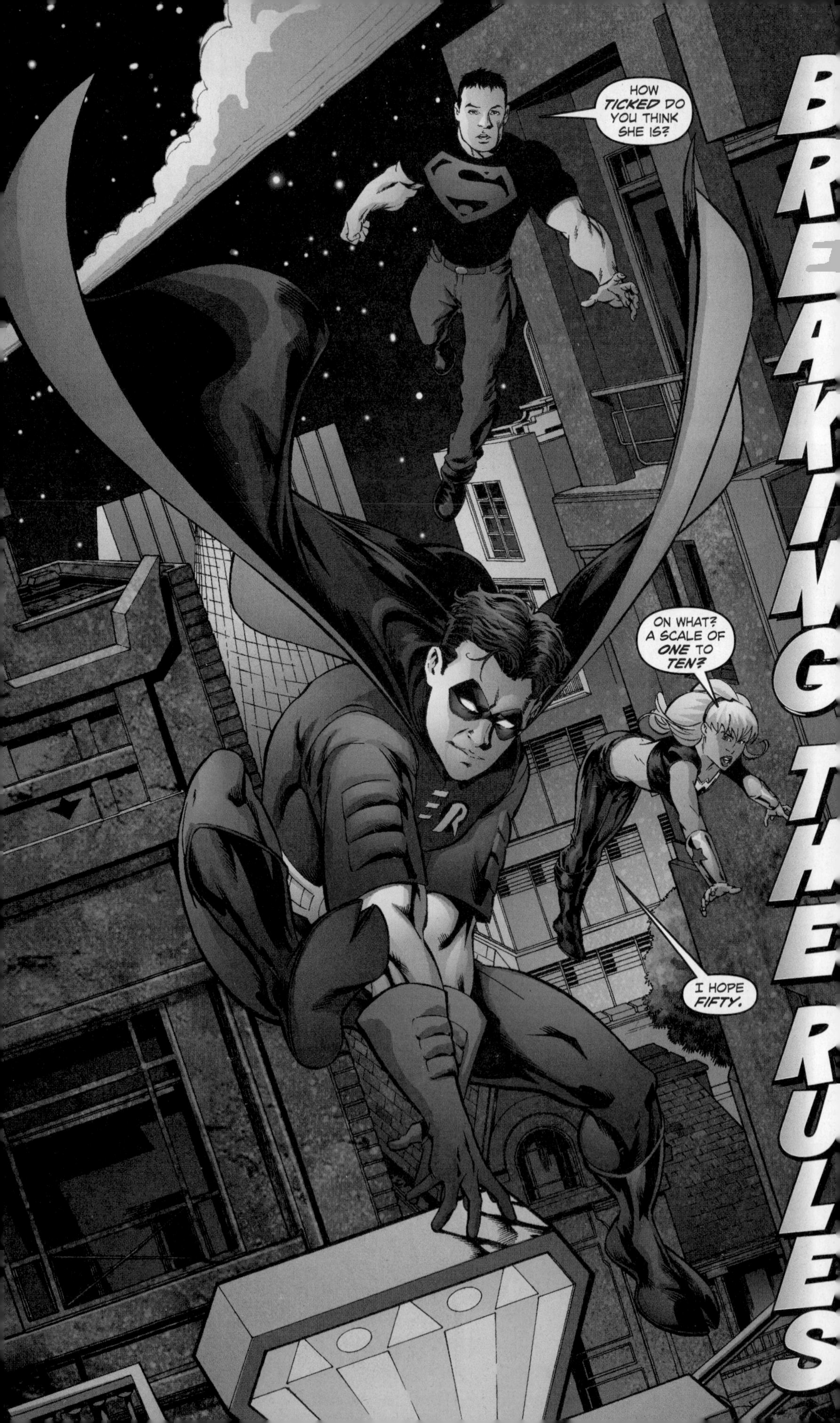
BREAKING THE RULES
HOW TICKED DO YOU THINK SHE IS?
ON WHAT? A SCALE OF ONE TO TEN?
I HOPE FIFTY.

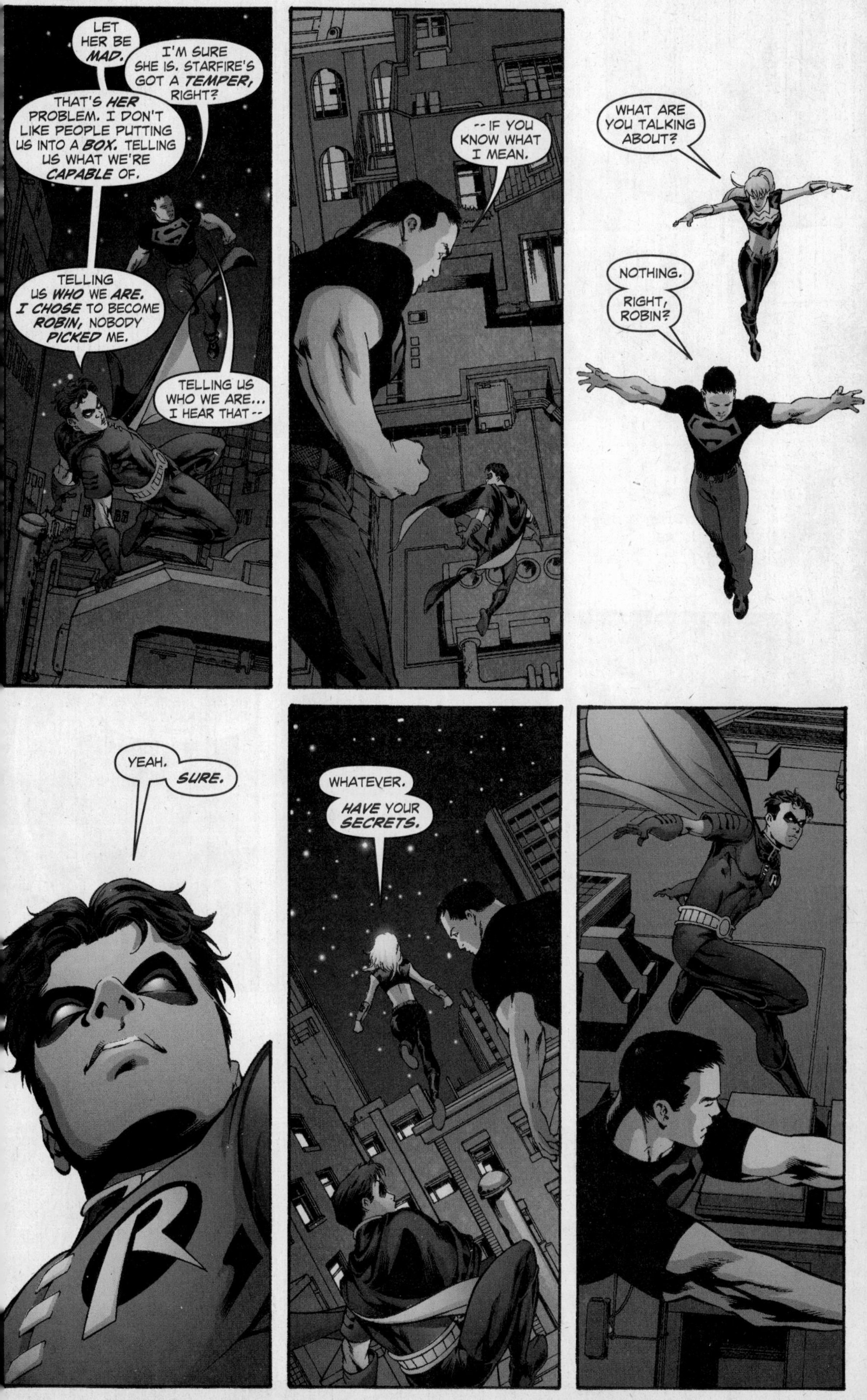
LET HER BE MAD.
I'M SURE SHE IS. STARFIRE'S GOT A TEMPER, RIGHT?
THAT'S HER PROBLEM. I DON'T LIKE PEOPLE PUTTING US INTO A BOX. TELLING US WHAT WE'RE CAPABLE OF.
TELLING US WHO WE ARE. I CHOSE TO BECOME ROBIN, NOBODY PICKED ME.
TELLING US WHO WE ARE... I HEAR THAT --
-- IF YOU KNOW WHAT I MEAN.
WHAT ARE YOU TALKING ABOUT?
NOTHING.
RIGHT, ROBIN?
YEAH.
SURE.
WHATEVER.
HAVE YOUR SECRETS.

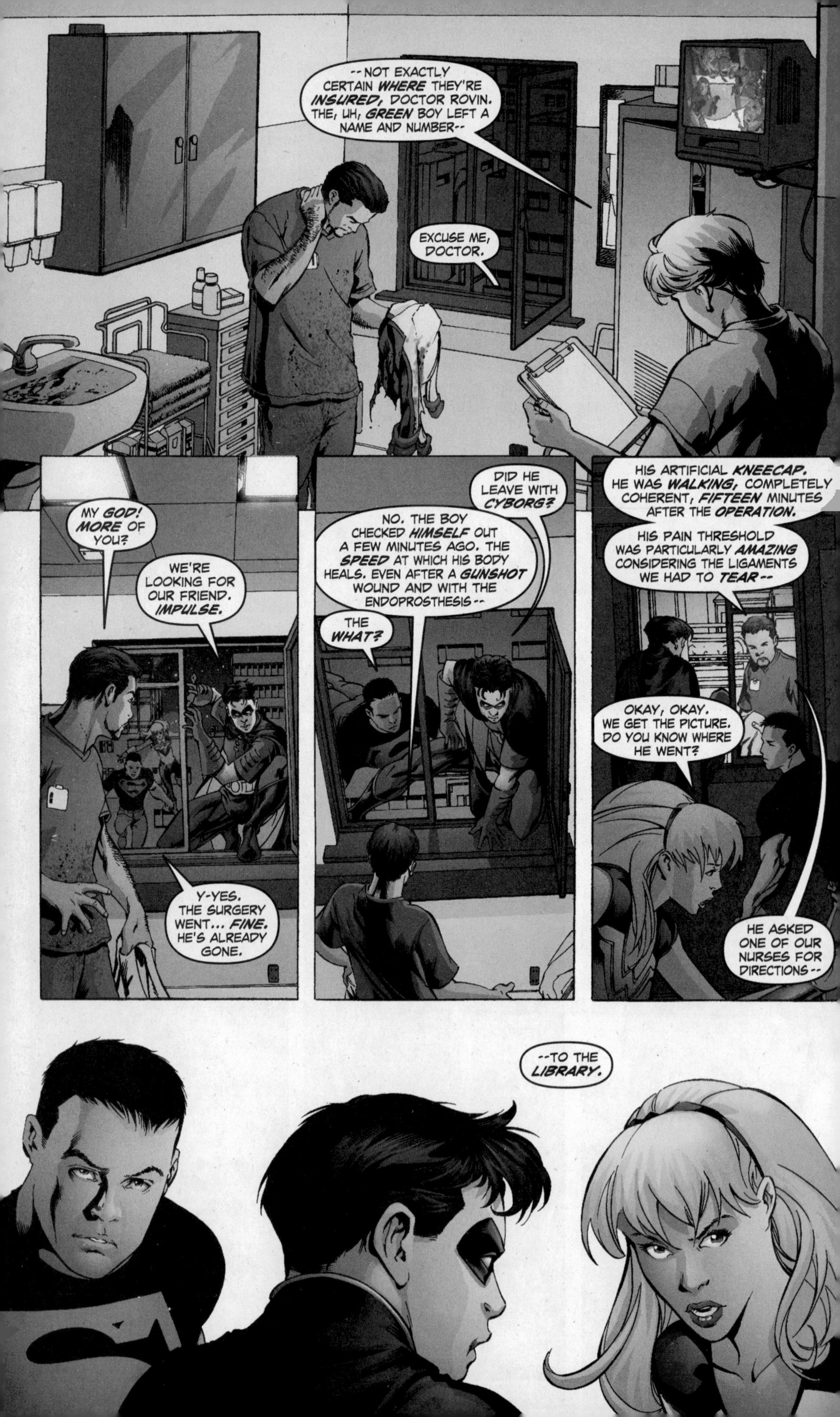
--NOT EXACTLY CERTAIN WHERE THEY'RE INSURED, DOCTOR ROVIN. THE, UH, GREEN BOY LEFT A NAME AND NUMBER--
EXCUSE ME, DOCTOR.
MY GOD! MORE OF YOU?
WE'RE LOOKING FOR OUR FRIEND. IMPULSE.
Y-YES. THE SURGERY WENT... FINE. HE'S ALREADY GONE.
DID HE LEAVE WITH CYBORG?
NO. THE BOY CHECKED HIMSELF OUT A FEW MINUTES AGO. THE SPEED AT WHICH HIS BODY HEALS. EVEN AFTER A GUNSHOT WOUND AND WITH THE ENDOPROSTHESIS--
THE WHAT?
HIS ARTIFICIAL KNEECAP. HE WAS WALKING, COMPLETELY COHERENT, FIFTEEN MINUTES AFTER THE OPERATION.
HIS PAIN THRESHOLD WAS PARTICULARLY AMAZING CONSIDERING THE LIGAMENTS WE HAD TO TEAR--
OKAY, OKAY. WE GET THE PICTURE. DO YOU KNOW WHERE HE WENT?
HE ASKED ONE OF OUR NURSES FOR DIRECTIONS--
--TO THE LIBRARY.

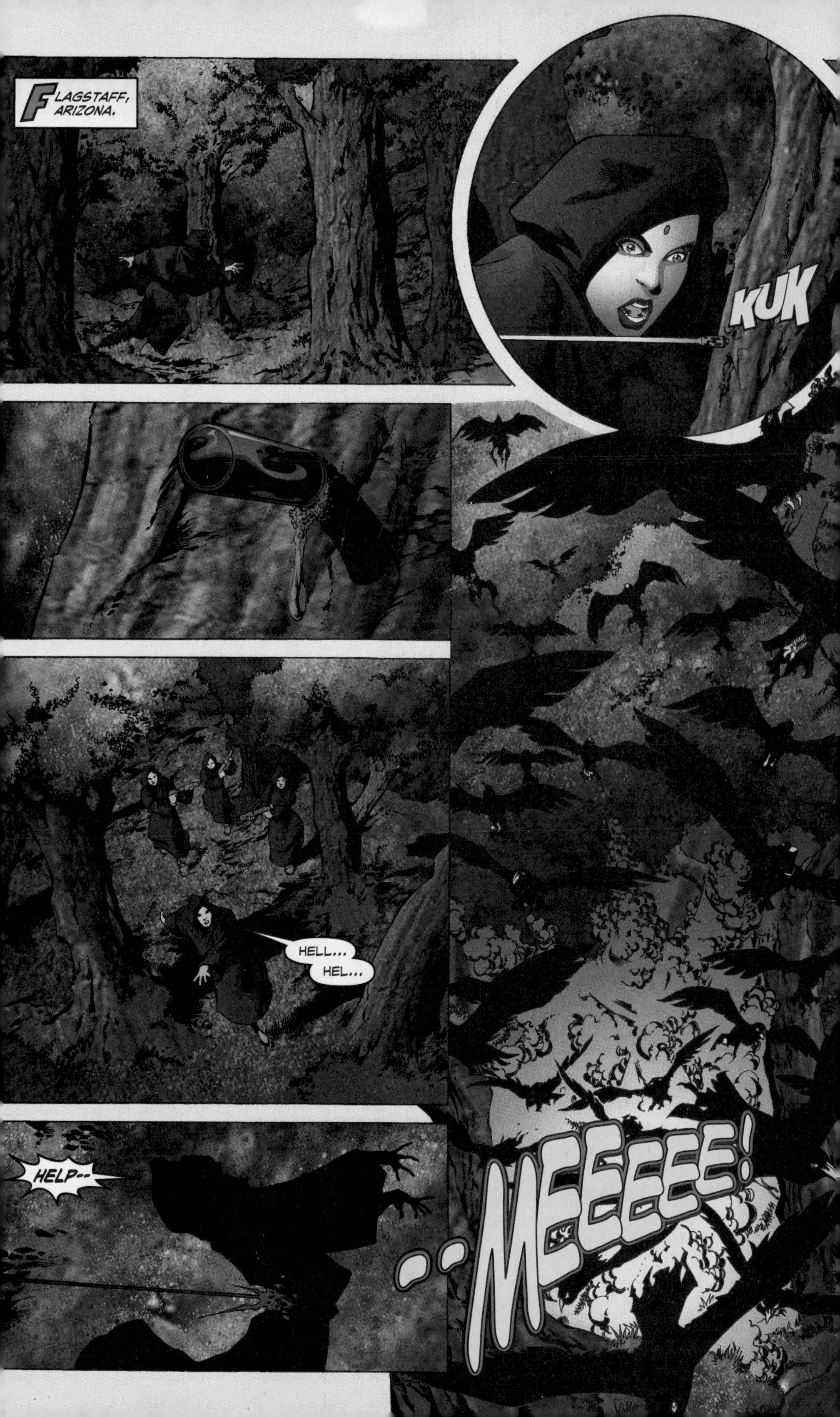
FLAGSTAFF, ARIZONA.
KUK
HELL...
HEL...
HELP--
--MEEEEEE!

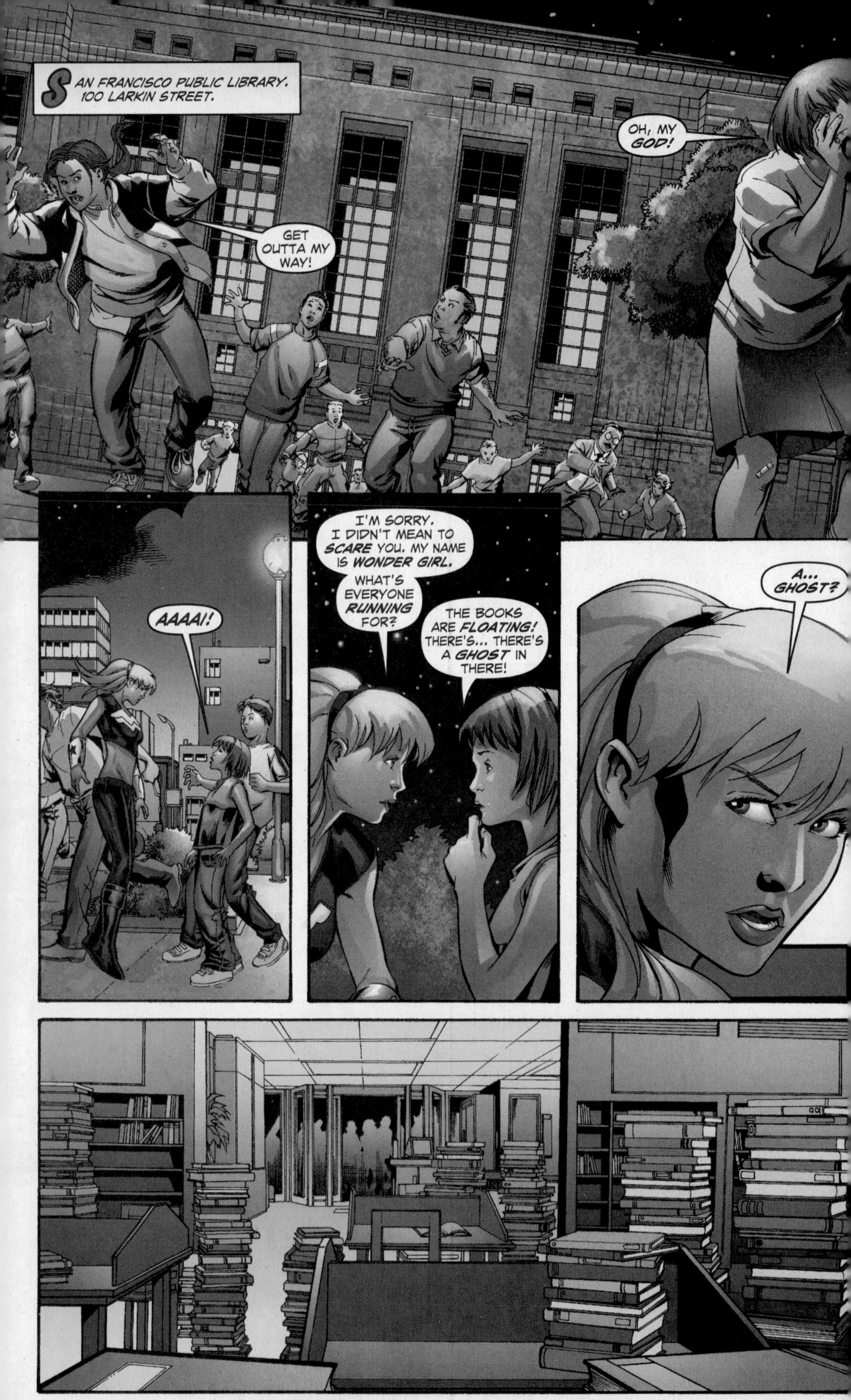
SAN FRANCISCO PUBLIC LIBRARY. 100 LARKIN STREET.
GET OUTTA MY WAY!
OH, MY GOD!
AAAAI!
I'M SORRY. I DIDN'T MEAN TO SCARE YOU. MY NAME IS WONDER GIRL.
WHAT'S EVERYONE RUNNING FOR?
THE BOOKS ARE FLOATING! THERE'S... THERE'S A GHOST IN THERE!
A... GHOST?

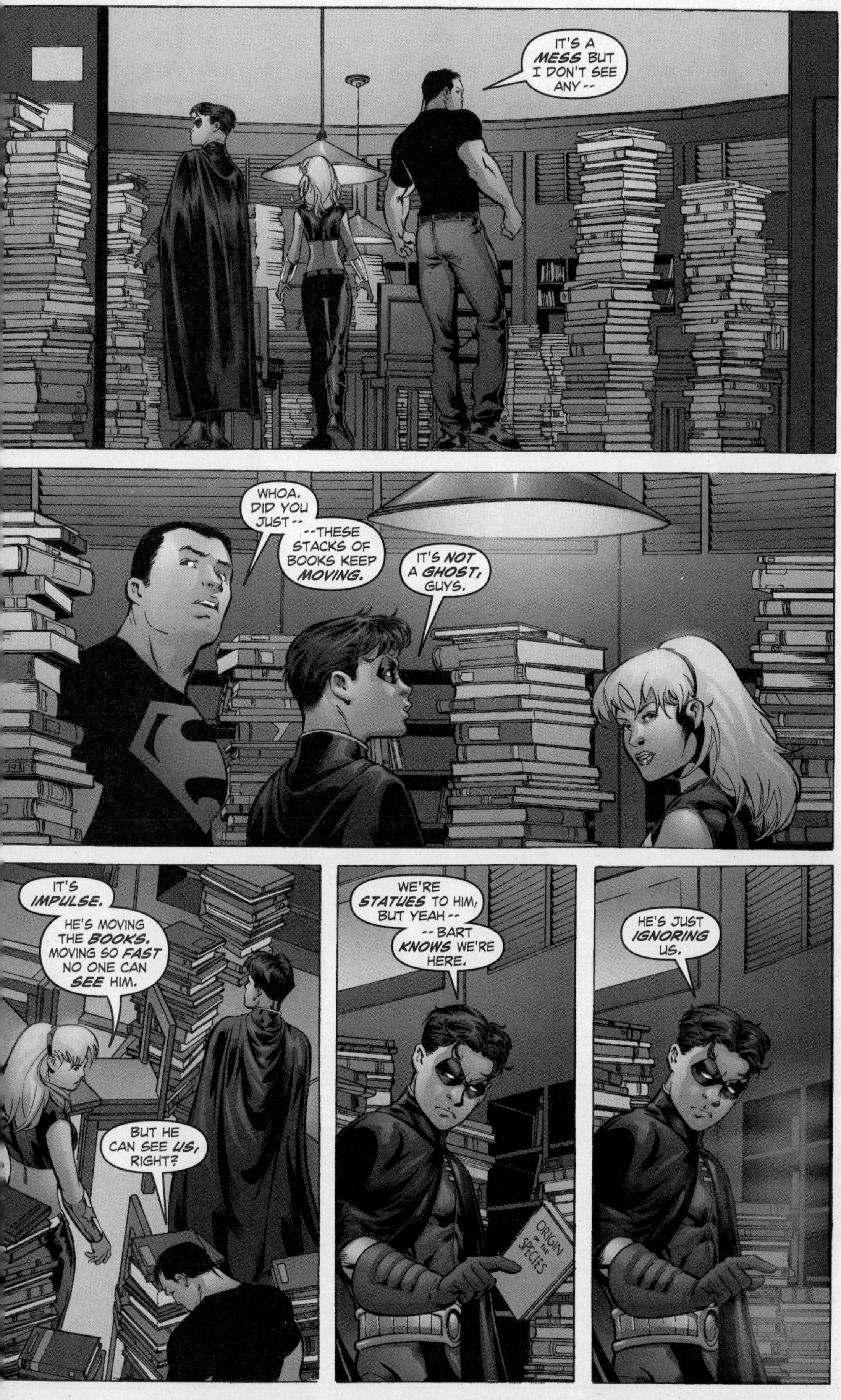
IT'S A MESS BUT I DON'T SEE ANY --
WHOA. DID YOU JUST --
--THESE STACKS OF BOOKS KEEP MOVING.
IT'S NOT A GHOST, GUYS.
IT'S IMPULSE.
HE'S MOVING THE BOOKS. MOVING SO FAST NO ONE CAN SEE HIM.
BUT HE CAN SEE US, RIGHT?
WE'RE STATUES TO HIM, BUT YEAH --
-- BART KNOWS WE'RE HERE.
ORIGIN OF THE SPECIES
HE'S JUST IGNORING US.

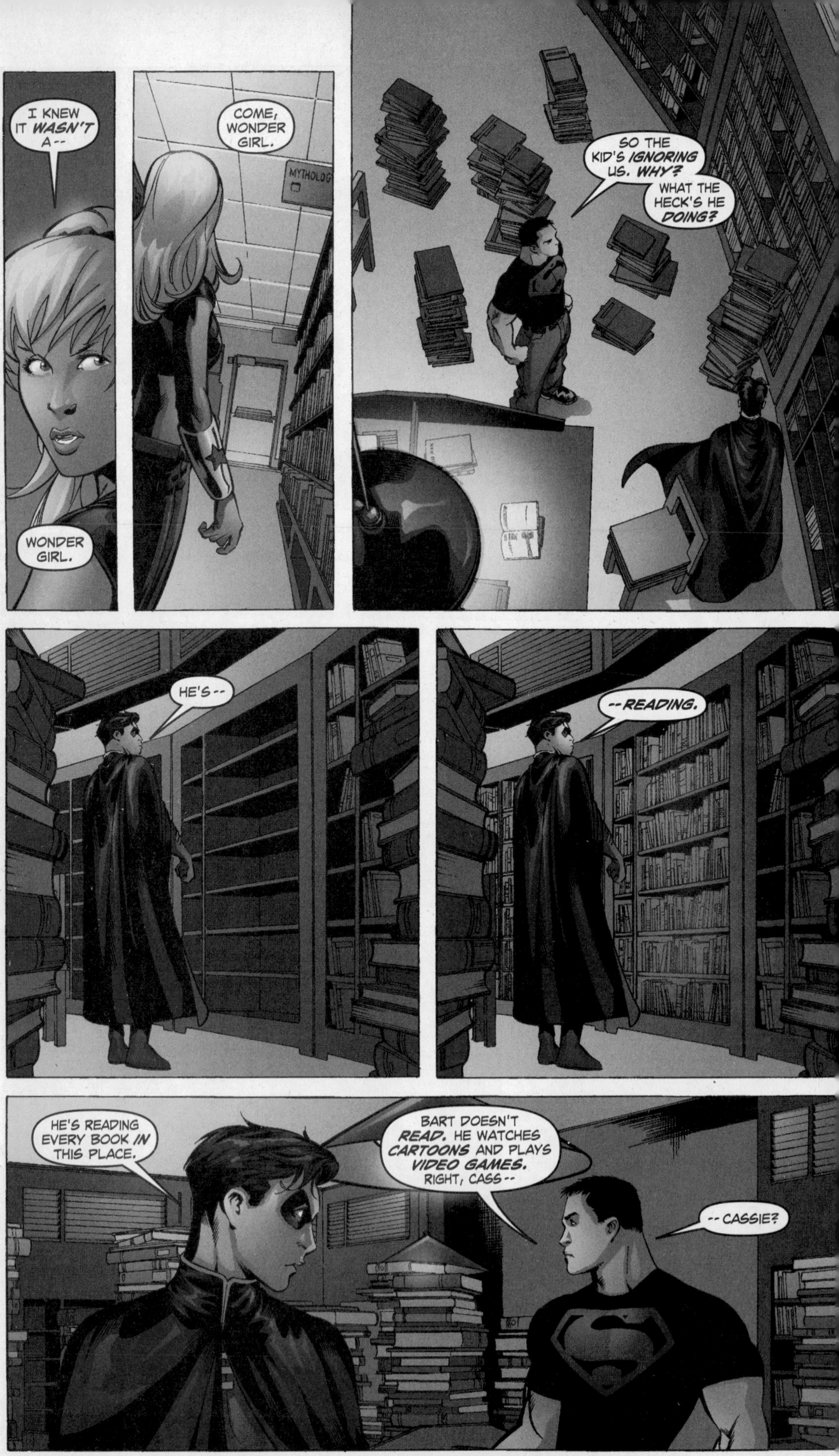
I KNEW IT WASN'T A--
WONDER GIRL.
COME, WONDER GIRL.
MYTHOLOG
SO THE KID'S IGNORING US. WHY?
WHAT THE HECK'S HE DOING?
HE'S--
--READING.
HE'S READING EVERY BOOK IN THIS PLACE.
BART DOESN'T READ. HE WATCHES CARTOONS AND PLAYS VIDEO GAMES. RIGHT, CASS--
--CASSIE?

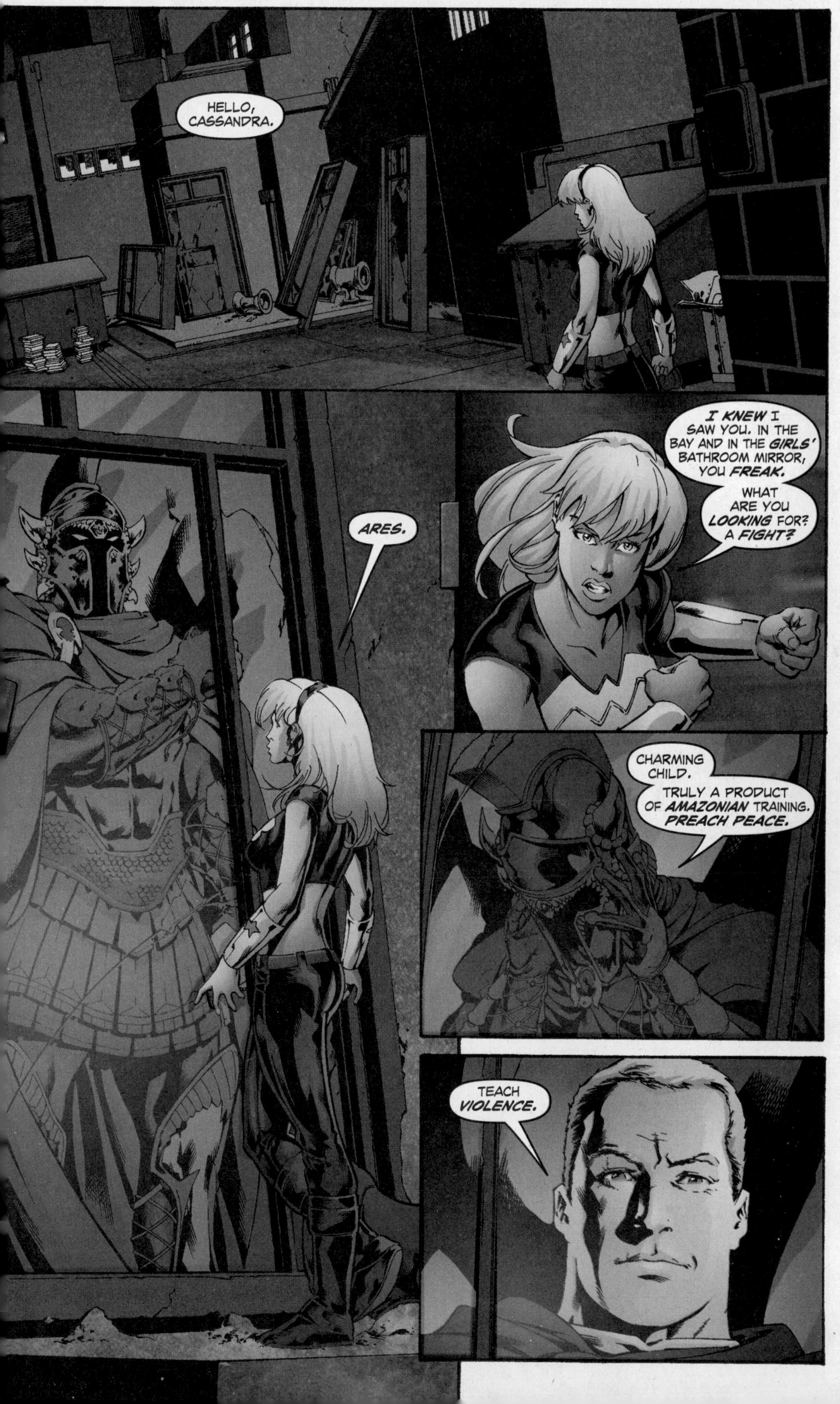
HELLO, CASSANDRA.
ARES.
I KNEW I SAW YOU. IN THE BAY AND IN THE GIRLS' BATHROOM MIRROR, YOU FREAK.
WHAT ARE YOU LOOKING FOR? A FIGHT?
CHARMING CHILD.
TRULY A PRODUCT OF AMAZONIAN TRAINING. PREACH PEACE.
TEACH VIOLENCE.

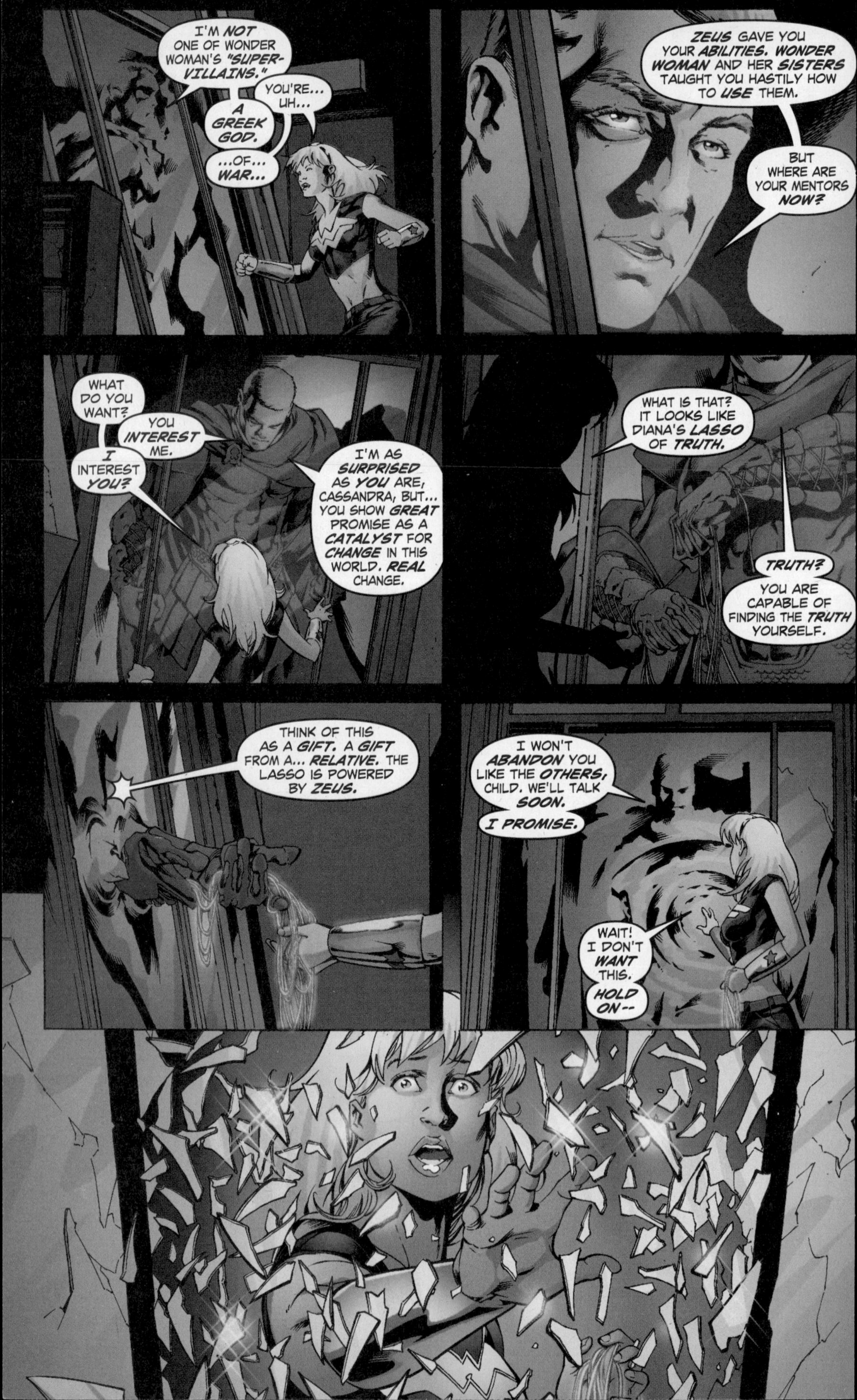
I'M NOT ONE OF WONDER WOMAN'S "SUPER-VILLAINS."
YOU'RE... UH...
A GREEK GOD.
...OF... WAR...
ZEUS GAVE YOU YOUR ABILITIES. WONDER WOMAN AND HER SISTERS TAUGHT YOU HASTILY HOW TO USE THEM.
BUT WHERE ARE YOUR MENTORS NOW?
WHAT DO YOU WANT?
YOU INTEREST ME.
I INTEREST YOU?
I'M AS SURPRISED AS YOU ARE, CASSANDRA, BUT... YOU SHOW GREAT PROMISE AS A CATALYST FOR CHANGE IN THIS WORLD. REAL CHANGE.
WHAT IS THAT? IT LOOKS LIKE DIANA'S LASSO OF TRUTH.
TRUTH?
YOU ARE CAPABLE OF FINDING THE TRUTH YOURSELF.
THINK OF THIS AS A GIFT. A GIFT FROM A... RELATIVE. THE LASSO IS POWERED BY ZEUS.
I WON'T ABANDON YOU LIKE THE OTHERS, CHILD. WE'LL TALK SOON.
I PROMISE.
WAIT! I DON'T WANT THIS.
HOLD ON--

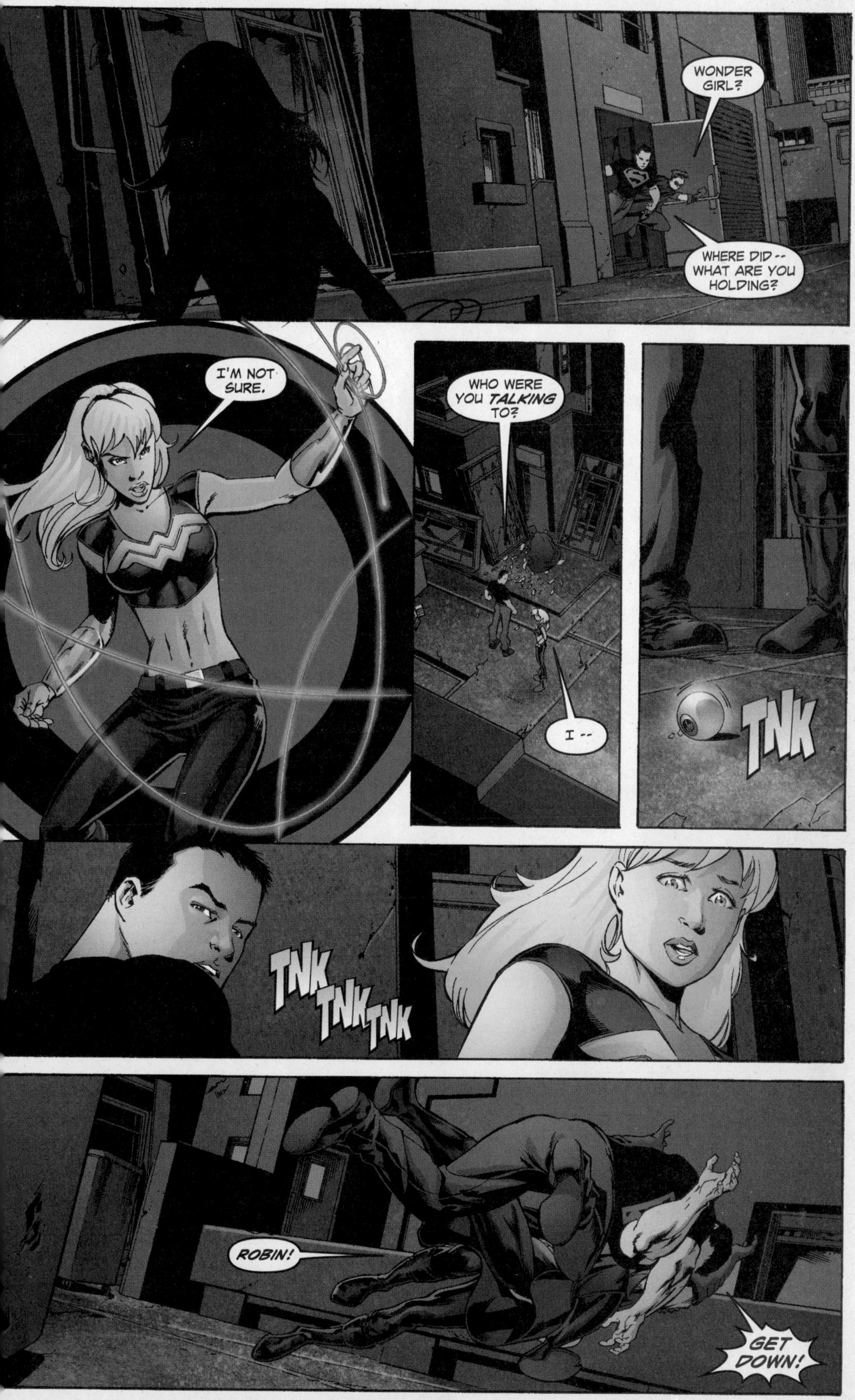
WONDER GIRL?
WHERE DID -- WHAT ARE YOU HOLDING?
I'M NOT SURE.
WHO WERE YOU *TALKING* TO?
I --
TNK
TNK TNK TNK
ROBIN!
GET DOWN!

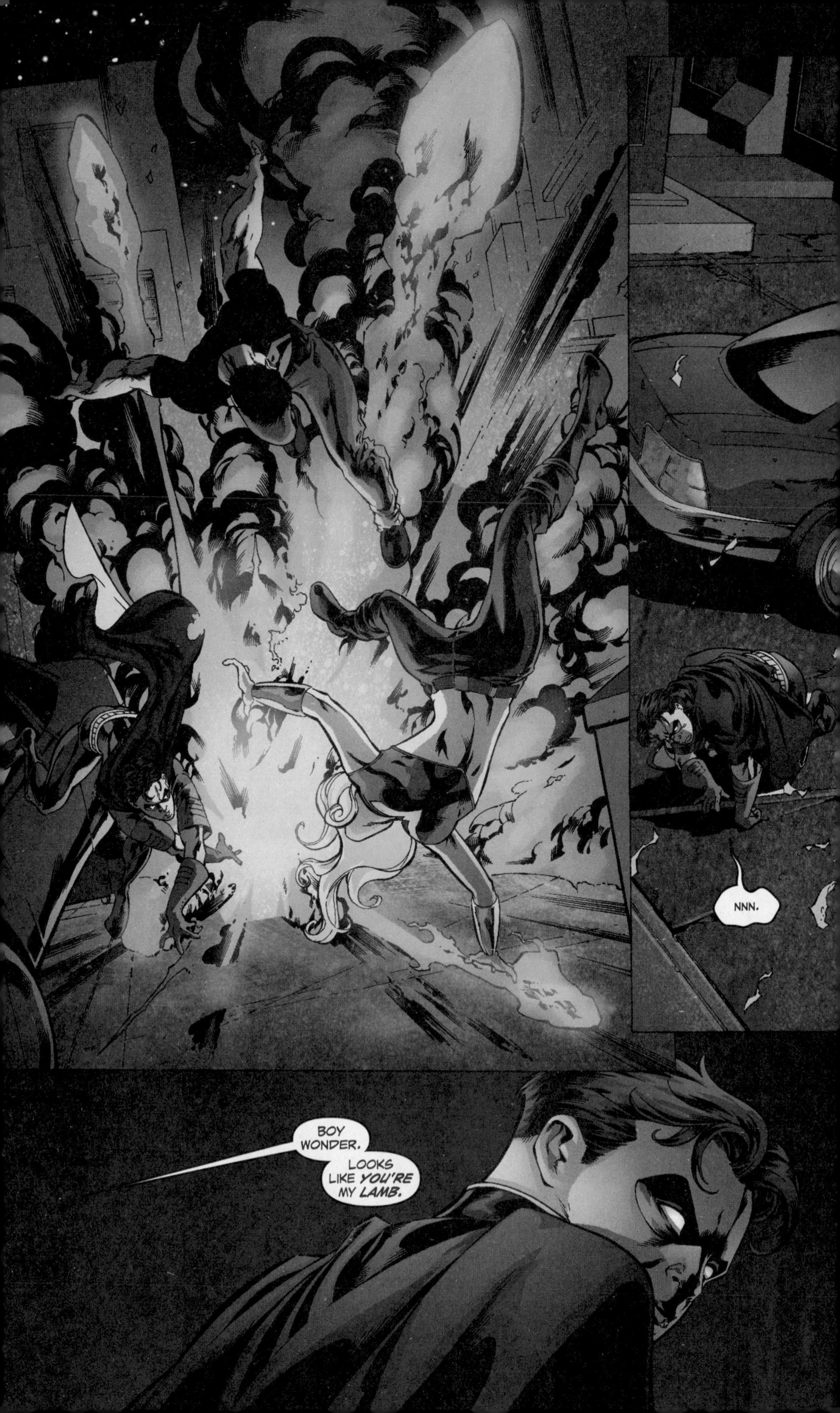
NNN.
BOY WONDER.
LOOKS LIKE YOU'RE MY LAMB.

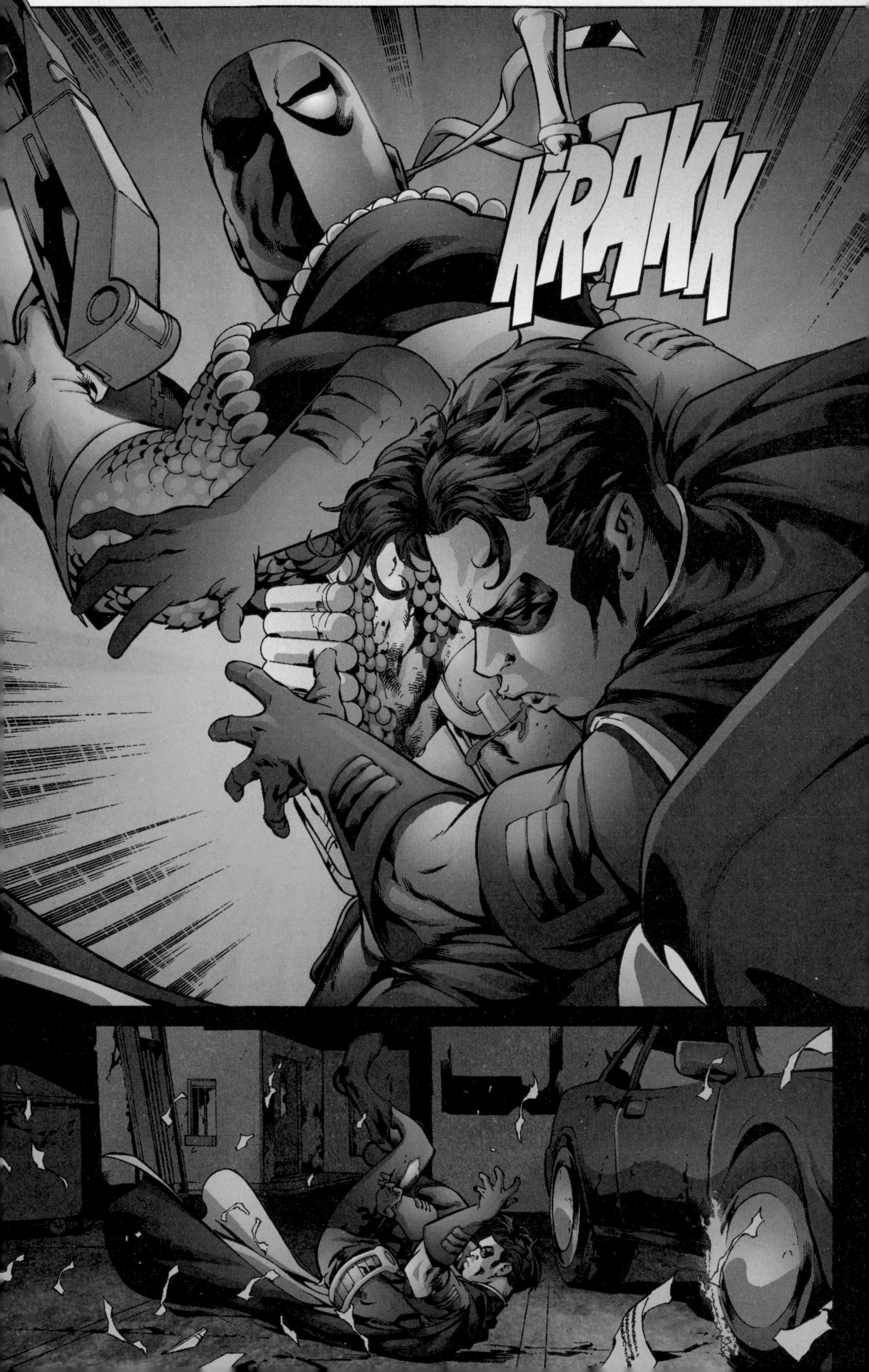
KRAKK

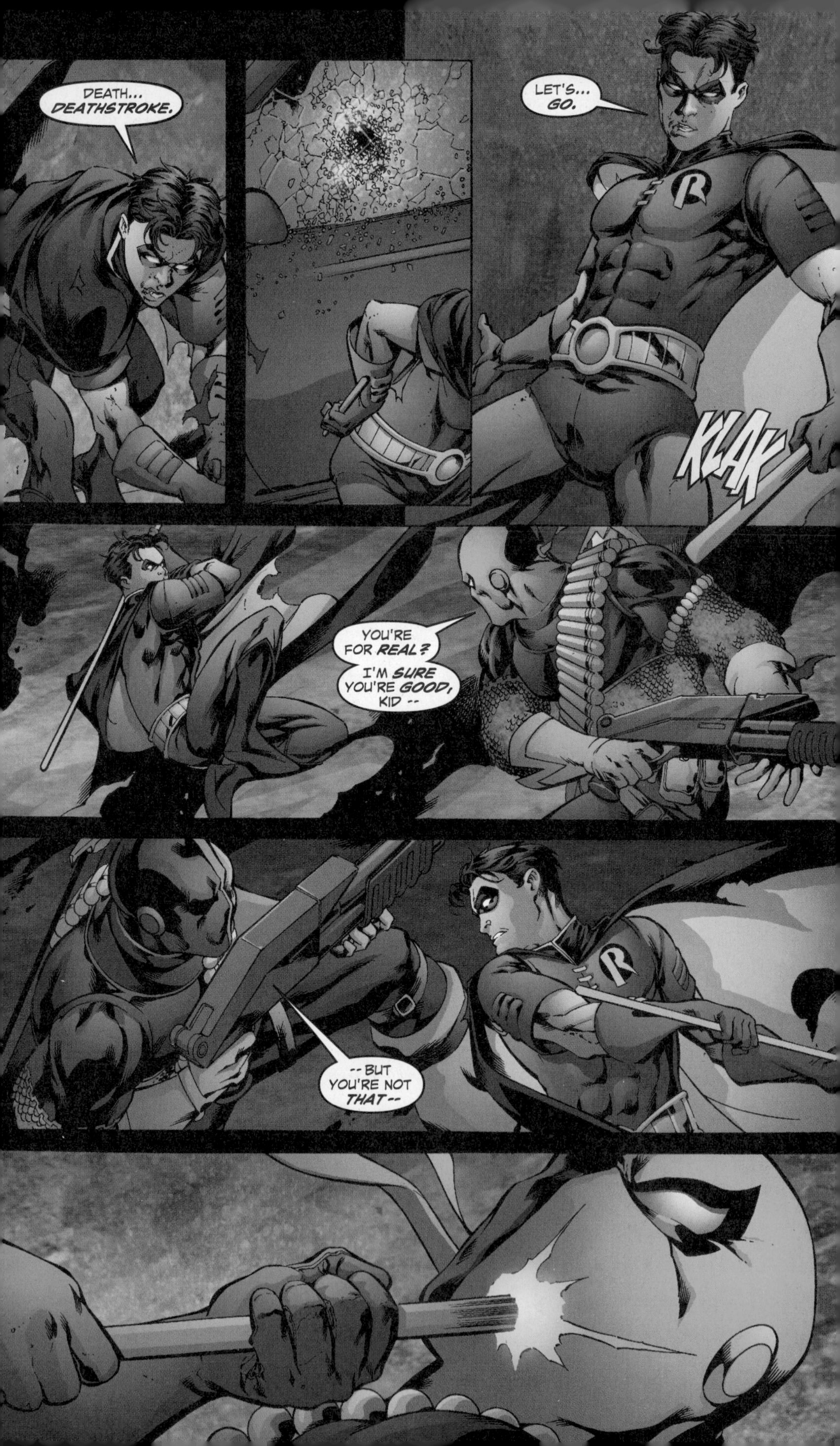
DEATH... DEATHSTROKE.
LET'S... GO.
KLAK
YOU'RE FOR REAL?
I'M SURE YOU'RE GOOD, KID --
-- BUT YOU'RE NOT THAT --

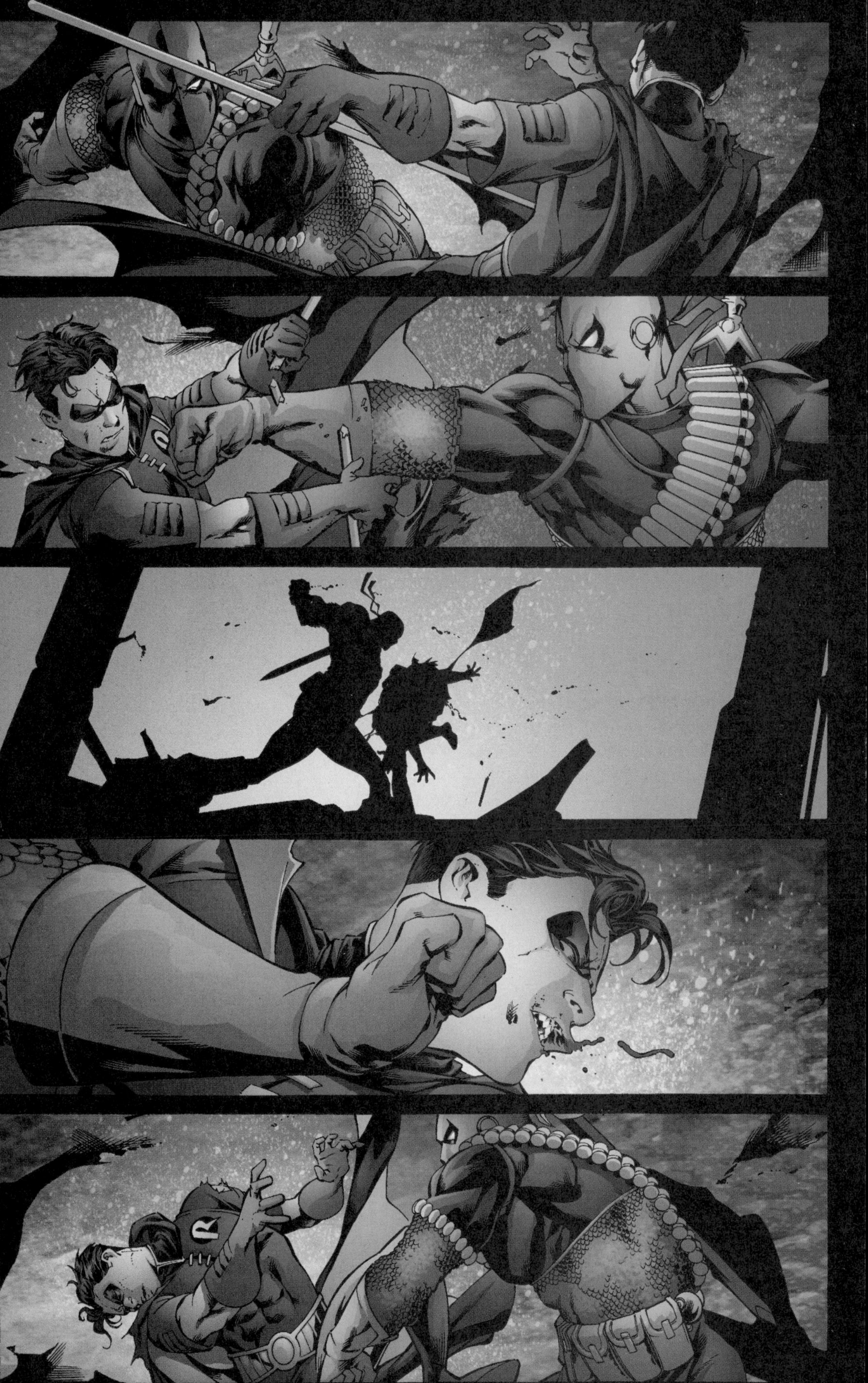

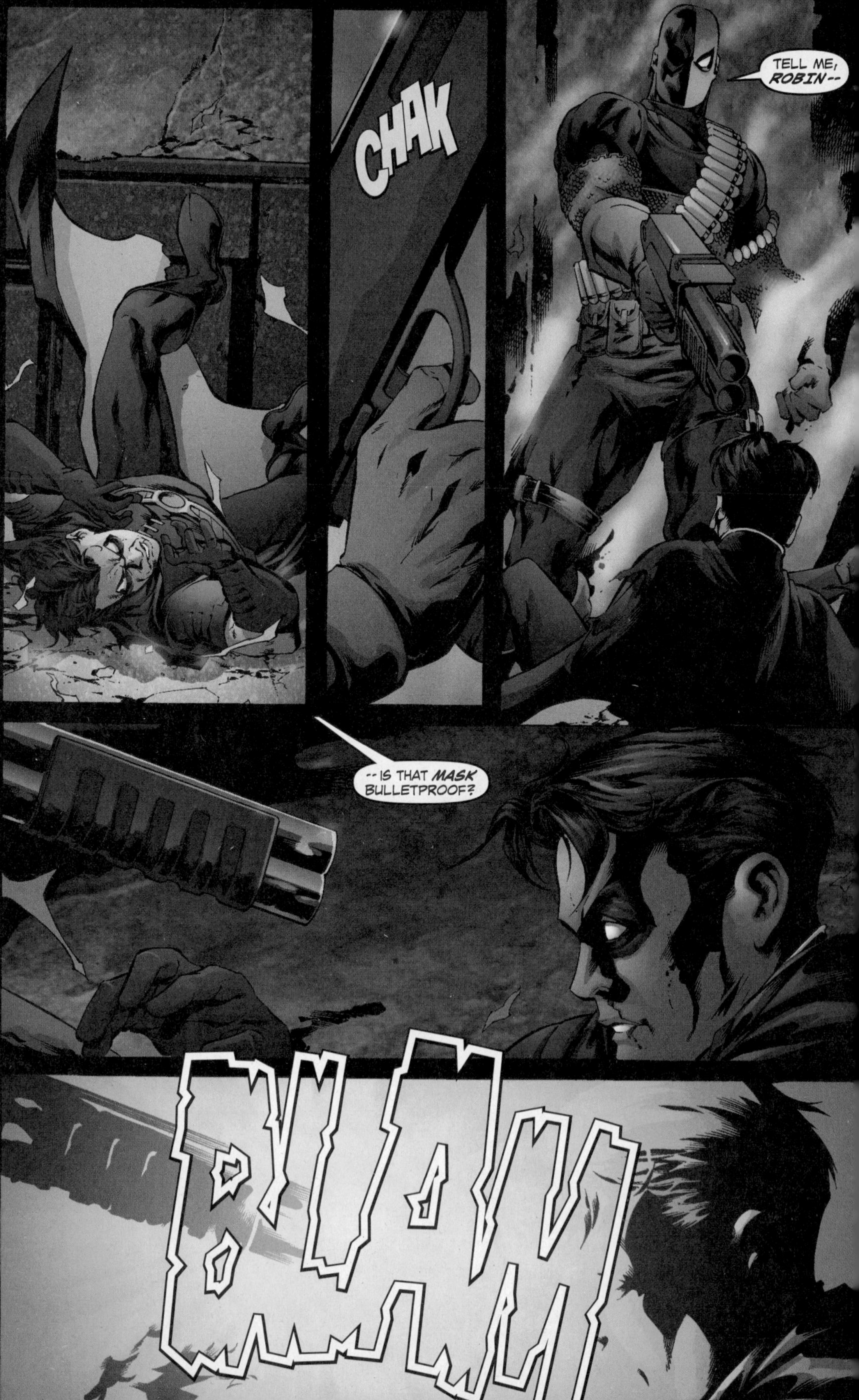
CHAK
TELL ME, *ROBIN*--
--IS THAT *MASK* BULLETPROOF?
BLAM

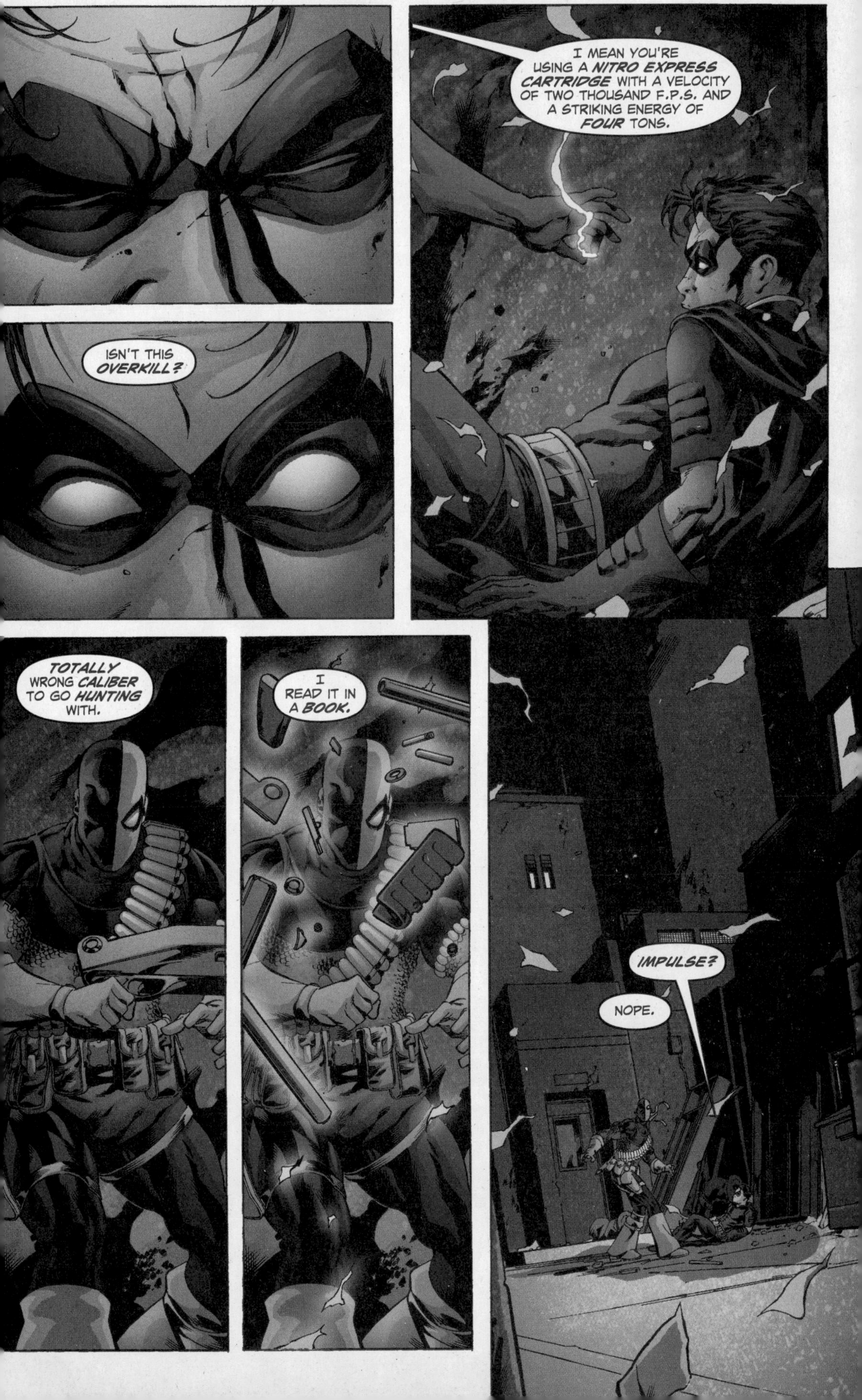
I MEAN YOU'RE USING A NITRO EXPRESS CARTRIDGE WITH A VELOCITY OF TWO THOUSAND F.P.S. AND A STRIKING ENERGY OF FOUR TONS.
ISN'T THIS OVERKILL?
TOTALLY WRONG CALIBER TO GO HUNTING WITH.
I READ IT IN A BOOK.
IMPULSE?
NOPE.

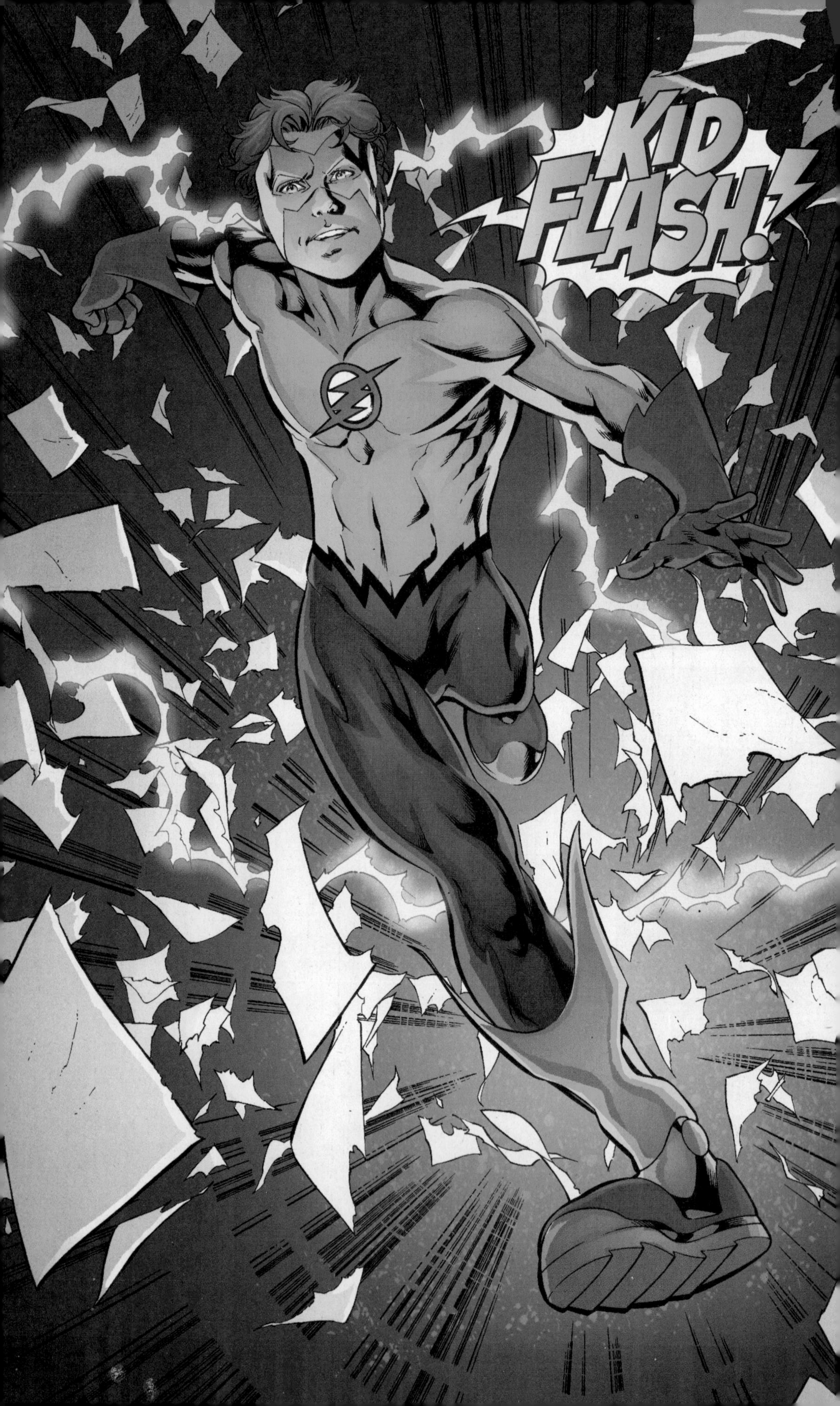
KID FLASH!

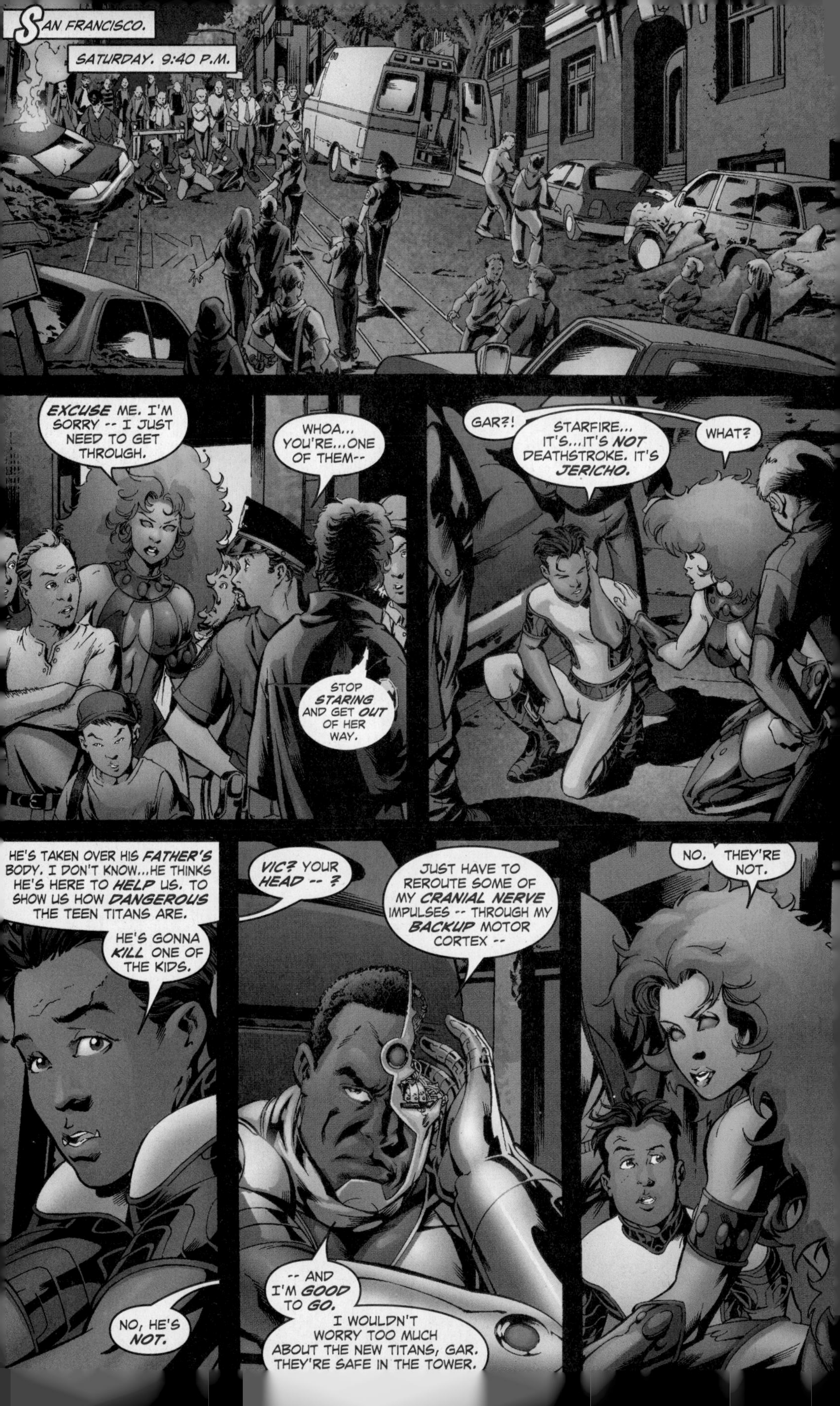
SAN FRANCISCO.
SATURDAY. 9:40 P.M.
EXCUSE ME. I'M SORRY -- I JUST NEED TO GET THROUGH.
WHOA... YOU'RE...ONE OF THEM--
STOP STARING AND GET OUT OF HER WAY.
GAR?!
STARFIRE... IT'S...IT'S NOT DEATHSTROKE. IT'S JERICHO.
WHAT?
HE'S TAKEN OVER HIS FATHER'S BODY. I DON'T KNOW...HE THINKS HE'S HERE TO HELP US. TO SHOW US HOW DANGEROUS THE TEEN TITANS ARE.
HE'S GONNA KILL ONE OF THE KIDS.
NO, HE'S NOT.
VIC? YOUR HEAD -- ?
JUST HAVE TO REROUTE SOME OF MY CRANIAL NERVE IMPULSES -- THROUGH MY BACKUP MOTOR CORTEX --
-- AND I'M GOOD TO GO.
I WOULDN'T WORRY TOO MUCH ABOUT THE NEW TITANS, GAR. THEY'RE SAFE IN THE TOWER.
NO.
THEY'RE NOT.

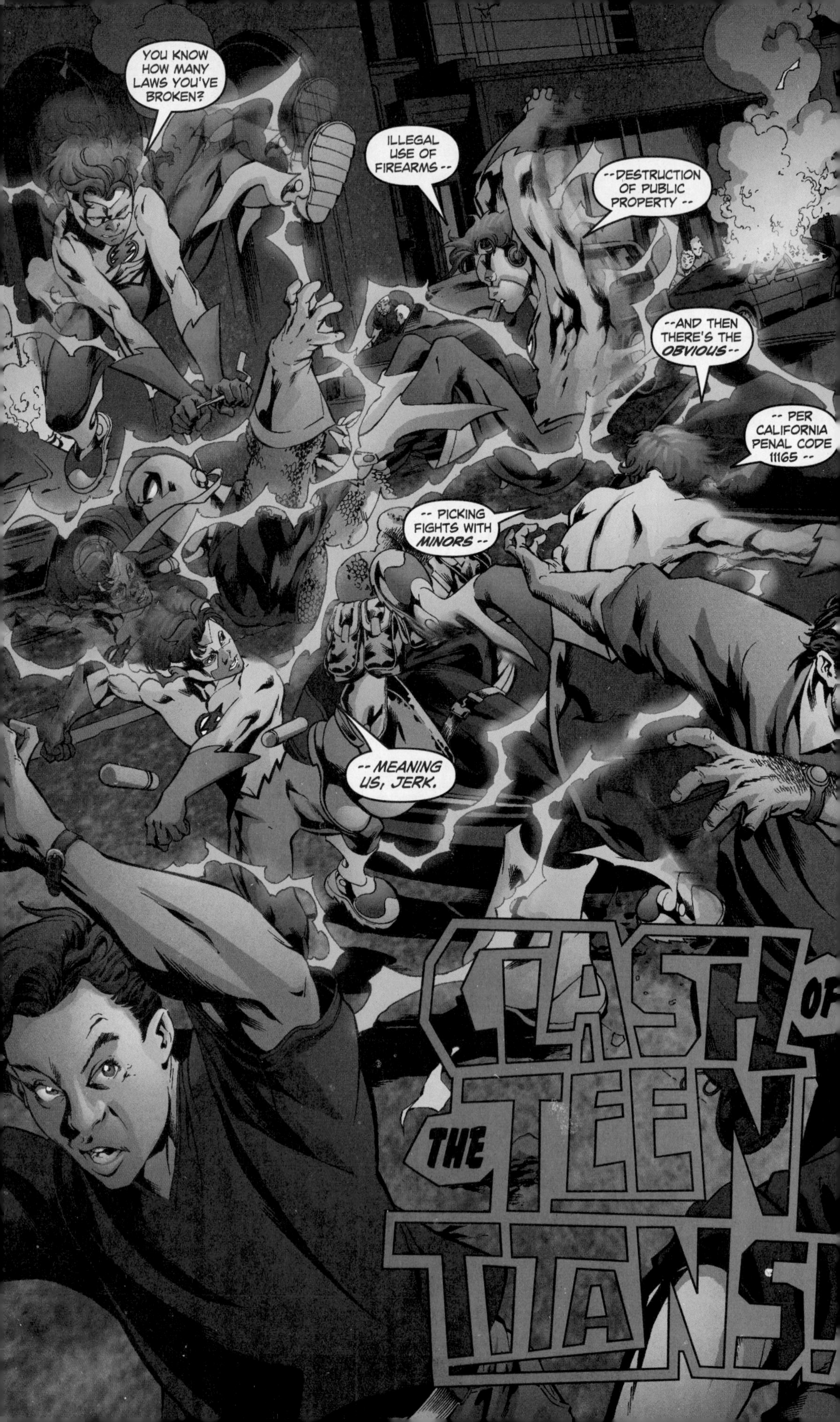
YOU KNOW HOW MANY LAWS YOU'VE BROKEN?
ILLEGAL USE OF FIREARMS--
--DESTRUCTION OF PUBLIC PROPERTY--
--AND THEN THERE'S THE *OBVIOUS*--
--PER CALIFORNIA PENAL CODE 11165--
--PICKING FIGHTS WITH *MINORS*--
--*MEANING US, JERK.*
CLASH OF THE TEEN TITANS!

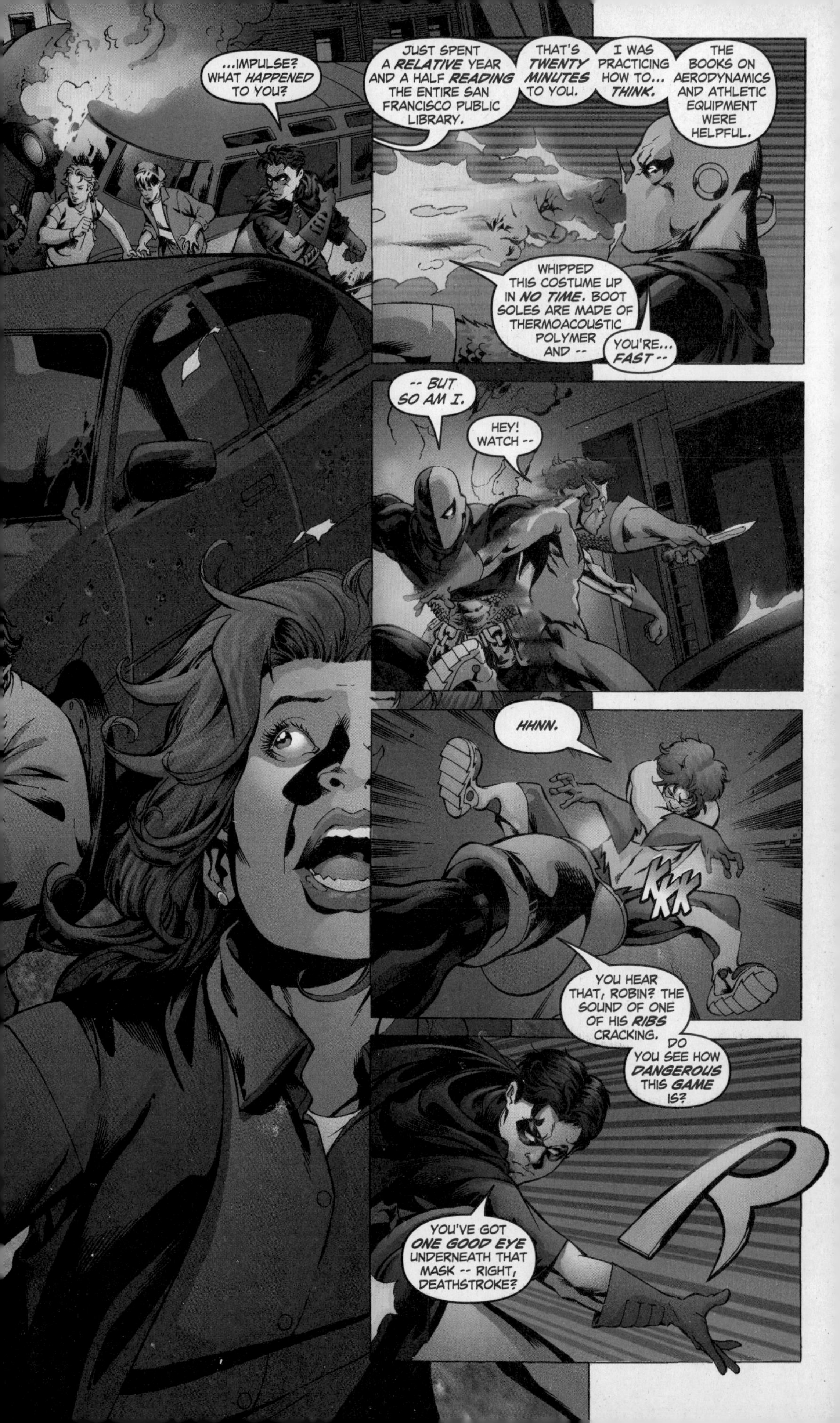
...IMPULSE? WHAT HAPPENED TO YOU?
JUST SPENT A RELATIVE YEAR AND A HALF READING THE ENTIRE SAN FRANCISCO PUBLIC LIBRARY.
THAT'S TWENTY MINUTES TO YOU.
I WAS PRACTICING HOW TO... THINK.
THE BOOKS ON AERODYNAMICS AND ATHLETIC EQUIPMENT WERE HELPFUL.
WHIPPED THIS COSTUME UP IN NO TIME. BOOT SOLES ARE MADE OF THERMOACOUSTIC POLYMER AND --
YOU'RE... FAST --
-- BUT SO AM I.
HEY! WATCH --
HHNN.
KKK
YOU HEAR THAT, ROBIN? THE SOUND OF ONE OF HIS RIBS CRACKING.
DO YOU SEE HOW DANGEROUS THIS GAME IS?
YOU'VE GOT ONE GOOD EYE UNDERNEATH THAT MASK -- RIGHT, DEATHSTROKE?

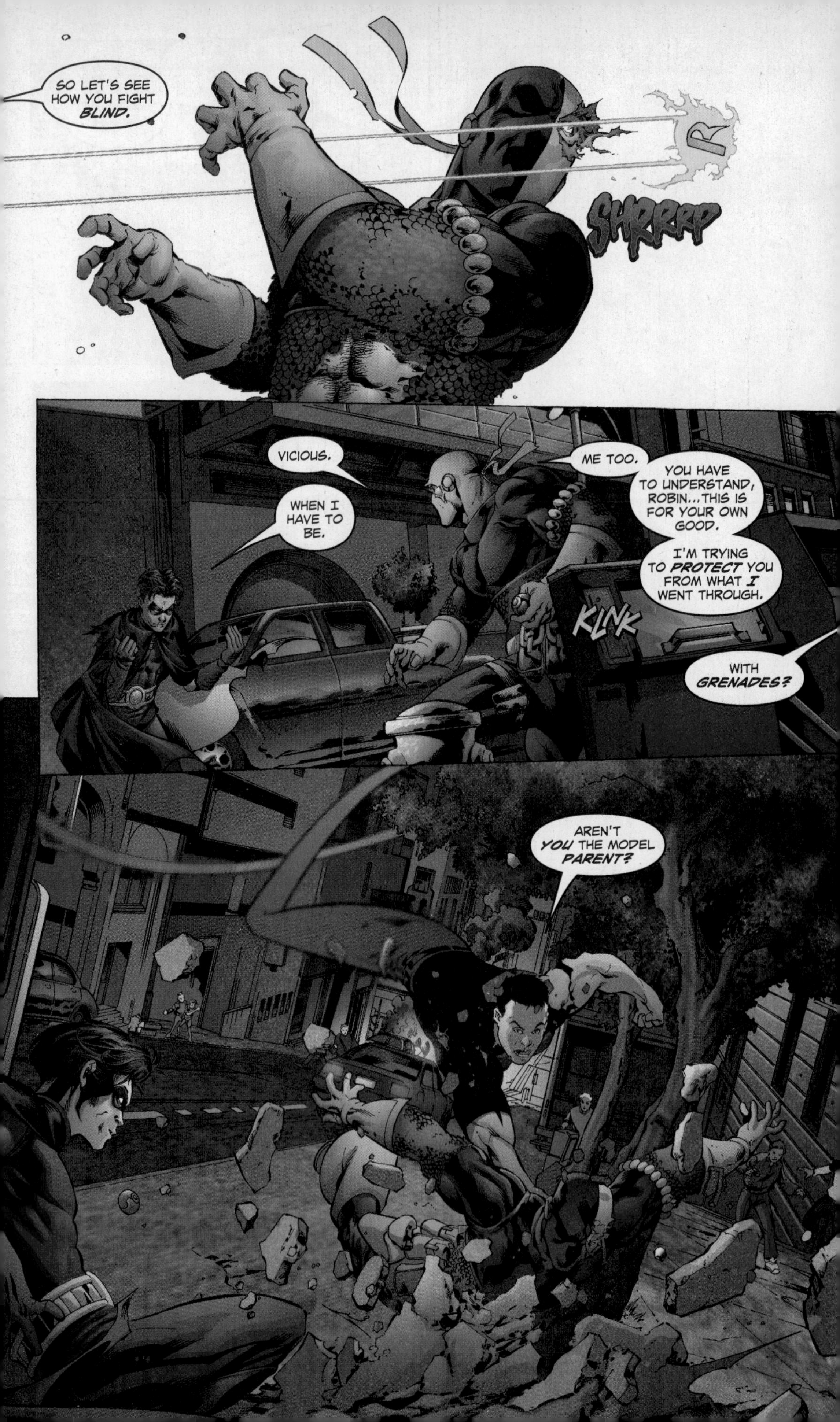
SO LET'S SEE HOW YOU FIGHT BLIND.
SHRRRP
VICIOUS.
WHEN I HAVE TO BE.
ME TOO.
YOU HAVE TO UNDERSTAND, ROBIN...THIS IS FOR YOUR OWN GOOD.
I'M TRYING TO PROTECT YOU FROM WHAT I WENT THROUGH.
KLINK
WITH GRENADES?
AREN'T YOU THE MODEL PARENT?

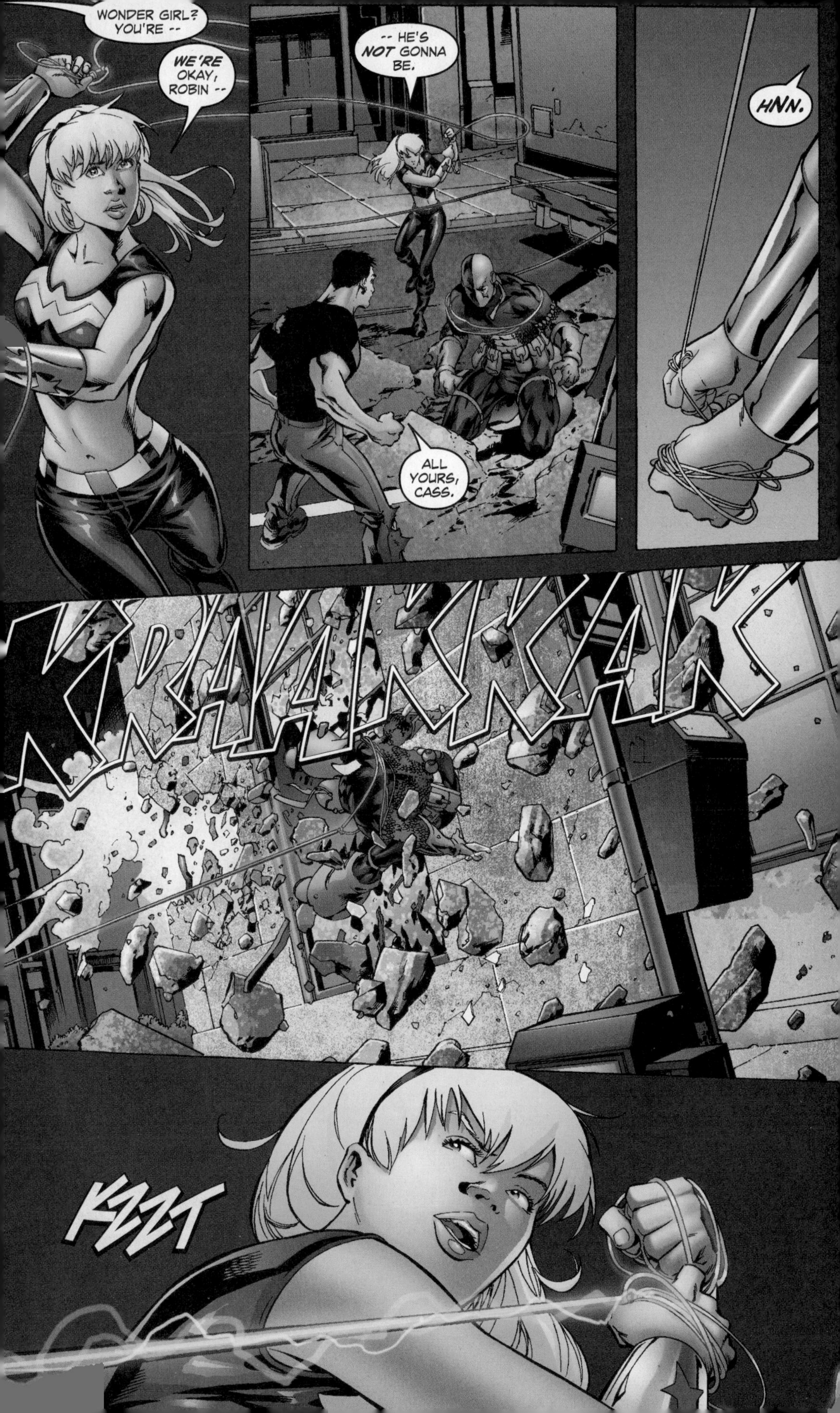
WONDER GIRL? YOU'RE --
WE'RE OKAY, ROBIN --
-- HE'S NOT GONNA BE.
ALL YOURS, CASS.
HNN.
KRAKAKKAKK
KZZT

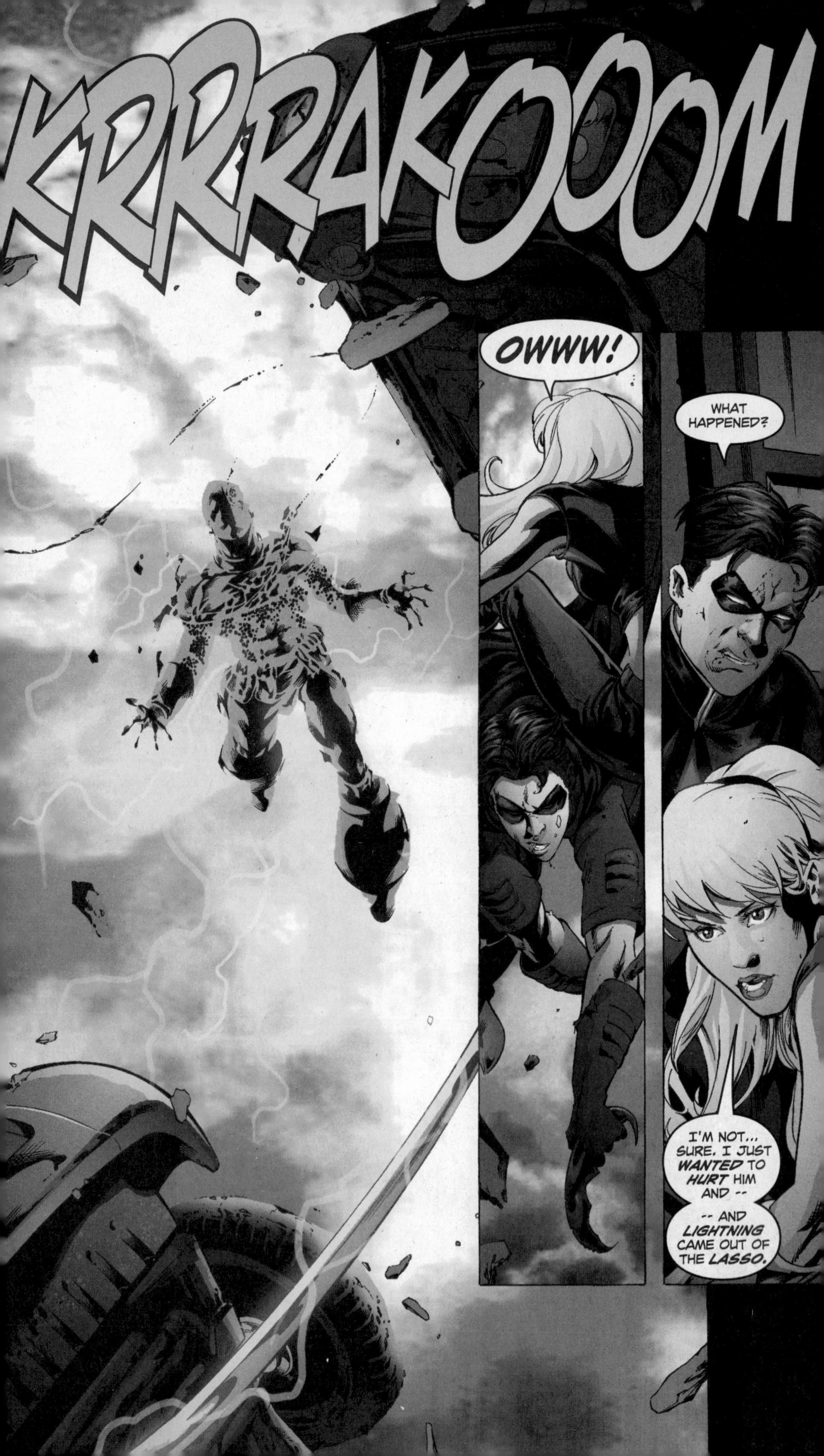
KRRRAKOOOOM
OWWW!
WHAT HAPPENED?
I'M NOT... SURE. I JUST WANTED TO HURT HIM AND --
-- AND LIGHTNING CAME OUT OF THE LASSO.

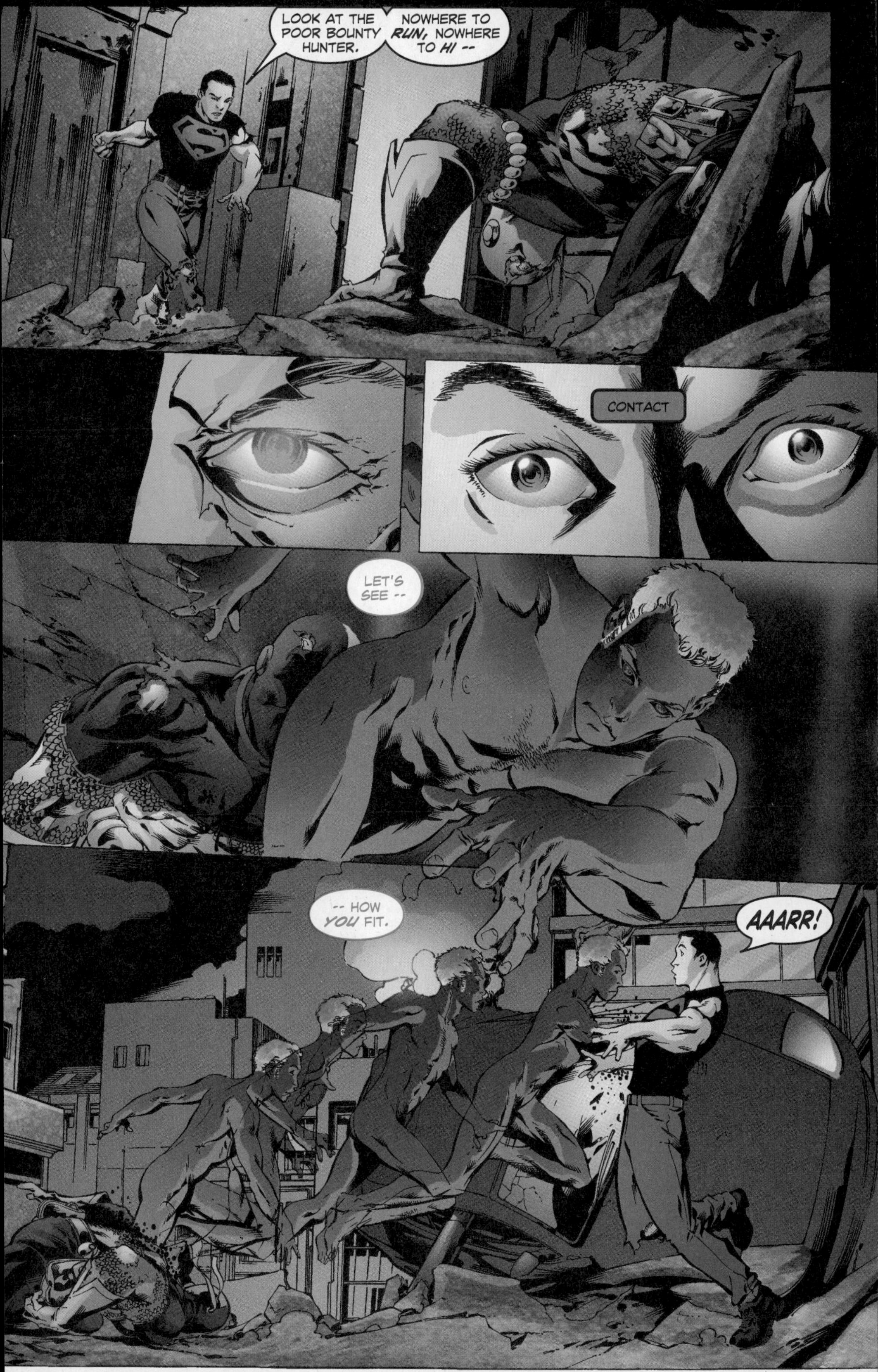
LOOK AT THE POOR BOUNTY HUNTER.
NOWHERE TO *RUN,* NOWHERE TO *HI* --
CONTACT
LET'S SEE --
-- HOW *YOU* FIT.
AAARR!

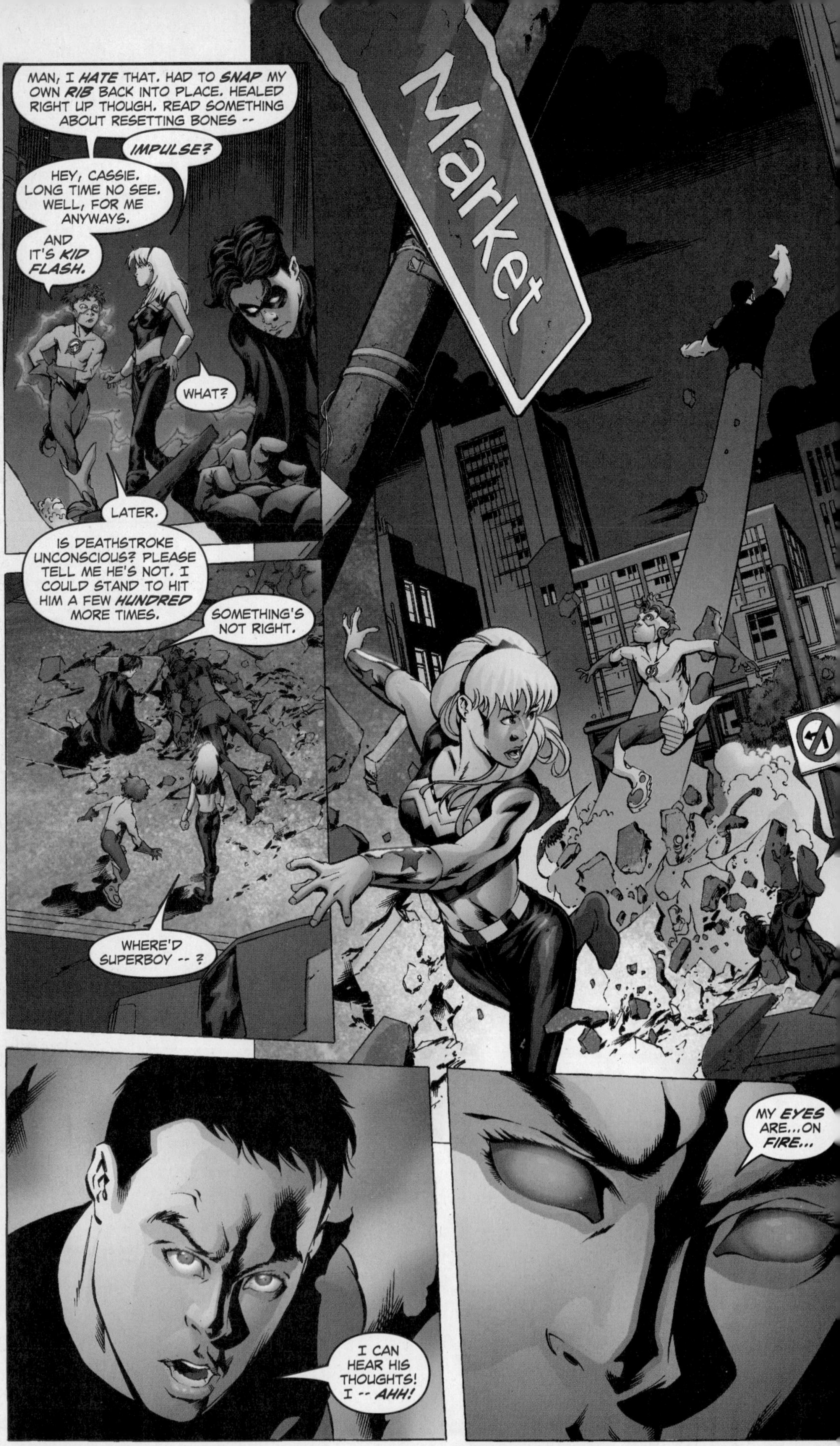

MAN, I *HATE* THAT. HAD TO *SNAP* MY OWN *RIB* BACK INTO PLACE. HEALED RIGHT UP THOUGH. READ SOMETHING ABOUT RESETTING BONES --
IMPULSE?
HEY, CASSIE. LONG TIME NO SEE. WELL, FOR ME ANYWAYS.
AND IT'S *KID FLASH.*
WHAT?
LATER.
Market
IS DEATHSTROKE UNCONSCIOUS? PLEASE TELL ME HE'S NOT. I COULD STAND TO HIT HIM A FEW *HUNDRED* MORE TIMES.
SOMETHING'S NOT RIGHT.
WHERE'D SUPERBOY -- ?
I CAN HEAR HIS THOUGHTS! I -- *AHH!*
MY *EYES* ARE...ON *FIRE...*

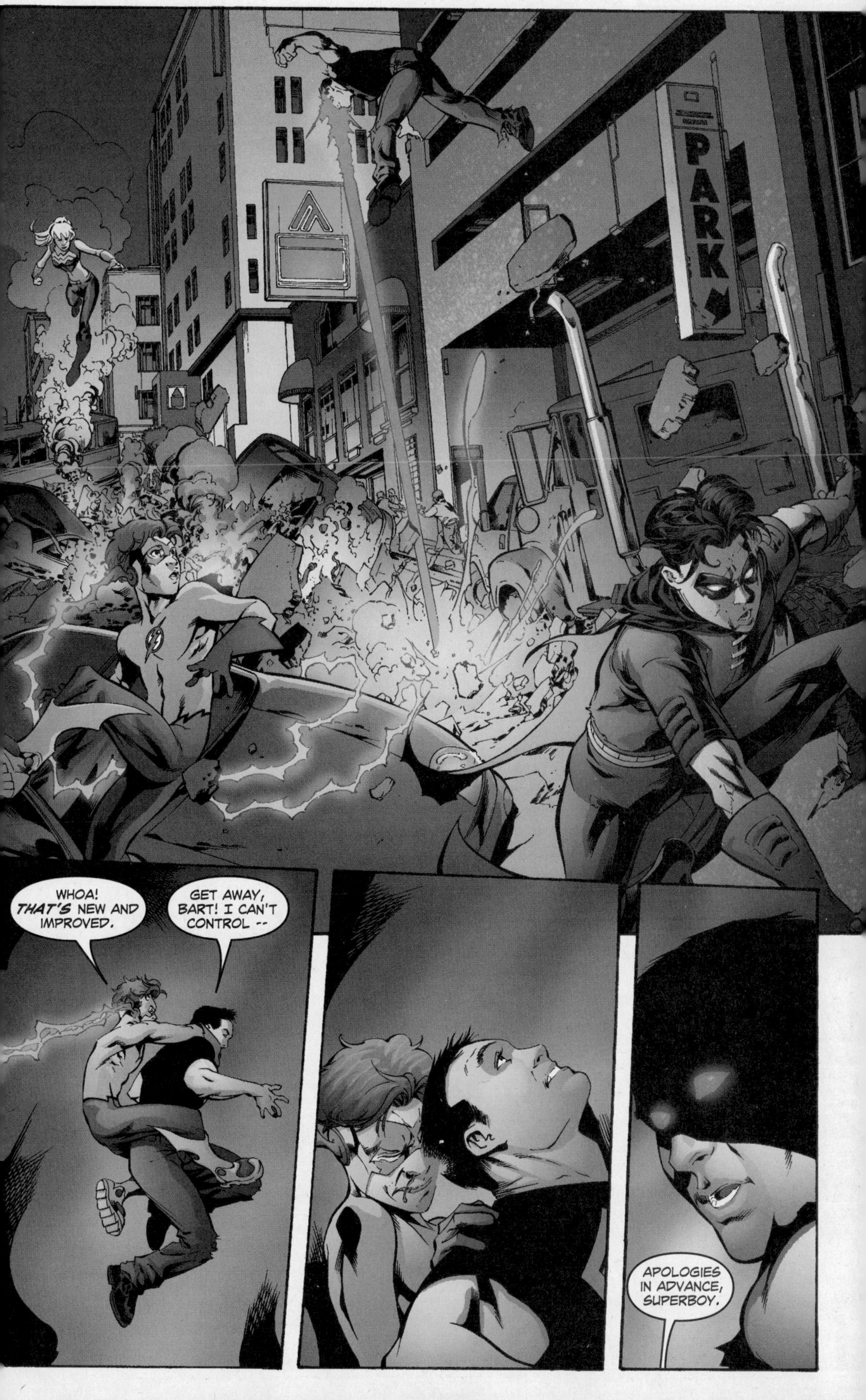
WHOA! THAT'S NEW AND IMPROVED.
GET AWAY, BART! I CAN'T CONTROL --
APOLOGIES IN ADVANCE, SUPERBOY.

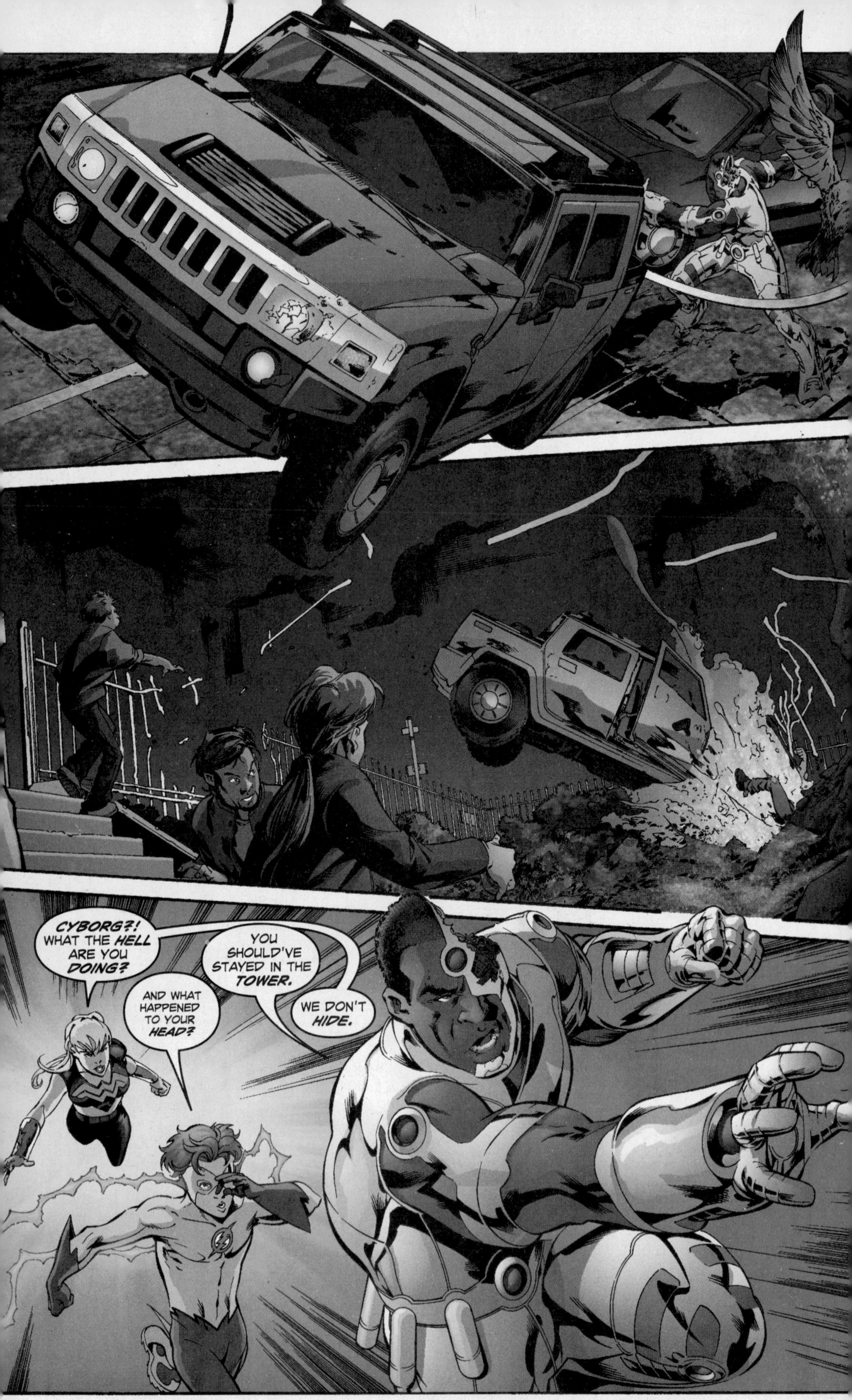
CYBORG?! WHAT THE HELL ARE YOU DOING?
AND WHAT HAPPENED TO YOUR HEAD?
YOU SHOULD'VE STAYED IN THE TOWER.
WE DON'T HIDE.

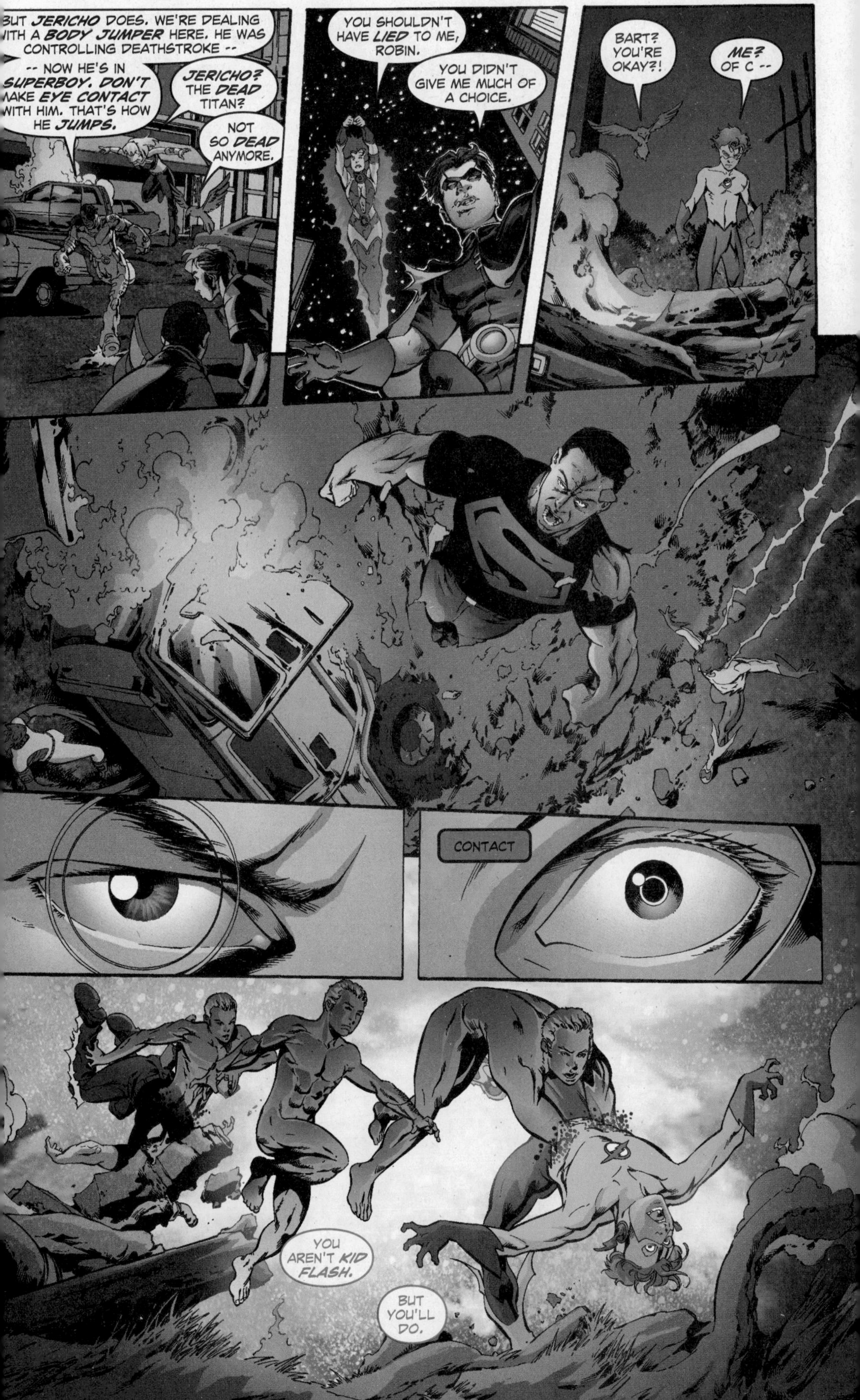
BUT JERICHO DOES. WE'RE DEALING WITH A BODY JUMPER HERE. HE WAS CONTROLLING DEATHSTROKE --
-- NOW HE'S IN SUPERBOY. DON'T MAKE EYE CONTACT WITH HIM. THAT'S HOW HE JUMPS.
JERICHO? THE DEAD TITAN?
NOT SO DEAD ANYMORE.
YOU SHOULDN'T HAVE LIED TO ME, ROBIN.
YOU DIDN'T GIVE ME MUCH OF A CHOICE.
BART? YOU'RE OKAY?!
ME? OF C --
CONTACT
YOU AREN'T KID FLASH.
BUT YOU'LL DO.

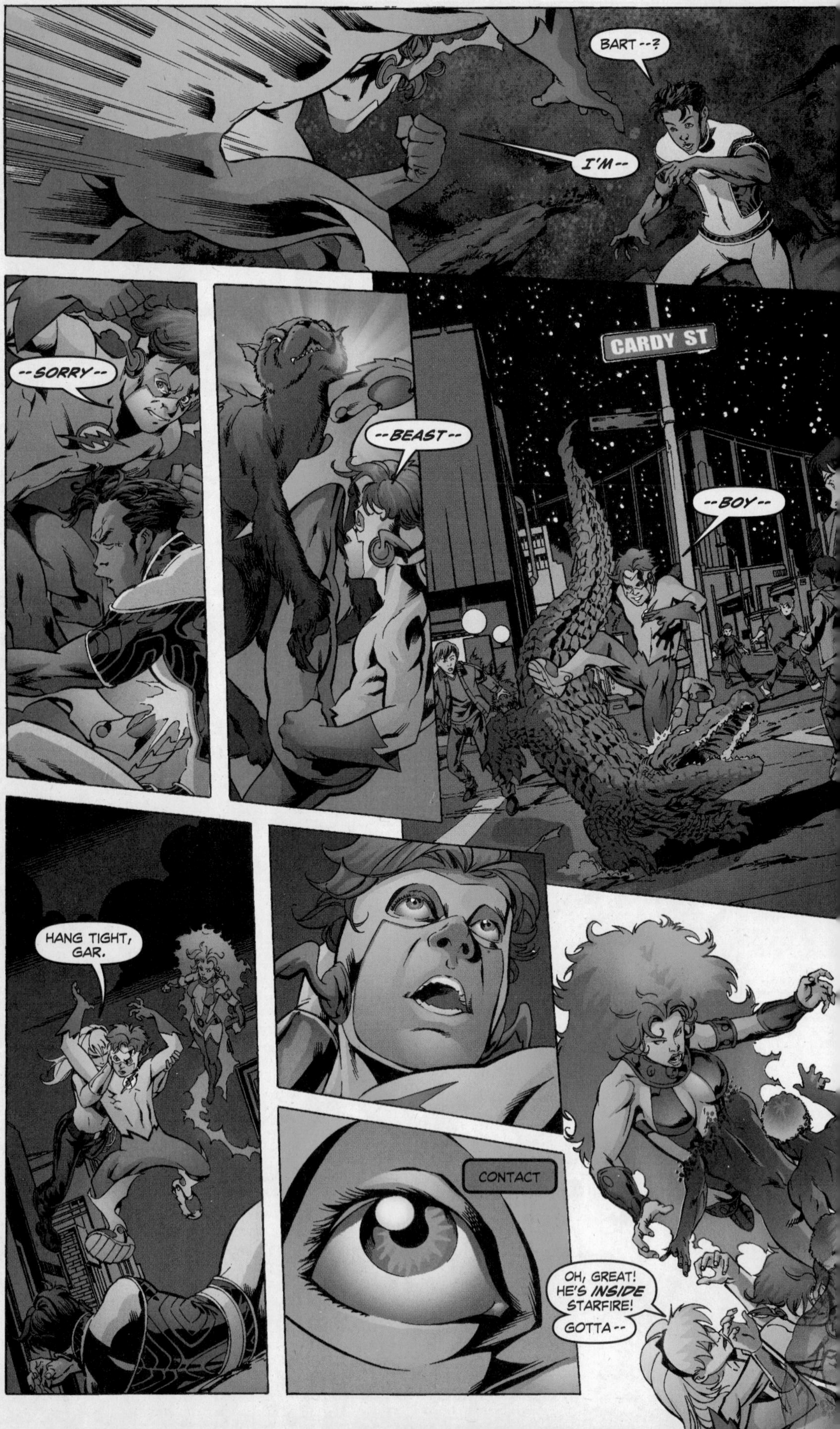
BART --?
I'M--
--SORRY--
--BEAST--
CARDY ST
--BOY--
HANG TIGHT, GAR.
CONTACT
OH, GREAT! HE'S INSIDE STARFIRE!
GOTTA--

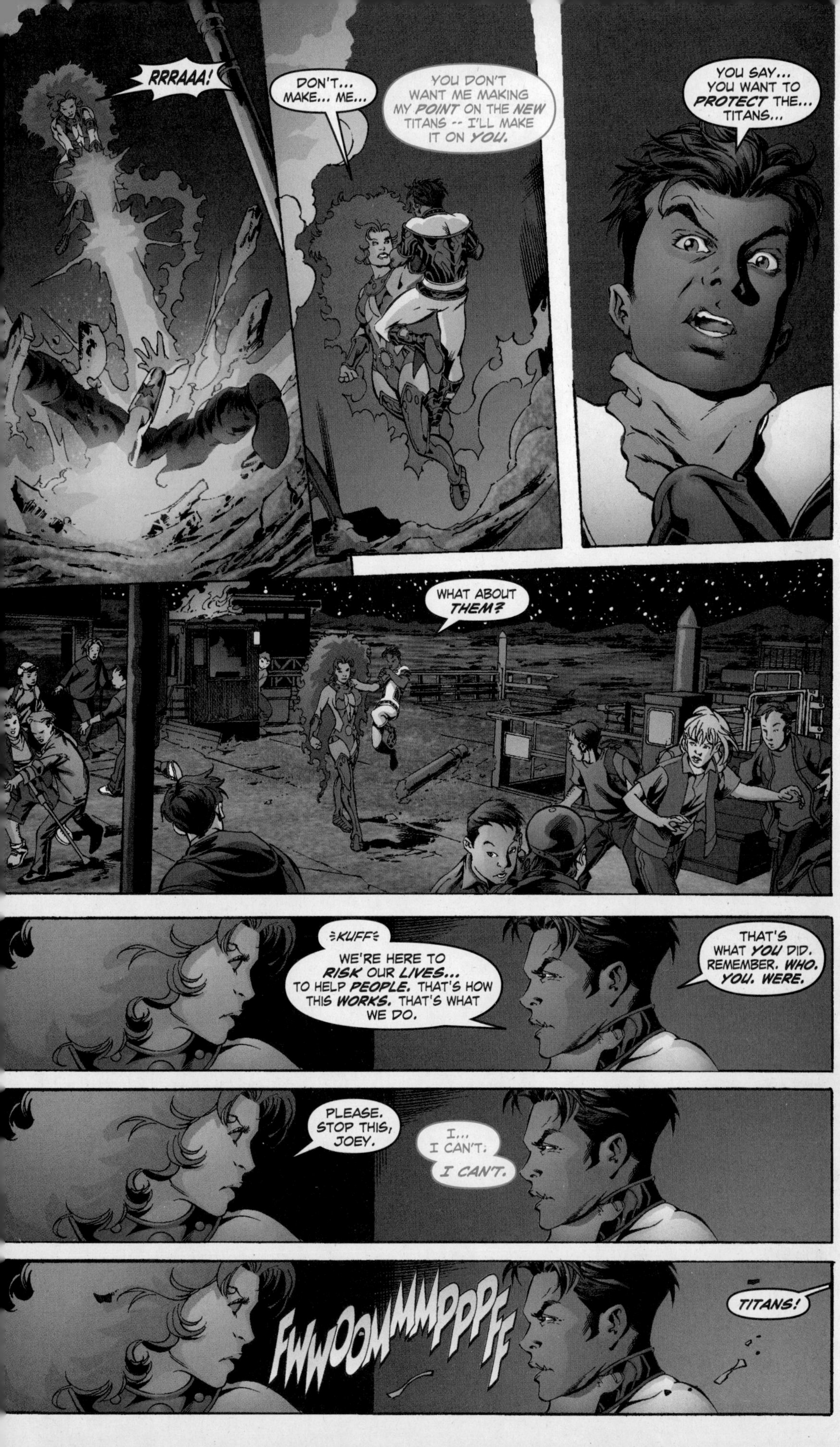
RRRAAA!
DON'T... MAKE... ME...
YOU DON'T WANT ME MAKING MY POINT ON THE NEW TITANS -- I'LL MAKE IT ON YOU.
YOU SAY... YOU WANT TO PROTECT THE... TITANS...
WHAT ABOUT THEM?
KUFF
WE'RE HERE TO RISK OUR LIVES... TO HELP PEOPLE. THAT'S HOW THIS WORKS. THAT'S WHAT WE DO.
THAT'S WHAT YOU DID. REMEMBER. WHO. YOU. WERE.
PLEASE. STOP THIS, JOEY.
I... I CAN'T. I CAN'T.
FWWOOMMMPPPFF
TITANS!

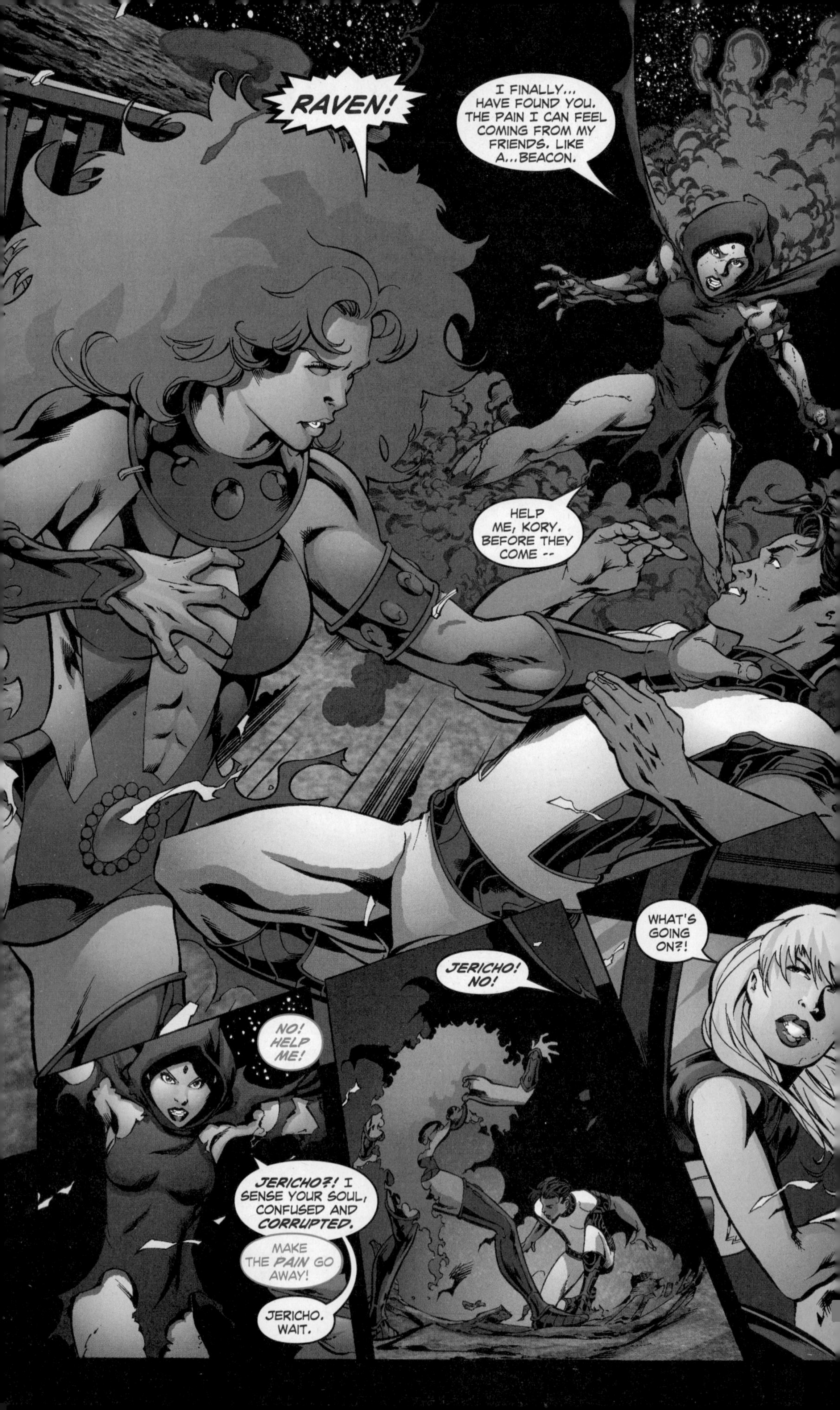
RAVEN!
I FINALLY... HAVE FOUND YOU. THE PAIN I CAN FEEL COMING FROM MY FRIENDS. LIKE A...BEACON.
HELP ME, KORY. BEFORE THEY COME --
WHAT'S GOING ON?!
JERICHO! NO!
NO! HELP ME!
JERICHO?! I SENSE YOUR SOUL, CONFUSED AND CORRUPTED.
MAKE THE PAIN GO AWAY!
JERICHO. WAIT.

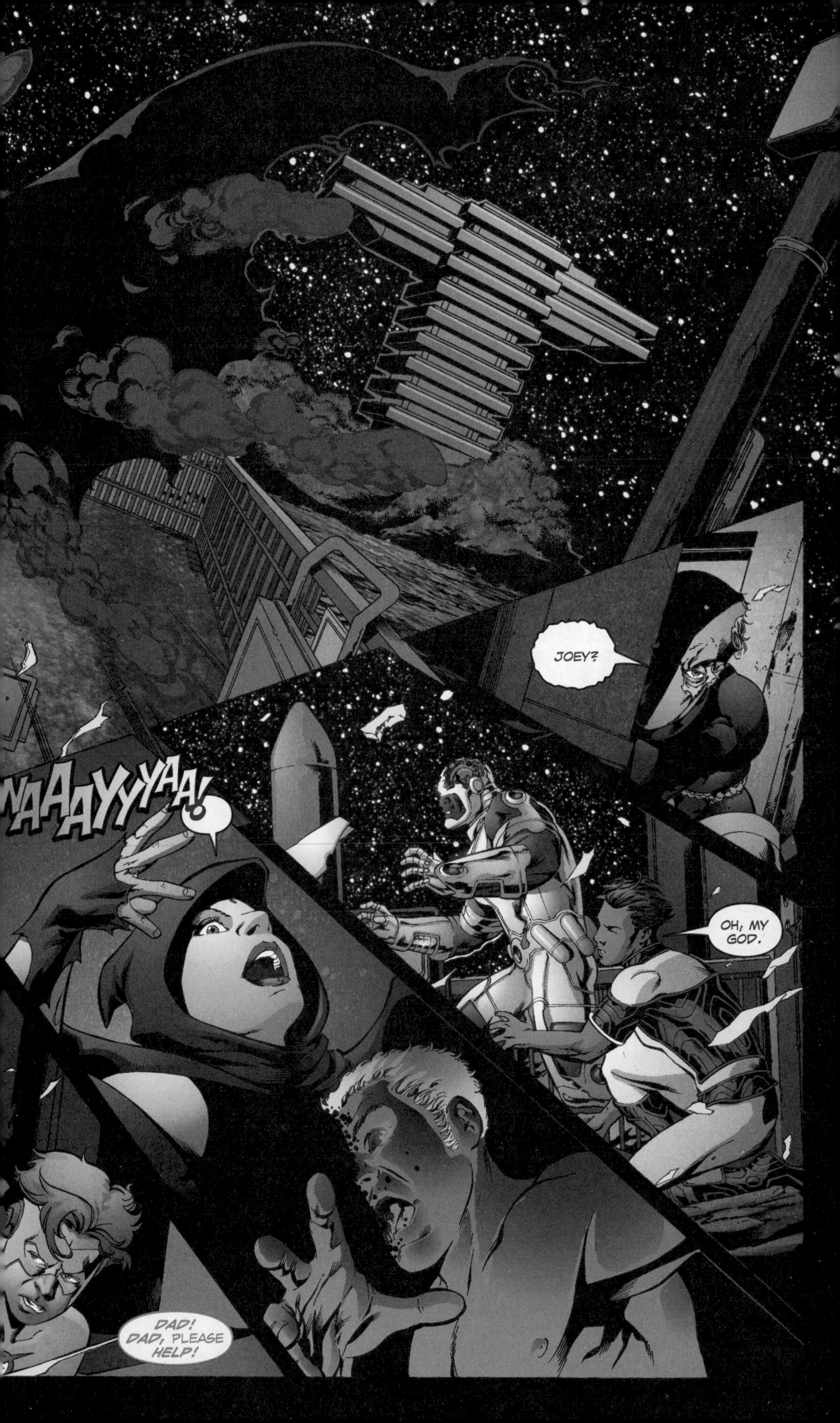
JOEY?
NAAAAYYYAA!
OH, MY GOD.
DAD! DAD, PLEASE HELP!

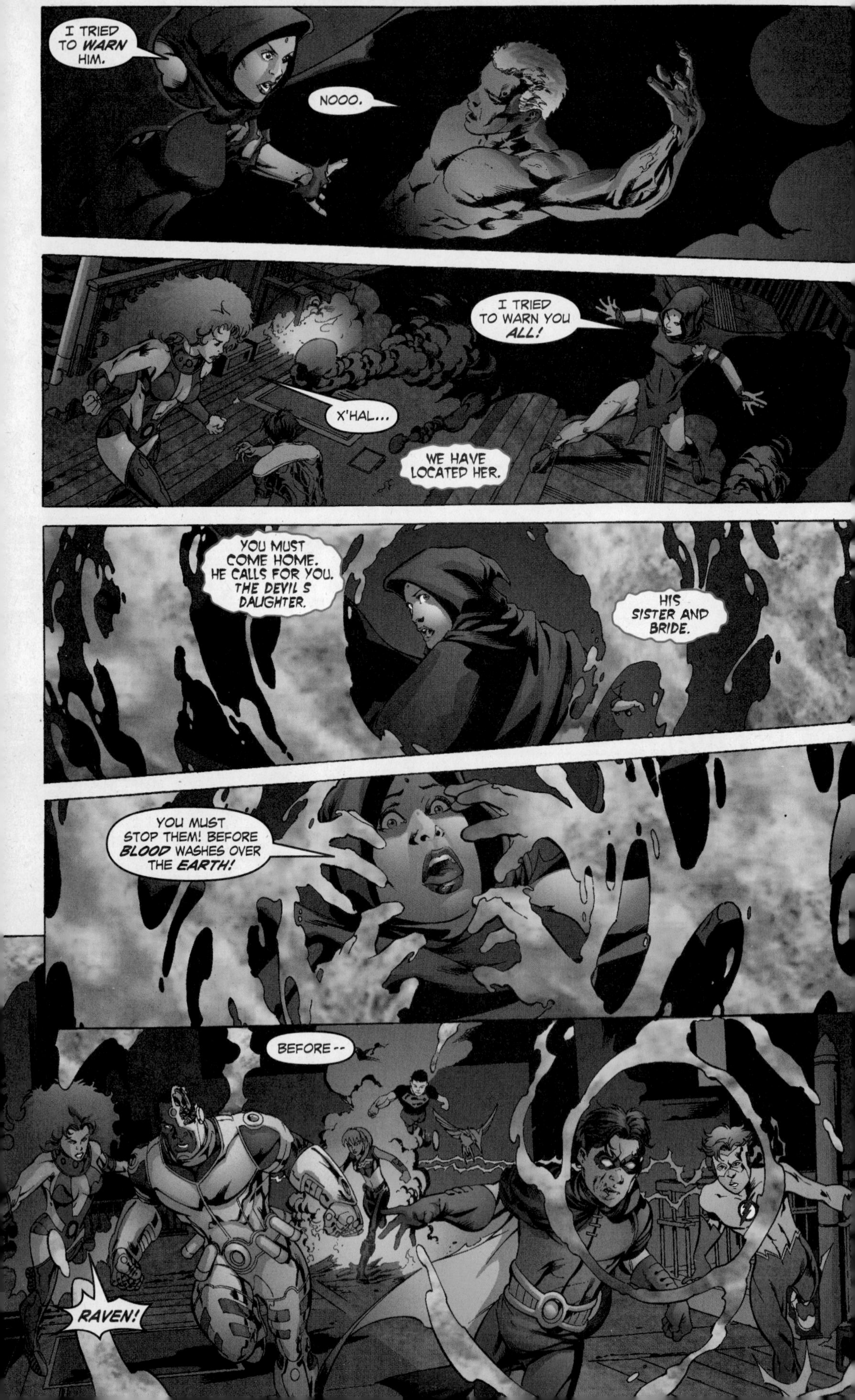
I TRIED TO *WARN* HIM.
NOOO.
I TRIED TO WARN YOU *ALL!*
X'HAL...
WE HAVE LOCATED HER.
YOU MUST COME HOME. HE CALLS FOR YOU. *THE DEVIL S DAUGHTER.*
HIS SISTER AND BRIDE.
YOU MUST STOP THEM! BEFORE *BLOOD* WASHES OVER THE *EARTH!*
BEFORE --
RAVEN!

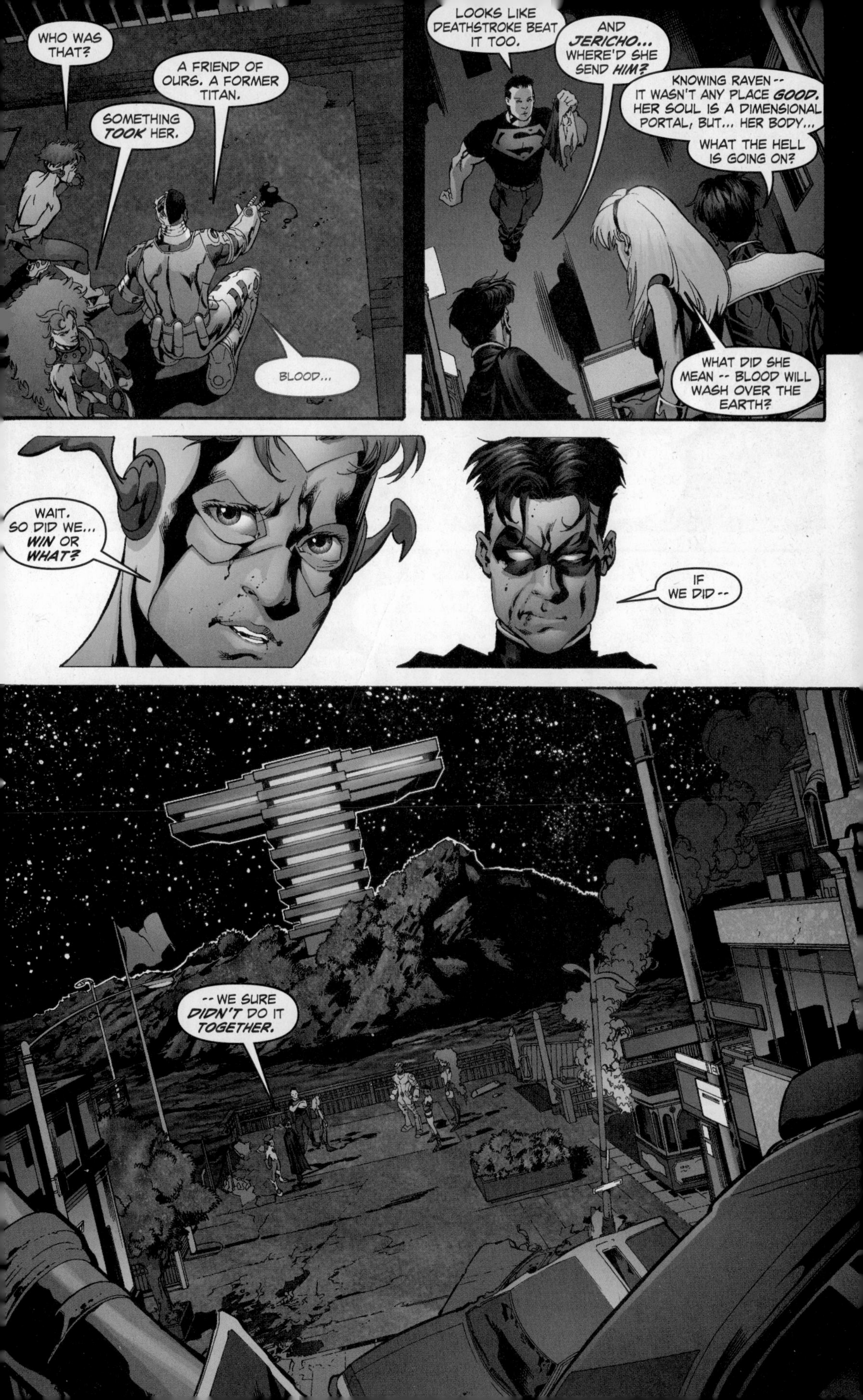
WHO WAS THAT?
A FRIEND OF OURS. A FORMER TITAN.
SOMETHING TOOK HER.
BLOOD...
LOOKS LIKE DEATHSTROKE BEAT IT TOO.
AND JERICHO... WHERE'D SHE SEND HIM?
KNOWING RAVEN -- IT WASN'T ANY PLACE GOOD. HER SOUL IS A DIMENSIONAL PORTAL, BUT... HER BODY...
WHAT THE HELL IS GOING ON?
WHAT DID SHE MEAN -- BLOOD WILL WASH OVER THE EARTH?
WAIT. SO DID WE... WIN OR WHAT?
IF WE DID --
-- WE SURE DIDN'T DO IT TOGETHER.

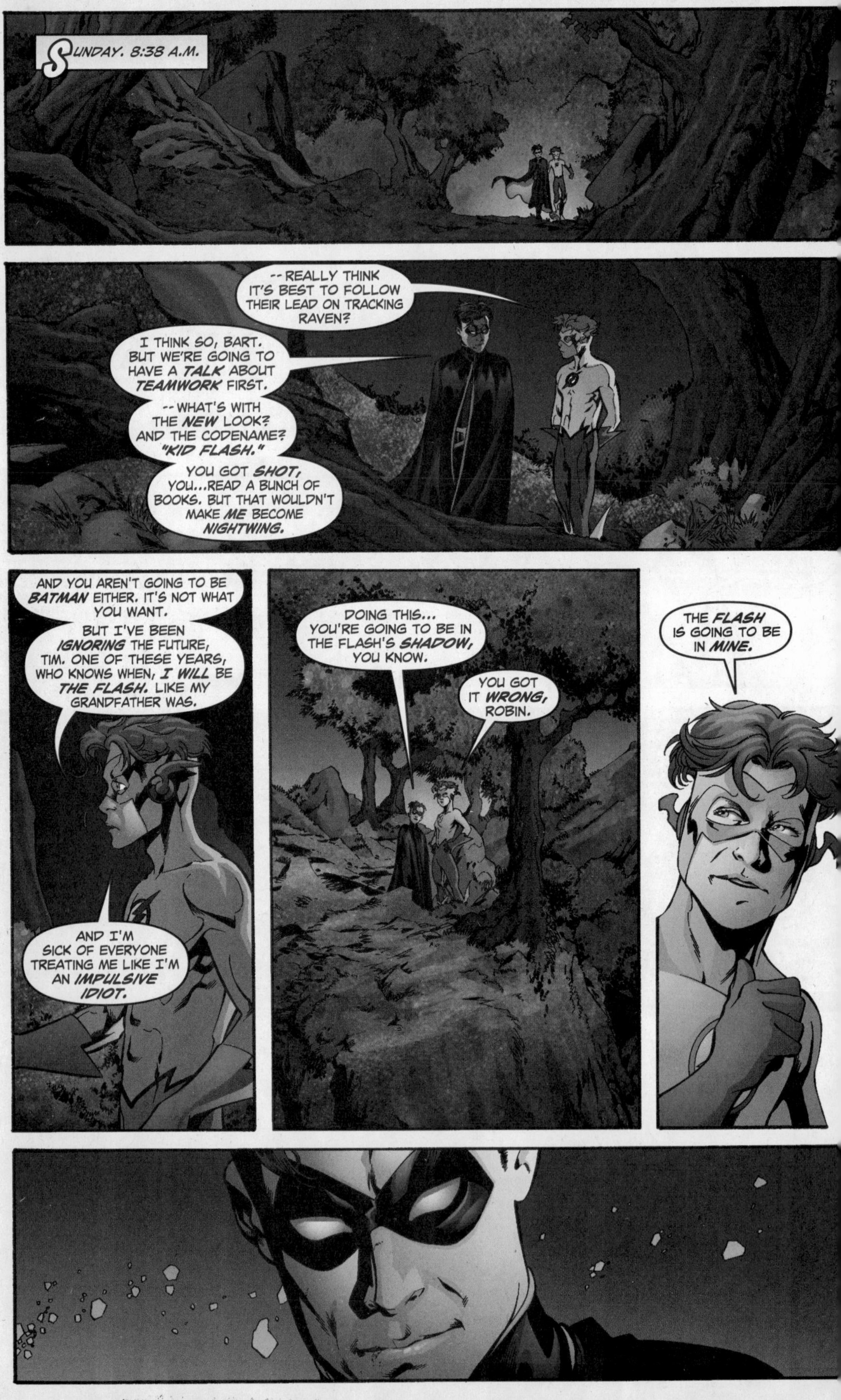
SUNDAY. 8:38 A.M.
--REALLY THINK IT'S BEST TO FOLLOW THEIR LEAD ON TRACKING RAVEN?
I THINK SO, BART. BUT WE'RE GOING TO HAVE A TALK ABOUT TEAMWORK FIRST.
--WHAT'S WITH THE NEW LOOK? AND THE CODENAME? "KID FLASH."
YOU GOT SHOT, YOU...READ A BUNCH OF BOOKS. BUT THAT WOULDN'T MAKE ME BECOME NIGHTWING.
AND YOU AREN'T GOING TO BE BATMAN EITHER. IT'S NOT WHAT YOU WANT.
BUT I'VE BEEN IGNORING THE FUTURE, TIM. ONE OF THESE YEARS, WHO KNOWS WHEN, I WILL BE THE FLASH. LIKE MY GRANDFATHER WAS.
AND I'M SICK OF EVERYONE TREATING ME LIKE I'M AN IMPULSIVE IDIOT.
DOING THIS... YOU'RE GOING TO BE IN THE FLASH'S SHADOW, YOU KNOW.
YOU GOT IT WRONG, ROBIN.
THE FLASH IS GOING TO BE IN MINE.

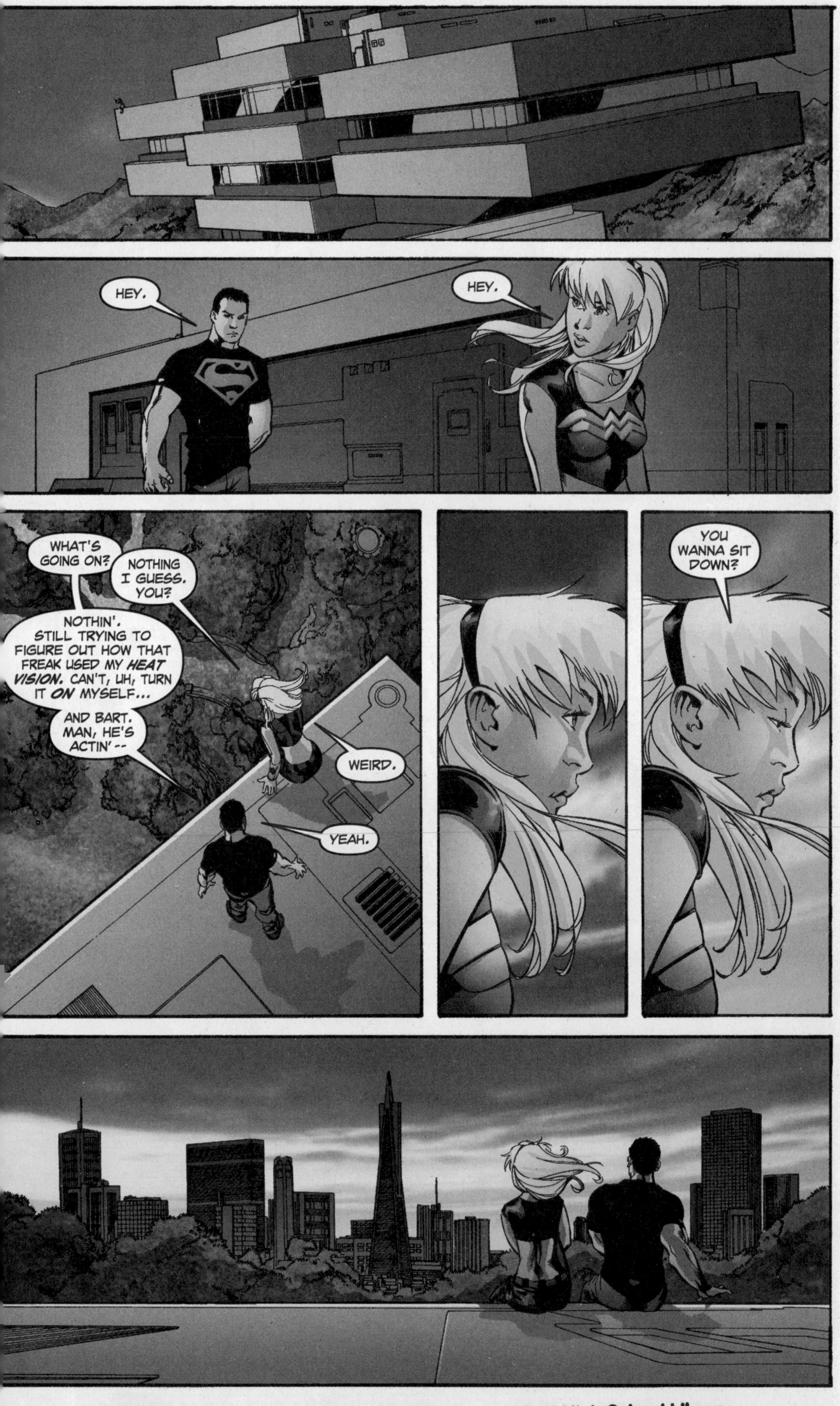
HEY.
HEY.
WHAT'S GOING ON?
NOTHING I GUESS. YOU?
NOTHIN'. STILL TRYING TO FIGURE OUT HOW THAT FREAK USED MY **HEAT VISION.** CAN'T, UH, TURN IT **ON** MYSELF...
AND BART. MAN, HE'S ACTIN' --
WEIRD.
YEAH.
YOU WANNA SIT DOWN?

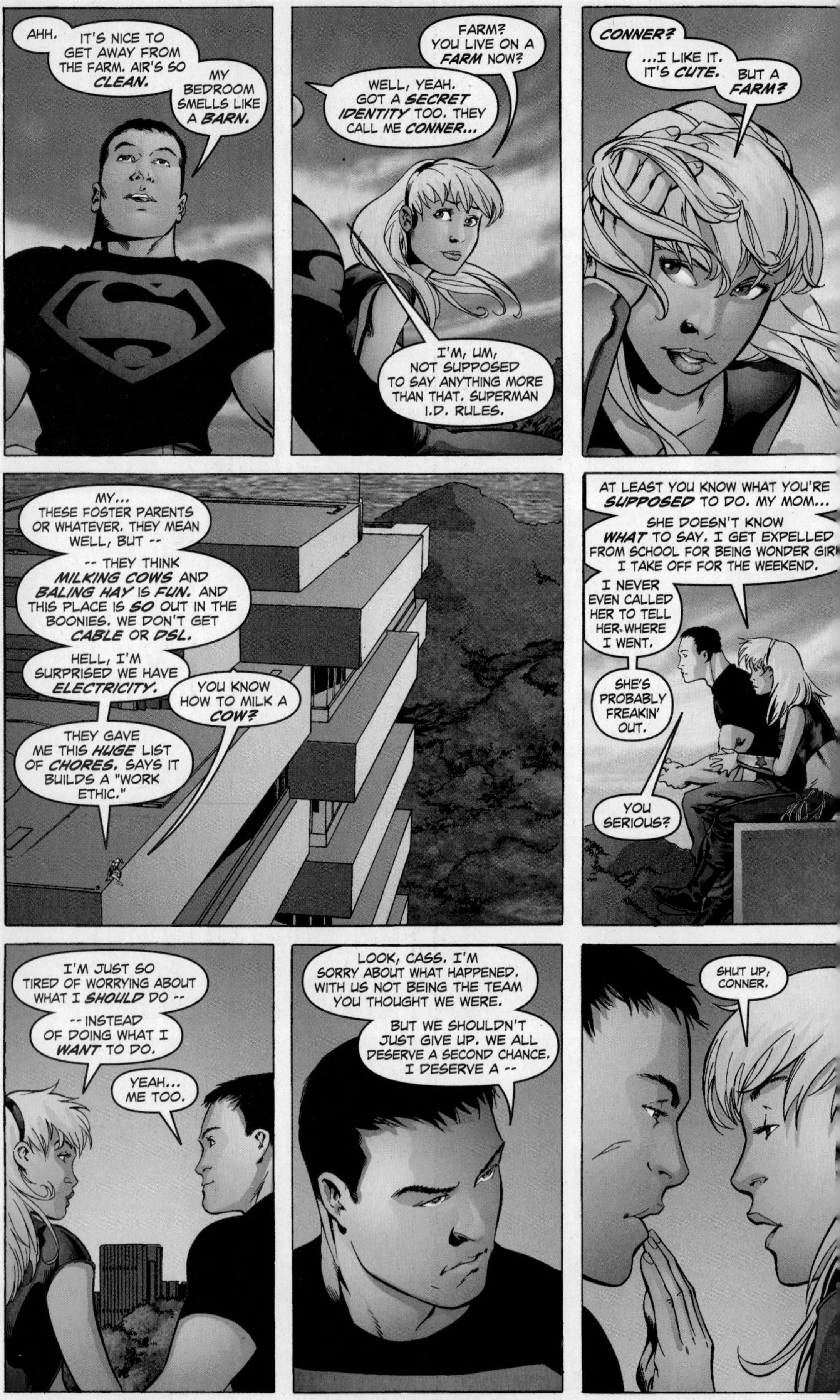
AHH.
IT'S NICE TO GET AWAY FROM THE FARM. AIR'S SO CLEAN.
MY BEDROOM SMELLS LIKE A BARN.
FARM? YOU LIVE ON A FARM NOW?
WELL, YEAH. GOT A SECRET IDENTITY TOO. THEY CALL ME CONNER...
I'M, UM, NOT SUPPOSED TO SAY ANYTHING MORE THAN THAT. SUPERMAN I.D. RULES.
CONNER?
...I LIKE IT. IT'S CUTE.
BUT A FARM?
MY... THESE FOSTER PARENTS OR WHATEVER. THEY MEAN WELL, BUT --
-- THEY THINK MILKING COWS AND BALING HAY IS FUN. AND THIS PLACE IS SO OUT IN THE BOONIES. WE DON'T GET CABLE OR DSL.
HELL, I'M SURPRISED WE HAVE ELECTRICITY.
YOU KNOW HOW TO MILK A COW?
THEY GAVE ME THIS HUGE LIST OF CHORES. SAYS IT BUILDS A "WORK ETHIC."
AT LEAST YOU KNOW WHAT YOU'RE SUPPOSED TO DO. MY MOM...
SHE DOESN'T KNOW WHAT TO SAY. I GET EXPELLED FROM SCHOOL FOR BEING WONDER GIR
I TAKE OFF FOR THE WEEKEND.
I NEVER EVEN CALLED HER TO TELL HER WHERE I WENT.
SHE'S PROBABLY FREAKIN' OUT.
YOU SERIOUS?
I'M JUST SO TIRED OF WORRYING ABOUT WHAT I SHOULD DO --
-- INSTEAD OF DOING WHAT I WANT TO DO.
YEAH... ME TOO.
LOOK, CASS. I'M SORRY ABOUT WHAT HAPPENED. WITH US NOT BEING THE TEAM YOU THOUGHT WE WERE.
BUT WE SHOULDN'T JUST GIVE UP. WE ALL DESERVE A SECOND CHANCE. I DESERVE A --
SHUT UP, CONNER.

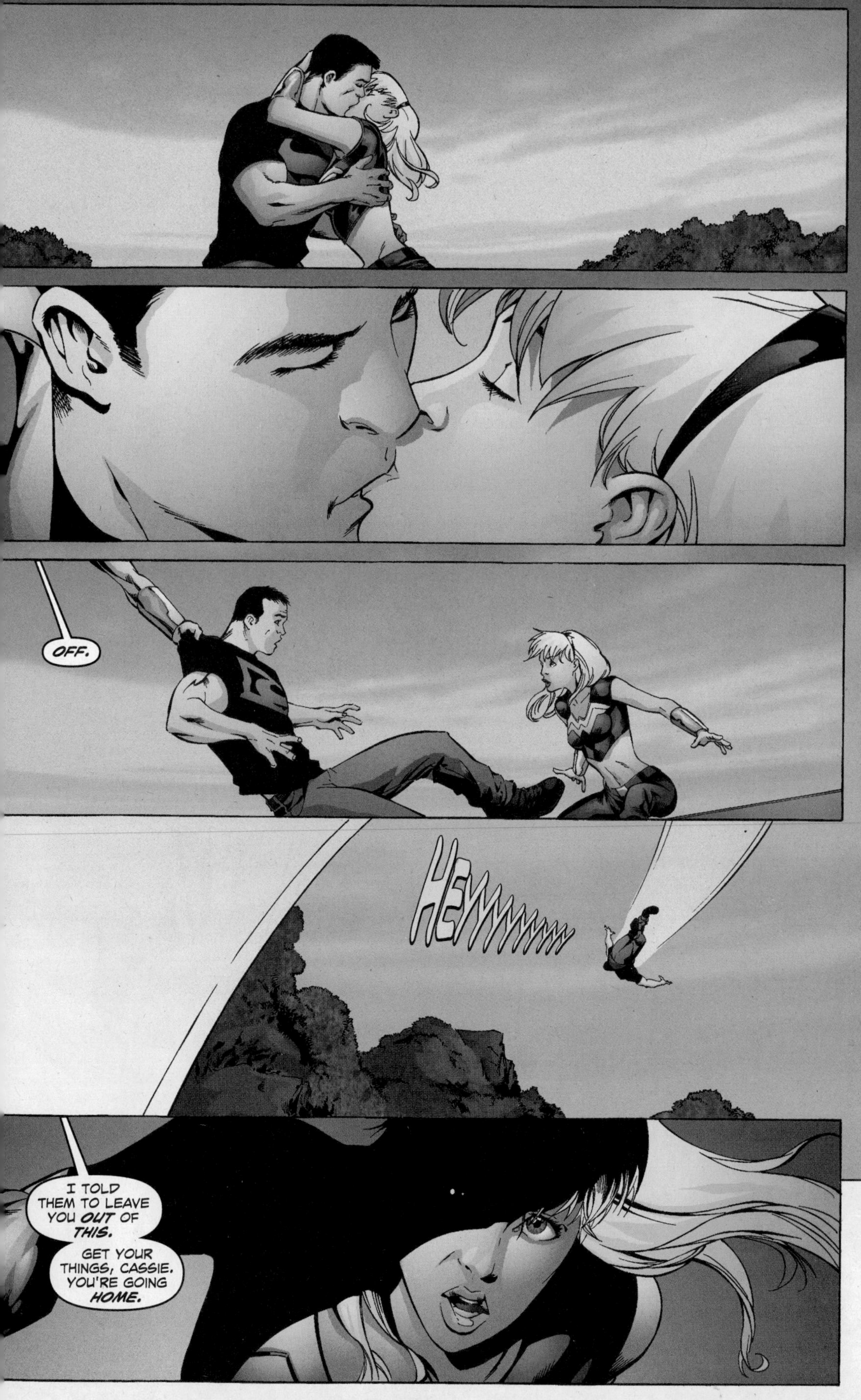
OFF.
HEYYYYYYY
I TOLD THEM TO LEAVE YOU OUT OF THIS.
GET YOUR THINGS, CASSIE. YOU'RE GOING HOME.

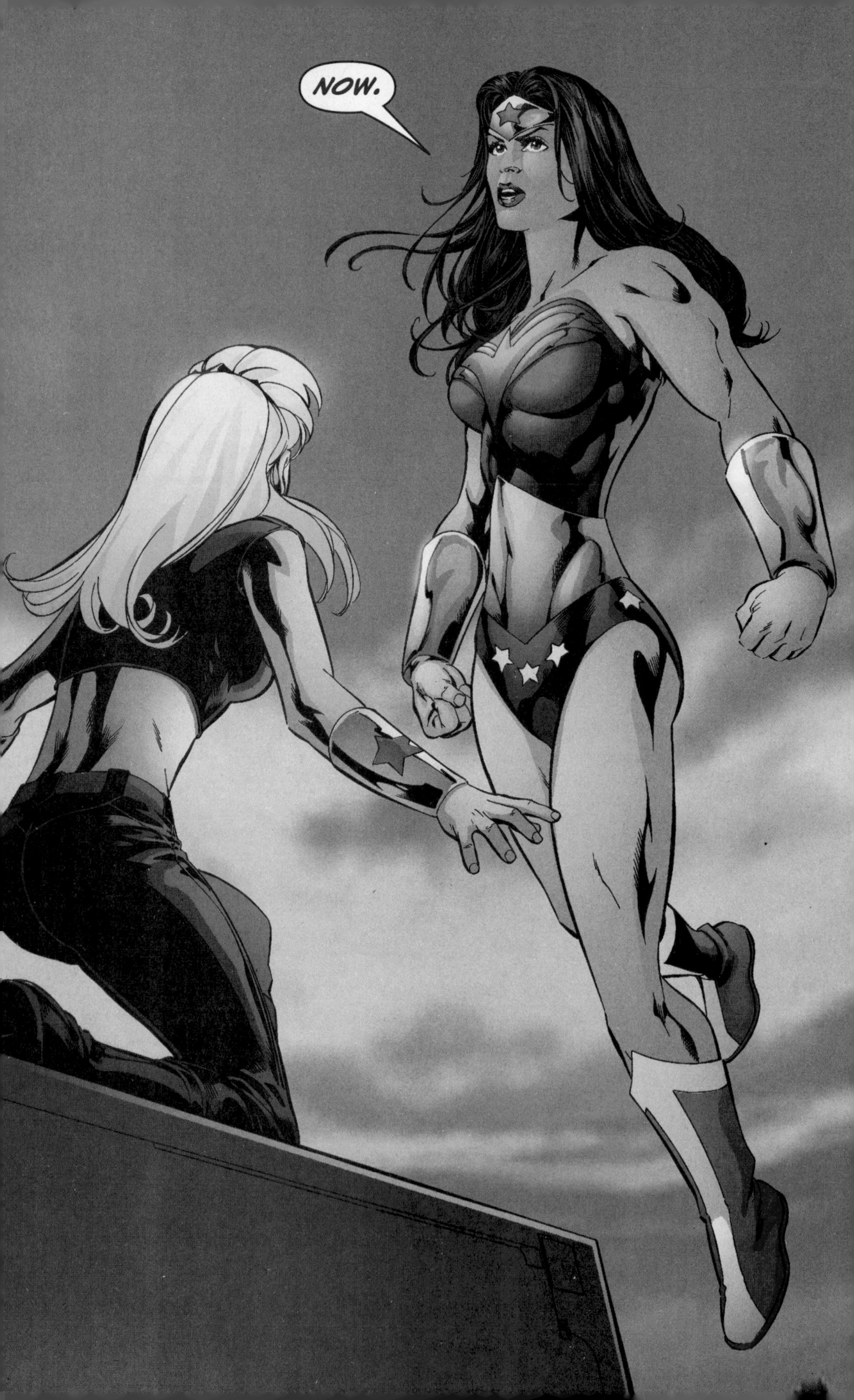
NOW.

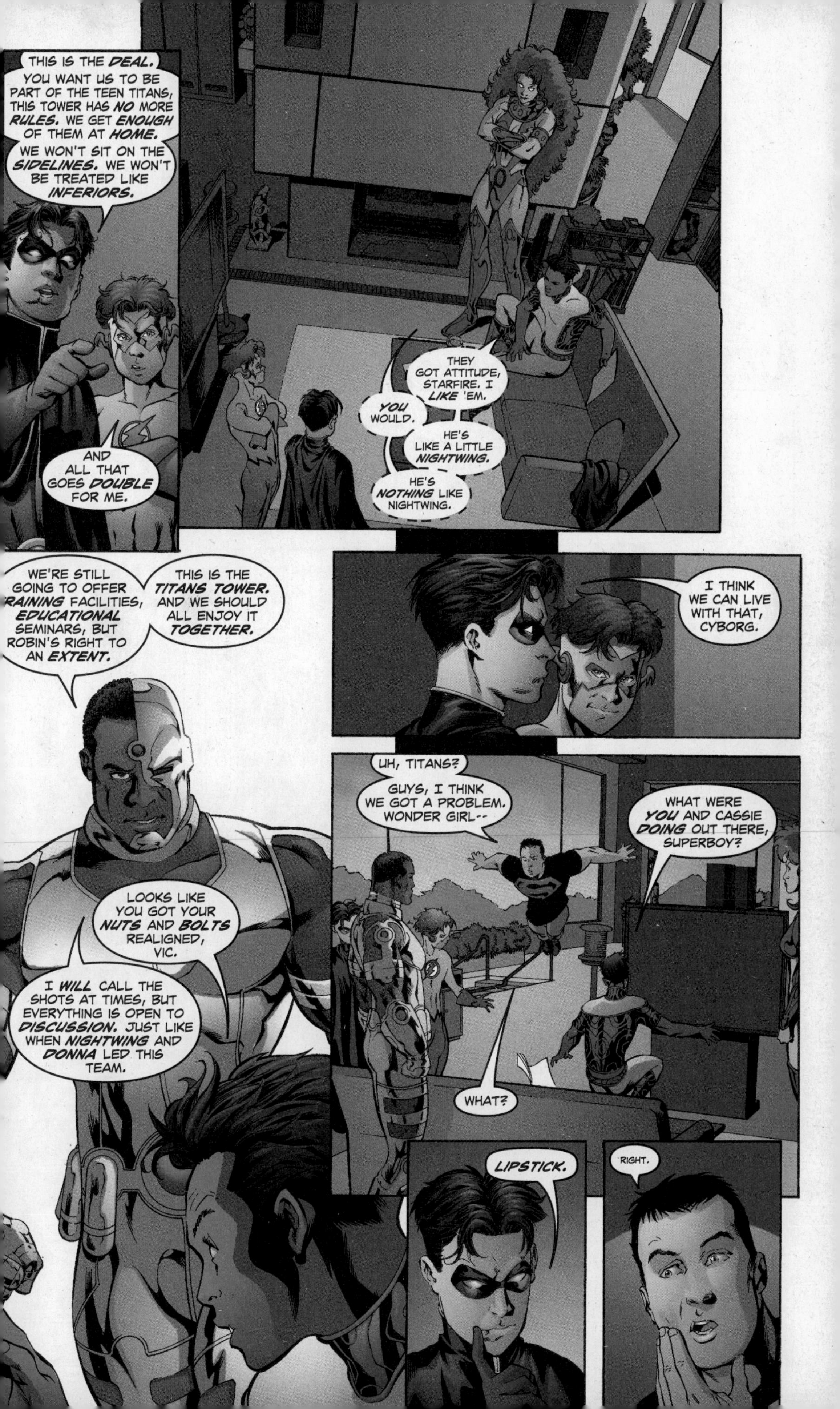
THIS IS THE DEAL.
YOU WANT US TO BE PART OF THE TEEN TITANS, THIS TOWER HAS NO MORE RULES. WE GET ENOUGH OF THEM AT HOME.
WE WON'T SIT ON THE SIDELINES. WE WON'T BE TREATED LIKE INFERIORS.
AND ALL THAT GOES DOUBLE FOR ME.
THEY GOT ATTITUDE, STARFIRE. I LIKE 'EM.
YOU WOULD.
HE'S LIKE A LITTLE NIGHTWING.
HE'S NOTHING LIKE NIGHTWING.
WE'RE STILL GOING TO OFFER TRAINING FACILITIES, EDUCATIONAL SEMINARS, BUT ROBIN'S RIGHT TO AN EXTENT.
THIS IS THE TITANS TOWER. AND WE SHOULD ALL ENJOY IT TOGETHER.
I WILL CALL THE SHOTS AT TIMES, BUT EVERYTHING IS OPEN TO DISCUSSION. JUST LIKE WHEN NIGHTWING AND DONNA LED THIS TEAM.
LOOKS LIKE YOU GOT YOUR NUTS AND BOLTS REALIGNED, VIC.
I THINK WE CAN LIVE WITH THAT, CYBORG.
UH, TITANS?
GUYS, I THINK WE GOT A PROBLEM. WONDER GIRL--
WHAT WERE YOU AND CASSIE DOING OUT THERE, SUPERBOY?
WHAT?
LIPSTICK.
RIGHT.

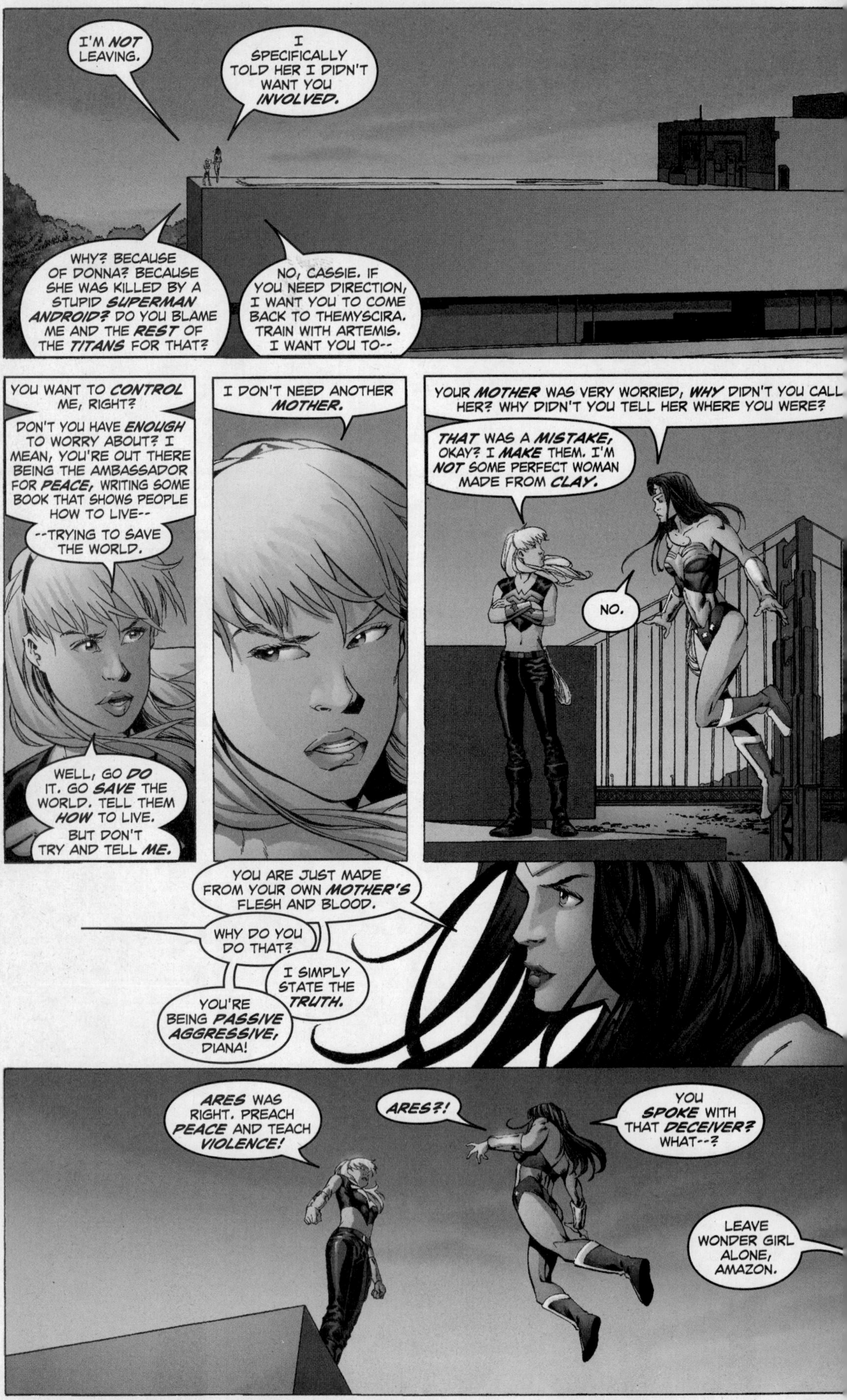

I'M NOT LEAVING.
I SPECIFICALLY TOLD HER I DIDN'T WANT YOU INVOLVED.
WHY? BECAUSE OF DONNA? BECAUSE SHE WAS KILLED BY A STUPID SUPERMAN ANDROID? DO YOU BLAME ME AND THE REST OF THE TITANS FOR THAT?
NO, CASSIE. IF YOU NEED DIRECTION, I WANT YOU TO COME BACK TO THEMYSCIRA. TRAIN WITH ARTEMIS. I WANT YOU TO--
YOU WANT TO CONTROL ME, RIGHT?
DON'T YOU HAVE ENOUGH TO WORRY ABOUT? I MEAN, YOU'RE OUT THERE BEING THE AMBASSADOR FOR PEACE, WRITING SOME BOOK THAT SHOWS PEOPLE HOW TO LIVE--
--TRYING TO SAVE THE WORLD.
WELL, GO DO IT. GO SAVE THE WORLD. TELL THEM HOW TO LIVE.
BUT DON'T TRY AND TELL ME.
I DON'T NEED ANOTHER MOTHER.
YOUR MOTHER WAS VERY WORRIED, WHY DIDN'T YOU CALL HER? WHY DIDN'T YOU TELL HER WHERE YOU WERE?
THAT WAS A MISTAKE, OKAY? I MAKE THEM. I'M NOT SOME PERFECT WOMAN MADE FROM CLAY.
NO.
YOU ARE JUST MADE FROM YOUR OWN MOTHER'S FLESH AND BLOOD.
WHY DO YOU DO THAT?
I SIMPLY STATE THE TRUTH.
YOU'RE BEING PASSIVE AGGRESSIVE, DIANA!
ARES WAS RIGHT. PREACH PEACE AND TEACH VIOLENCE!
ARES?!
YOU SPOKE WITH THAT DECEIVER? WHAT--?
LEAVE WONDER GIRL ALONE, AMAZON.

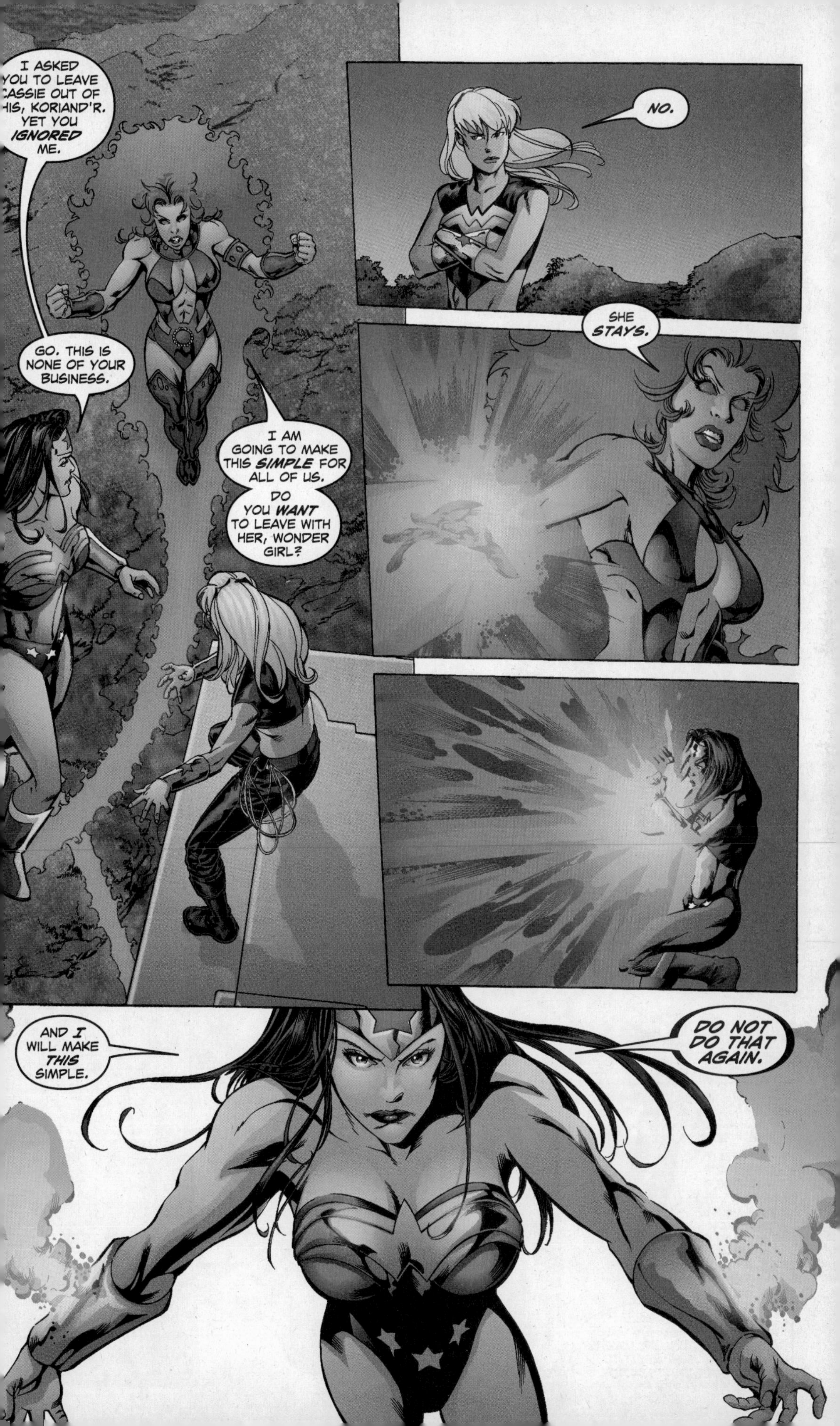
I ASKED YOU TO LEAVE CASSIE OUT OF THIS, KORIAND'R. YET YOU IGNORED ME.
GO. THIS IS NONE OF YOUR BUSINESS.
I AM GOING TO MAKE THIS SIMPLE FOR ALL OF US.
DO YOU WANT TO LEAVE WITH HER, WONDER GIRL?
NO.
SHE STAYS.
AND I WILL MAKE THIS SIMPLE.
DO NOT DO THAT AGAIN.

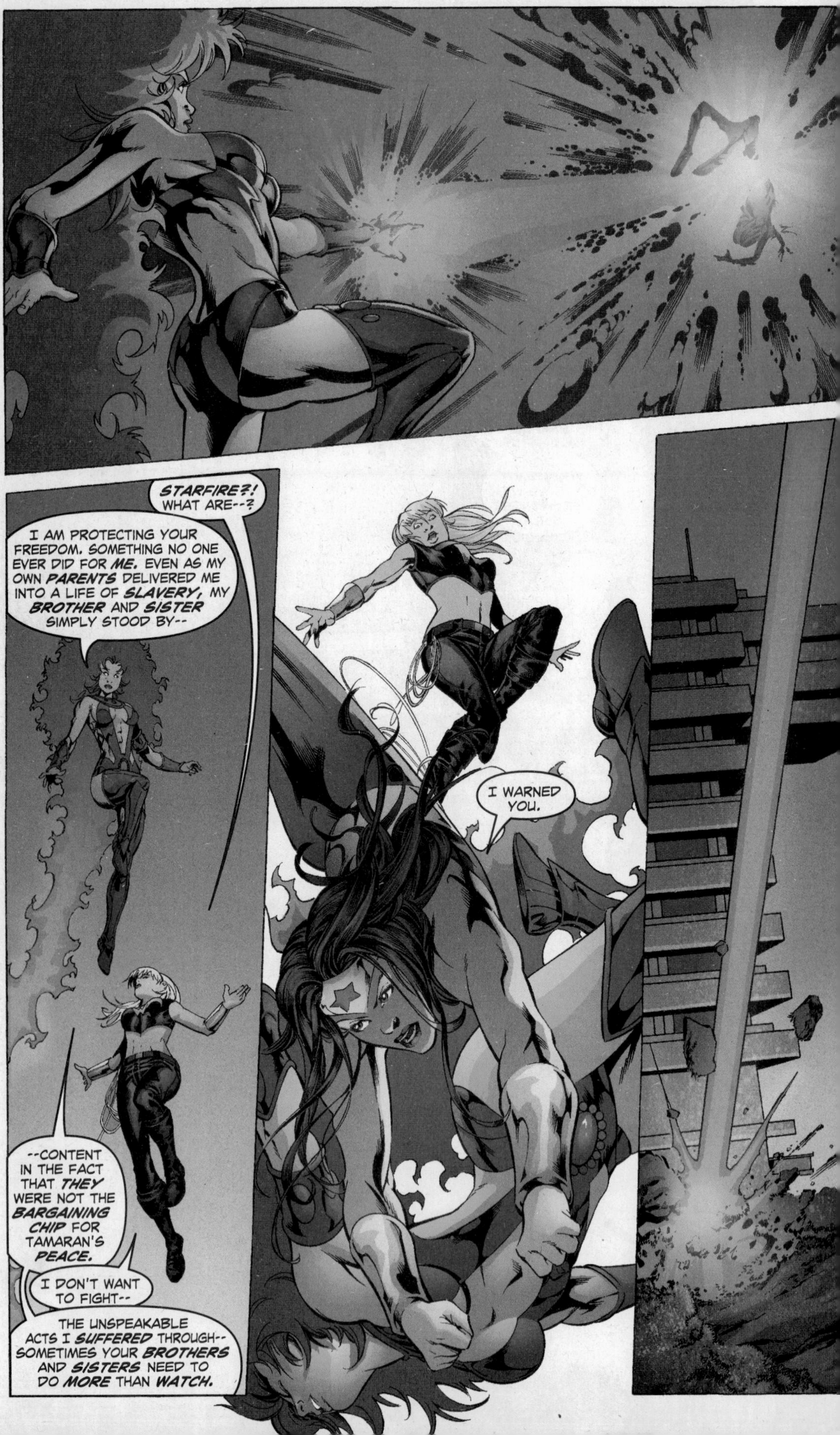
STARFIRE?! WHAT ARE--?
I AM PROTECTING YOUR FREEDOM. SOMETHING NO ONE EVER DID FOR ME. EVEN AS MY OWN PARENTS DELIVERED ME INTO A LIFE OF SLAVERY, MY BROTHER AND SISTER SIMPLY STOOD BY--
--CONTENT IN THE FACT THAT THEY WERE NOT THE BARGAINING CHIP FOR TAMARAN'S PEACE.
I DON'T WANT TO FIGHT--
THE UNSPEAKABLE ACTS I SUFFERED THROUGH-- SOMETIMES YOUR BROTHERS AND SISTERS NEED TO DO MORE THAN WATCH.
I WARNED YOU.

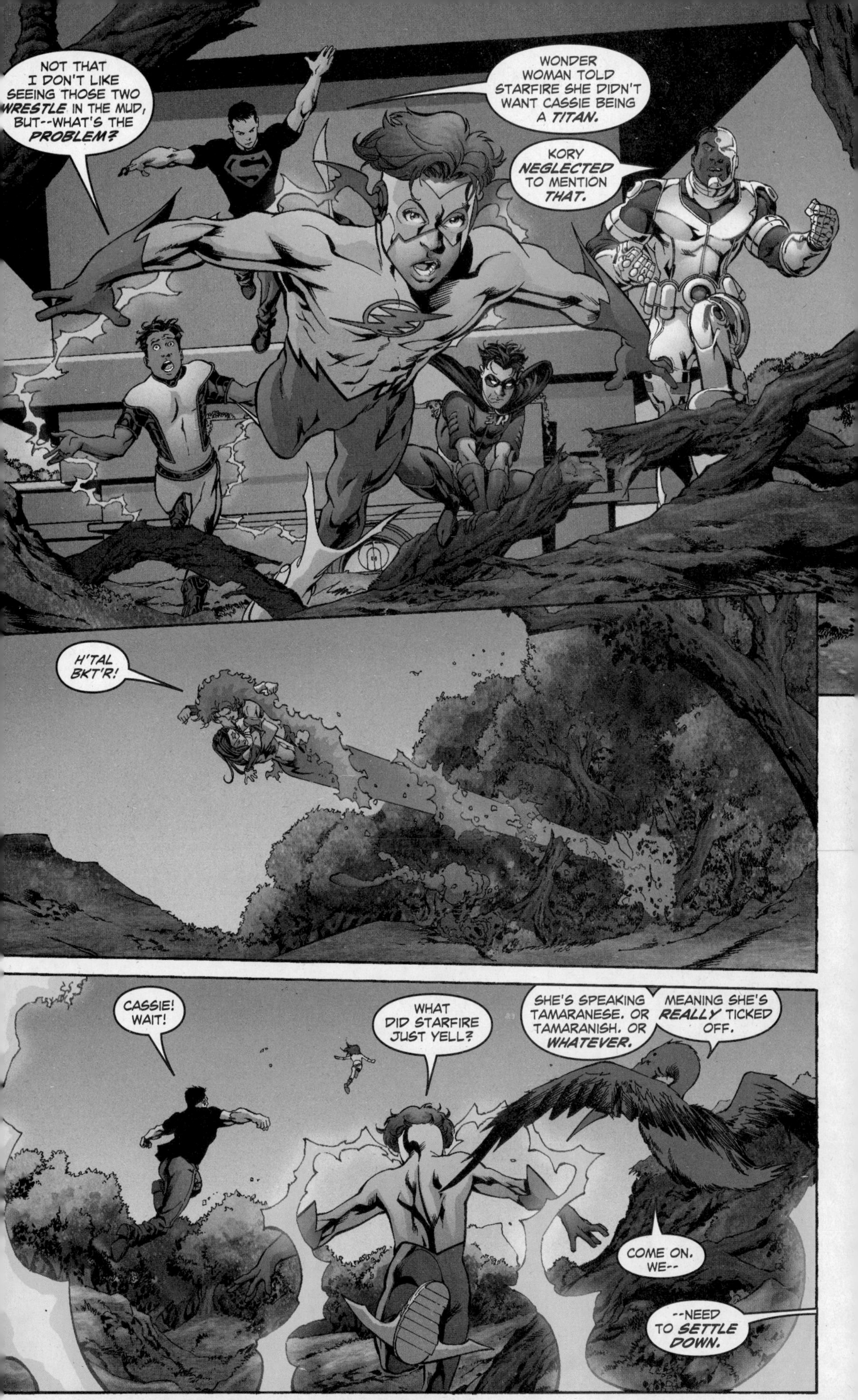
NOT THAT I DON'T LIKE SEEING THOSE TWO WRESTLE IN THE MUD, BUT--WHAT'S THE PROBLEM?
WONDER WOMAN TOLD STARFIRE SHE DIDN'T WANT CASSIE BEING A TITAN.
KORY NEGLECTED TO MENTION THAT.
H'TAL BKT'R!
CASSIE! WAIT!
WHAT DID STARFIRE JUST YELL?
SHE'S SPEAKING TAMARANESE. OR TAMARANISH. OR WHATEVER.
MEANING SHE'S REALLY TICKED OFF.
COME ON. WE--
--NEED TO SETTLE DOWN.

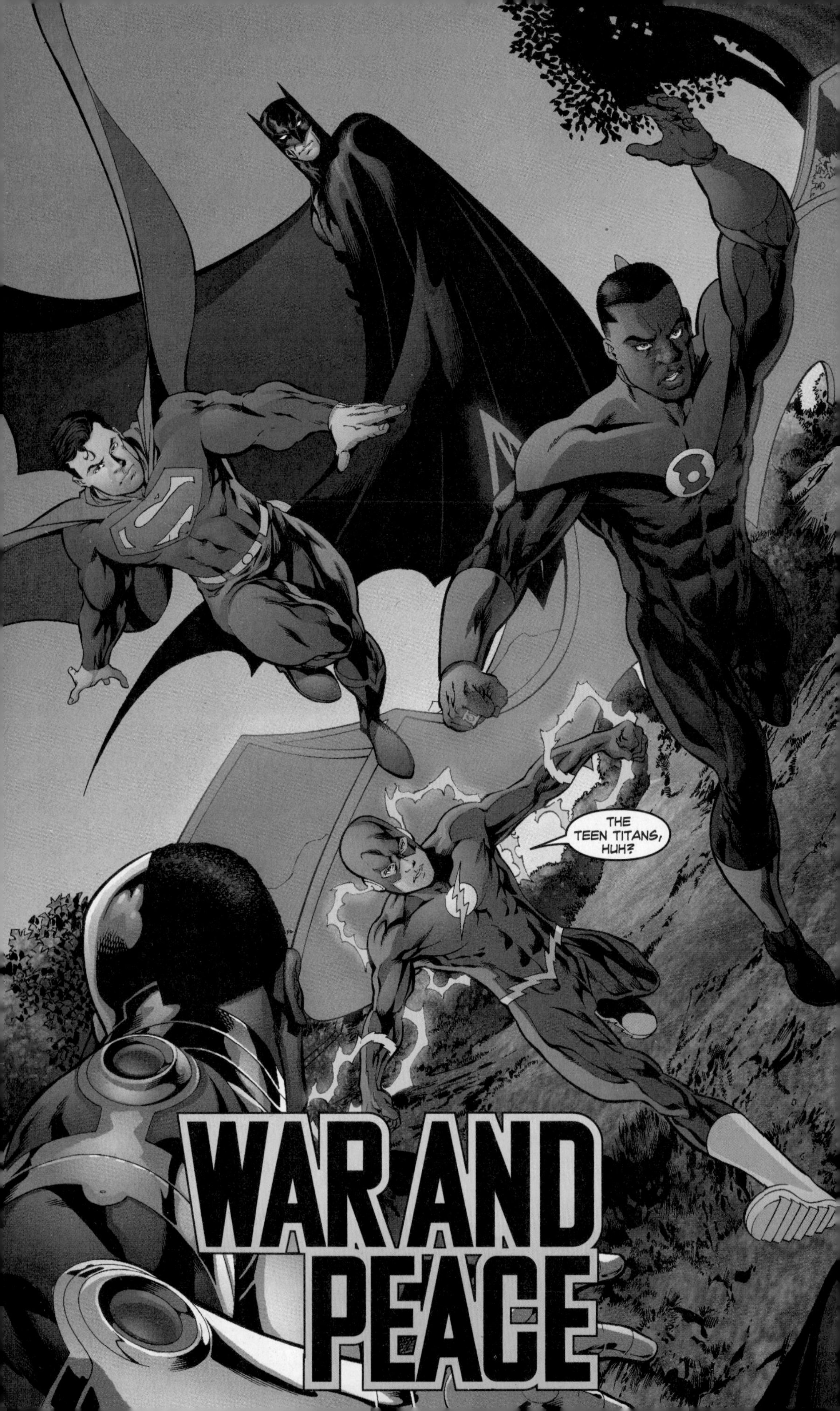
THE TEEN TITANS, HUH?
WAR AND PEACE

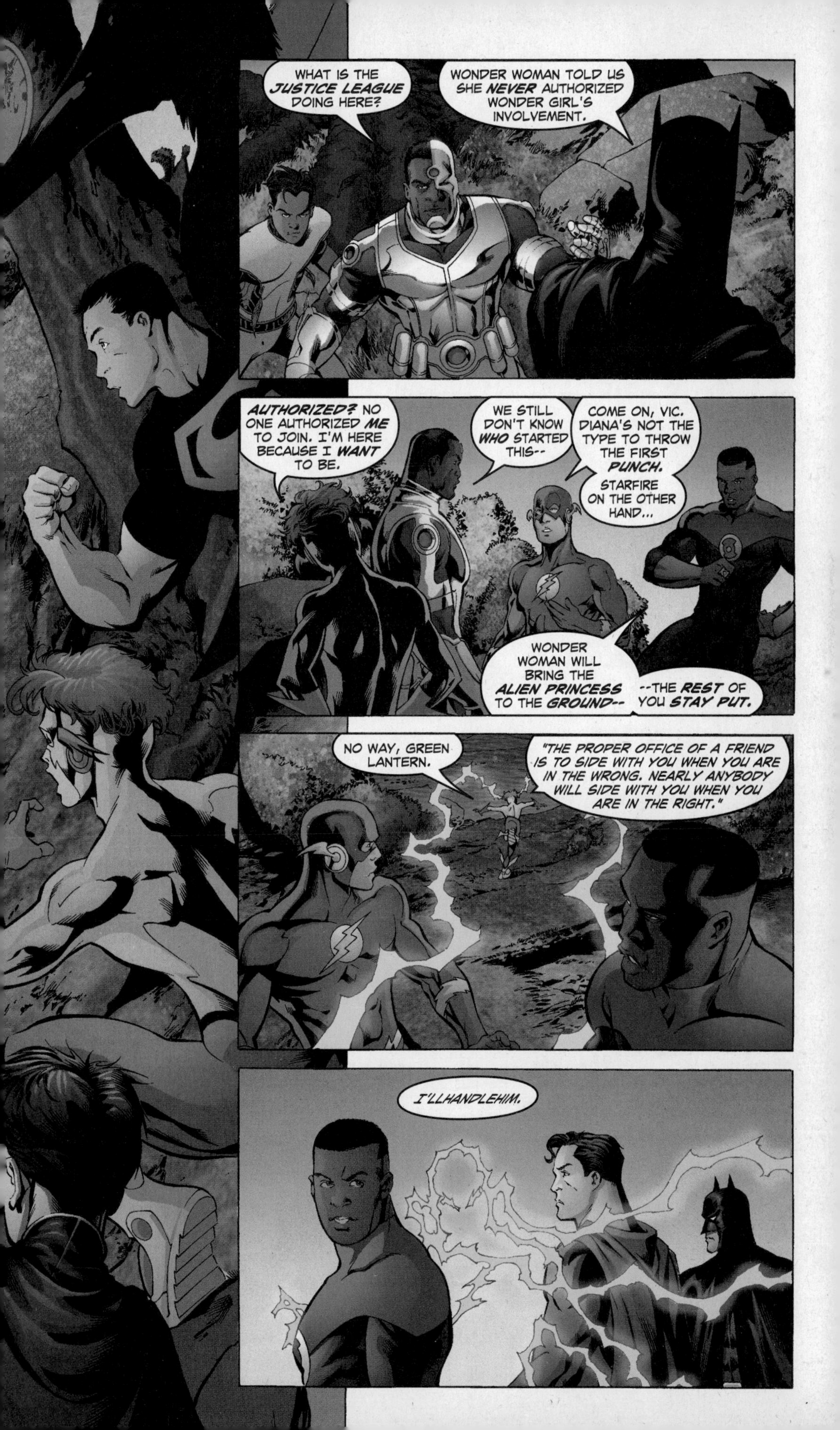

WHAT IS THE JUSTICE LEAGUE DOING HERE?
WONDER WOMAN TOLD US SHE NEVER AUTHORIZED WONDER GIRL'S INVOLVEMENT.
AUTHORIZED? NO ONE AUTHORIZED ME TO JOIN. I'M HERE BECAUSE I WANT TO BE.
WE STILL DON'T KNOW WHO STARTED THIS--
COME ON, VIC. DIANA'S NOT THE TYPE TO THROW THE FIRST PUNCH.
STARFIRE ON THE OTHER HAND...
WONDER WOMAN WILL BRING THE ALIEN PRINCESS TO THE GROUND--
--THE REST OF YOU STAY PUT.
NO WAY, GREEN LANTERN.
"THE PROPER OFFICE OF A FRIEND IS TO SIDE WITH YOU WHEN YOU ARE IN THE WRONG. NEARLY ANYBODY WILL SIDE WITH YOU WHEN YOU ARE IN THE RIGHT."
I'LLHANDLEHIM.

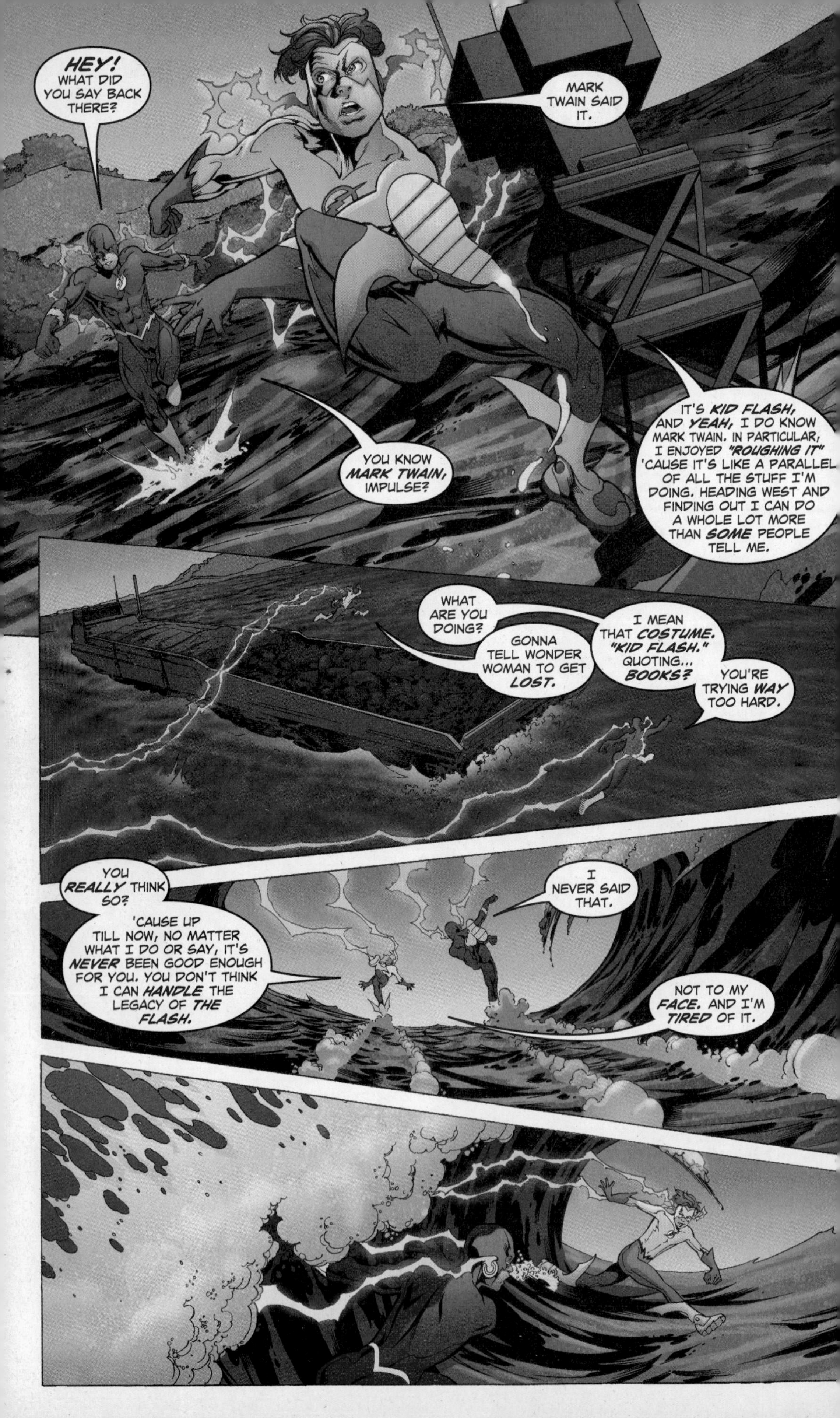
HEY! WHAT DID YOU SAY BACK THERE?
MARK TWAIN SAID IT.
YOU KNOW MARK TWAIN, IMPULSE?
IT'S KID FLASH, AND YEAH, I DO KNOW MARK TWAIN. IN PARTICULAR, I ENJOYED "ROUGHING IT" 'CAUSE IT'S LIKE A PARALLEL OF ALL THE STUFF I'M DOING. HEADING WEST AND FINDING OUT I CAN DO A WHOLE LOT MORE THAN SOME PEOPLE TELL ME.
WHAT ARE YOU DOING?
GONNA TELL WONDER WOMAN TO GET LOST.
I MEAN THAT COSTUME. "KID FLASH." QUOTING... BOOKS?
YOU'RE TRYING WAY TOO HARD.
YOU REALLY THINK SO?
'CAUSE UP TILL NOW, NO MATTER WHAT I DO OR SAY, IT'S NEVER BEEN GOOD ENOUGH FOR YOU. YOU DON'T THINK I CAN HANDLE THE LEGACY OF THE FLASH.
I NEVER SAID THAT.
NOT TO MY FACE. AND I'M TIRED OF IT.

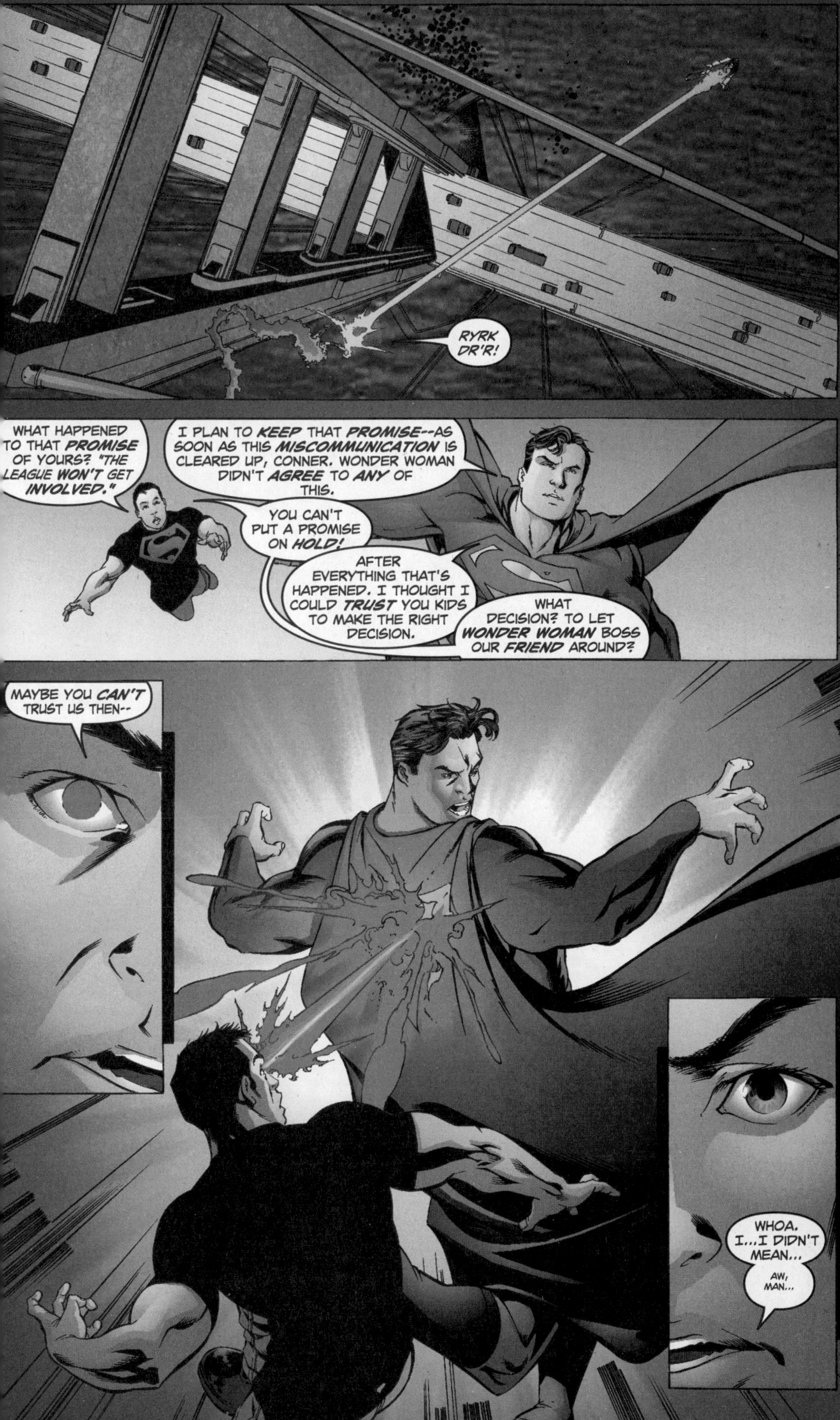
RYRK DR'R!
WHAT HAPPENED TO THAT PROMISE OF YOURS? "THE LEAGUE WON'T GET INVOLVED."
I PLAN TO KEEP THAT PROMISE--AS SOON AS THIS MISCOMMUNICATION IS CLEARED UP, CONNER. WONDER WOMAN DIDN'T AGREE TO ANY OF THIS.
YOU CAN'T PUT A PROMISE ON HOLD!
AFTER EVERYTHING THAT'S HAPPENED. I THOUGHT I COULD TRUST YOU KIDS TO MAKE THE RIGHT DECISION.
WHAT DECISION? TO LET WONDER WOMAN BOSS OUR FRIEND AROUND?
MAYBE YOU CAN'T TRUST US THEN--
WHOA. I...I DIDN'T MEAN...
AW, MAN...

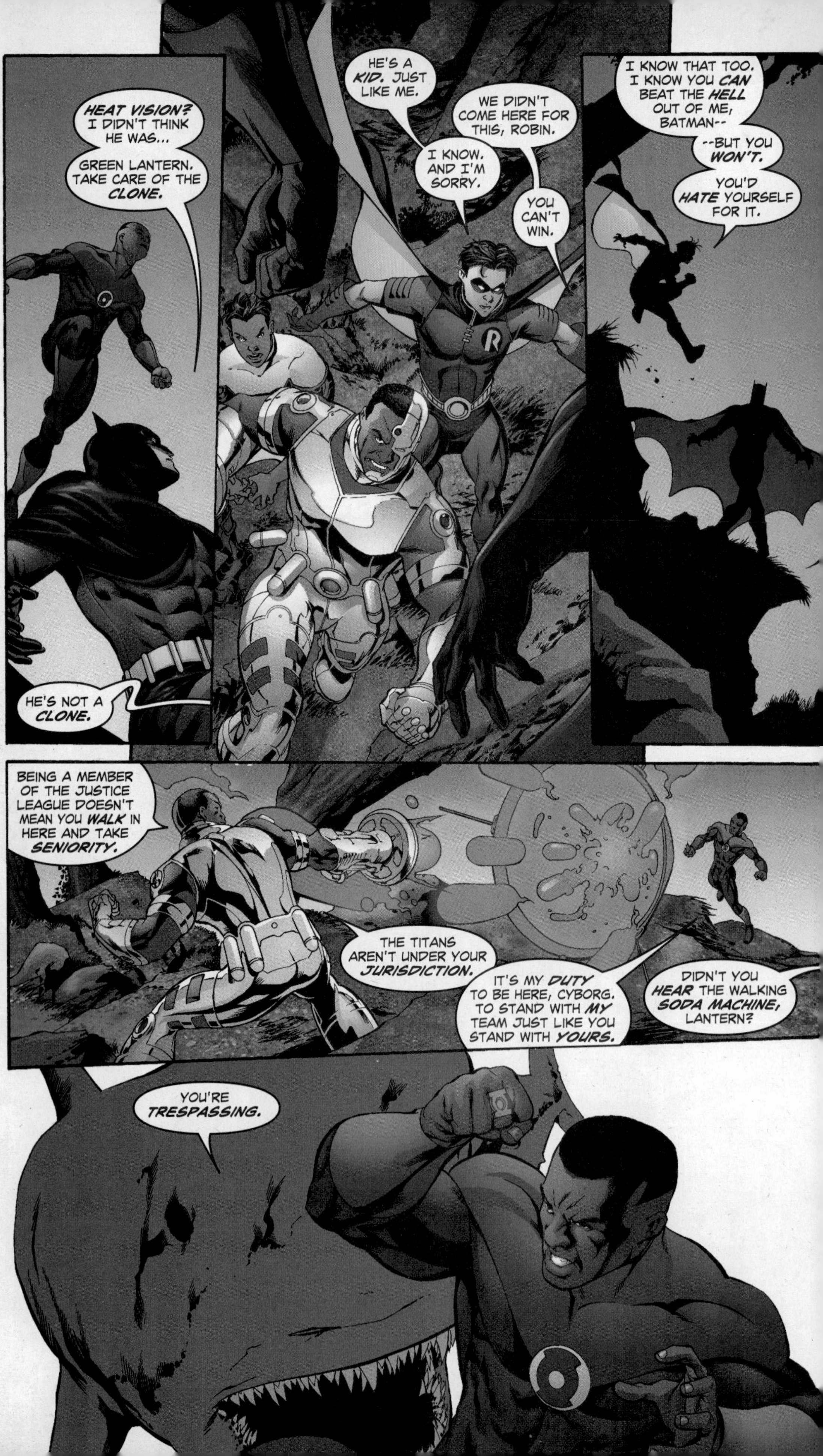
HEAT VISION? I DIDN'T THINK HE WAS...
GREEN LANTERN. TAKE CARE OF THE CLONE.
HE'S NOT A CLONE.
HE'S A KID. JUST LIKE ME.
WE DIDN'T COME HERE FOR THIS, ROBIN.
I KNOW. AND I'M SORRY.
YOU CAN'T WIN.
I KNOW THAT TOO. I KNOW YOU CAN BEAT THE HELL OUT OF ME, BATMAN--
--BUT YOU WON'T.
YOU'D HATE YOURSELF FOR IT.
BEING A MEMBER OF THE JUSTICE LEAGUE DOESN'T MEAN YOU WALK IN HERE AND TAKE SENIORITY.
THE TITANS AREN'T UNDER YOUR JURISDICTION.
IT'S MY DUTY TO BE HERE, CYBORG. TO STAND WITH MY TEAM JUST LIKE YOU STAND WITH YOURS.
DIDN'T YOU HEAR THE WALKING SODA MACHINE, LANTERN?
YOU'RE TRESPASSING.

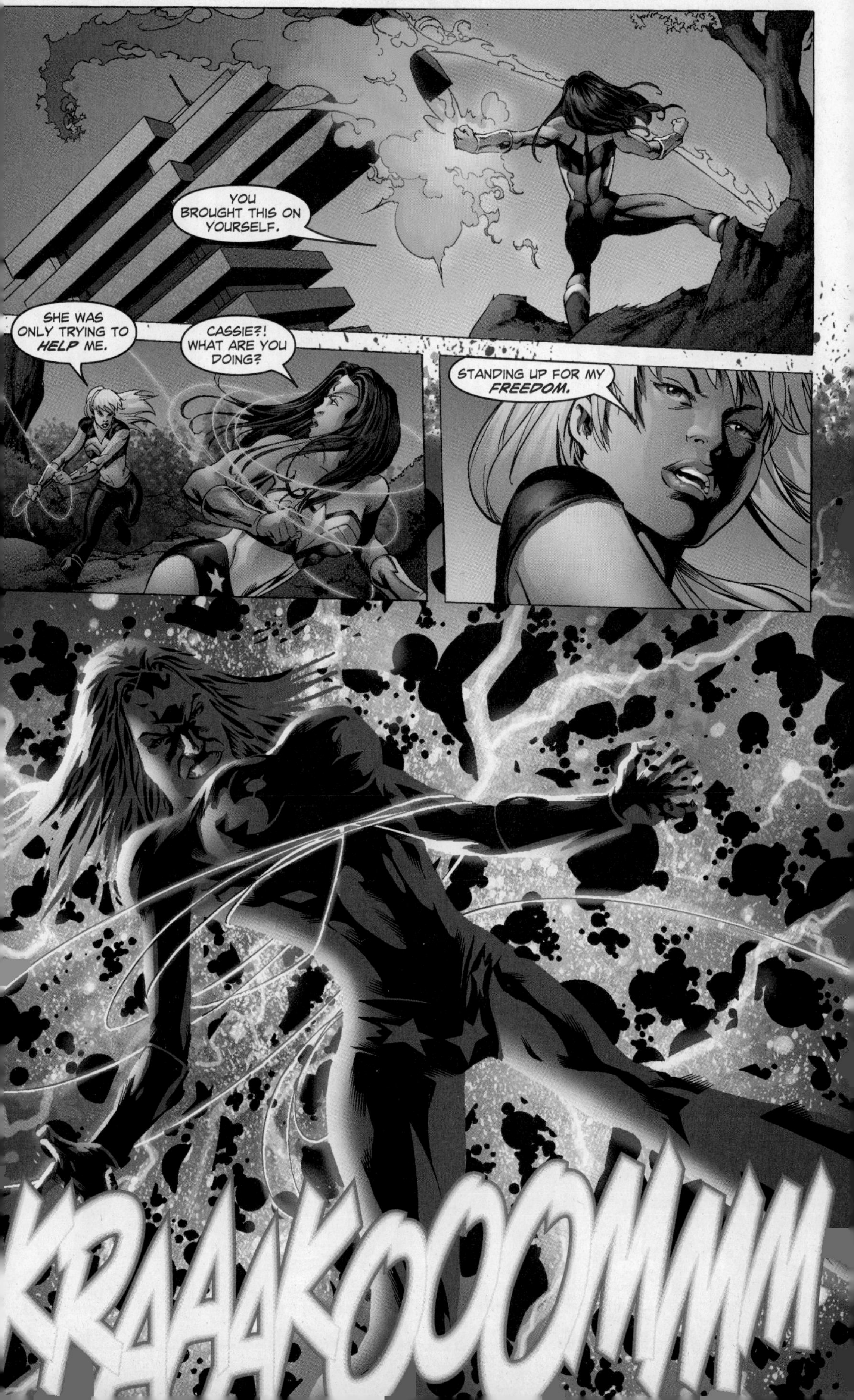
YOU BROUGHT THIS ON YOURSELF.
SHE WAS ONLY TRYING TO HELP ME.
CASSIE?! WHAT ARE YOU DOING?
STANDING UP FOR MY FREEDOM.
KRAAKOOOMMM

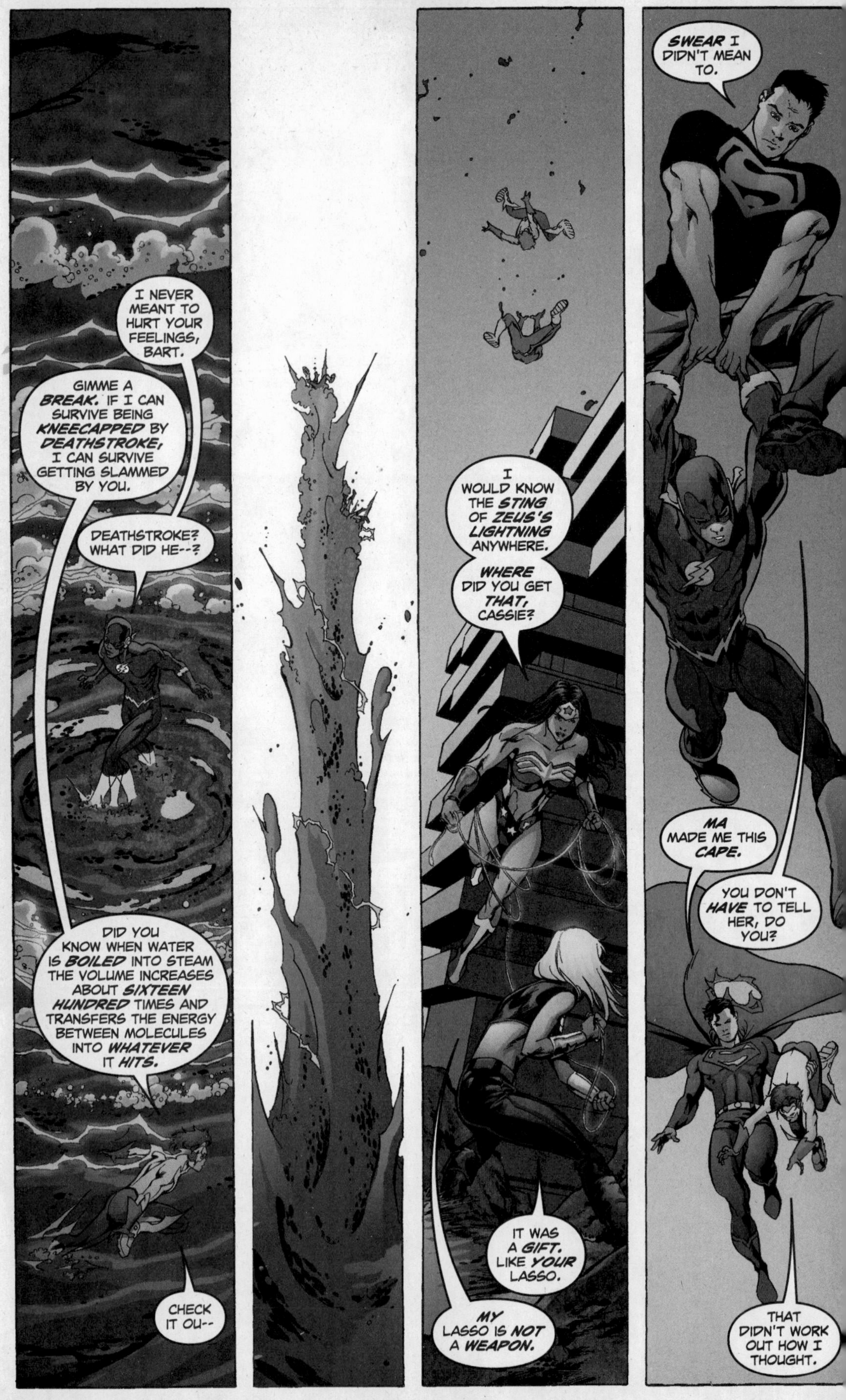
I NEVER MEANT TO HURT YOUR FEELINGS, BART.
GIMME A BREAK. IF I CAN SURVIVE BEING KNEECAPPED BY DEATHSTROKE, I CAN SURVIVE GETTING SLAMMED BY YOU.
DEATHSTROKE? WHAT DID HE--?
DID YOU KNOW WHEN WATER IS BOILED INTO STEAM THE VOLUME INCREASES ABOUT SIXTEEN HUNDRED TIMES AND TRANSFERS THE ENERGY BETWEEN MOLECULES INTO WHATEVER IT HITS.
CHECK IT OU--
I WOULD KNOW THE STING OF ZEUS'S LIGHTNING ANYWHERE.
WHERE DID YOU GET THAT, CASSIE?
IT WAS A GIFT. LIKE YOUR LASSO.
MY LASSO IS NOT A WEAPON.
SWEAR I DIDN'T MEAN TO.
MA MADE ME THIS CAPE.
YOU DON'T HAVE TO TELL HER, DO YOU?
THAT DIDN'T WORK OUT HOW I THOUGHT.

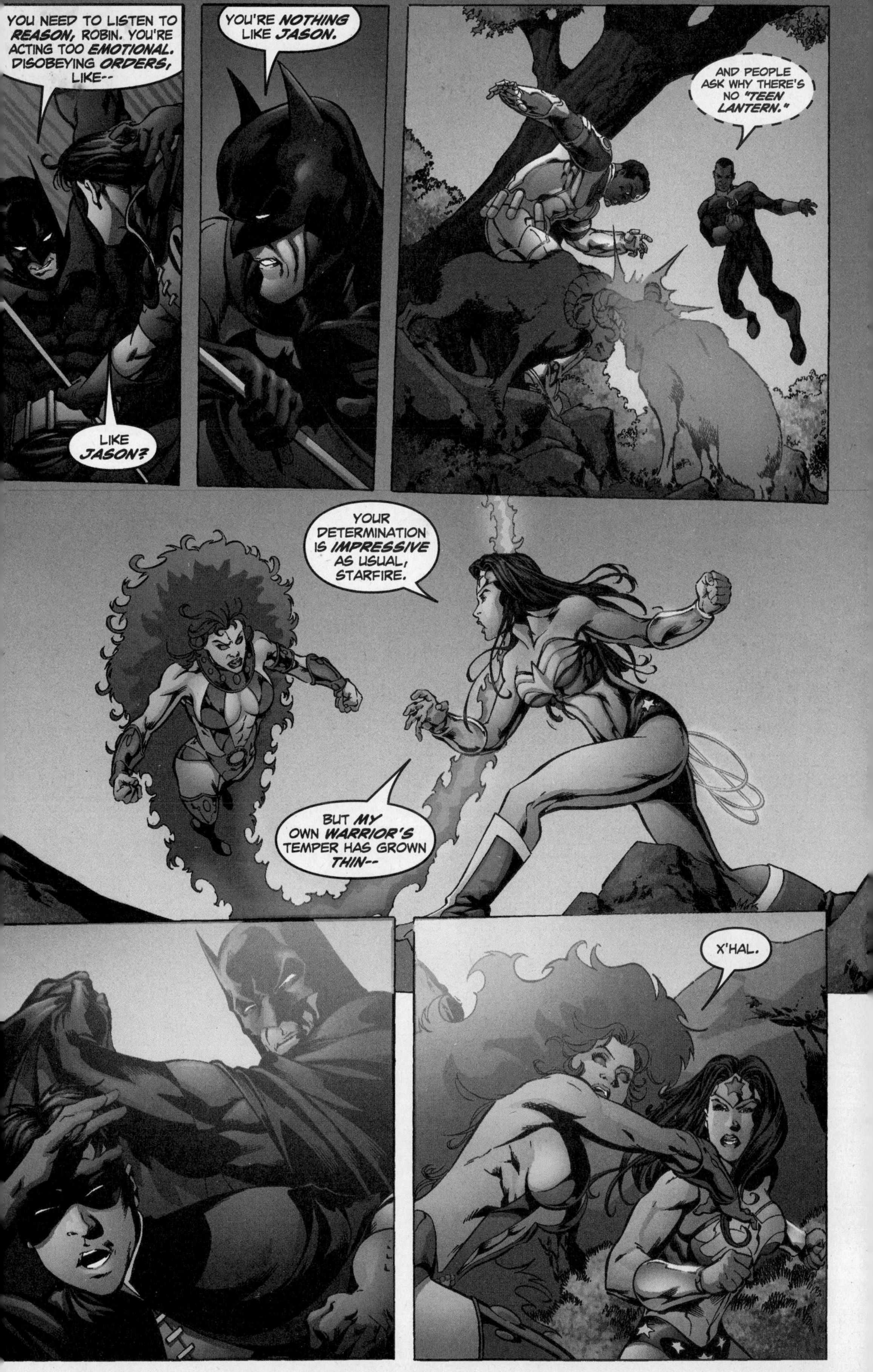

YOU NEED TO LISTEN TO REASON, ROBIN. YOU'RE ACTING TOO EMOTIONAL. DISOBEYING ORDERS, LIKE--
LIKE JASON?
YOU'RE NOTHING LIKE JASON.
AND PEOPLE ASK WHY THERE'S NO "TEEN LANTERN."
YOUR DETERMINATION IS IMPRESSIVE AS USUAL, STARFIRE.
BUT MY OWN WARRIOR'S TEMPER HAS GROWN THIN--
X'HAL.

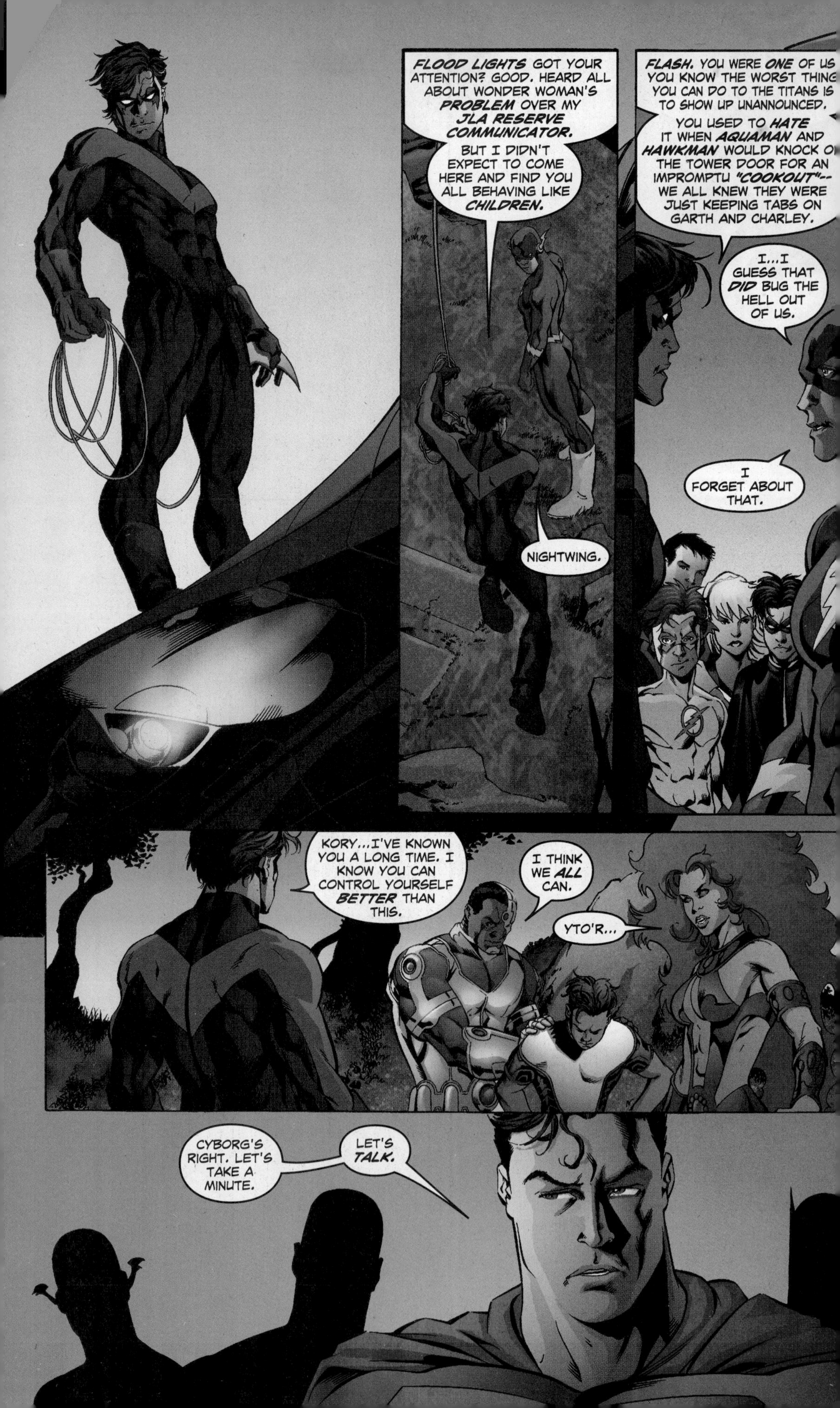

FLOOD LIGHTS GOT YOUR ATTENTION? GOOD. HEARD ALL ABOUT WONDER WOMAN'S PROBLEM OVER MY JLA RESERVE COMMUNICATOR.
BUT I DIDN'T EXPECT TO COME HERE AND FIND YOU ALL BEHAVING LIKE CHILDREN.
NIGHTWING.
FLASH. YOU WERE ONE OF US. YOU KNOW THE WORST THING YOU CAN DO TO THE TITANS IS TO SHOW UP UNANNOUNCED.
YOU USED TO HATE IT WHEN AQUAMAN AND HAWKMAN WOULD KNOCK ON THE TOWER DOOR FOR AN IMPROMPTU "COOKOUT"-- WE ALL KNEW THEY WERE JUST KEEPING TABS ON GARTH AND CHARLEY.
I...I GUESS THAT DID BUG THE HELL OUT OF US.
I FORGET ABOUT THAT.
KORY...I'VE KNOWN YOU A LONG TIME. I KNOW YOU CAN CONTROL YOURSELF BETTER THAN THIS.
I THINK WE ALL CAN.
YTO'R...
CYBORG'S RIGHT. LET'S TAKE A MINUTE.
LET'S TALK.

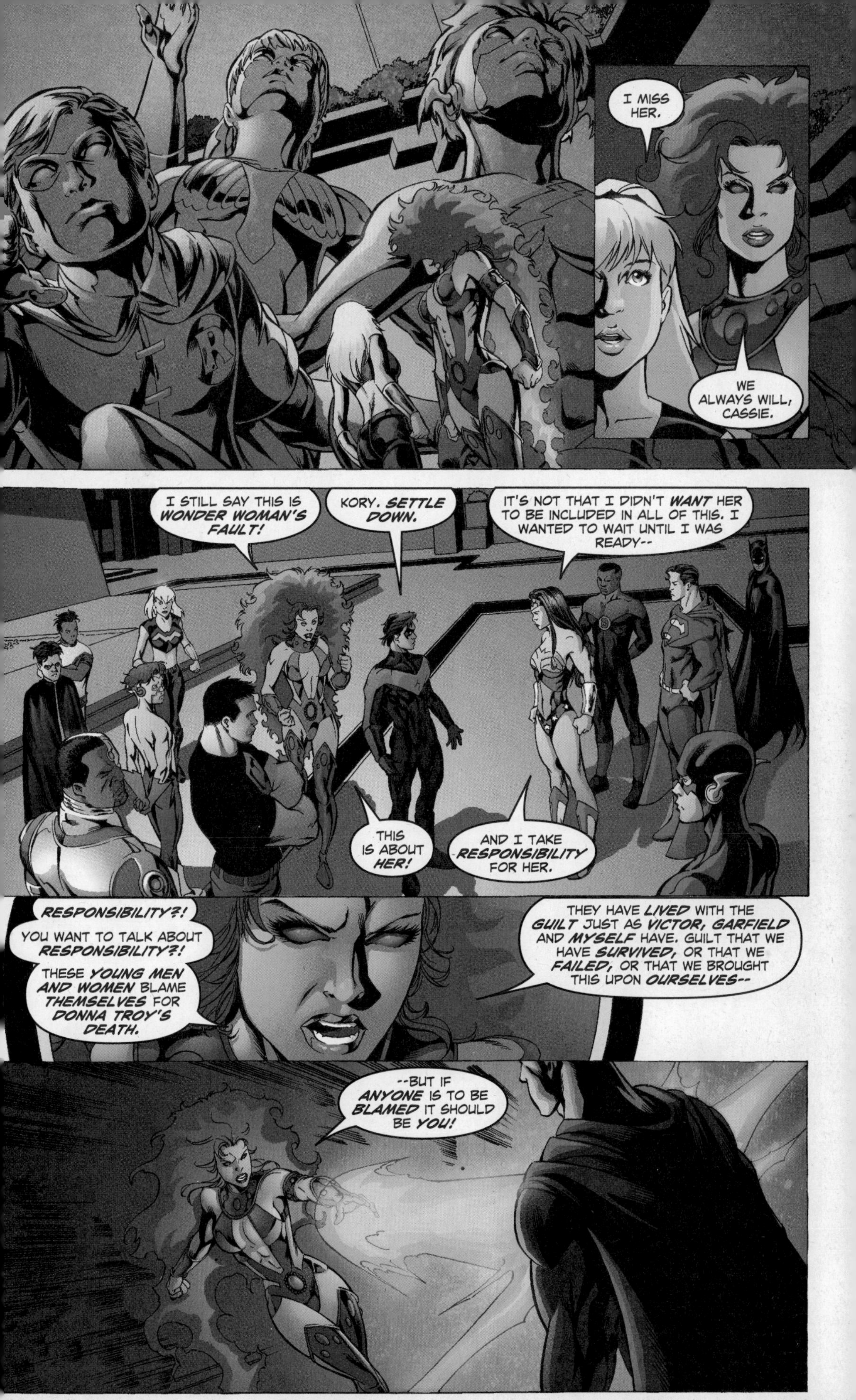

I MISS HER.
WE ALWAYS WILL, CASSIE.
I STILL SAY THIS IS WONDER WOMAN'S FAULT!
KORY. SETTLE DOWN.
IT'S NOT THAT I DIDN'T WANT HER TO BE INCLUDED IN ALL OF THIS. I WANTED TO WAIT UNTIL I WAS READY--
THIS IS ABOUT HER!
AND I TAKE RESPONSIBILITY FOR HER.
RESPONSIBILITY?!
YOU WANT TO TALK ABOUT RESPONSIBILITY?!
THESE YOUNG MEN AND WOMEN BLAME THEMSELVES FOR DONNA TROY'S DEATH.
THEY HAVE LIVED WITH THE GUILT JUST AS VICTOR, GARFIELD AND MYSELF HAVE. GUILT THAT WE HAVE SURVIVED, OR THAT WE FAILED, OR THAT WE BROUGHT THIS UPON OURSELVES--
--BUT IF ANYONE IS TO BE BLAMED IT SHOULD BE YOU!

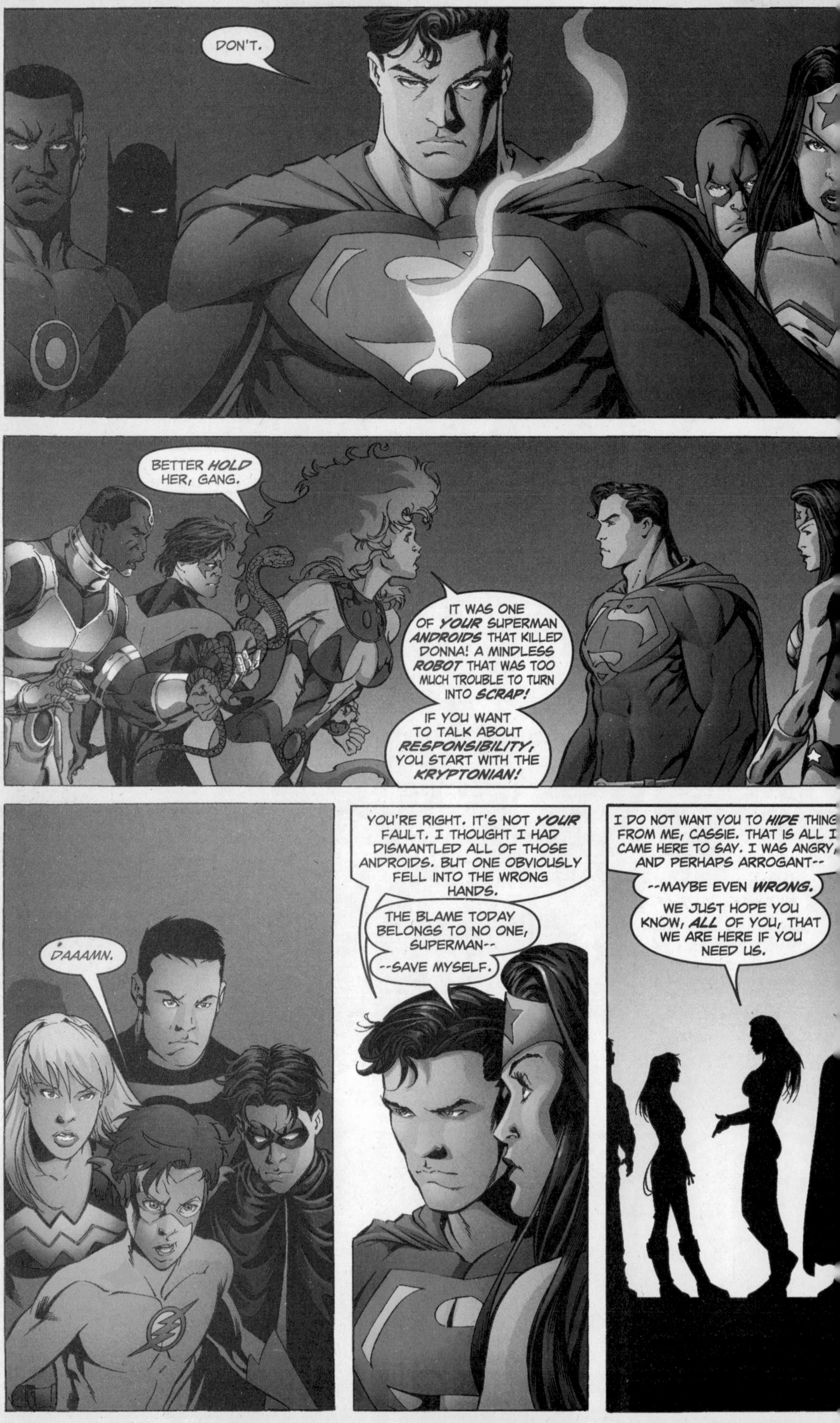
DON'T.
BETTER HOLD HER, GANG.
IT WAS ONE OF YOUR SUPERMAN ANDROIDS THAT KILLED DONNA! A MINDLESS ROBOT THAT WAS TOO MUCH TROUBLE TO TURN INTO SCRAP!
IF YOU WANT TO TALK ABOUT RESPONSIBILITY, YOU START WITH THE KRYPTONIAN!
DAAAMN.
YOU'RE RIGHT. IT'S NOT YOUR FAULT. I THOUGHT I HAD DISMANTLED ALL OF THOSE ANDROIDS. BUT ONE OBVIOUSLY FELL INTO THE WRONG HANDS.
THE BLAME TODAY BELONGS TO NO ONE, SUPERMAN--
--SAVE MYSELF.
I DO NOT WANT YOU TO HIDE THING FROM ME, CASSIE. THAT IS ALL I CAME HERE TO SAY. I WAS ANGRY, AND PERHAPS ARROGANT--
--MAYBE EVEN WRONG.
WE JUST HOPE YOU KNOW, ALL OF YOU, THAT WE ARE HERE IF YOU NEED US.

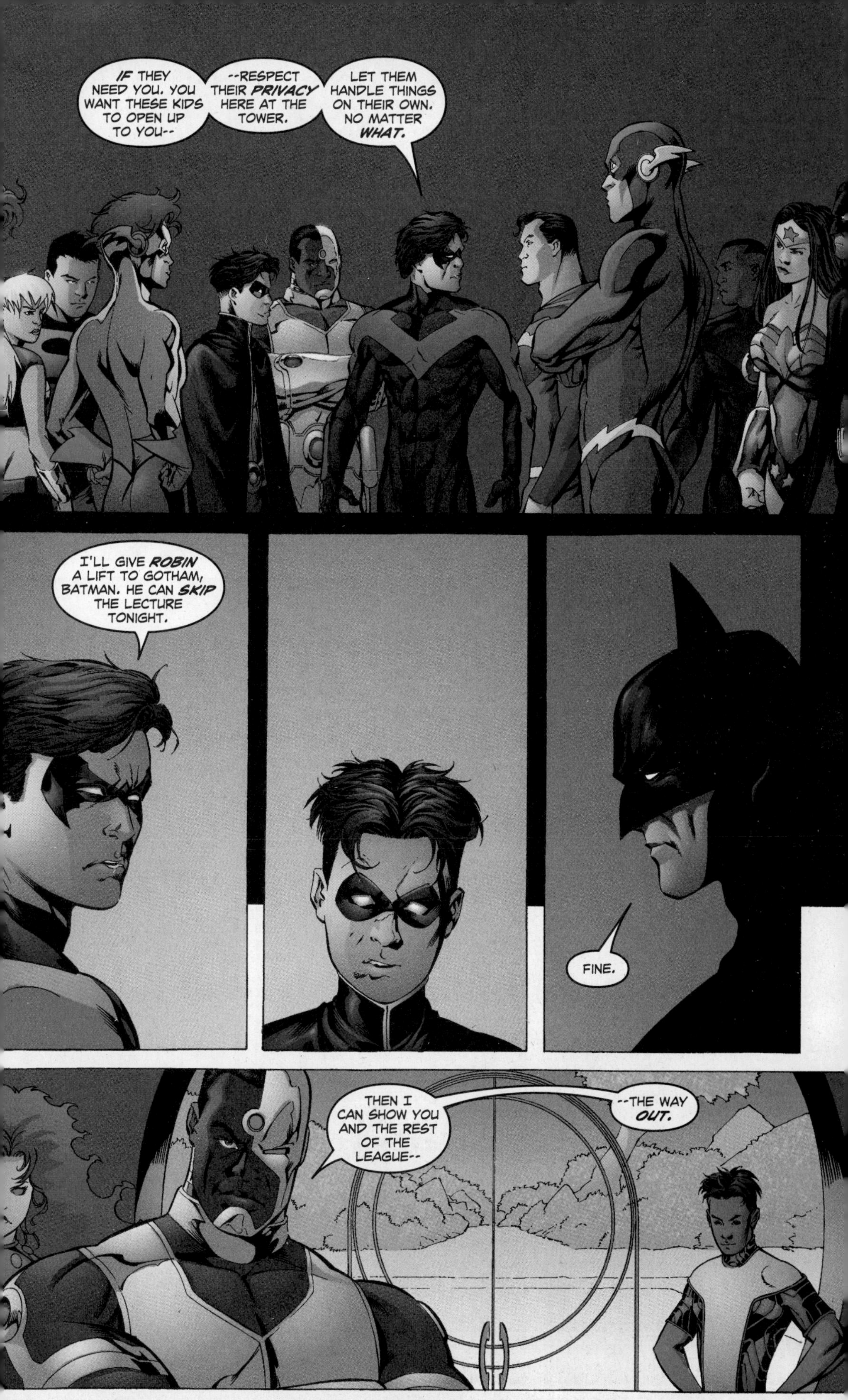
IF THEY NEED YOU. YOU WANT THESE KIDS TO OPEN UP TO YOU--
--RESPECT THEIR PRIVACY HERE AT THE TOWER.
LET THEM HANDLE THINGS ON THEIR OWN. NO MATTER WHAT.
I'LL GIVE ROBIN A LIFT TO GOTHAM, BATMAN. HE CAN SKIP THE LECTURE TONIGHT.
FINE.
THEN I CAN SHOW YOU AND THE REST OF THE LEAGUE--
--THE WAY OUT.

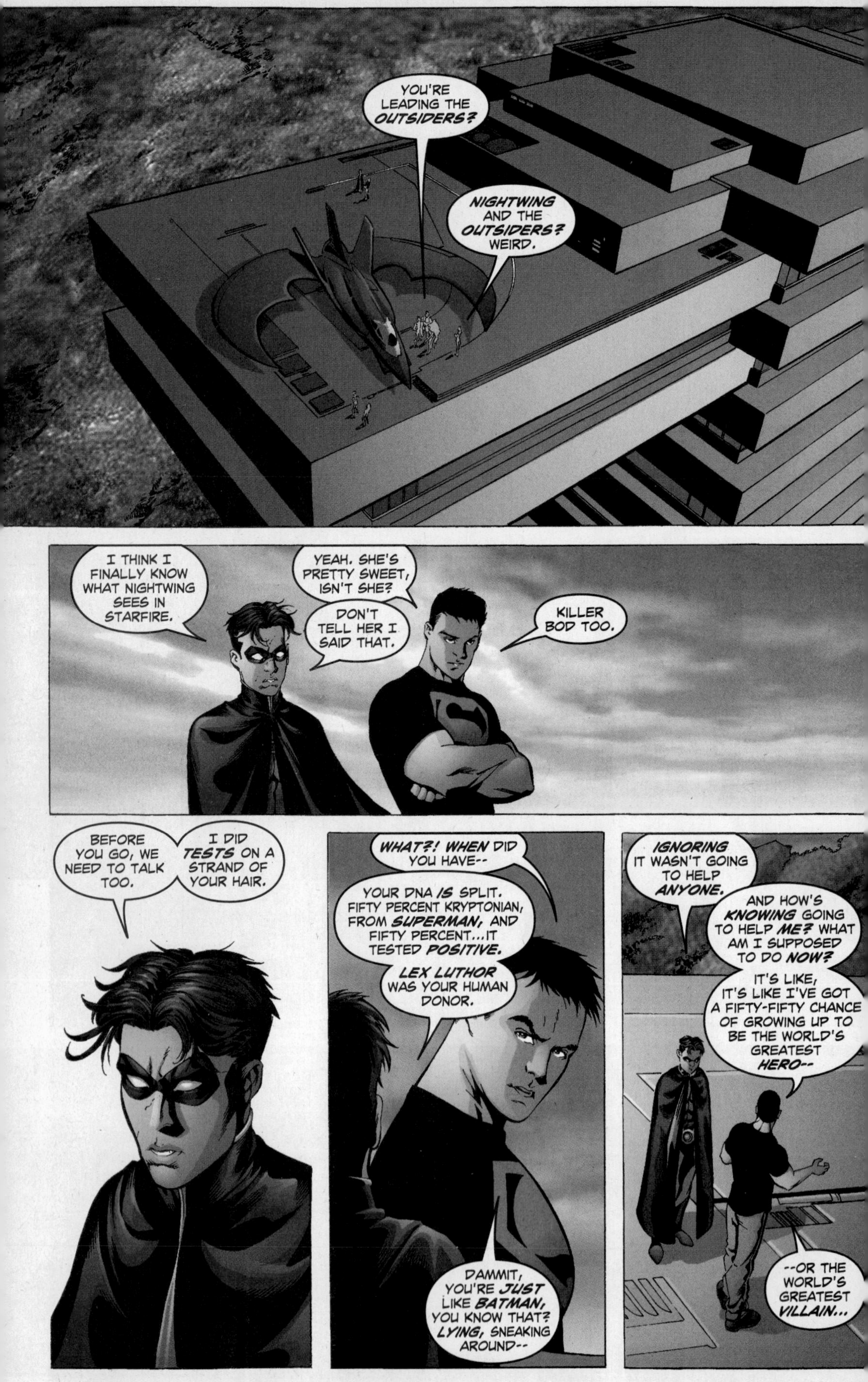

YOU'RE LEADING THE OUTSIDERS?
NIGHTWING AND THE OUTSIDERS? WEIRD.
I THINK I FINALLY KNOW WHAT NIGHTWING SEES IN STARFIRE.
YEAH. SHE'S PRETTY SWEET, ISN'T SHE?
DON'T TELL HER I SAID THAT.
KILLER BOD TOO.
BEFORE YOU GO, WE NEED TO TALK TOO.
I DID TESTS ON A STRAND OF YOUR HAIR.
WHAT?! WHEN DID YOU HAVE--
YOUR DNA IS SPLIT. FIFTY PERCENT KRYPTONIAN, FROM SUPERMAN, AND FIFTY PERCENT...IT TESTED POSITIVE.
LEX LUTHOR WAS YOUR HUMAN DONOR.
DAMMIT, YOU'RE JUST LIKE BATMAN, YOU KNOW THAT? LYING, SNEAKING AROUND--
IGNORING IT WASN'T GOING TO HELP ANYONE.
AND HOW'S KNOWING GOING TO HELP ME? WHAT AM I SUPPOSED TO DO NOW?
IT'S LIKE, IT'S LIKE I'VE GOT A FIFTY-FIFTY CHANCE OF GROWING UP TO BE THE WORLD'S GREATEST HERO--
--OR THE WORLD'S GREATEST VILLAIN...

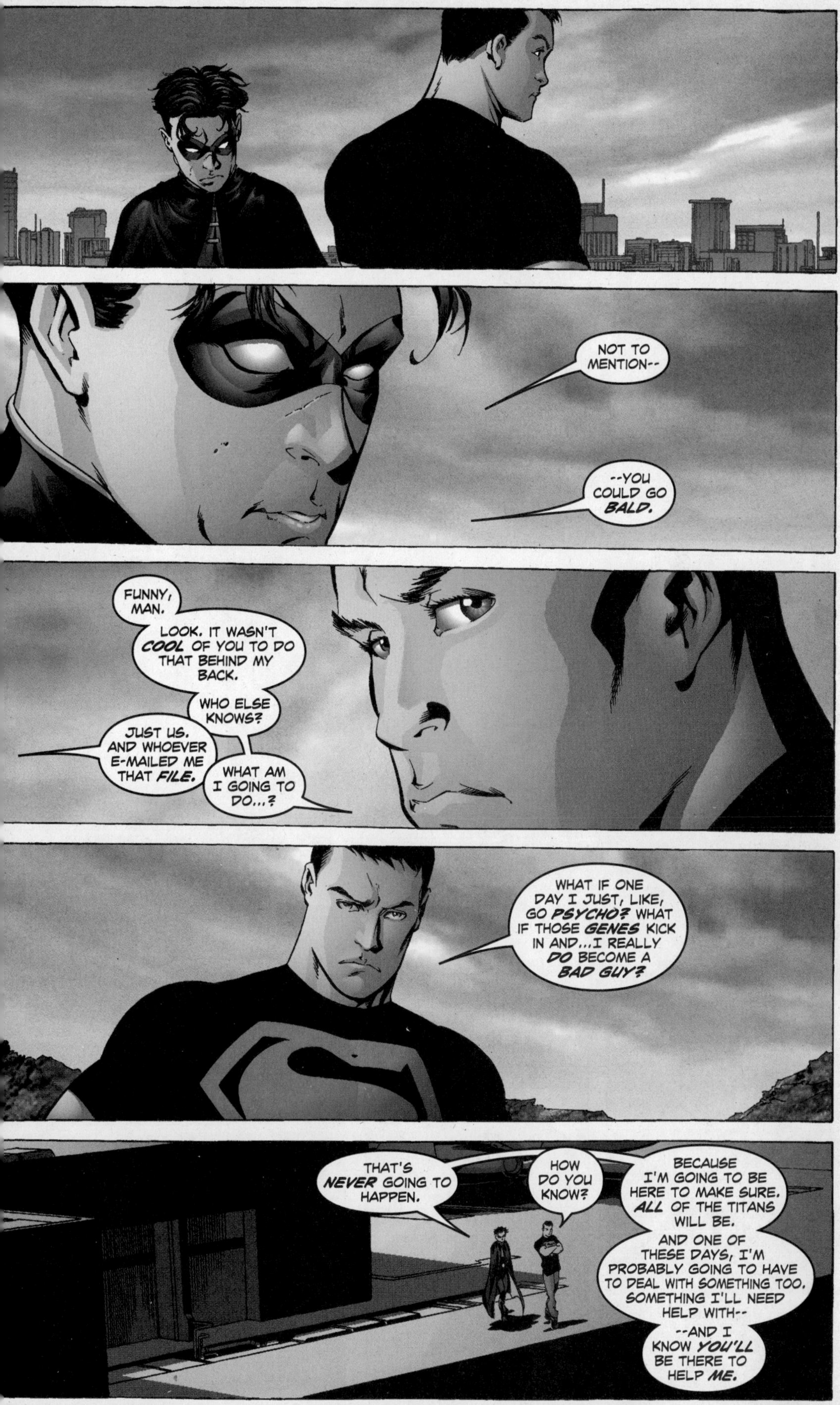
NOT TO MENTION--
--YOU COULD GO BALD.
FUNNY, MAN.
LOOK. IT WASN'T COOL OF YOU TO DO THAT BEHIND MY BACK.
WHO ELSE KNOWS?
JUST US. AND WHOEVER E-MAILED ME THAT FILE.
WHAT AM I GOING TO DO...?
WHAT IF ONE DAY I JUST, LIKE, GO PSYCHO? WHAT IF THOSE GENES KICK IN AND...I REALLY DO BECOME A BAD GUY?
THAT'S NEVER GOING TO HAPPEN.
HOW DO YOU KNOW?
BECAUSE I'M GOING TO BE HERE TO MAKE SURE. ALL OF THE TITANS WILL BE.
AND ONE OF THESE DAYS, I'M PROBABLY GOING TO HAVE TO DEAL WITH SOMETHING TOO. SOMETHING I'LL NEED HELP WITH--
--AND I KNOW YOU'LL BE THERE TO HELP ME.

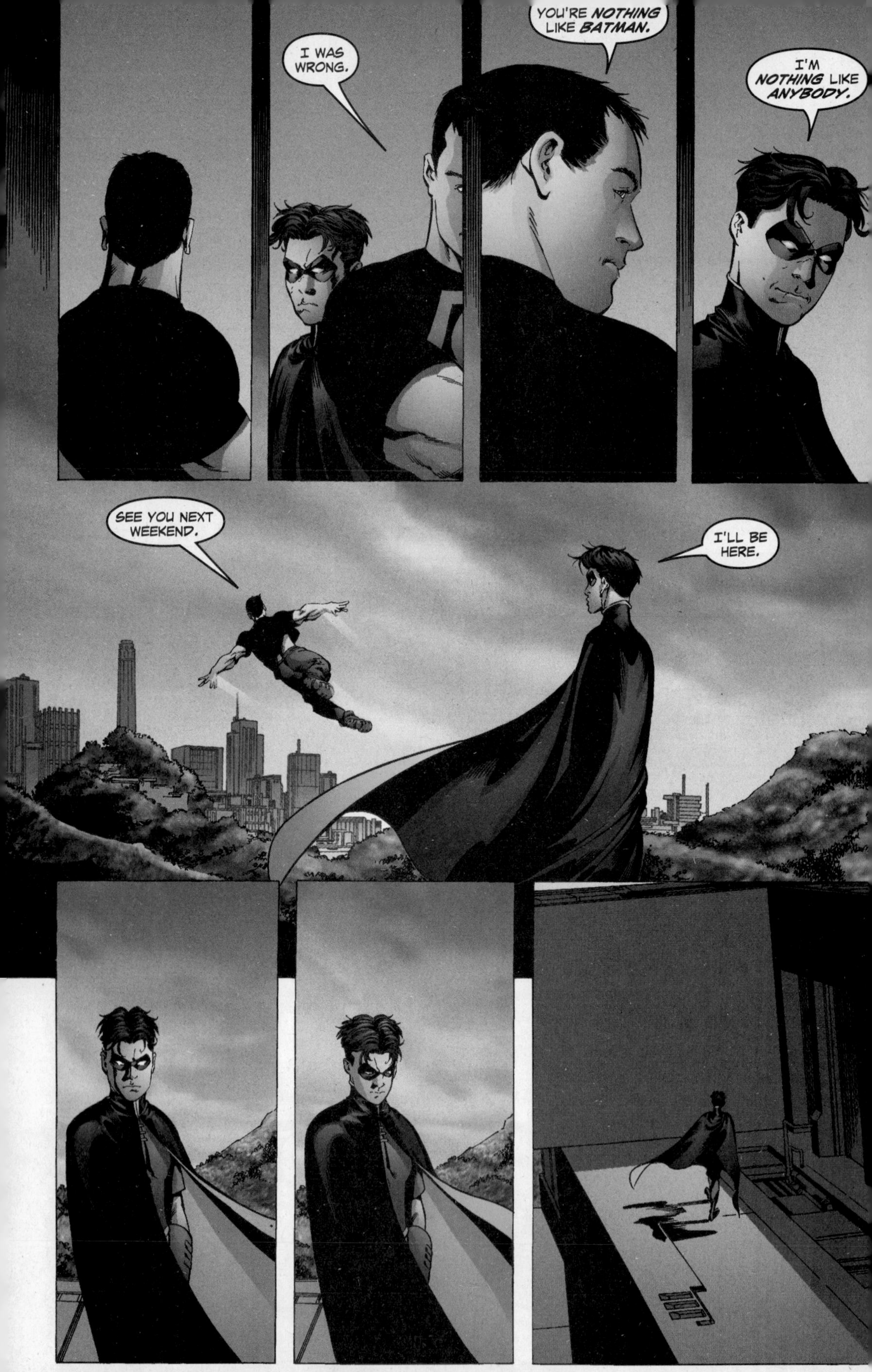
I WAS WRONG.
YOU'RE NOTHING LIKE BATMAN.
I'M NOTHING LIKE ANYBODY.
SEE YOU NEXT WEEKEND.
I'LL BE HERE.

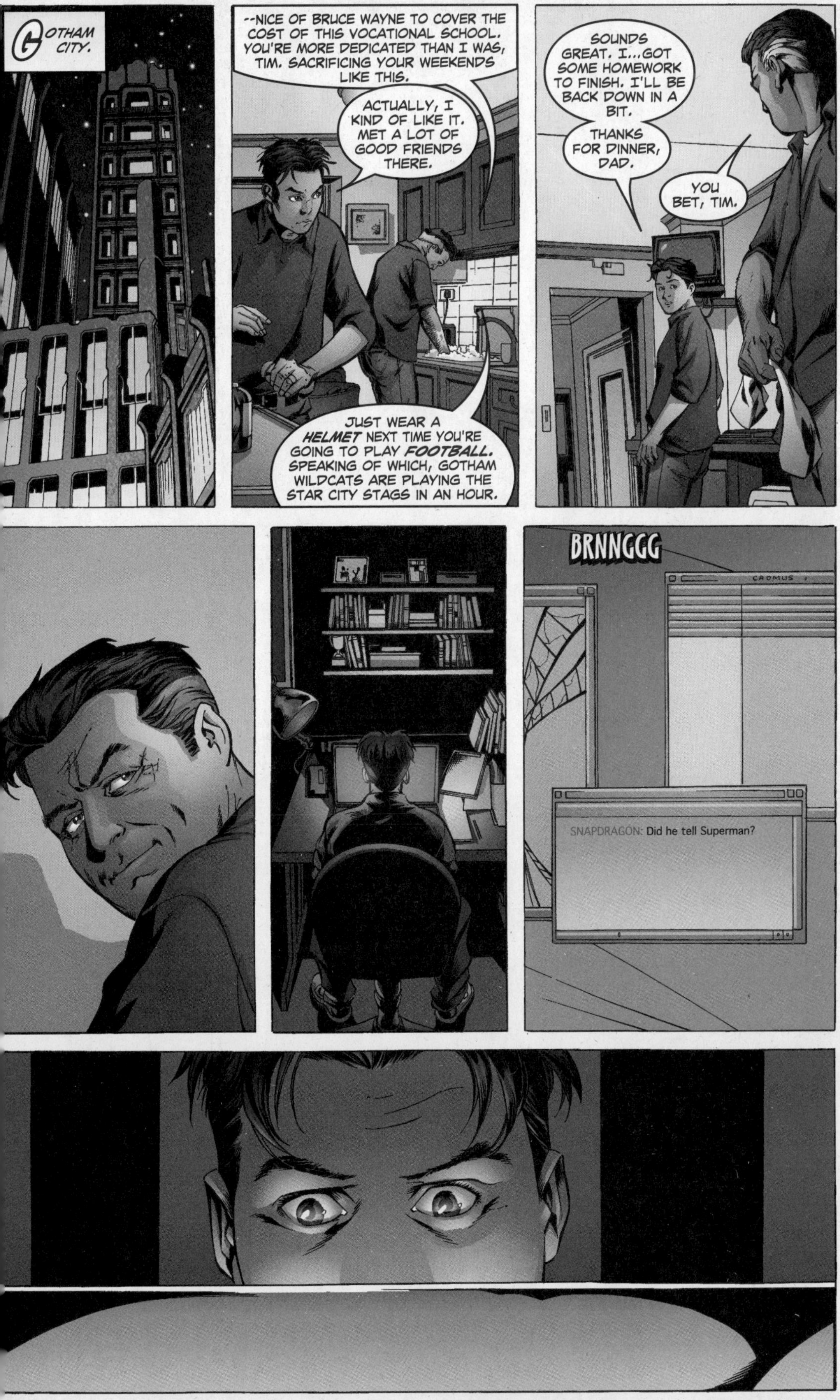
GOTHAM CITY.
--NICE OF BRUCE WAYNE TO COVER THE COST OF THIS VOCATIONAL SCHOOL. YOU'RE MORE DEDICATED THAN I WAS, TIM. SACRIFICING YOUR WEEKENDS LIKE THIS.
ACTUALLY, I KIND OF LIKE IT. MET A LOT OF GOOD FRIENDS THERE.
JUST WEAR A HELMET NEXT TIME YOU'RE GOING TO PLAY FOOTBALL. SPEAKING OF WHICH, GOTHAM WILDCATS ARE PLAYING THE STAR CITY STAGS IN AN HOUR.
SOUNDS GREAT. I...GOT SOME HOMEWORK TO FINISH. I'LL BE BACK DOWN IN A BIT.
THANKS FOR DINNER, DAD.
YOU BET, TIM.
BRNNGGG
CADMUS
SNAPDRAGON: Did he tell Superman?

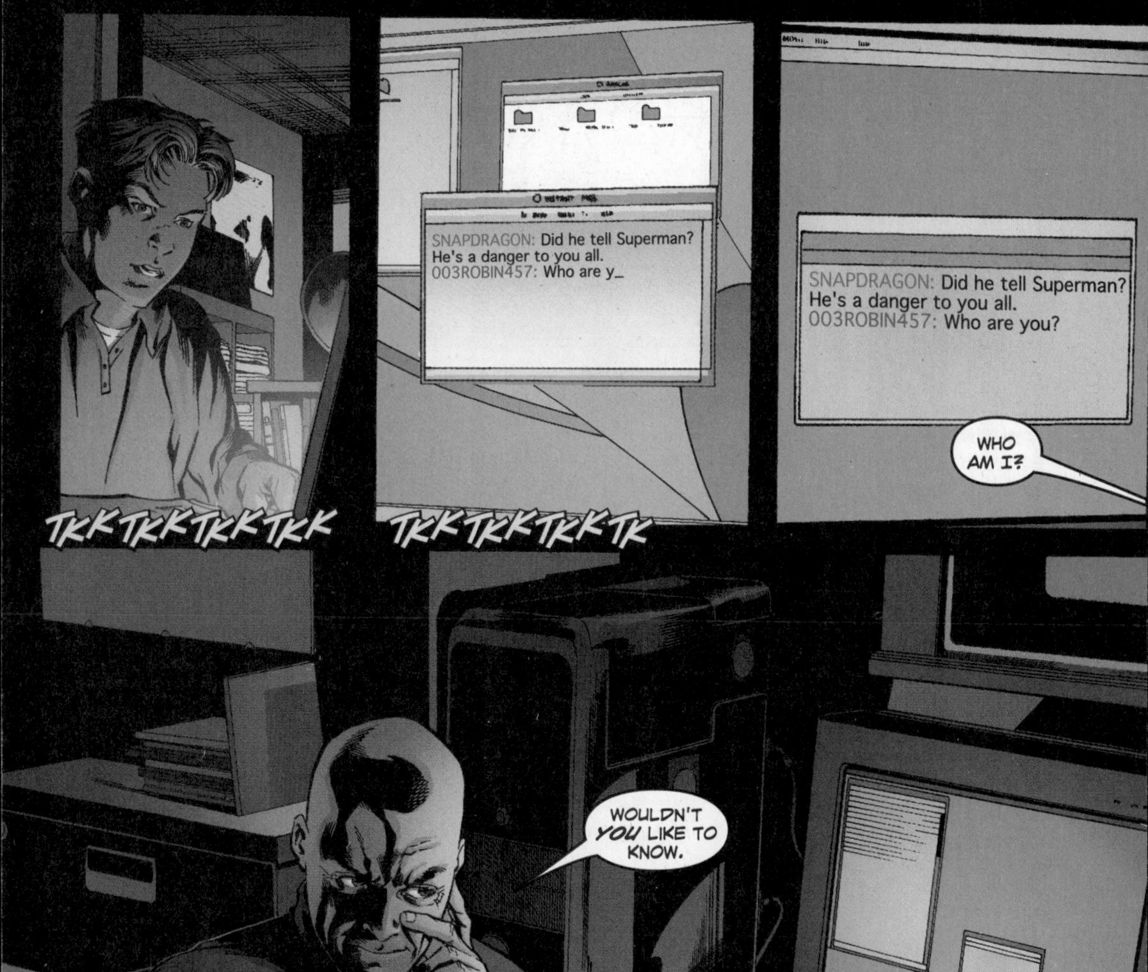
TKKTKKTKKTKK
SNAPDRAGON: Did he tell Superman? He's a danger to you all. 003ROBIN457: Who are y_
TKKTKKTKKTK
SNAPDRAGON: Did he tell Superman? He's a danger to you all. 003ROBIN457: Who are you?
WHO AM I?
WOULDN'T YOU LIKE TO KNOW.
THE END.

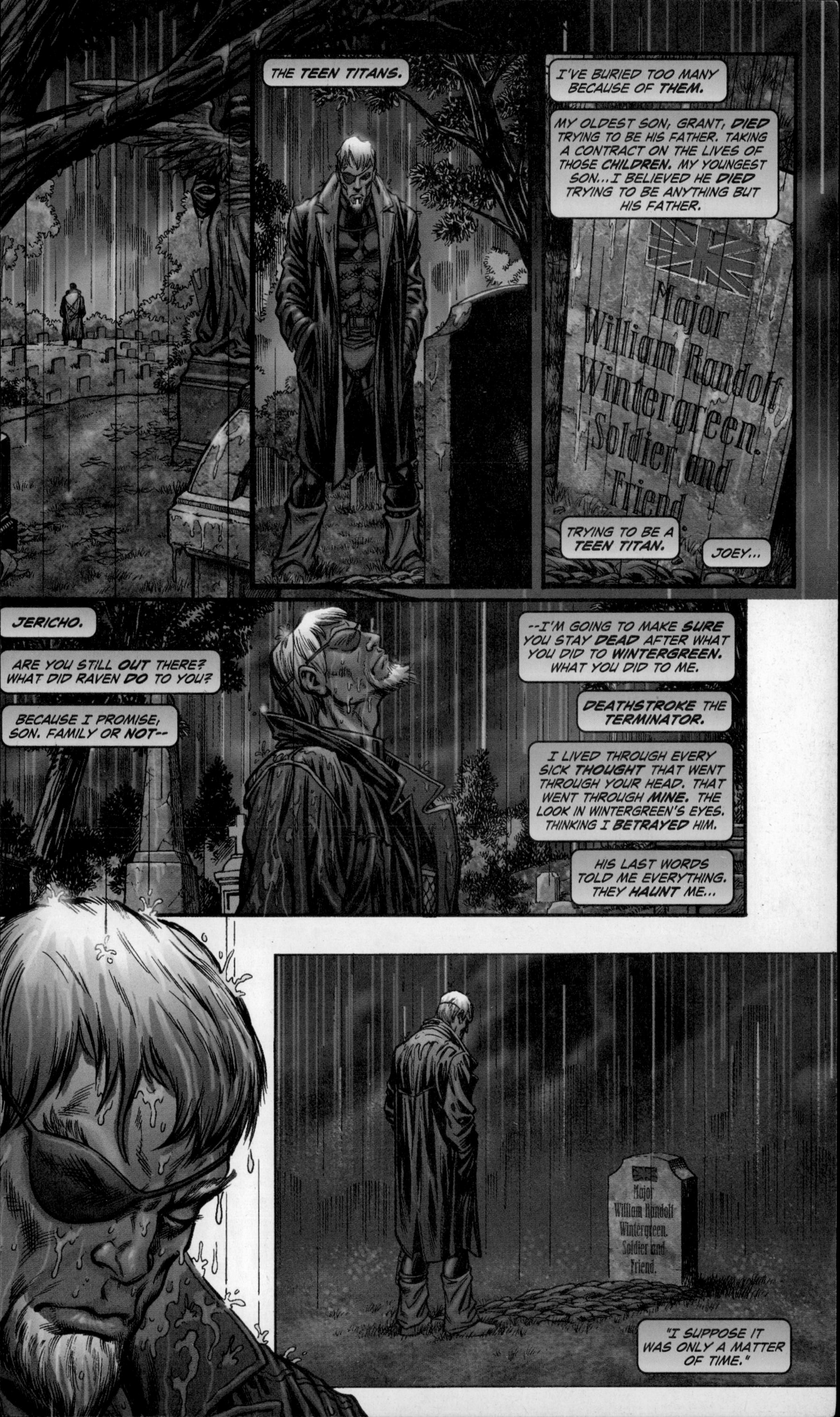
THE TEEN TITANS.
I'VE BURIED TOO MANY BECAUSE OF THEM.
MY OLDEST SON, GRANT, DIED TRYING TO BE HIS FATHER. TAKING A CONTRACT ON THE LIVES OF THOSE CHILDREN. MY YOUNGEST SON... I BELIEVED HE DIED TRYING TO BE ANYTHING BUT HIS FATHER.
Major William Randolf Wintergreen. Soldier and Friend.
TRYING TO BE A TEEN TITAN.
JOEY...
JERICHO.
ARE YOU STILL OUT THERE? WHAT DID RAVEN DO TO YOU?
BECAUSE I PROMISE, SON. FAMILY OR NOT--
--I'M GOING TO MAKE SURE YOU STAY DEAD AFTER WHAT YOU DID TO WINTERGREEN. WHAT YOU DID TO ME.
DEATHSTROKE THE TERMINATOR.
I LIVED THROUGH EVERY SICK THOUGHT THAT WENT THROUGH YOUR HEAD. THAT WENT THROUGH MINE. THE LOOK IN WINTERGREEN'S EYES. THINKING I BETRAYED HIM.
HIS LAST WORDS TOLD ME EVERYTHING. THEY HAUNT ME...
Major William Randolf Wintergreen. Soldier and Friend.
"I SUPPOSE IT WAS ONLY A MATTER OF TIME."

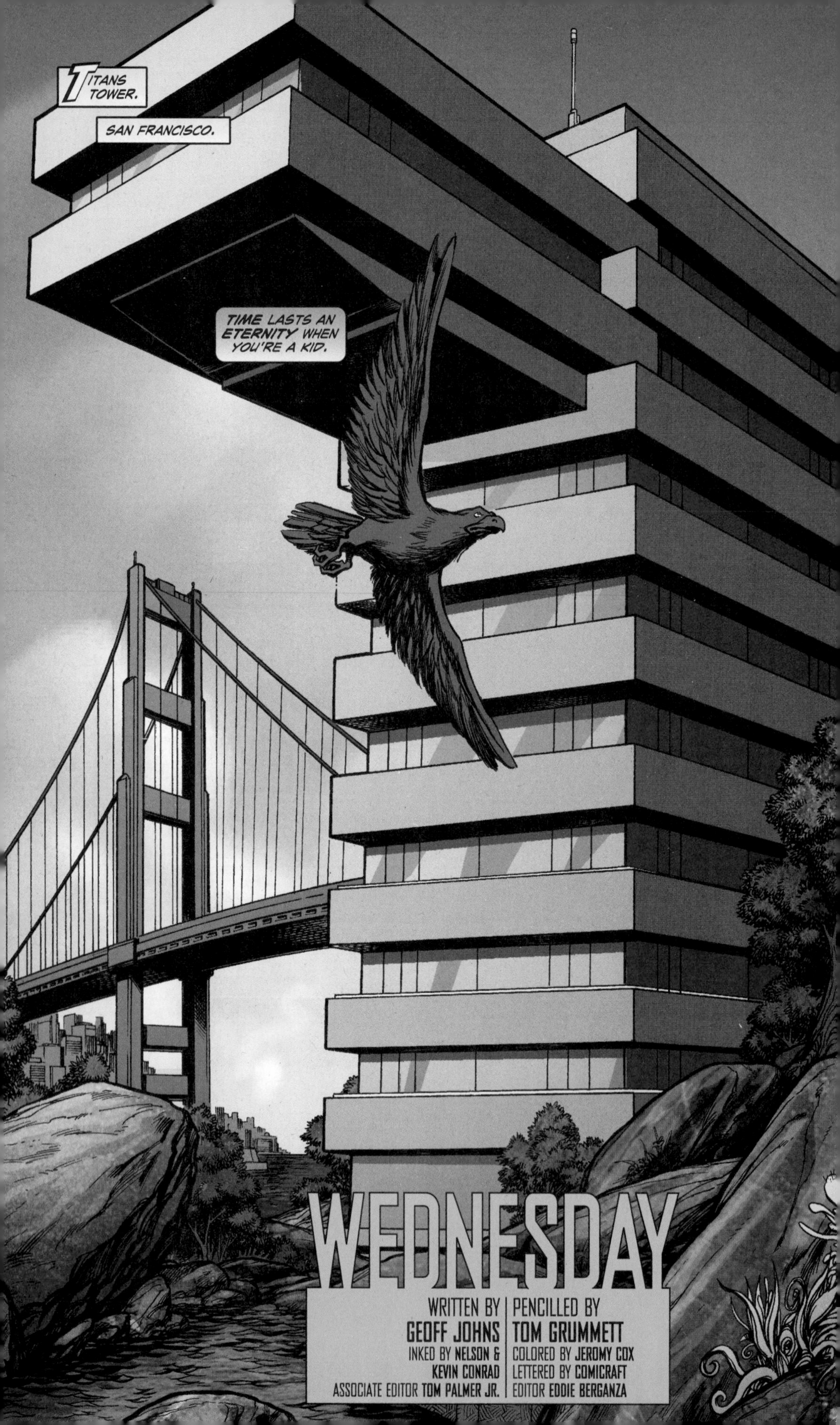
TITANS TOWER.
SAN FRANCISCO.
TIME LASTS AN ETERNITY WHEN YOU'RE A KID.
WEDNESDAY
WRITTEN BY GEOFF JOHNS
PENCILLED BY TOM GRUMMETT
INKED BY NELSON & KEVIN CONRAD
COLORED BY JEROMY COX
LETTERED BY COMICRAFT
ASSOCIATE EDITOR TOM PALMER JR.
EDITOR EDDIE BERGANZA

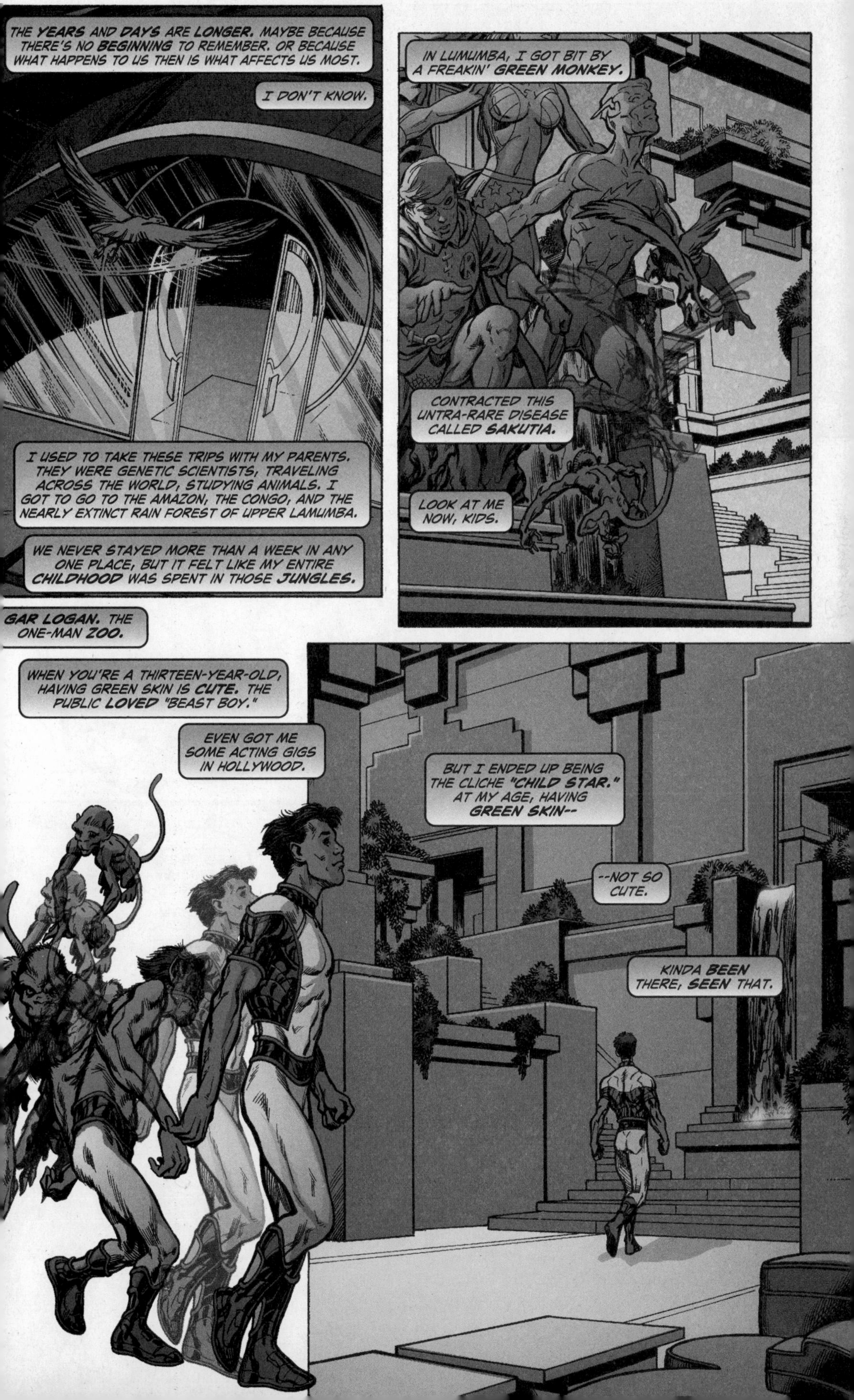
THE YEARS AND DAYS ARE LONGER. MAYBE BECAUSE THERE'S NO BEGINNING TO REMEMBER. OR BECAUSE WHAT HAPPENS TO US THEN IS WHAT AFFECTS US MOST.
I DON'T KNOW.
I USED TO TAKE THESE TRIPS WITH MY PARENTS. THEY WERE GENETIC SCIENTISTS, TRAVELING ACROSS THE WORLD, STUDYING ANIMALS. I GOT TO GO TO THE AMAZON, THE CONGO, AND THE NEARLY EXTINCT RAIN FOREST OF UPPER LAMUMBA.
WE NEVER STAYED MORE THAN A WEEK IN ANY ONE PLACE, BUT IT FELT LIKE MY ENTIRE CHILDHOOD WAS SPENT IN THOSE JUNGLES.
IN LUMUMBA, I GOT BIT BY A FREAKIN' GREEN MONKEY.
CONTRACTED THIS UNTRA-RARE DISEASE CALLED SAKUTIA.
LOOK AT ME NOW, KIDS.
GAR LOGAN. THE ONE-MAN ZOO.
WHEN YOU'RE A THIRTEEN-YEAR-OLD, HAVING GREEN SKIN IS CUTE. THE PUBLIC LOVED "BEAST BOY."
EVEN GOT ME SOME ACTING GIGS IN HOLLYWOOD.
BUT I ENDED UP BEING THE CLICHE "CHILD STAR." AT MY AGE, HAVING GREEN SKIN--
--NOT SO CUTE.
KINDA BEEN THERE, SEEN THAT.

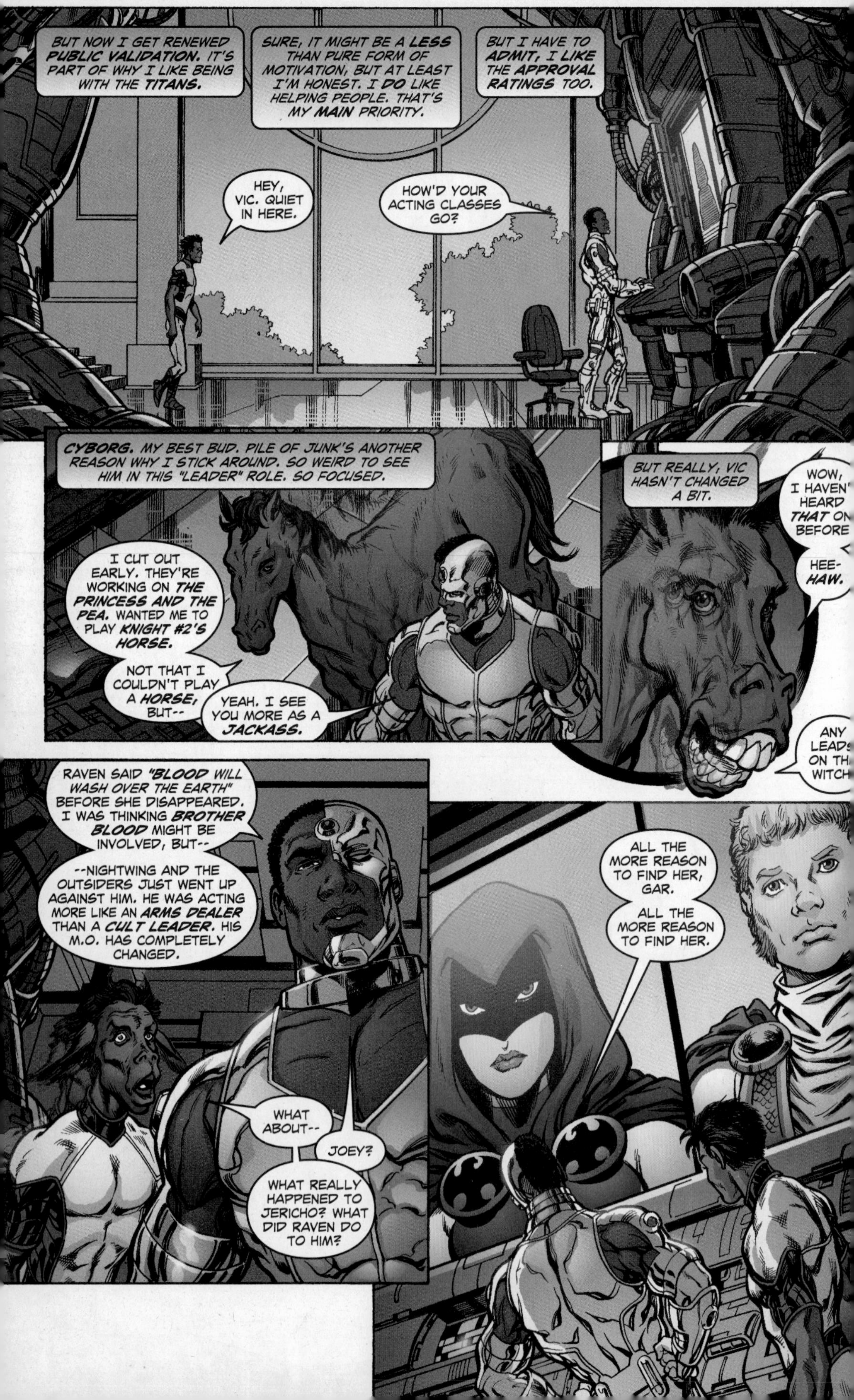
BUT NOW I GET RENEWED PUBLIC VALIDATION. IT'S PART OF WHY I LIKE BEING WITH THE TITANS.
SURE, IT MIGHT BE A LESS THAN PURE FORM OF MOTIVATION, BUT AT LEAST I'M HONEST. I DO LIKE HELPING PEOPLE. THAT'S MY MAIN PRIORITY.
BUT I HAVE TO ADMIT, I LIKE THE APPROVAL RATINGS TOO.
HEY, VIC. QUIET IN HERE.
HOW'D YOUR ACTING CLASSES GO?
CYBORG. MY BEST BUD. PILE OF JUNK'S ANOTHER REASON WHY I STICK AROUND. SO WEIRD TO SEE HIM IN THIS "LEADER" ROLE. SO FOCUSED.
I CUT OUT EARLY. THEY'RE WORKING ON THE PRINCESS AND THE PEA. WANTED ME TO PLAY KNIGHT #2'S HORSE.
NOT THAT I COULDN'T PLAY A HORSE, BUT--
YEAH. I SEE YOU MORE AS A JACKASS.
BUT REALLY, VIC HASN'T CHANGED A BIT.
WOW, I HAVEN' HEARD THAT ON BEFORE
HEE-HAW.
ANY LEADS ON TH WITCH
RAVEN SAID "BLOOD WILL WASH OVER THE EARTH" BEFORE SHE DISAPPEARED. I WAS THINKING BROTHER BLOOD MIGHT BE INVOLVED, BUT--
--NIGHTWING AND THE OUTSIDERS JUST WENT UP AGAINST HIM. HE WAS ACTING MORE LIKE AN ARMS DEALER THAN A CULT LEADER. HIS M.O. HAS COMPLETELY CHANGED.
WHAT ABOUT--
JOEY?
WHAT REALLY HAPPENED TO JERICHO? WHAT DID RAVEN DO TO HIM?
ALL THE MORE REASON TO FIND HER, GAR.
ALL THE MORE REASON TO FIND HER.

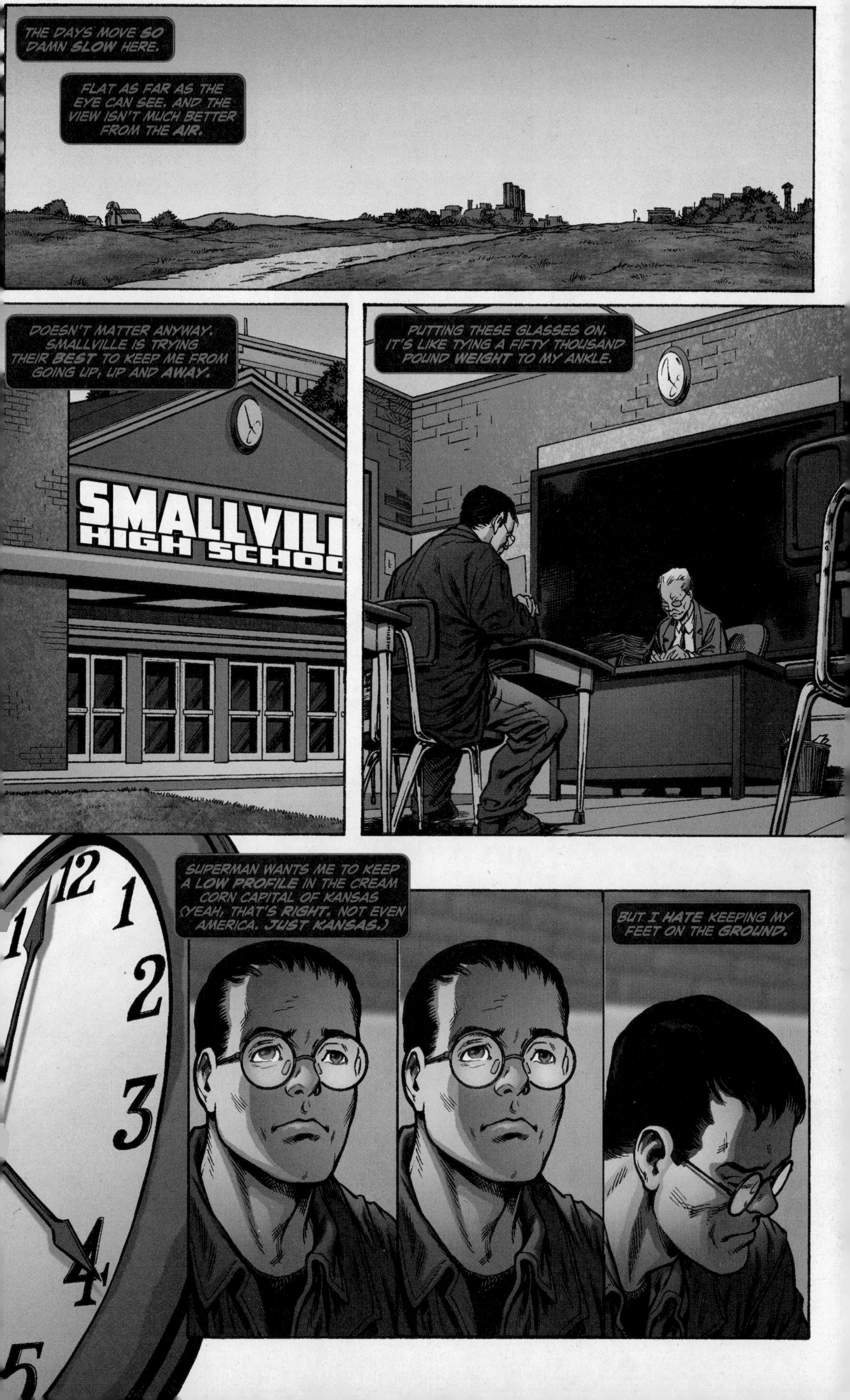
THE DAYS MOVE SO DAMN SLOW HERE.
FLAT AS FAR AS THE EYE CAN SEE. AND THE VIEW ISN'T MUCH BETTER FROM THE AIR.
DOESN'T MATTER ANYWAY. SMALLVILLE IS TRYING THEIR BEST TO KEEP ME FROM GOING UP, UP AND AWAY.
SMALLVILL
HIGH SCHOO
PUTTING THESE GLASSES ON. IT'S LIKE TYING A FIFTY THOUSAND POUND WEIGHT TO MY ANKLE.
SUPERMAN WANTS ME TO KEEP A LOW PROFILE IN THE CREAM CORN CAPITAL OF KANSAS (YEAH, THAT'S RIGHT, NOT EVEN AMERICA. JUST KANSAS.)
BUT I HATE KEEPING MY FEET ON THE GROUND.

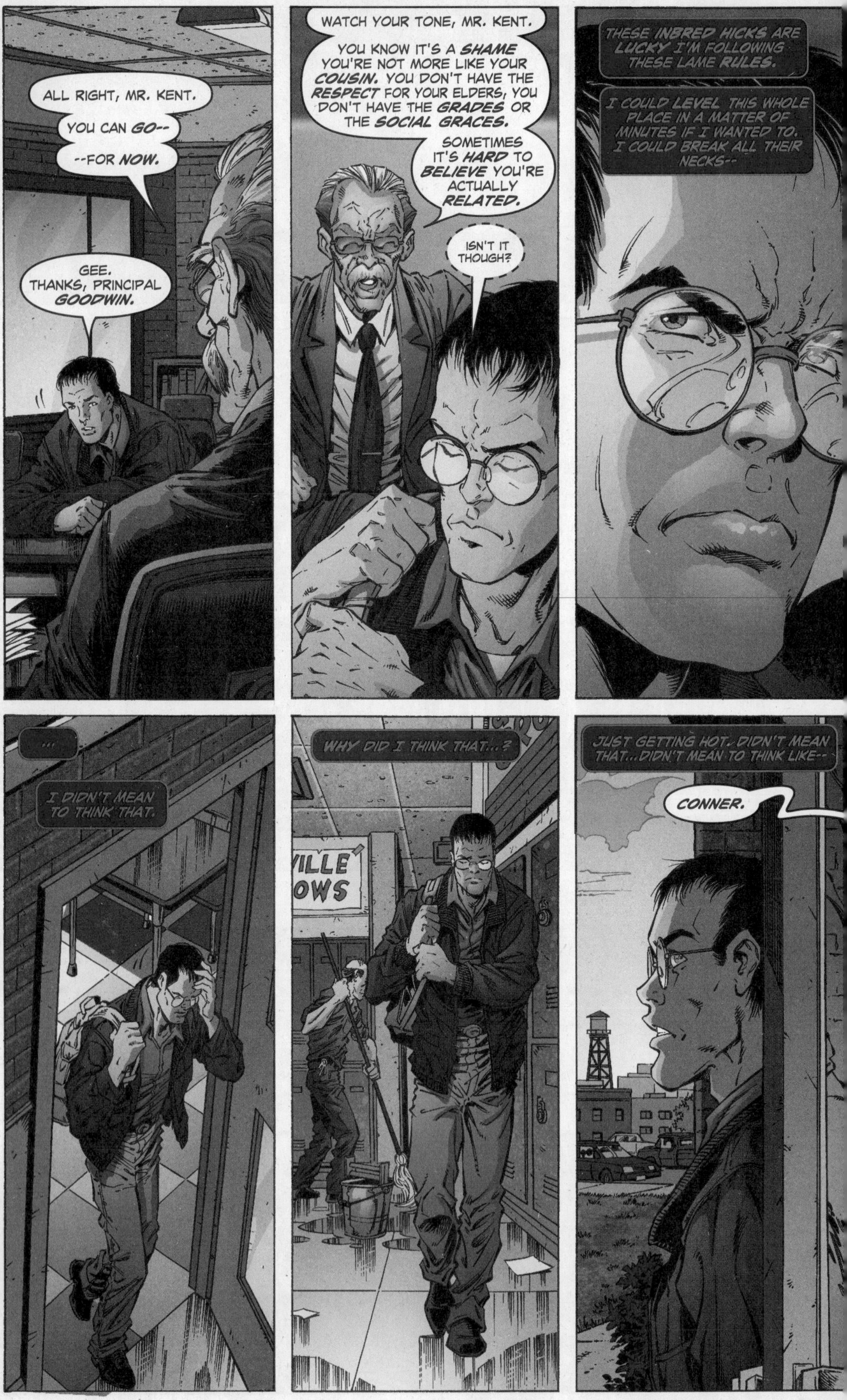
ALL RIGHT, MR. KENT.
YOU CAN GO--
--FOR NOW.
GEE. THANKS, PRINCIPAL GOODWIN.
WATCH YOUR TONE, MR. KENT.
YOU KNOW IT'S A SHAME YOU'RE NOT MORE LIKE YOUR COUSIN. YOU DON'T HAVE THE RESPECT FOR YOUR ELDERS, YOU DON'T HAVE THE GRADES OR THE SOCIAL GRACES.
SOMETIMES IT'S HARD TO BELIEVE YOU'RE ACTUALLY RELATED.
ISN'T IT THOUGH?
THESE INBRED HICKS ARE LUCKY I'M FOLLOWING THESE LAME RULES.
I COULD LEVEL THIS WHOLE PLACE IN A MATTER OF MINUTES IF I WANTED TO. I COULD BREAK ALL THEIR NECKS--
...
I DIDN'T MEAN TO THINK THAT.
WHY DID I THINK THAT...?
VILLE
OWS
JUST GETTING HOT. DIDN'T MEAN THAT...DIDN'T MEAN TO THINK LIKE--
CONNER.

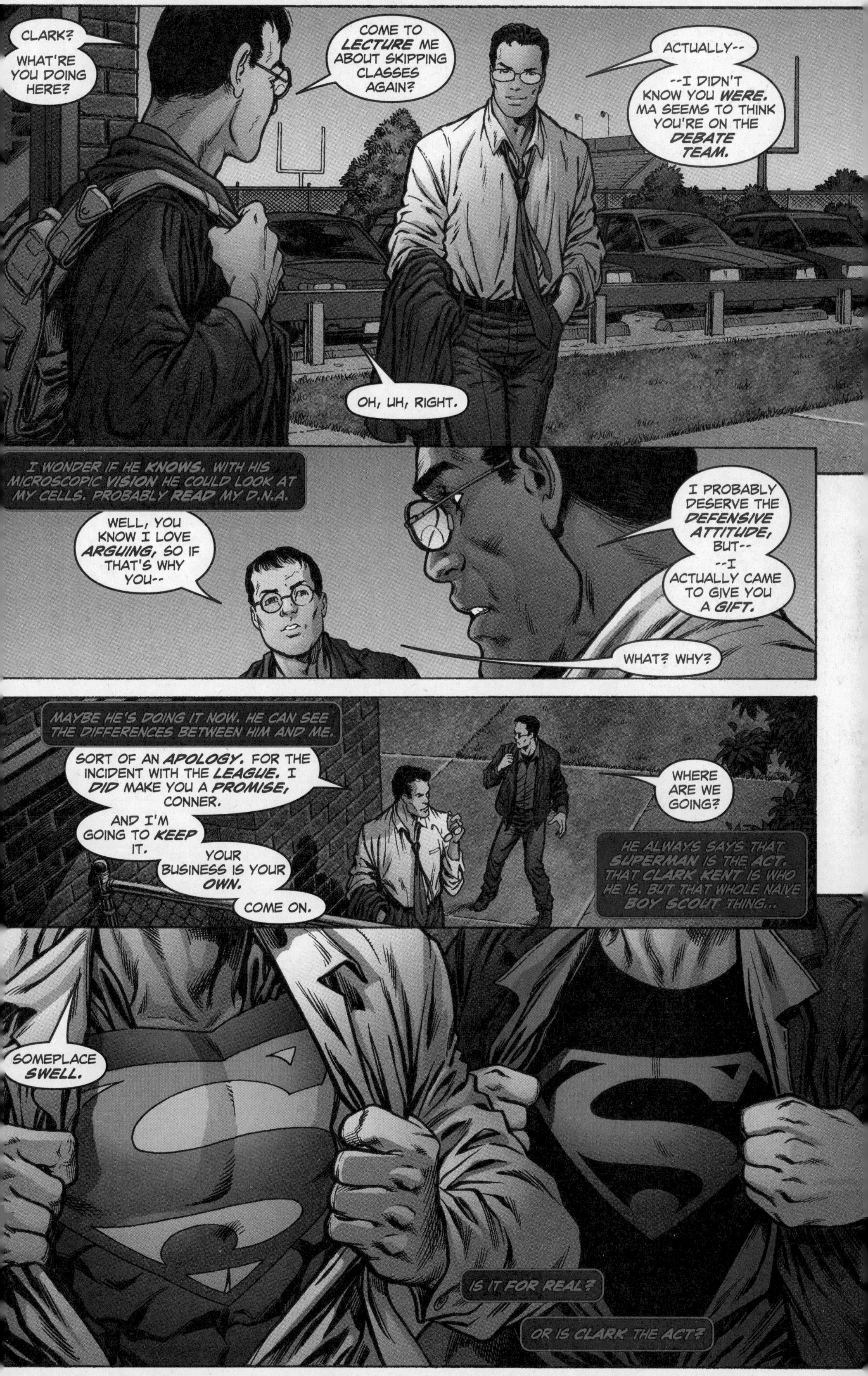
CLARK? WHAT'RE YOU DOING HERE?
COME TO LECTURE ME ABOUT SKIPPING CLASSES AGAIN?
ACTUALLY--
--I DIDN'T KNOW YOU WERE. MA SEEMS TO THINK YOU'RE ON THE DEBATE TEAM.
OH, UH, RIGHT.
I WONDER IF HE KNOWS. WITH HIS MICROSCOPIC VISION HE COULD LOOK AT MY CELLS. PROBABLY READ MY D.N.A.
WELL, YOU KNOW I LOVE ARGUING, SO IF THAT'S WHY YOU--
I PROBABLY DESERVE THE DEFENSIVE ATTITUDE, BUT--
--I ACTUALLY CAME TO GIVE YOU A GIFT.
WHAT? WHY?
MAYBE HE'S DOING IT NOW. HE CAN SEE THE DIFFERENCES BETWEEN HIM AND ME.
SORT OF AN APOLOGY. FOR THE INCIDENT WITH THE LEAGUE. I DID MAKE YOU A PROMISE, CONNER.
AND I'M GOING TO KEEP IT.
YOUR BUSINESS IS YOUR OWN.
COME ON.
WHERE ARE WE GOING?
HE ALWAYS SAYS THAT SUPERMAN IS THE ACT. THAT CLARK KENT IS WHO HE IS. BUT THAT WHOLE NAIVE BOY SCOUT THING...
SOMEPLACE SWELL.
IS IT FOR REAL?
OR IS CLARK THE ACT?

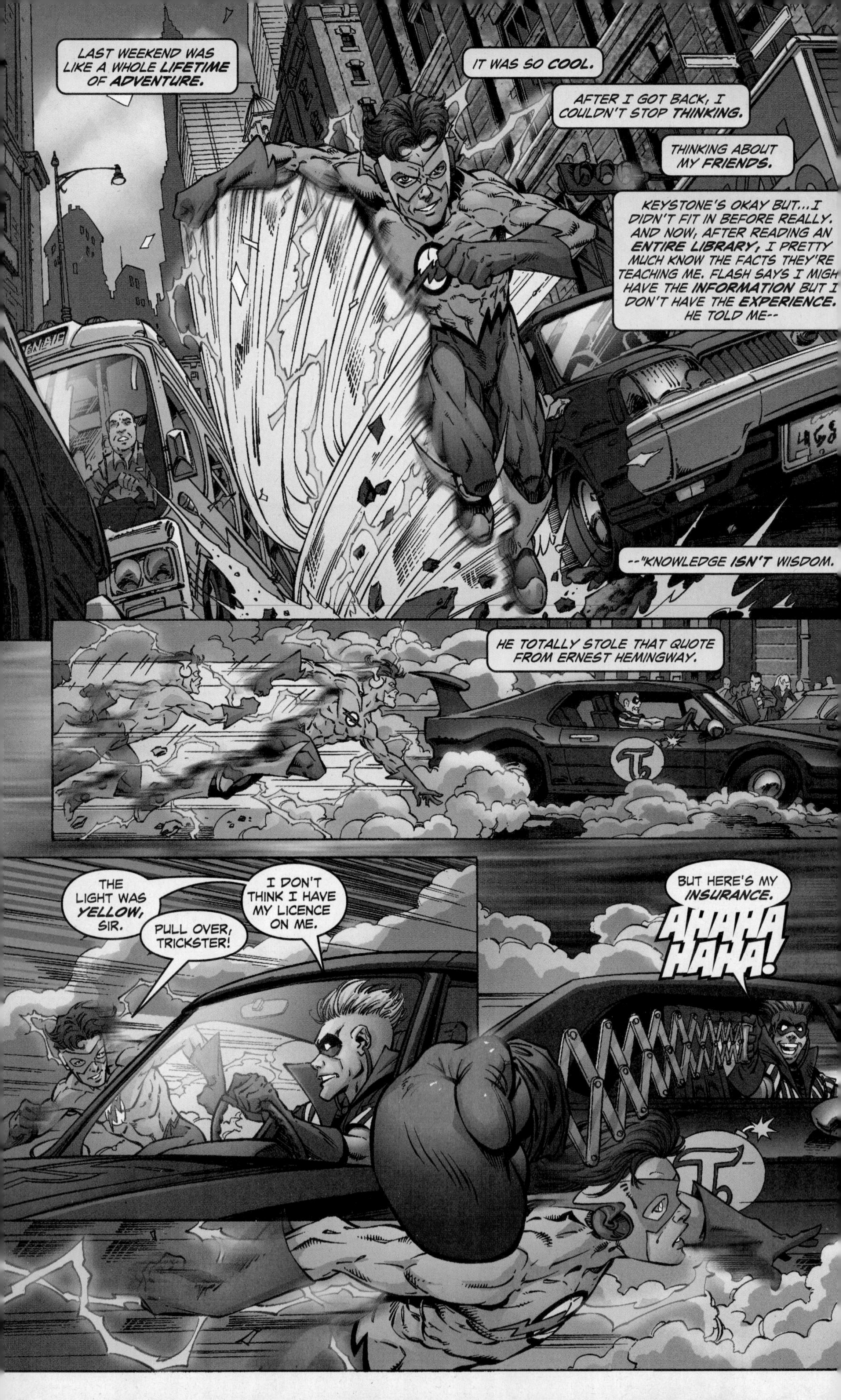
LAST WEEKEND WAS LIKE A WHOLE LIFETIME OF ADVENTURE.
IT WAS SO COOL.
AFTER I GOT BACK, I COULDN'T STOP THINKING.
THINKING ABOUT MY FRIENDS.
KEYSTONE'S OKAY BUT...I DIDN'T FIT IN BEFORE REALLY. AND NOW, AFTER READING AN ENTIRE LIBRARY, I PRETTY MUCH KNOW THE FACTS THEY'RE TEACHING ME. FLASH SAYS I MIGH HAVE THE INFORMATION BUT I DON'T HAVE THE EXPERIENCE. HE TOLD ME--
--"KNOWLEDGE ISN'T WISDOM.
HE TOTALLY STOLE THAT QUOTE FROM ERNEST HEMINGWAY.
PULL OVER, TRICKSTER!
THE LIGHT WAS YELLOW, SIR.
I DON'T THINK I HAVE MY LICENCE ON ME.
BUT HERE'S MY INSURANCE.
AHAHA HAHA!

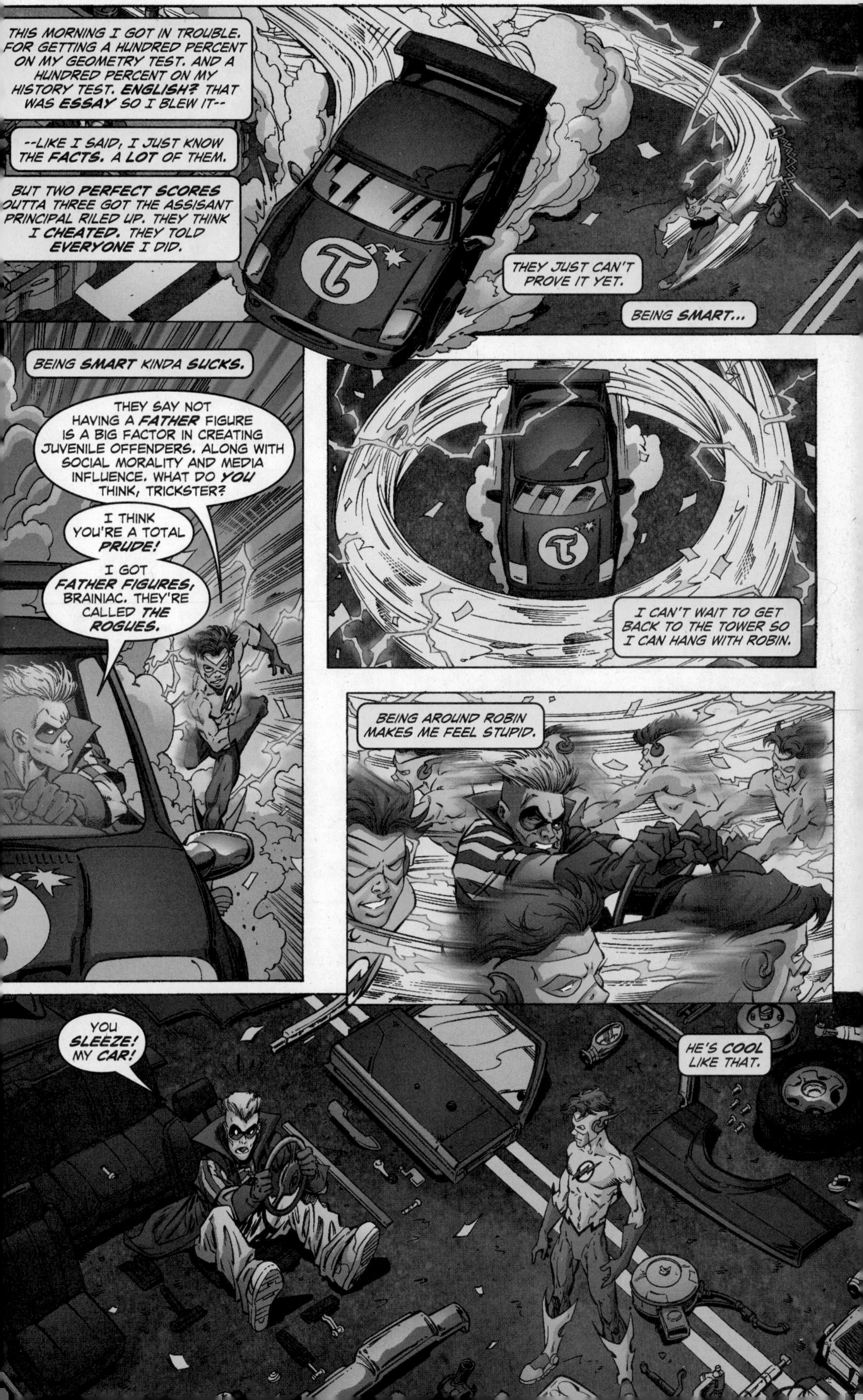
THIS MORNING I GOT IN TROUBLE. FOR GETTING A HUNDRED PERCENT ON MY GEOMETRY TEST. AND A HUNDRED PERCENT ON MY HISTORY TEST. ENGLISH? THAT WAS ESSAY SO I BLEW IT--
--LIKE I SAID, I JUST KNOW THE FACTS. A LOT OF THEM.
BUT TWO PERFECT SCORES OUTTA THREE GOT THE ASSISANT PRINCIPAL RILED UP. THEY THINK I CHEATED. THEY TOLD EVERYONE I DID.
THEY JUST CAN'T PROVE IT YET.
BEING SMART...
BEING SMART KINDA SUCKS.
THEY SAY NOT HAVING A FATHER FIGURE IS A BIG FACTOR IN CREATING JUVENILE OFFENDERS. ALONG WITH SOCIAL MORALITY AND MEDIA INFLUENCE. WHAT DO YOU THINK, TRICKSTER?
I THINK YOU'RE A TOTAL PRUDE!
I GOT FATHER FIGURES, BRAINIAC. THEY'RE CALLED THE ROGUES.
I CAN'T WAIT TO GET BACK TO THE TOWER SO I CAN HANG WITH ROBIN.
BEING AROUND ROBIN MAKES ME FEEL STUPID.
YOU SLEEZE! MY CAR!
HE'S COOL LIKE THAT.

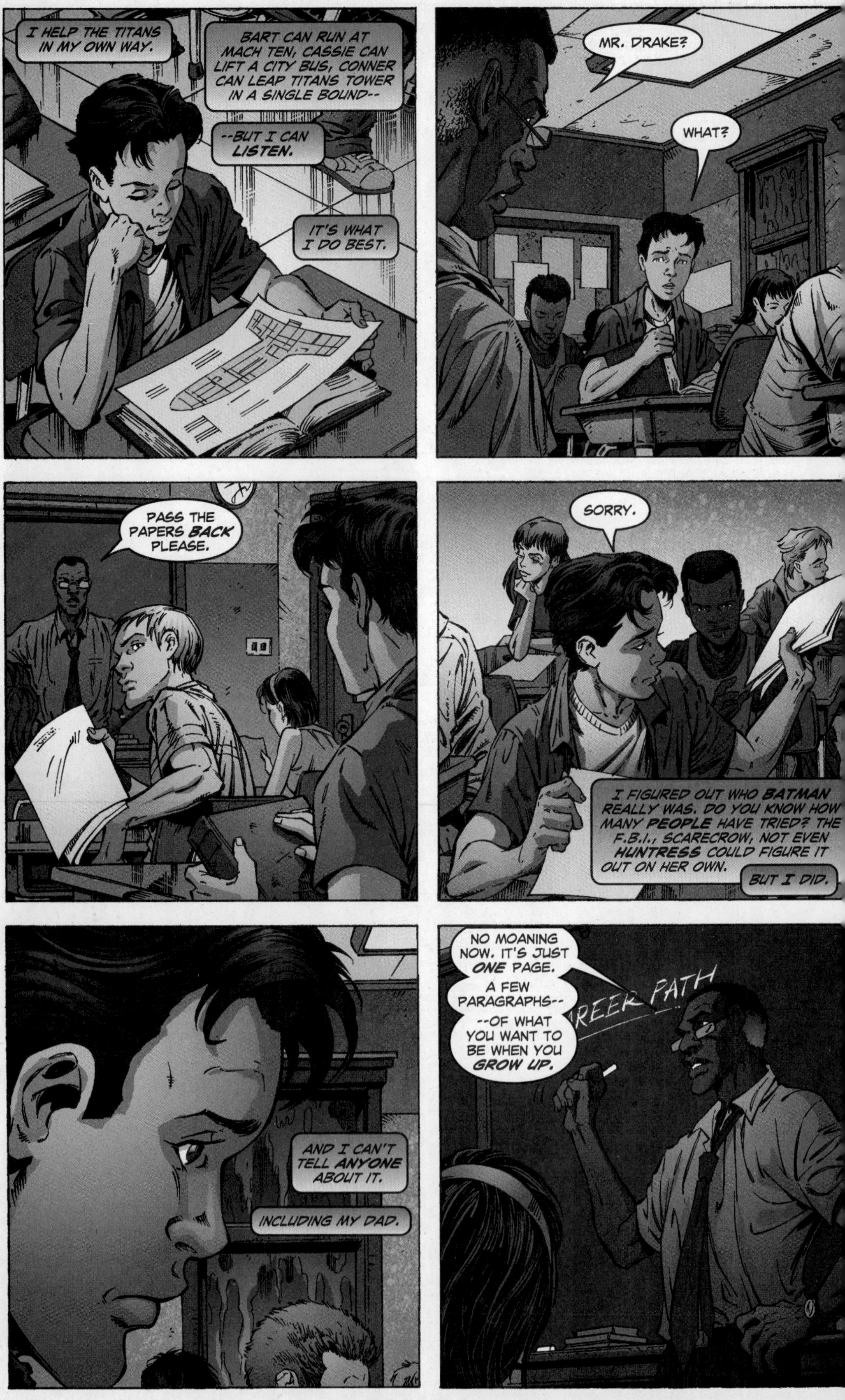
I HELP THE TITANS IN MY OWN WAY.
BART CAN RUN AT MACH TEN, CASSIE CAN LIFT A CITY BUS, CONNER CAN LEAP TITANS TOWER IN A SINGLE BOUND--
--BUT I CAN LISTEN.
IT'S WHAT I DO BEST.
MR. DRAKE?
WHAT?
PASS THE PAPERS BACK PLEASE.
SORRY.
I FIGURED OUT WHO BATMAN REALLY WAS. DO YOU KNOW HOW MANY PEOPLE HAVE TRIED? THE F.B.I., SCARECROW, NOT EVEN HUNTRESS COULD FIGURE IT OUT ON HER OWN.
BUT I DID.
AND I CAN'T TELL ANYONE ABOUT IT.
INCLUDING MY DAD.
NO MOANING NOW. IT'S JUST ONE PAGE.
A FEW PARAGRAPHS--
--OF WHAT YOU WANT TO BE WHEN YOU GROW UP.
CAREER PATH

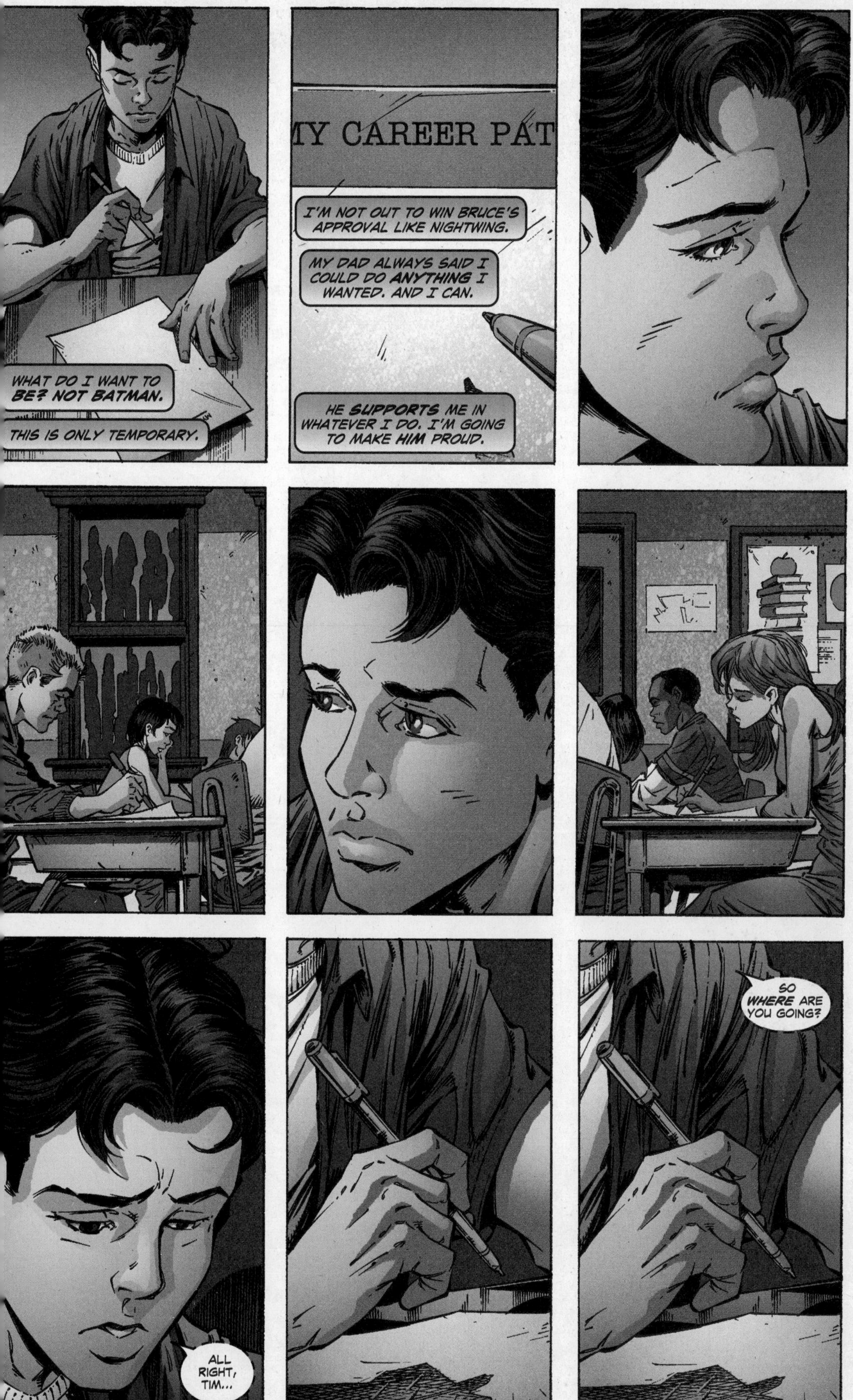
WHAT DO I WANT TO BE? NOT BATMAN.
THIS IS ONLY TEMPORARY.
MY CAREER PAT
I'M NOT OUT TO WIN BRUCE'S APPROVAL LIKE NIGHTWING.
MY DAD ALWAYS SAID I COULD DO ANYTHING I WANTED. AND I CAN.
HE SUPPORTS ME IN WHATEVER I DO. I'M GOING TO MAKE HIM PROUD.
ALL RIGHT, TIM...
SO WHERE ARE YOU GOING?

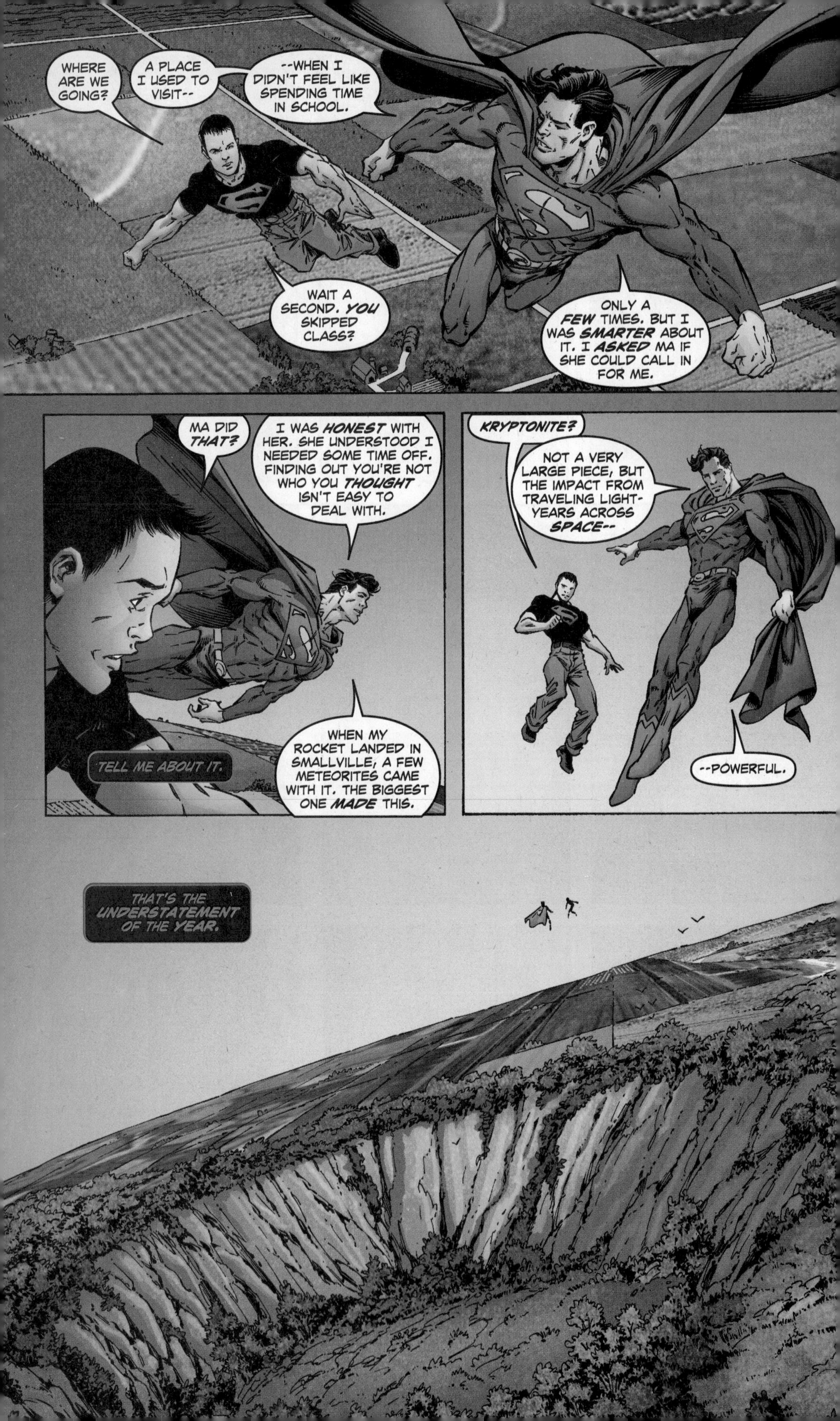
WHERE ARE WE GOING?
A PLACE I USED TO VISIT--
--WHEN I DIDN'T FEEL LIKE SPENDING TIME IN SCHOOL.
WAIT A SECOND. YOU SKIPPED CLASS?
ONLY A FEW TIMES. BUT I WAS SMARTER ABOUT IT. I ASKED MA IF SHE COULD CALL IN FOR ME.
MA DID THAT?
I WAS HONEST WITH HER. SHE UNDERSTOOD I NEEDED SOME TIME OFF. FINDING OUT YOU'RE NOT WHO YOU THOUGHT ISN'T EASY TO DEAL WITH.
TELL ME ABOUT IT.
WHEN MY ROCKET LANDED IN SMALLVILLE, A FEW METEORITES CAME WITH IT. THE BIGGEST ONE MADE THIS.
KRYPTONITE?
NOT A VERY LARGE PIECE, BUT THE IMPACT FROM TRAVELING LIGHT-YEARS ACROSS SPACE--
--POWERFUL.
THAT'S THE UNDERSTATEMENT OF THE YEAR.

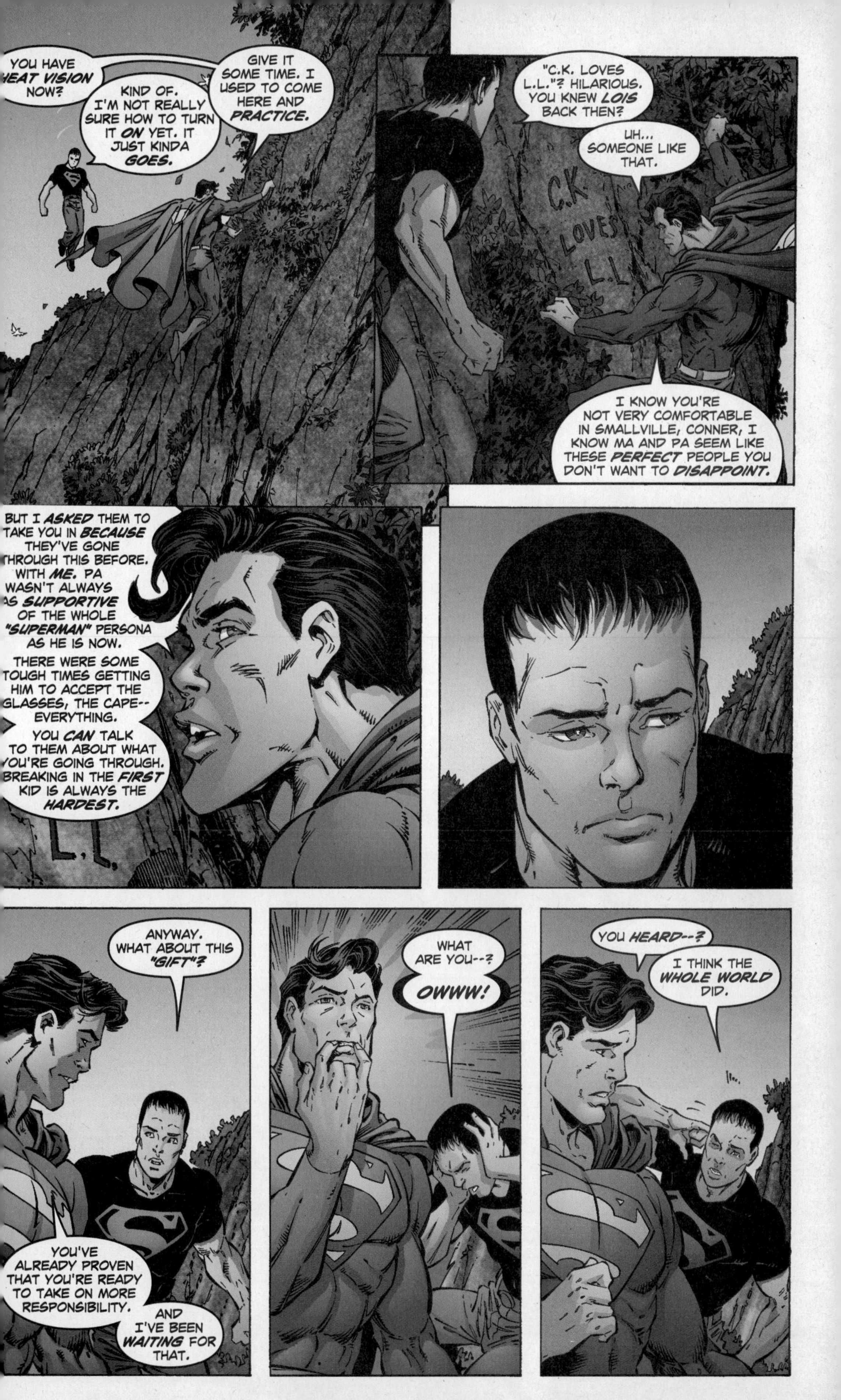

YOU HAVE HEAT VISION NOW?
KIND OF. I'M NOT REALLY SURE HOW TO TURN IT ON YET. IT JUST KINDA GOES.
GIVE IT SOME TIME. I USED TO COME HERE AND PRACTICE.
"C.K. LOVES L.L."? HILARIOUS. YOU KNEW LOIS BACK THEN?
UH... SOMEONE LIKE THAT.
C.K. LOVES L.L.
I KNOW YOU'RE NOT VERY COMFORTABLE IN SMALLVILLE, CONNER, I KNOW MA AND PA SEEM LIKE THESE PERFECT PEOPLE YOU DON'T WANT TO DISAPPOINT.
BUT I ASKED THEM TO TAKE YOU IN BECAUSE THEY'VE GONE THROUGH THIS BEFORE. WITH ME. PA WASN'T ALWAYS AS SUPPORTIVE OF THE WHOLE "SUPERMAN" PERSONA AS HE IS NOW.
THERE WERE SOME TOUGH TIMES GETTING HIM TO ACCEPT THE GLASSES, THE CAPE-- EVERYTHING.
YOU CAN TALK TO THEM ABOUT WHAT YOU'RE GOING THROUGH. BREAKING IN THE FIRST KID IS ALWAYS THE HARDEST.
ANYWAY. WHAT ABOUT THIS "GIFT"?
YOU'VE ALREADY PROVEN THAT YOU'RE READY TO TAKE ON MORE RESPONSIBILITY.
AND I'VE BEEN WAITING FOR THAT.
WHAT ARE YOU--?
OWWW!
YOU HEARD--?
I THINK THE WHOLE WORLD DID.

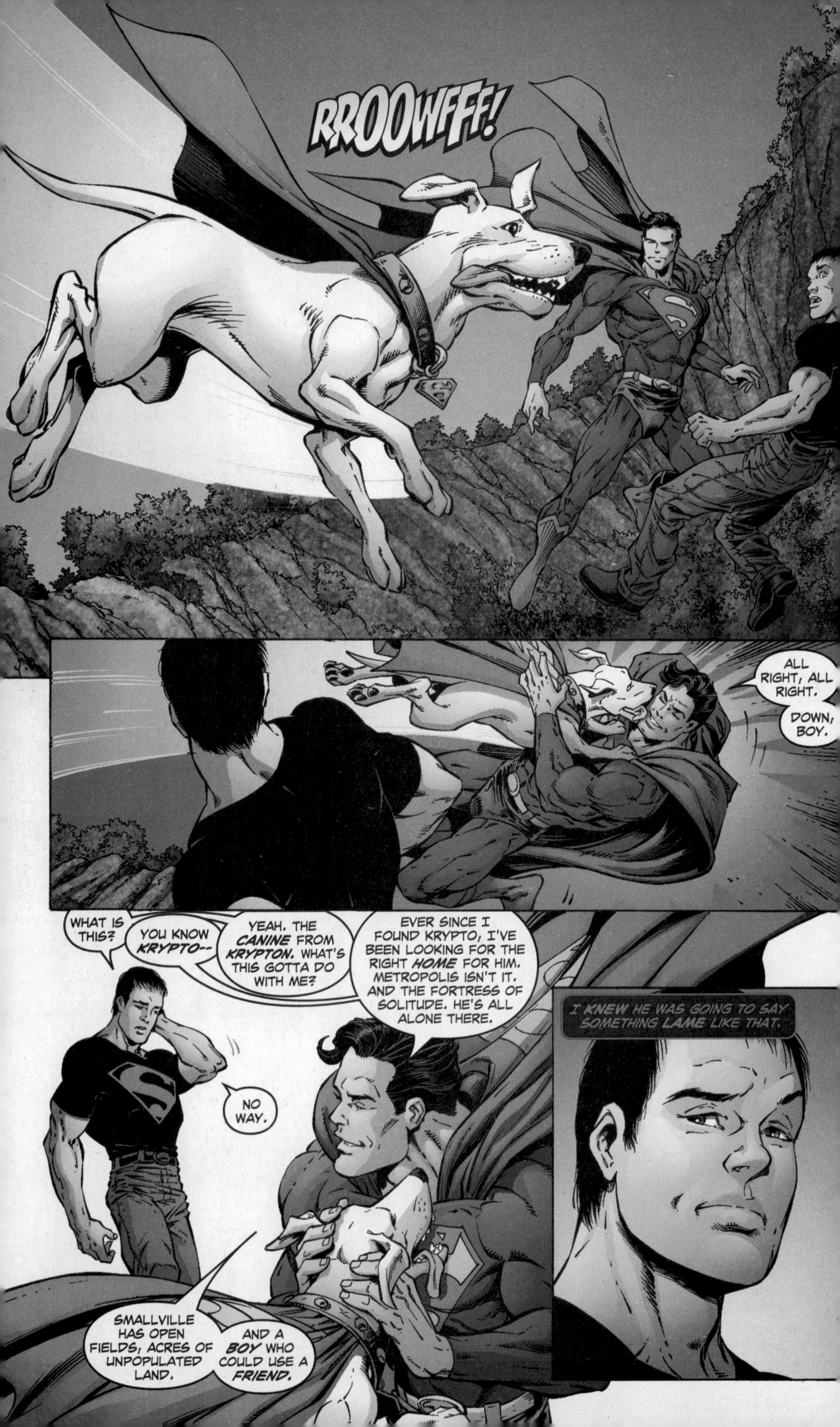
RROOWFFF!
ALL RIGHT, ALL RIGHT.
DOWN, BOY.
WHAT IS THIS?
YOU KNOW KRYPTO--
YEAH. THE CANINE FROM KRYPTON. WHAT'S THIS GOTTA DO WITH ME?
EVER SINCE I FOUND KRYPTO, I'VE BEEN LOOKING FOR THE RIGHT HOME FOR HIM. METROPOLIS ISN'T IT. AND THE FORTRESS OF SOLITUDE. HE'S ALL ALONE THERE.
NO WAY.
SMALLVILLE HAS OPEN FIELDS, ACRES OF UNPOPULATED LAND.
AND A BOY WHO COULD USE A FRIEND.
I KNEW HE WAS GOING TO SAY SOMETHING LAME LIKE THAT.

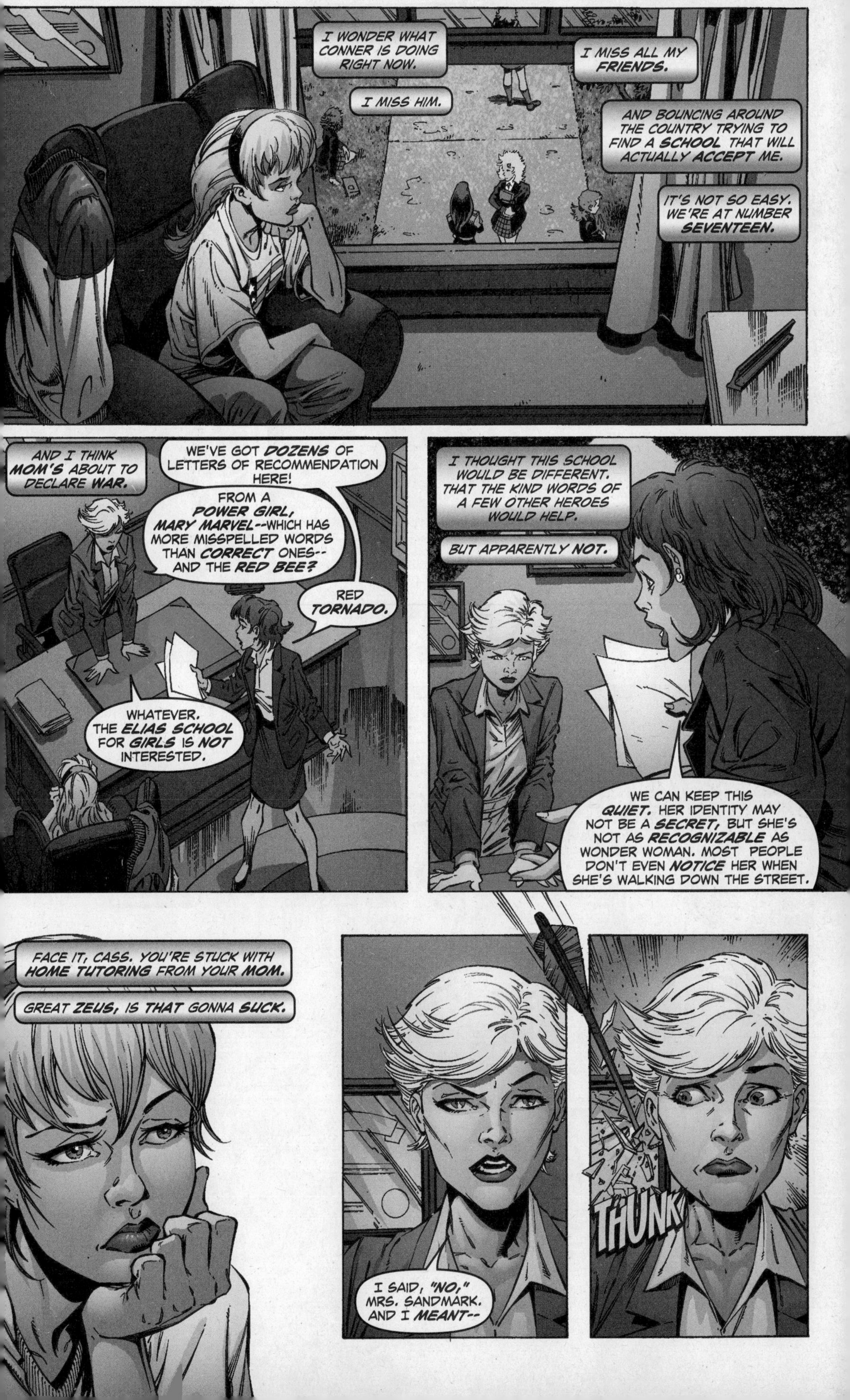
I WONDER WHAT CONNER IS DOING RIGHT NOW.
I MISS HIM.
I MISS ALL MY FRIENDS.
AND BOUNCING AROUND THE COUNTRY TRYING TO FIND A SCHOOL THAT WILL ACTUALLY ACCEPT ME.
IT'S NOT SO EASY. WE'RE AT NUMBER SEVENTEEN.
AND I THINK MOM'S ABOUT TO DECLARE WAR.
WE'VE GOT DOZENS OF LETTERS OF RECOMMENDATION HERE!
FROM A POWER GIRL, MARY MARVEL--WHICH HAS MORE MISSPELLED WORDS THAN CORRECT ONES-- AND THE RED BEE?
RED TORNADO.
WHATEVER. THE ELIAS SCHOOL FOR GIRLS IS NOT INTERESTED.
I THOUGHT THIS SCHOOL WOULD BE DIFFERENT. THAT THE KIND WORDS OF A FEW OTHER HEROES WOULD HELP.
BUT APPARENTLY NOT.
WE CAN KEEP THIS QUIET. HER IDENTITY MAY NOT BE A SECRET, BUT SHE'S NOT AS RECOGNIZABLE AS WONDER WOMAN. MOST PEOPLE DON'T EVEN NOTICE HER WHEN SHE'S WALKING DOWN THE STREET.
FACE IT, CASS. YOU'RE STUCK WITH HOME TUTORING FROM YOUR MOM.
GREAT ZEUS, IS THAT GONNA SUCK.
I SAID, "NO," MRS. SANDMARK. AND I MEANT--
THUNK

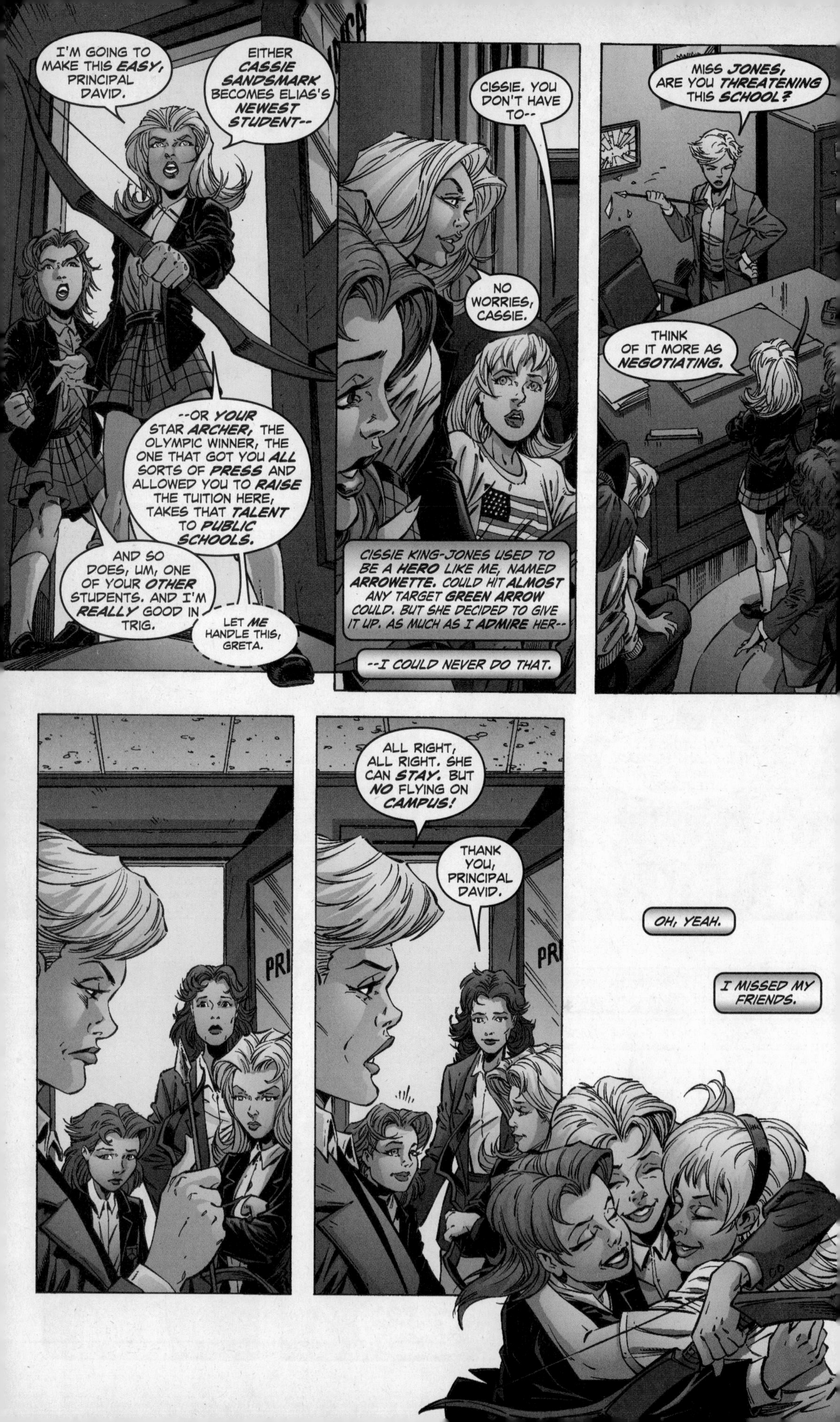
I'M GOING TO MAKE THIS EASY, PRINCIPAL DAVID.
EITHER CASSIE SANDSMARK BECOMES ELIAS'S NEWEST STUDENT--
--OR YOUR STAR ARCHER, THE OLYMPIC WINNER, THE ONE THAT GOT YOU ALL SORTS OF PRESS AND ALLOWED YOU TO RAISE THE TUITION HERE, TAKES THAT TALENT TO PUBLIC SCHOOLS.
AND SO DOES, UM, ONE OF YOUR OTHER STUDENTS. AND I'M REALLY GOOD IN TRIG.
LET ME HANDLE THIS, GRETA.
CISSIE. YOU DON'T HAVE TO--
NO WORRIES, CASSIE.
CISSIE KING-JONES USED TO BE A HERO LIKE ME, NAMED ARROWETTE. COULD HIT ALMOST ANY TARGET GREEN ARROW COULD. BUT SHE DECIDED TO GIVE IT UP. AS MUCH AS I ADMIRE HER--
--I COULD NEVER DO THAT.
MISS JONES, ARE YOU THREATENING THIS SCHOOL?
THINK OF IT MORE AS NEGOTIATING.
ALL RIGHT, ALL RIGHT. SHE CAN STAY. BUT NO FLYING ON CAMPUS!
THANK YOU, PRINCIPAL DAVID.
OH, YEAH.
I MISSED MY FRIENDS.

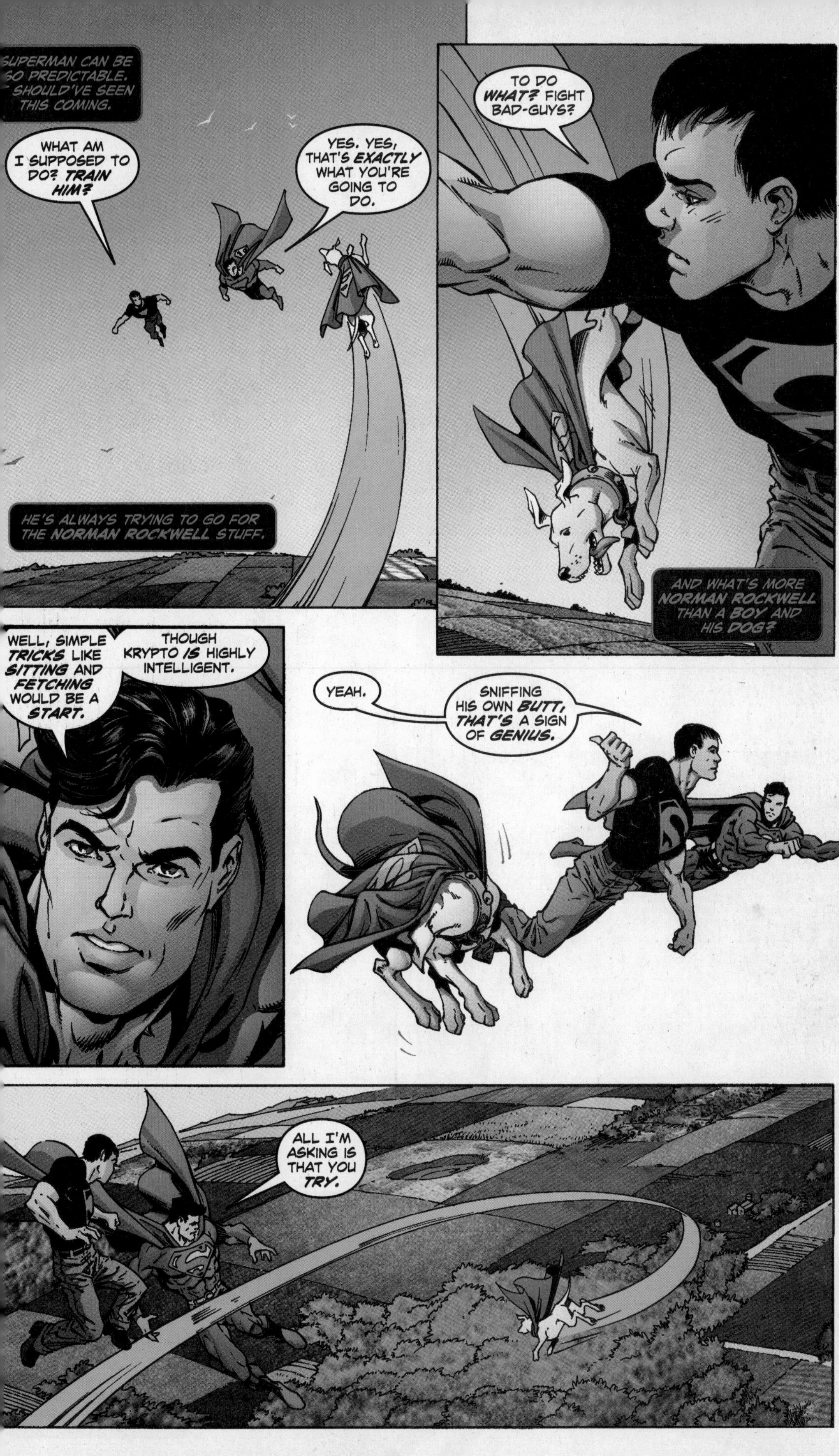

SUPERMAN CAN BE SO PREDICTABLE. I SHOULD'VE SEEN THIS COMING.
WHAT AM I SUPPOSED TO DO? TRAIN HIM?
YES. YES, THAT'S EXACTLY WHAT YOU'RE GOING TO DO.
HE'S ALWAYS TRYING TO GO FOR THE NORMAN ROCKWELL STUFF.
TO DO WHAT? FIGHT BAD-GUYS?
AND WHAT'S MORE NORMAN ROCKWELL THAN A BOY AND HIS DOG?
WELL, SIMPLE TRICKS LIKE SITTING AND FETCHING WOULD BE A START.
THOUGH KRYPTO IS HIGHLY INTELLIGENT.
YEAH.
SNIFFING HIS OWN BUTT, THAT'S A SIGN OF GENIUS.
ALL I'M ASKING IS THAT YOU TRY.

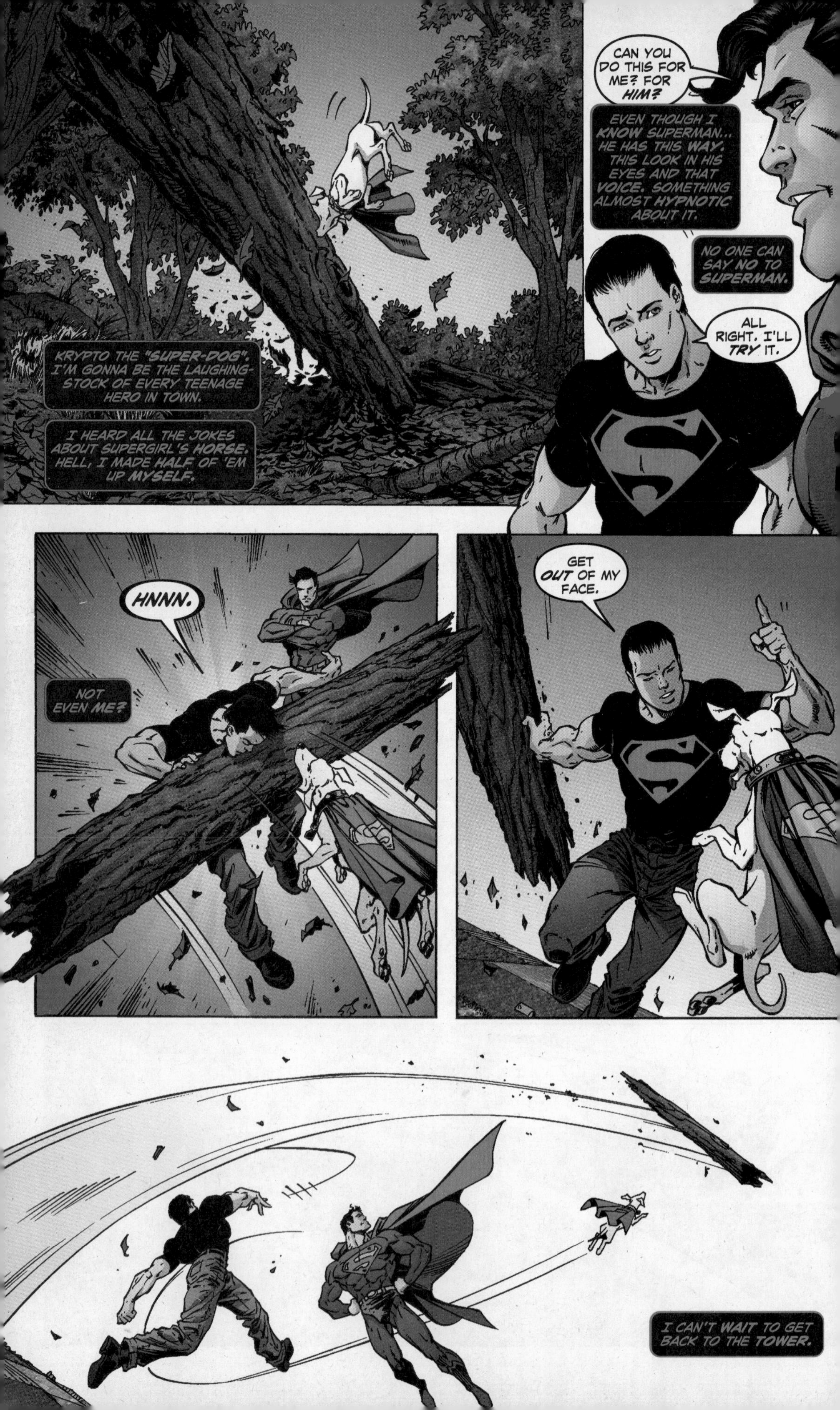
KRYPTO THE "SUPER-DOG". I'M GONNA BE THE LAUGHING-STOCK OF EVERY TEENAGE HERO IN TOWN.
I HEARD ALL THE JOKES ABOUT SUPERGIRL'S HORSE. HELL, I MADE HALF OF 'EM UP MYSELF.
CAN YOU DO THIS FOR ME? FOR HIM?
EVEN THOUGH I KNOW SUPERMAN... HE HAS THIS WAY. THIS LOOK IN HIS EYES AND THAT VOICE. SOMETHING ALMOST HYPNOTIC ABOUT IT.
NO ONE CAN SAY NO TO SUPERMAN.
ALL RIGHT. I'LL TRY IT.
HNNN.
NOT EVEN ME?
GET OUT OF MY FACE.
I CAN'T WAIT TO GET BACK TO THE TOWER.

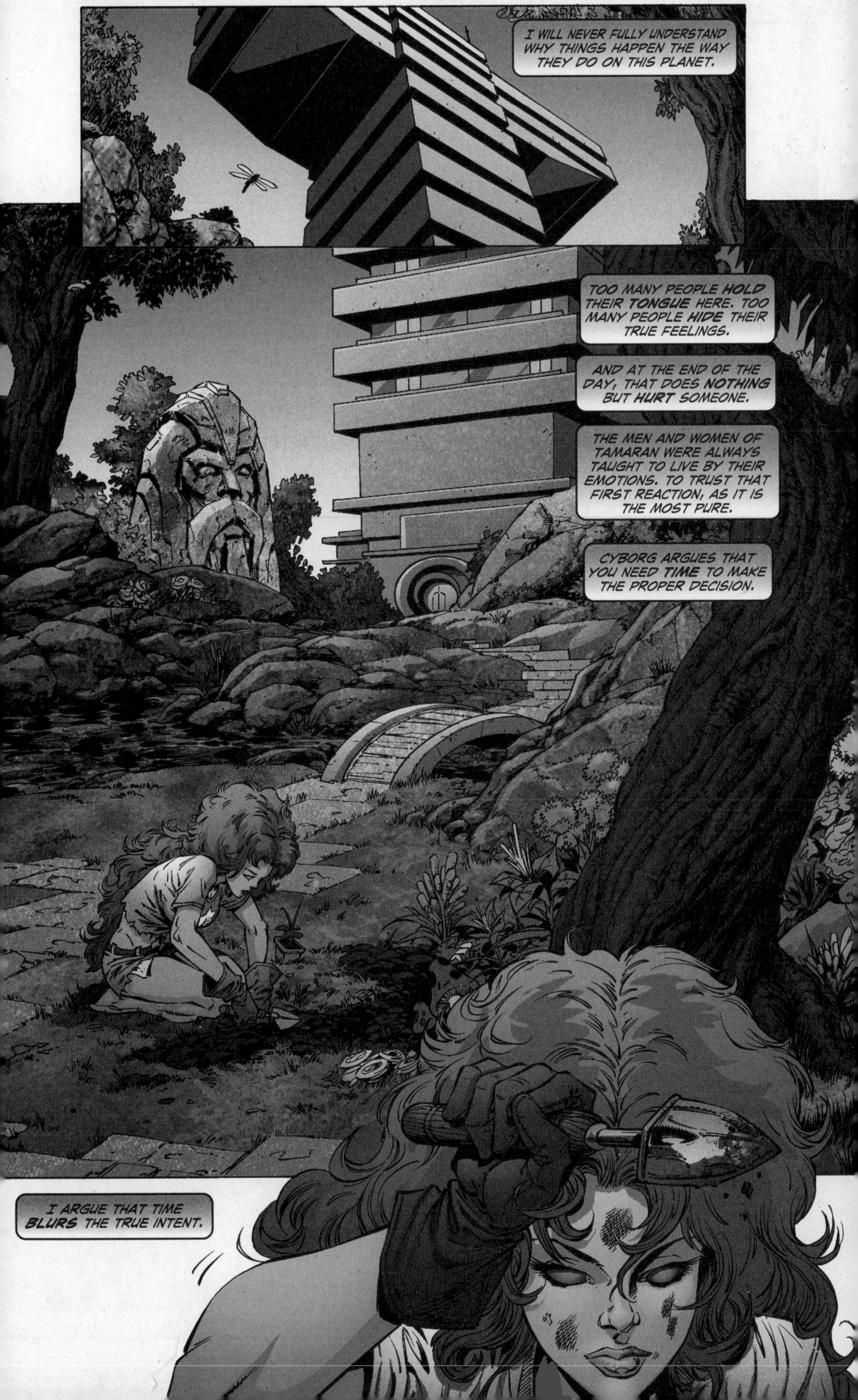
I WILL NEVER FULLY UNDERSTAND WHY THINGS HAPPEN THE WAY THEY DO ON THIS PLANET.
TOO MANY PEOPLE **HOLD** THEIR **TONGUE** HERE. TOO MANY PEOPLE **HIDE** THEIR TRUE FEELINGS.
AND AT THE END OF THE DAY, THAT DOES **NOTHING** BUT **HURT** SOMEONE.
THE MEN AND WOMEN OF TAMARAN WERE ALWAYS TAUGHT TO LIVE BY THEIR EMOTIONS. TO TRUST THAT FIRST REACTION, AS IT IS THE MOST PURE.
CYBORG ARGUES THAT YOU NEED **TIME** TO MAKE THE PROPER DECISION.
I ARGUE THAT TIME **BLURS** THE TRUE INTENT.

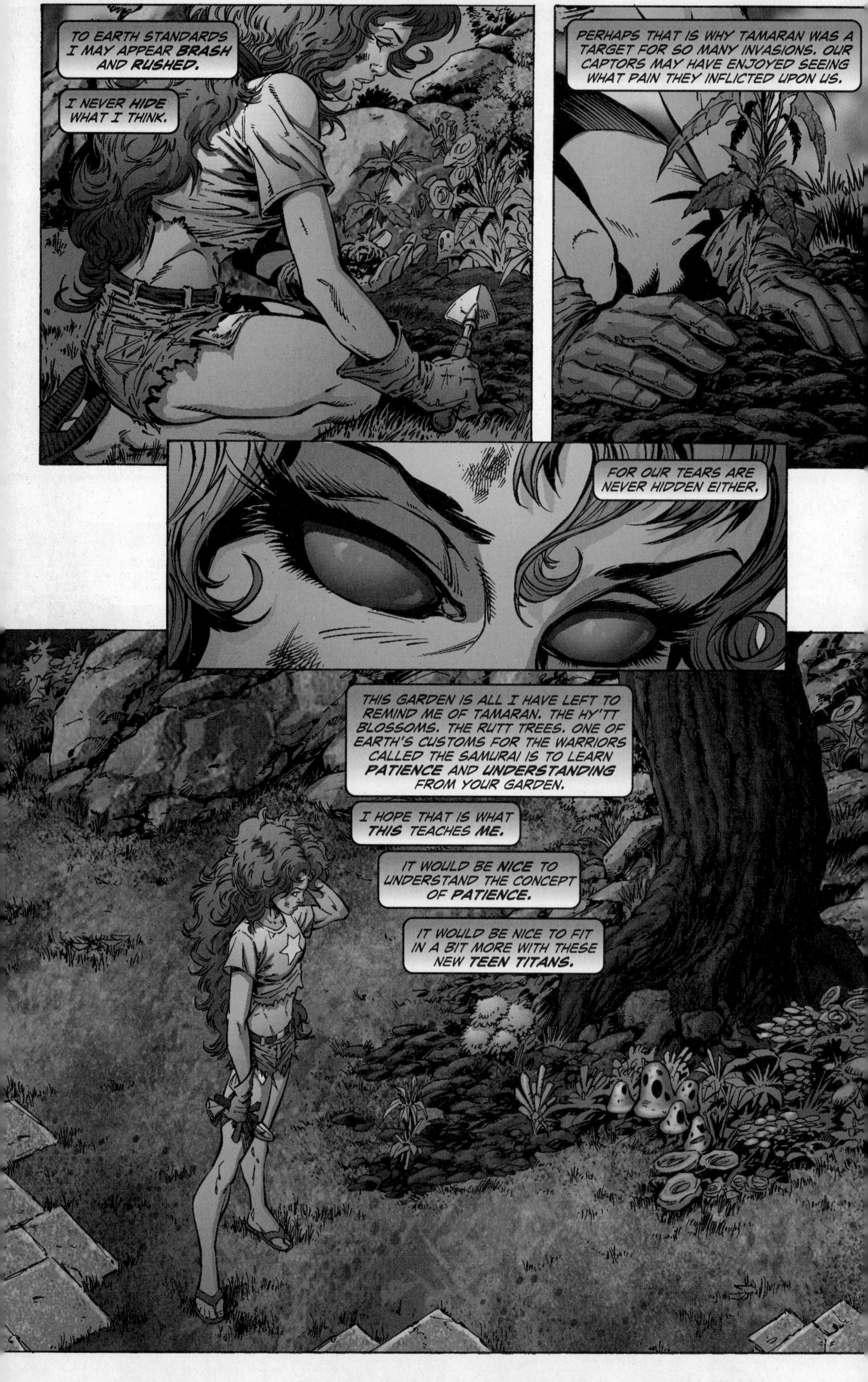
TO EARTH STANDARDS I MAY APPEAR BRASH AND RUSHED.
I NEVER HIDE WHAT I THINK.
PERHAPS THAT IS WHY TAMARAN WAS A TARGET FOR SO MANY INVASIONS. OUR CAPTORS MAY HAVE ENJOYED SEEING WHAT PAIN THEY INFLICTED UPON US.
FOR OUR TEARS ARE NEVER HIDDEN EITHER.
THIS GARDEN IS ALL I HAVE LEFT TO REMIND ME OF TAMARAN. THE HY'TT BLOSSOMS. THE RUTT TREES. ONE OF EARTH'S CUSTOMS FOR THE WARRIORS CALLED THE SAMURAI IS TO LEARN PATIENCE AND UNDERSTANDING FROM YOUR GARDEN.
I HOPE THAT IS WHAT THIS TEACHES ME.
IT WOULD BE NICE TO UNDERSTAND THE CONCEPT OF PATIENCE.
IT WOULD BE NICE TO FIT IN A BIT MORE WITH THESE NEW TEEN TITANS.

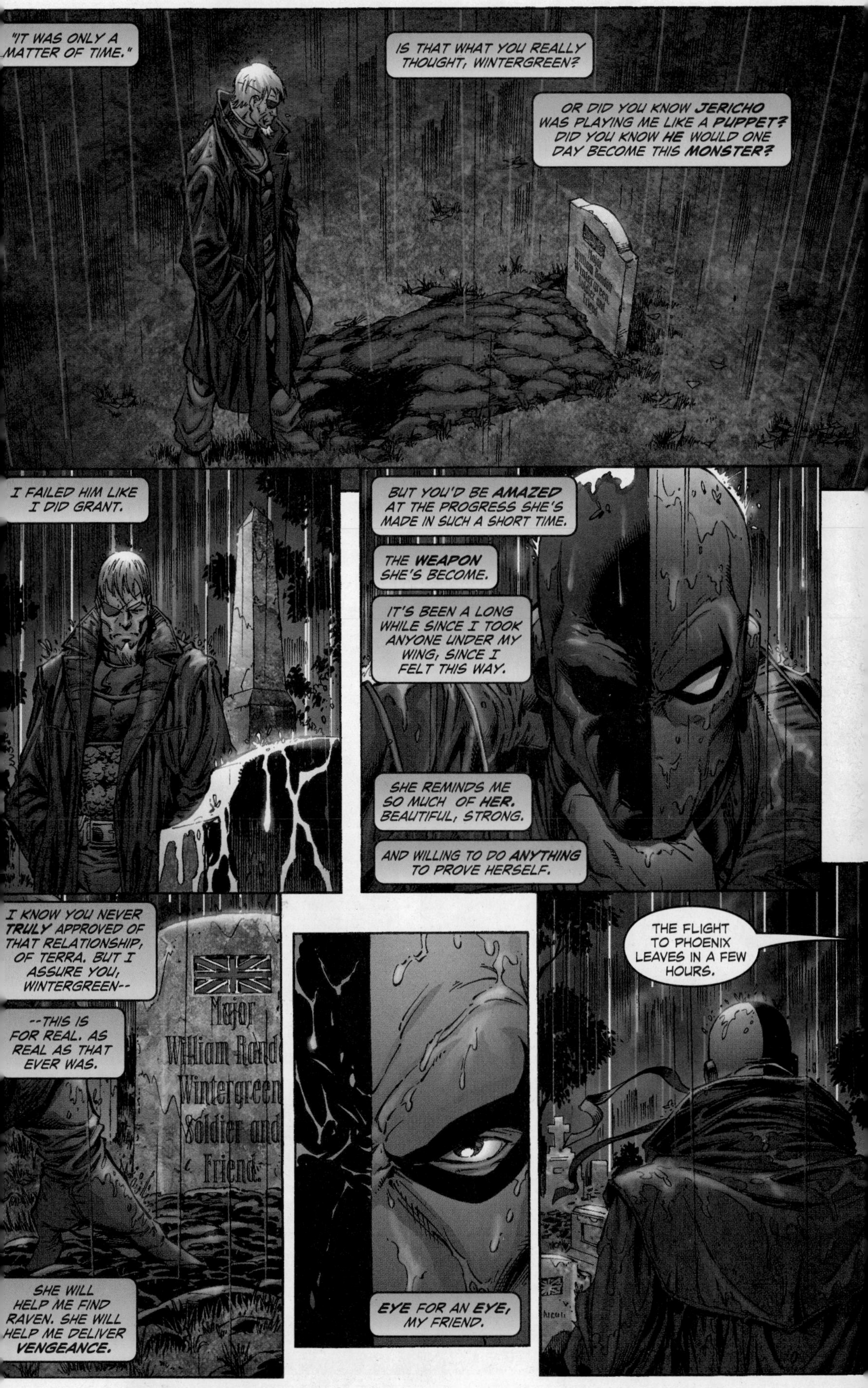
"IT WAS ONLY A MATTER OF TIME."
IS THAT WHAT YOU REALLY THOUGHT, WINTERGREEN?
OR DID YOU KNOW JERICHO WAS PLAYING ME LIKE A PUPPET? DID YOU KNOW HE WOULD ONE DAY BECOME THIS MONSTER?
I FAILED HIM LIKE I DID GRANT.
BUT YOU'D BE AMAZED AT THE PROGRESS SHE'S MADE IN SUCH A SHORT TIME.
THE WEAPON SHE'S BECOME.
IT'S BEEN A LONG WHILE SINCE I TOOK ANYONE UNDER MY WING, SINCE I FELT THIS WAY.
SHE REMINDS ME SO MUCH OF HER. BEAUTIFUL, STRONG.
AND WILLING TO DO ANYTHING TO PROVE HERSELF.
I KNOW YOU NEVER TRULY APPROVED OF THAT RELATIONSHIP, OF TERRA. BUT I ASSURE YOU, WINTERGREEN--
--THIS IS FOR REAL. AS REAL AS THAT EVER WAS.
Major
William Rand
Wintergreen
Soldier and
Friend
SHE WILL HELP ME FIND RAVEN. SHE WILL HELP ME DELIVER VENGEANCE.
EYE FOR AN EYE, MY FRIEND.
THE FLIGHT TO PHOENIX LEAVES IN A FEW HOURS.

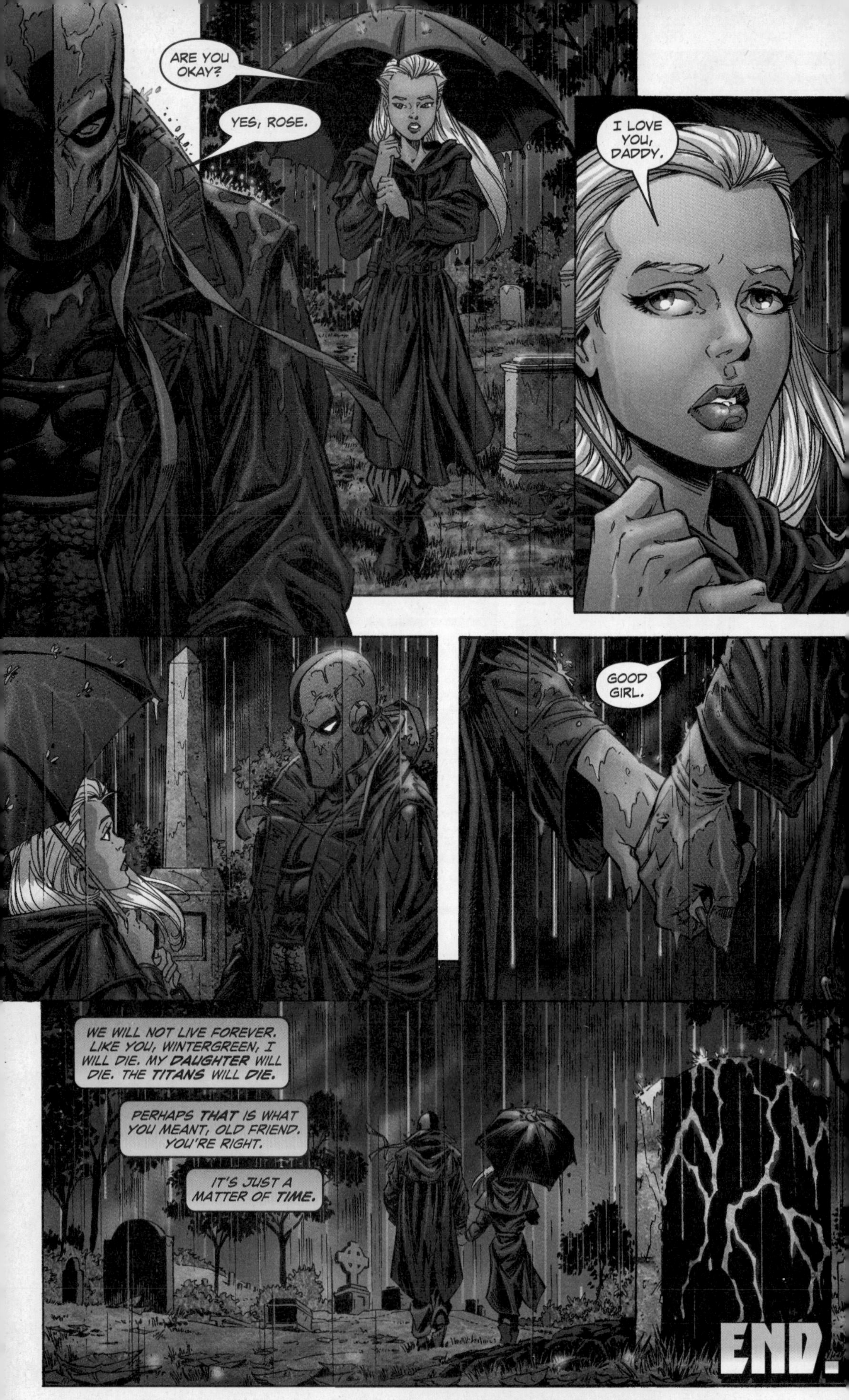
ARE YOU OKAY?
YES, ROSE.
I LOVE YOU, DADDY.
GOOD GIRL.
WE WILL NOT LIVE FOREVER. LIKE YOU, WINTERGREEN, I WILL DIE. MY DAUGHTER WILL DIE. THE TITANS WILL DIE.
PERHAPS THAT IS WHAT YOU MEANT, OLD FRIEND. YOU'RE RIGHT.
IT'S JUST A MATTER OF TIME.
END.

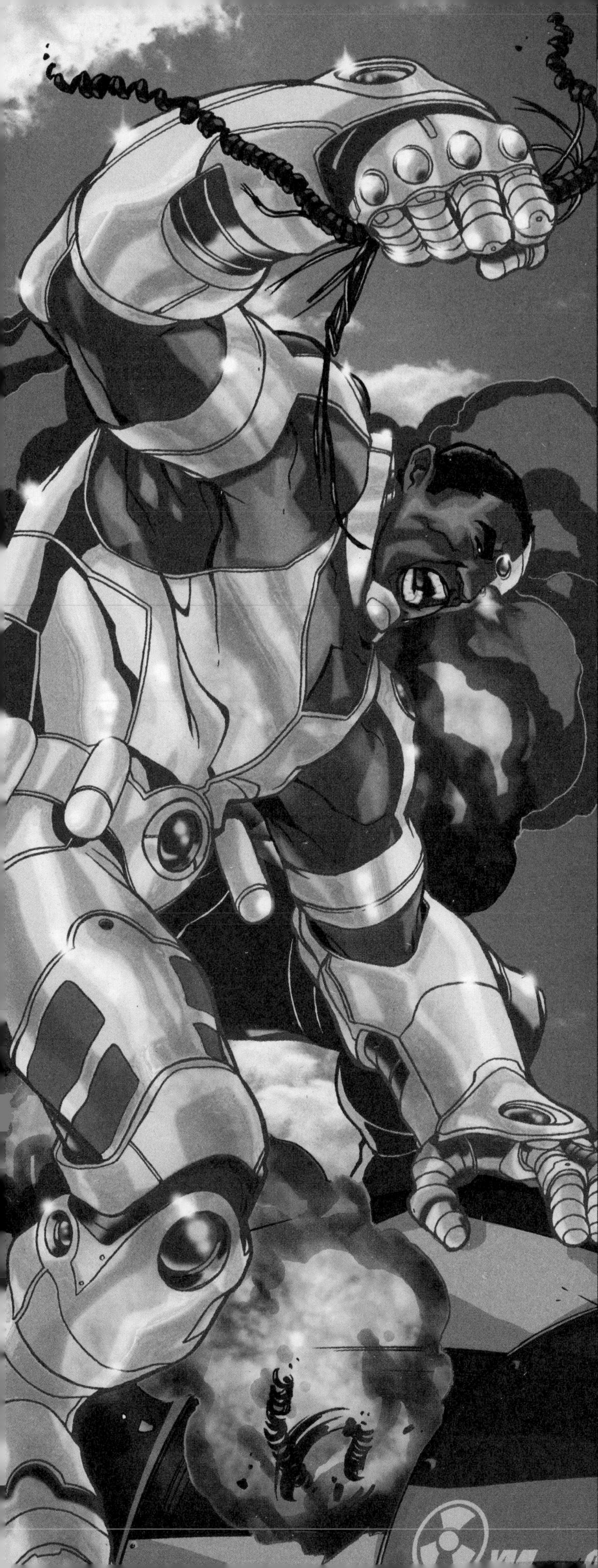

CYBORG

Real Name: Victor Stone
Marital Status: Single
Height: 6' 8"
Weight: 445 lbs.
Eyes: Brown
Hair: Black
First Appearance: DC Comics Presents #26 (October, 1980)

Victor Stone's parents were research scientists for S.T.A.R. Labs, a highly advanced technical institute nationally known throughout the United States. Although they encouraged their son to pursue interests of intellect, Victor found athletic activity far more captivating and devoted much of his time to sports, hoping to one day enter the Olympics.

During an experiment at S.T.A.R. Labs, Victor's mother accidentally unleashed a destructive force that killed her instantly and attacked Victor. If not for the interference of his father, Victor would have died as well, but his body was still almost completely destroyed. Victor's father rushed his son to his lab and desperately grafted cybernetic parts to his organs and computerized synthetic nerve bases to his spine. Once Victor was stable, his father followed through by replacing his limbs and part of his face with experimental molybdenum steel. Victor Stone became a true cyborg.

Horrified by his appearance and seeing himself as a complete outcast, Victor found himself cut off from the things he loved most in life, from playing sports to interacting with normal, everyday people. Thankfully, Victor was inducted into the newly re-formed Teen Titans soon after, restoring his sense of purpose and much of his good humor, though he still misses being completely human.

Currently, Cyborg has taken it upon himself to re-form the Teen Titans and usher in today's teenage superheroes at Titans Tower in San Francisco. Cyborg has one goal in mind: to help prepare these kids, and himself, for the future—a future they'll all get a glimpse of sooner than any of them expect.

Text: Geoff Johns Art & Color: Karl Kerschl

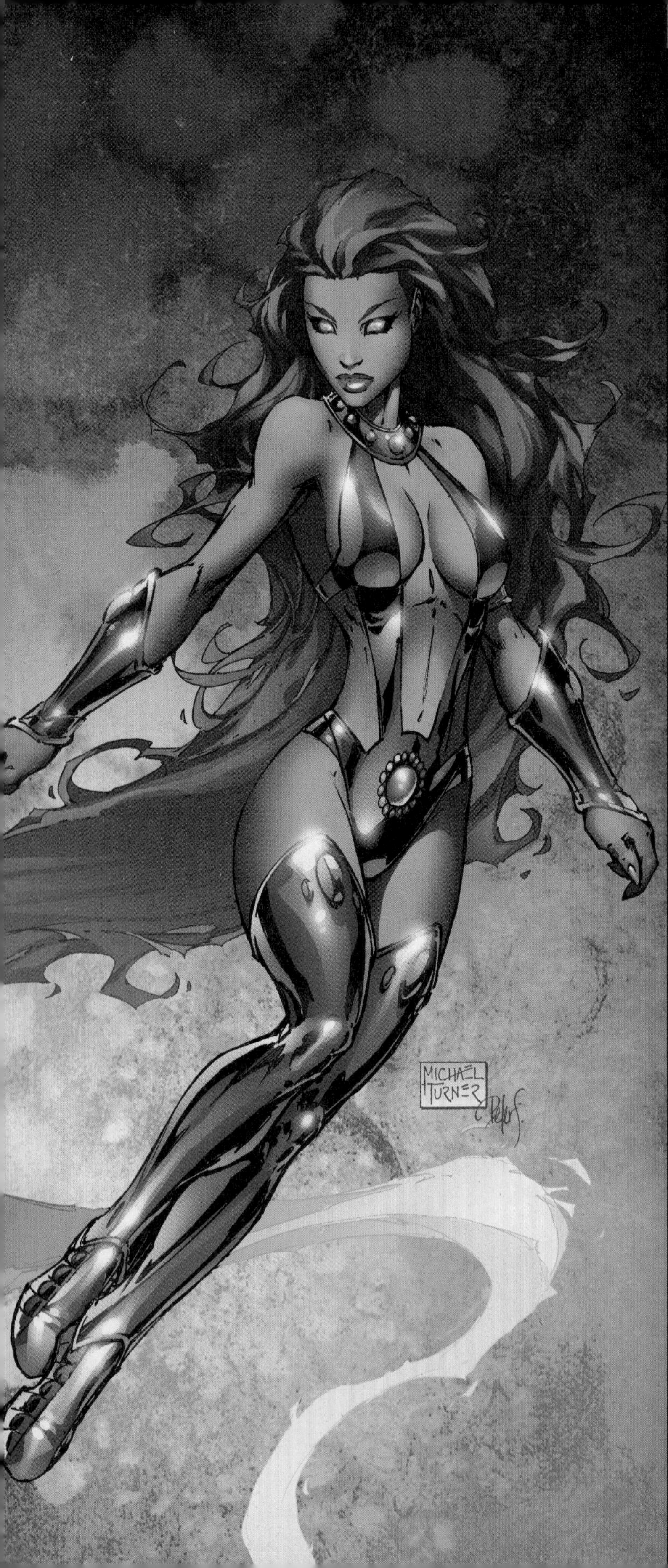
MICHAEL TURNER

STARFIRE

Real Name: Koriand'r
Occupation: Teen Titan
Marital Status: Twice widowed
Ht: 6' 4" **Wt:** 152 lbs.
Eyes: Green **Hair:** Auburn
First Appearance: DC COMIC PRESENTS #26 (October, 1980)

Starfire grew up on Tamarar the youngest daughter of the plar et's rulers. When her homeworl was invaded by a race of alien that threatened to destroy th entire planet, her people prove unable to fight off the invader despite their warrior heritage. A a "peace offering," Princes Koriand'r was given up to th invaders, taken away from he family and enslaved.

After suffering unspeakable ho rors, Starfire escaped he captors and fled to Earth. Her she encountered the Teen Titan and quickly became a membe Starfire is a living solar batter able to take the sun's energy an use it to enable her to fly and ger erate deadly starbolts. Starfire' alien physiology also gives her level of super-strength.

Early on, Starfire's siste Komand'r, came into conflict wit the Titans under the name c Blackfire. Recently, Tamaran wa destroyed, Blackfire seemingl along with it. Kory's other effort at making a family for herself hav failed, with two husbands tragica ly losing their lives and a planne marriage to Dick Grayson neve coming to pass.

Starfire tends to be impatien and that, combined with he disinterest in being anyone "teacher," has made her uncon fortable about her role on this ne team of Titans. Although she spent some time on Earth, Starfir is still naïve in many ways an fails to grasp the reasoning behin many of her adopted home's cus toms and laws. When she spenc time alone, Starfire prefers to ten to her garden on Titans Islanc which is made up of severa species of plant life saved fror her homeworld of Tamaran.

Text: Geoff Johns Art: Michael Turner
Color: Peter Steigerwald

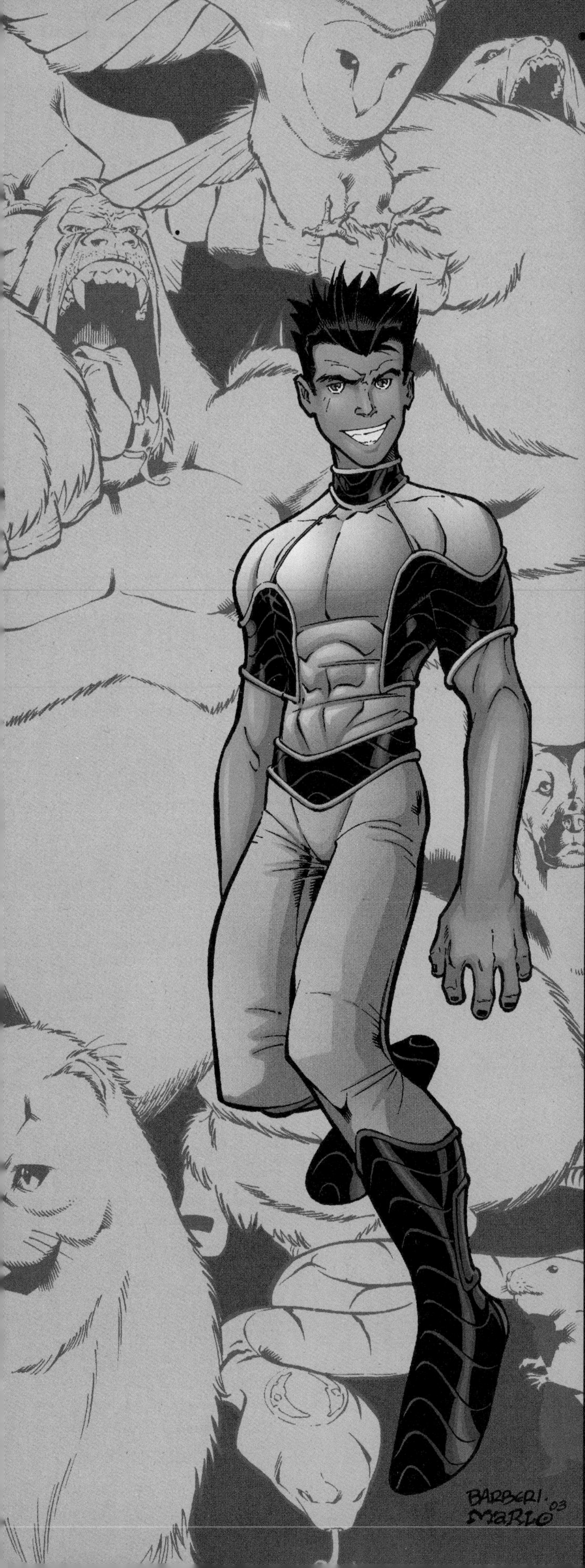
BARBERI. 03
MARLO

BEAST BOY

Real Name: Garfield Mark Logan
Occupation: Would-be actor
Marital Status: Single
Ht: 5' 8" **Wt:** 150 lbs.
Eyes: Green **Hair:** Green
First Appearance: DOOM PATROL #99 (November, 1965)

Young Garfield Logan, the son of two geneticists, went with his parents to Africa on one of their many expeditions. His parents were searching for a rare breed of green-colored primate, hoping to unlock the secrets of its resistance to disease. Unfortunately, one of these animals attacked young Garfield and bit him, passing on a lethal disease known as Sakutia. His parents treated Garfield with an experimental drug and saved their child's life.

But, the side effects of surviving Sakutia were beyond bizarre. Not only had Garfield's skin and hair turned a permanent green, the boy found he could reshape himself into virtually any animal he could imagine, from ones as large as an elephant to others as small as a bee.

After losing his parents in an accident, Garfield was taken in by the super-hero team known as the Doom Patrol and nicknamed "Beast Boy." Tragedy struck months later when the team was seemingly killed, save for young Garfield. Feeling lost, Gar fled to Hollywood in hopes of pursuing an acting career. It didn't work out, but soon after, Beast Boy learned about a group of teenaged heroes re-forming the Teen Titans. He became a charter member of the new team and quickly found his place again in the world.

At age 19, Beast Boy finds himself acting as the mediator between the older and younger Titans, a role he readily accepts. Gar has begun taking acting classes in San Francisco, though he claims this is more for fun than anything else.

One of these days, San Francisco will discover what makes Beast Boy so special. And they might not like it.

Text: Geoff Johns Art : Carlo Barbieri & Marlo Alquiza
Color: Tom McCraw

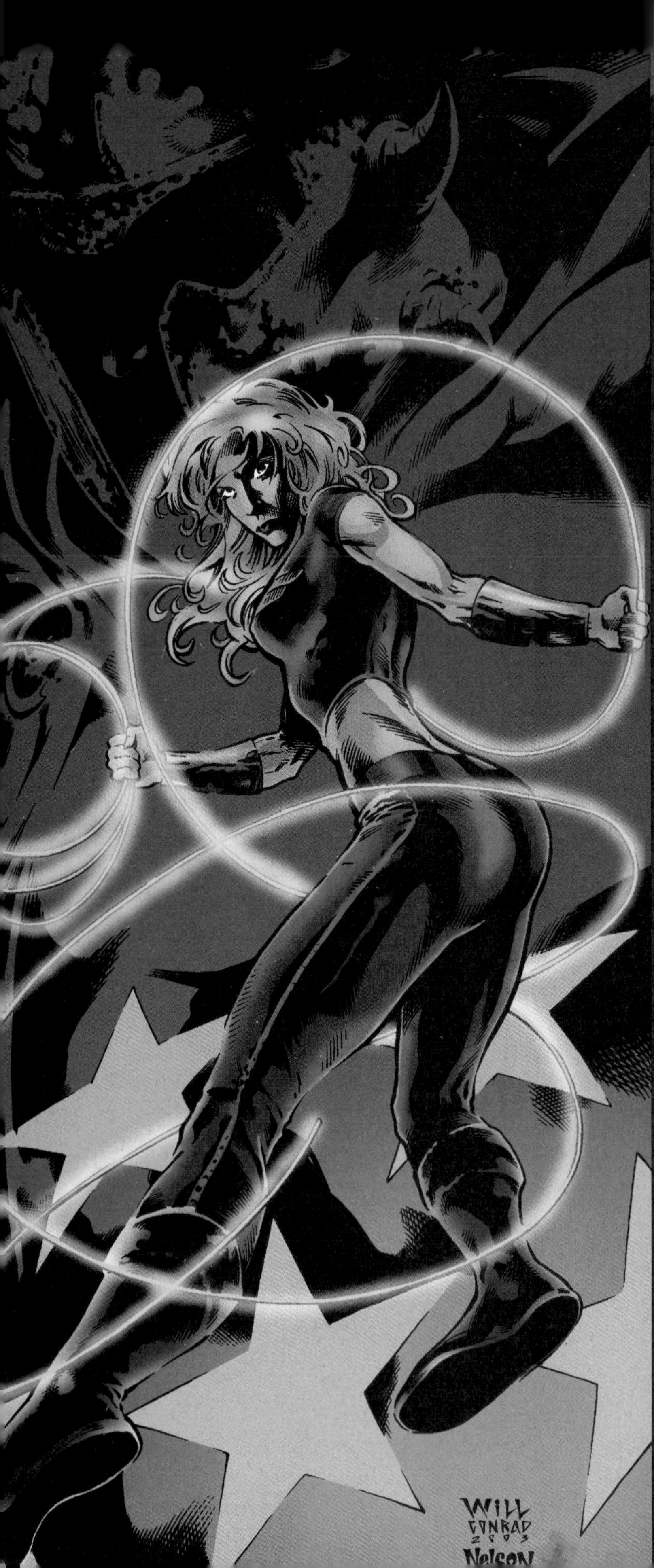
WILL
CONRAD
2003
NELSON

WONDER GIR

Real Name: Cassie Sandsmark
Marital Status: Single
Ht: 5' 3" **Wt:** 115 lbs.
Eyes: Blue **Hair:** Blonde
First Appearance: (as Cassie Sandsmark) WONDER WOMAN (current series) #105 (February, 1996); (as Wonder Girl) WONDER WOMAN (current series) #111 (July, 1996)

Cassie Sandsmark is the daug ter of archaeologist Hele Sandsmark. Her father has be missing most of Cassie's life, a even when Cassie finally met hi something felt wrong. She h dealt with being the daughter o single mother as best anyo could. If anything, in fact, i made her mature beyond her yea (albeit a bit headstrong).

Cassie first met Wonder Wom in her home of Gateway City wh the Amazon Princess briefly liv there. During one of Wonc Woman's battles, Cassie help her role model by "borrowing" t Sandals of Hermes and t Gauntlet of Atlas, which enabl her to fly and granted her a degr of super-strength. Soon aft Cassie spoke with Zeus hims asking for powers of her ow Zeus, seemingly impressed by t "mere mortal," bestowed Cas with super-strength and the pov of flight. Cassie took on the role Wonder Girl full-time, attempti to balance her academic a superheroic careers. She train with the Amazon Artemis up ur the death of Donna Troy, the fi Wonder Girl. Recently, Wonc Girl's secret identity was expos when her school came unc attack by the Silver Swan. Cas has been expelled from Gatew City High due to the increas security risk she brings to school.

Wonder Girl continues to gr into her role, discovering new li its to her powers and finding n allies and enemies lurking amo Ancient Myth, such as Ares, w recently bestowed her with unexpected gift: a lasso who powers, as much as the reason the gift itself, remain a mystery.

Text: Geoff Johns Art: Will Conrad & Nelson Color: Tom McC

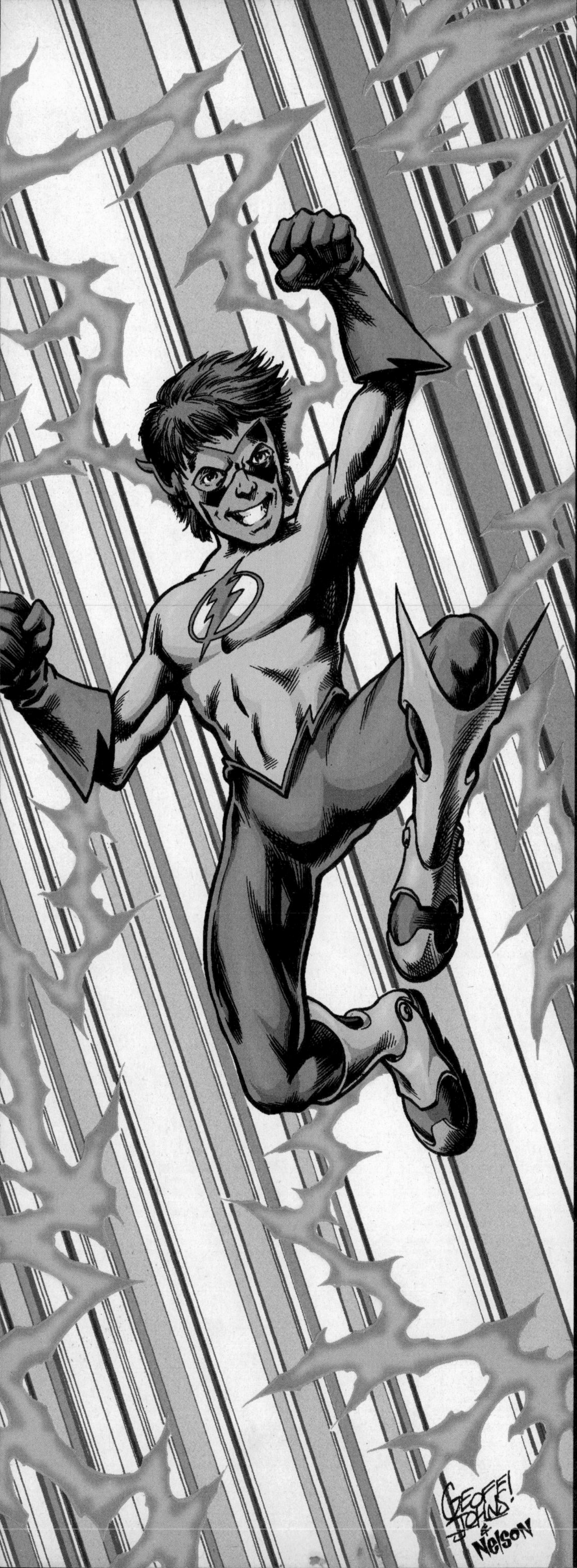
GEOFF! JOHNS & NELSON

KID FLASH

Real Name: Bart Allen
Marital Status: Single
Height: 5′ 2″
Weight: 115 lbs.
Eyes: Yellow
Hair: Brown
First Appearance: THE FLASH #91 (June, 1994)

Bart Allen — the grandson of Barry Allen, the second Flash, and Iris West — was brought back through time to our century after his father was killed. At Iris's request, Wally West, the current scarlet speedster, began to teach Bart how to fit into his new era and get a grasp on his powers. Frustrated by his nephew's lack of focus, Wally turned his attention elsewhere. Bart became known as Impulse and set out to become a super-hero in his own right.

Bart Allen's powers mirror those of Wally West, with one major exception: Bart also has the ability to remember everything he reads at super-speed. Currently, he resides in Keystone City with Jay Garrick — the original Flash — and Jay's wife Joan. Despite Wally West's misgivings, Bart accepted an invitation to join the new Teen Titans.

Recently, Bart was injured when Deathstroke put a shotgun to his leg. Thankfully, his accelerated healing enabled a handful of skeptical surgeons to replace his kneecap with an artificial one, and Bart was back on his feet in a matter of hours. But the effects of this encounter were much more than physical. Feeling unsure, and tired of being underestimated, Bart went to the local public library and read every single book in the building. He retained that knowledge, but what he'll do with it from here, and how it will balance with his lack of experience, is anyone's guess.

Text: Jeremy Johns Art: Geoff Johns & Nelson
Color: Tom McCraw

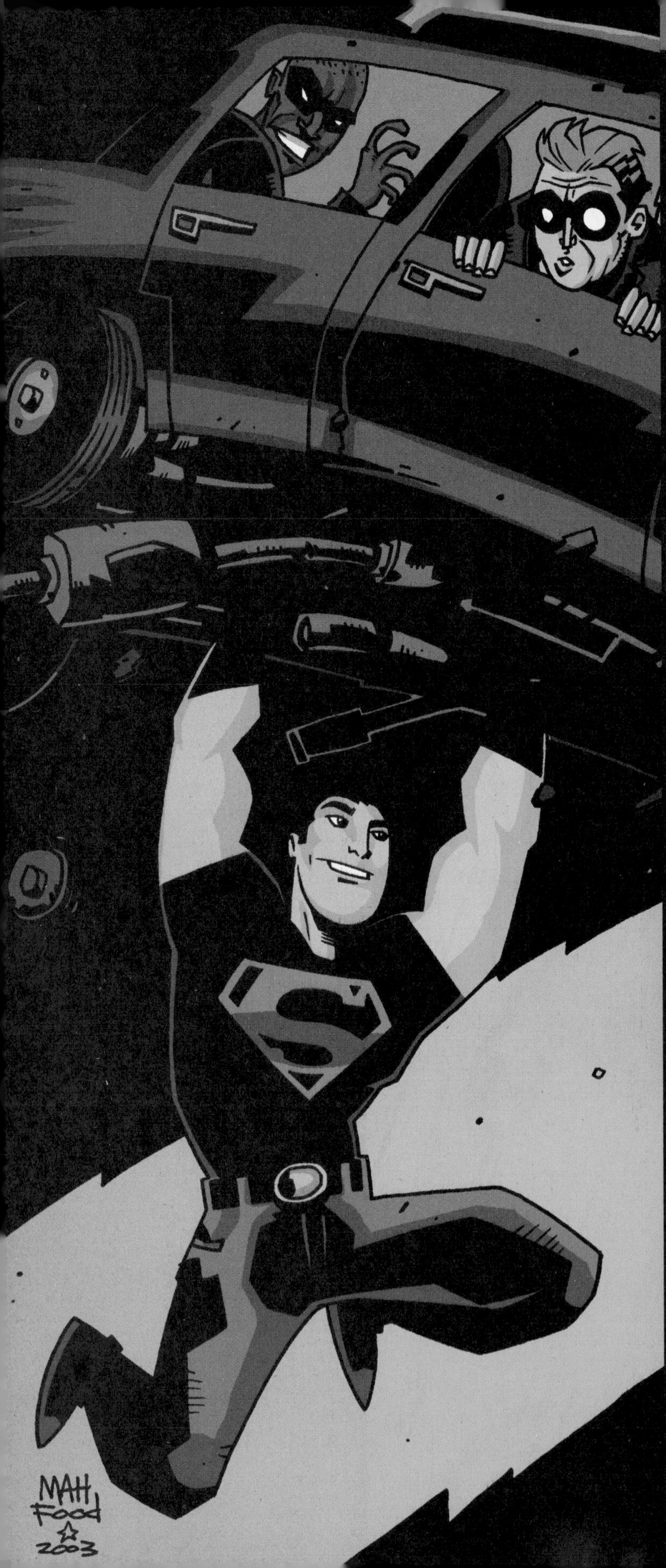
MAH Food 2003

SUPERBOY

Real Name: Conner Kent (a.k.a.
Kon-El)
Marital Status: Single
Ht: 5' 7" **Wt:** 145 lbs.
Eyes: Blue **Hair:** Black
First Appearance: ADVENTURES OF
SUPERMAN #500 (June, 1993)

The exact nature of Projec
Superboy is still somewhat of
mystery, but what is known is th
scientists were incapable of su
cessfully cloning Superman. Aft
several failed experiments, th
grafted what they could
Superman's DNA onto human DN
and that process stabilized t
extraterrestrial genes—th
Superboy was born, fifty perce
Kryptonian and fifty perce
human.

Because he is not an exact clo
of Superman, Superboy's abiliti
differ. His primary power is a li
ited form of telekinesis that mi
ics super-strength and flight. He
also able to disassemble obje
with a touch. As he's age
Superboy has manifested a certa
amount of non-psychically deriv
super-strength, but it remains
be seen if Superboy will devel
any other attributes that possess
the Man of Steel.

At the beginning of the n
school year, Superboy was taken
by Superman's Earth paren
Jonathan and Martha Kent, unc
the guise of Conner Kent, cous
to Clark. Now enrolled
Smallville High, Conner
attempting to live a more norm
life, though he finds it incredi
boring.

Conner recently discovered th
the human DNA that was graft
onto Superman's in creating h
may be that of criminal mast
mind Lex Luthor. Conner refus
to believe this possibility and h
only shared the rumor with Rob
However, there is one other pers
who knows this secret...and
absolutely willing to exploit it.

Text: Geoff Johns Art: Jim Mahfood Color: Tom McCraw

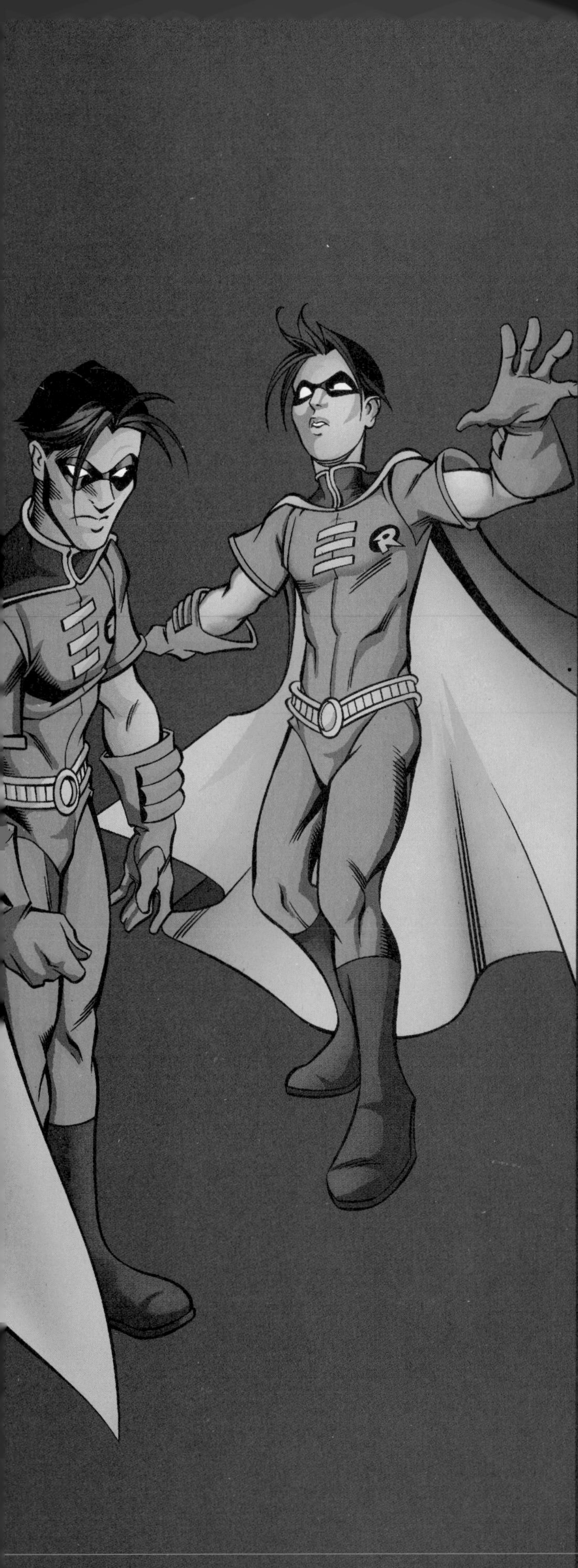

ROBIN

Real Name: Timothy Drake
Marital Status: Single
Height: 5' 5"
Weight: 125 lbs.
Eyes: Blue
Hair: Black
First Appearance: (as Tim) BATMAN #436 (August, 1989); (as Robin) BATMAN #457 (December, 1990)

Many see Robin as the straight-and-narrow kid striving to be perfect for his mentor, and that's just what he wants everyone to think.

Tim Drake was barely a teenager when he first became a detective, uncovering that Batman was in fact secretly Bruce Wayne. Batman recruited Tim to become the third person to bear the name of Robin, the Teen Wonder. Although Tim is not as natural an acrobat as was Dick Grayson, the first Robin, he is an incredibly quick learner and doesn't hesitate to rely on weapons or trickery to give himself an edge.

Tim currently lives with his father and stepmother, both unaware that Tim spends his nights protecting the streets of Gotham City. Tim has also been forced to lie to his father about where he's been spending his time when it comes to the Teen Titans, often citing weekend vocational schooling (which has been falsely created and verified by the hi-tech information hub known as Oracle). How long Tim can keep up this charade is anyone's guess, though the strain is beginning to show.

Robin remains a mystery to those around him. Even when the Teen Titans began to believe they could predict his next move, they found out they were mistaken. Robin will do anything he feels he must in order to insure the safety of those around him. He has never been one to just follow orders blindly, and will constantly challenge the elder Titans around him.

Text: Geoff Johns Art: Rick Mays & Aaron Sowd
Color: Tom McCraw

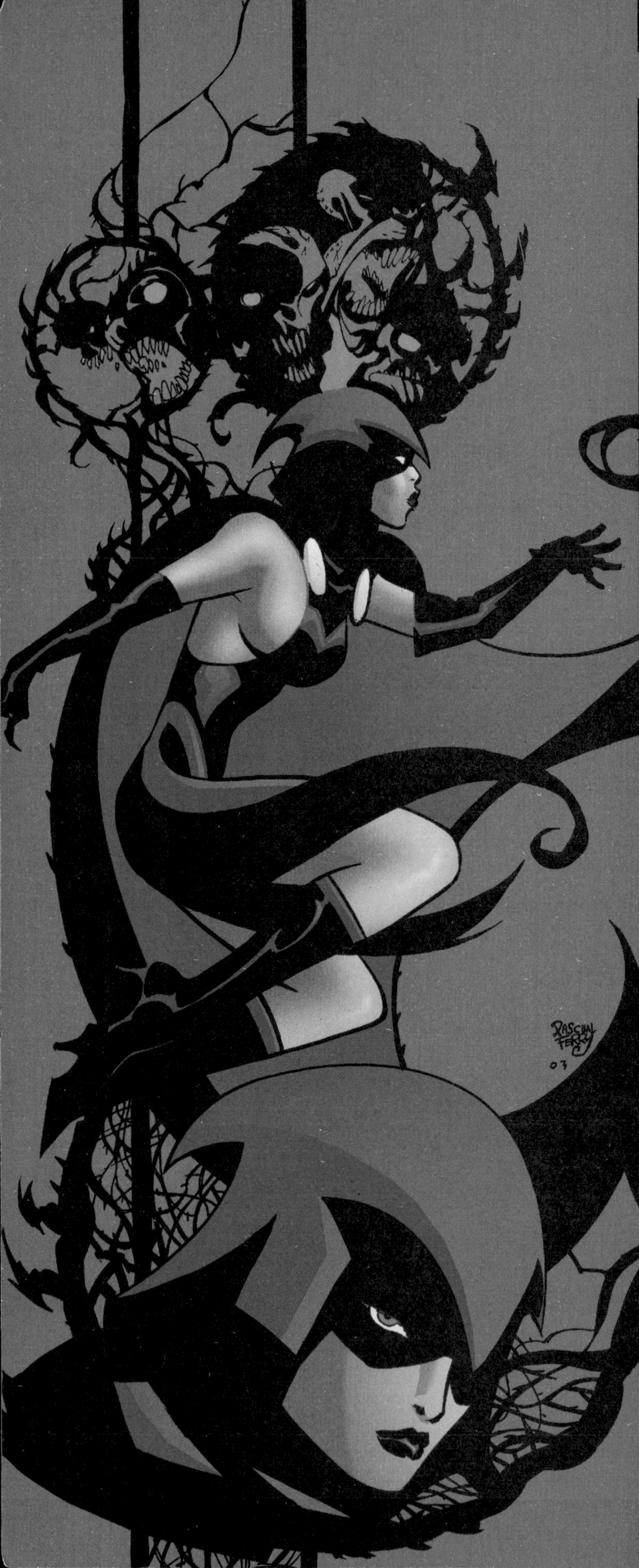
PASCUAL FERRY
03

RAVEN

Real Name: Raven
Marital Status: Single
Height: 5' 5"
Weight: 110 lbs.
Eyes: Indigo
Hair: Black
First Appearance: DC Comi
Presents #26 (October, 1980)

Raven has not had an ea existence. The daughter of earthborn woman and the dem called Trigon, she has spent mu of her life trying to escape h father's influence. Before Rav was born, her mother was taken the peaceful world of Azara where she spent her childhood r atively safe from Trigon's har She was taught how to use her t ents, including teleportation, h empathic ability of detecting a removing pain, and projecting h "soul-self," a powerful astral for capable of swallowing her enemi and forcing them to confront th own fears and sins.

Raven was always told to ke her anger and frustrations check, else she might give in to h father's demonic influence.

Raven traveled to Earth after s foresaw Trigon's attack on the m tal plane. She gathered togeth teenage heroes, eventually formi the new Teen Titans, and togeth they repelled Trigon's attack.

After countless battles with h daughter, Trigon was eventua killed. But soon after, Raven h self became subject to her fathe influence, even after his death, a became a dark version of herse In order to save Raven, her bo was destroyed, leaving her so self intact.

Without a body to inhab Raven's soul-self wandered t world aimlessly until recent when a new form of evil came claim her...an evil known Brother Blood.

Text: Geoff Johns Art: Pascual Ferry Color: Tom McCraw

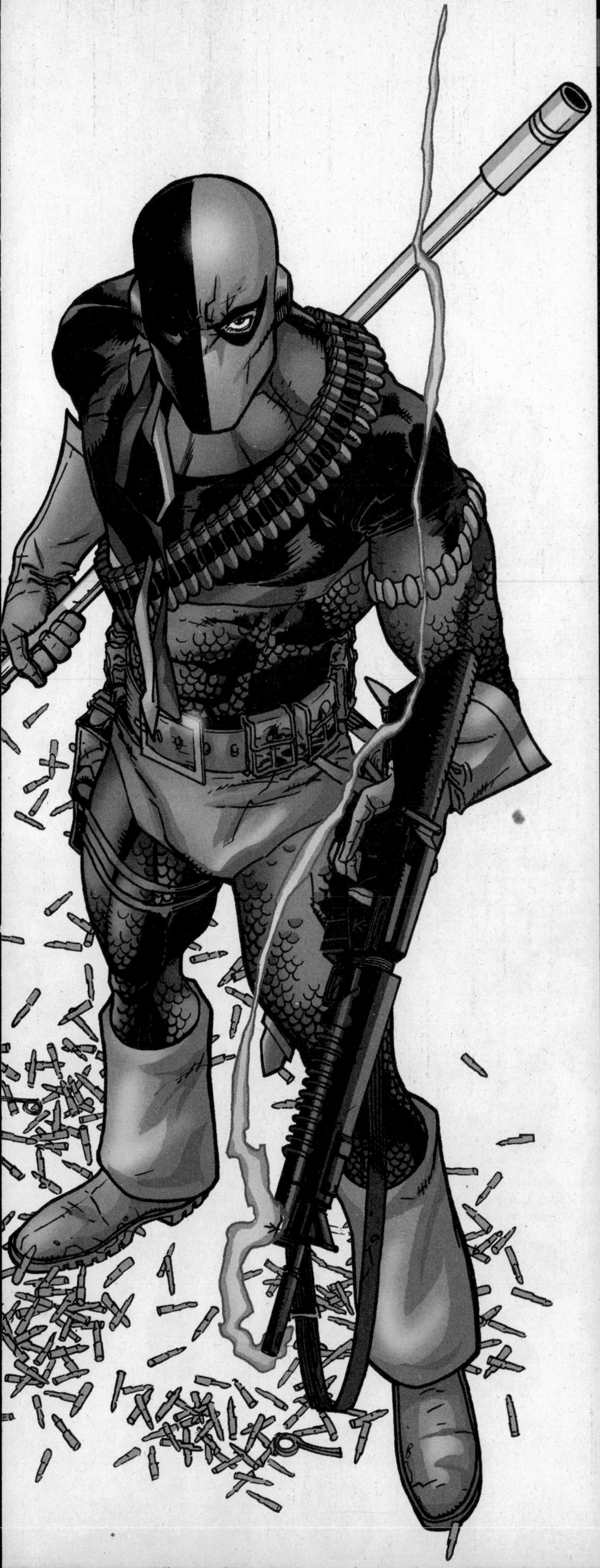

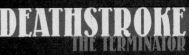

DEATHSTROKE
THE TERMINATOR

Real Name: Slade Wilson
Marital Status: Divorced
Ht: 6' 4" **Wt:** 220 lbs.
Eyes: Blue **Hair:** White
First Appearance: THE NEW TEEN TITANS #2 (December, 1980)

Deathstroke the Terminator is the deadliest mercenary in the world. During his time with the U.S Army, Slade Wilson underwent experiments that heightened his strength, speed, stamina and mind several times above normal levels. After his career in the military, Slade became an assassin, taking out contracts and hunting targets throughout the world. Trusting no one save his faithful friend Wintergreen, Slade cut most ties with his family.

Slade originally came into conflict with the Titans when his first son, Grant, died before fulfilling an assassination contract on the teenaged superheroes. Through a warped sense of honor, Slade took it upon himself to complete his son's contract. Slade's other son, Joe, joined the Titans (as Jericho) in an attempt to stop his father from harming the young heroes. Jericho had somehow gained the power to possess other people, possibly as a result of the experiments done on his father. Slade watched his son serve on the Titans for years, eventually killing him after Jericho seemed to have gone mad. Slades's only surviving family member is his estranged daughter, Rose.

Recently, Deathstroke discovered the spirit of his son, Jericho, had survived and taken refuge deep inside his body. With the help of Wintergreen, Deathstroke attempted to exorcise his son from him, but was quickly overpowered. Jericho lives inside his father, controlling his every move...for now.

In the future, Deathstroke will become a greater threat to the Titans and the hero community at large, focusing his hatred on one in particular.

Text: Geoff Johns Art: Kilian Plunkett Color: Tom McCraw

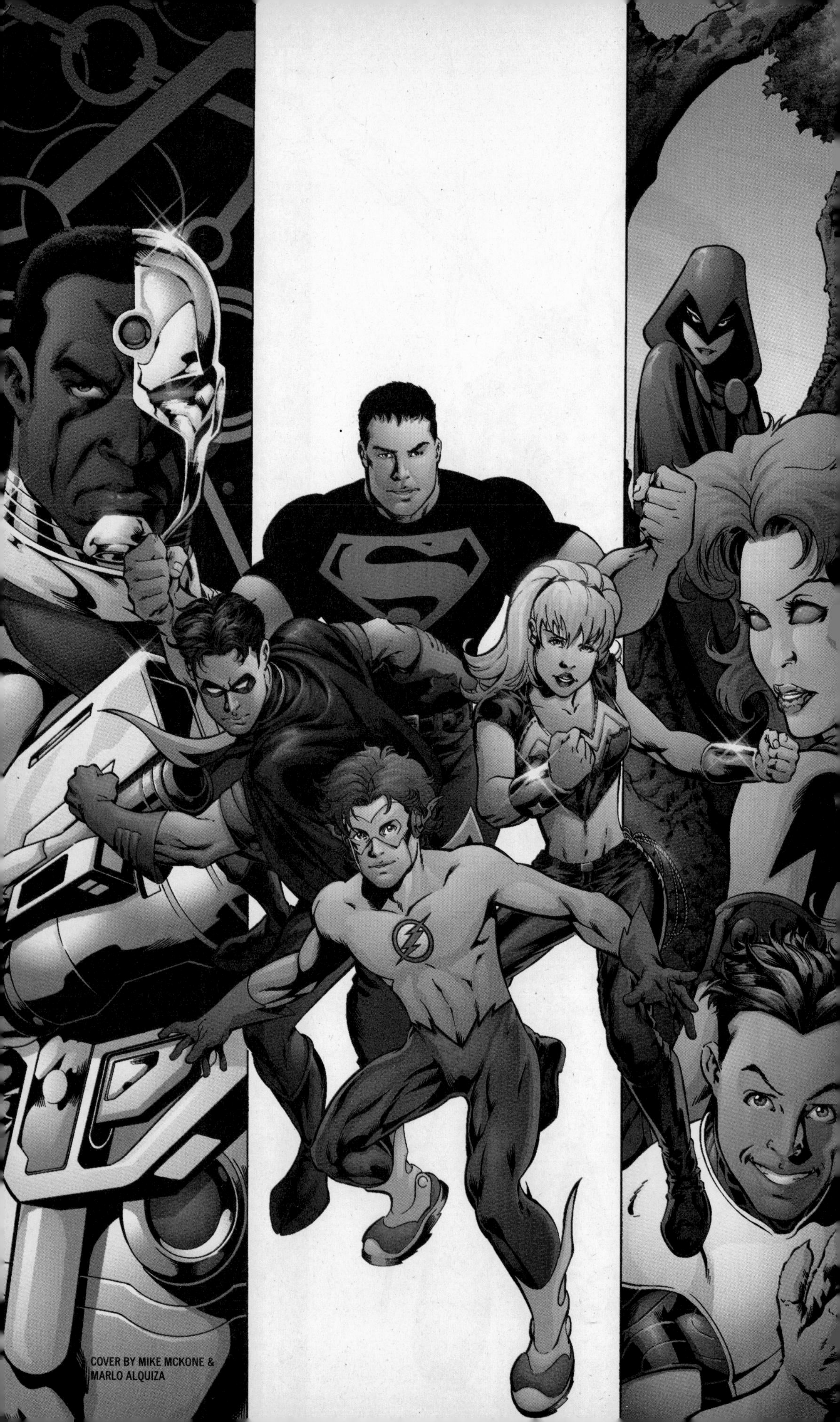

COVER BY MIKE MCKONE &
MARLO ALQUIZA

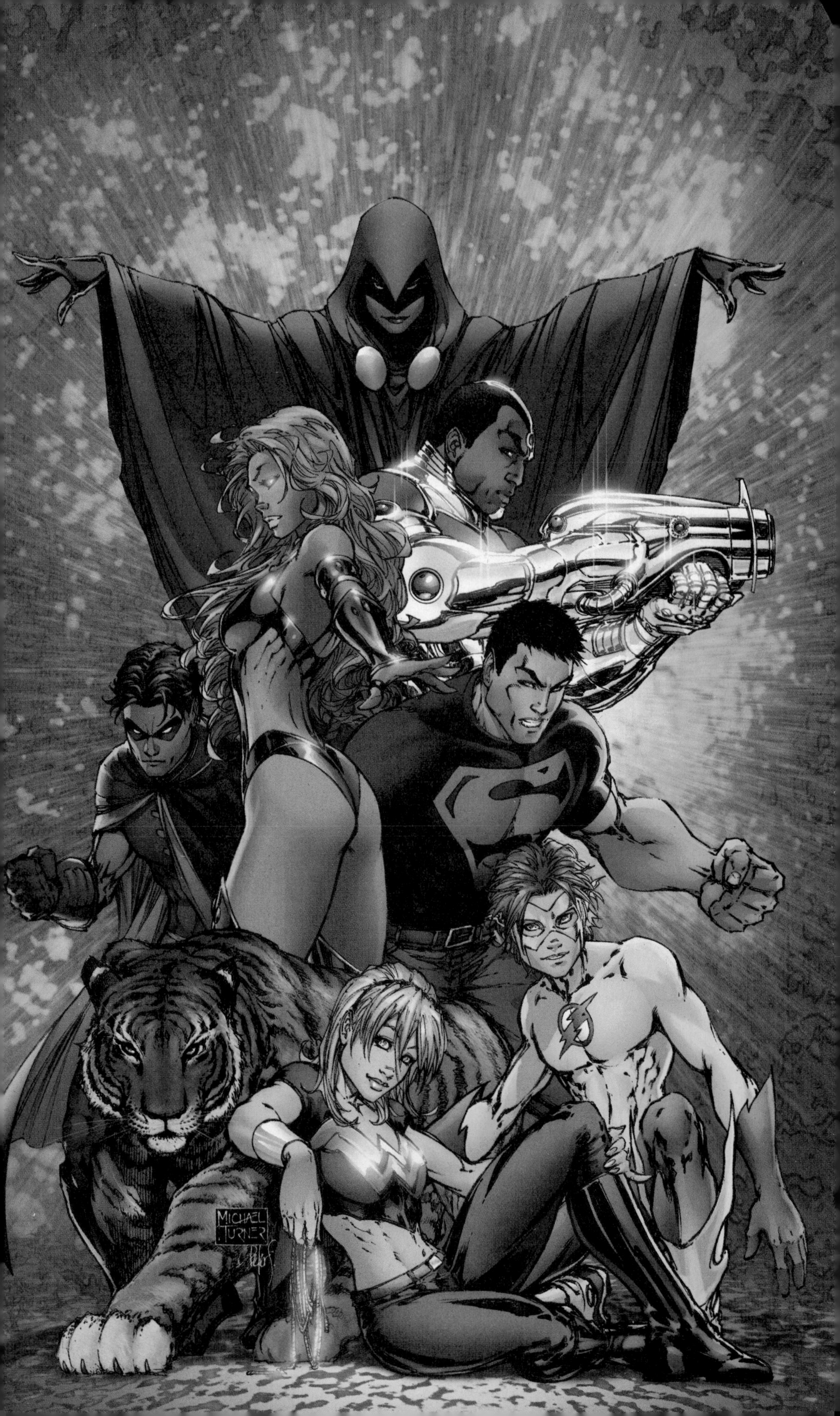
MICHAEL
TURNER

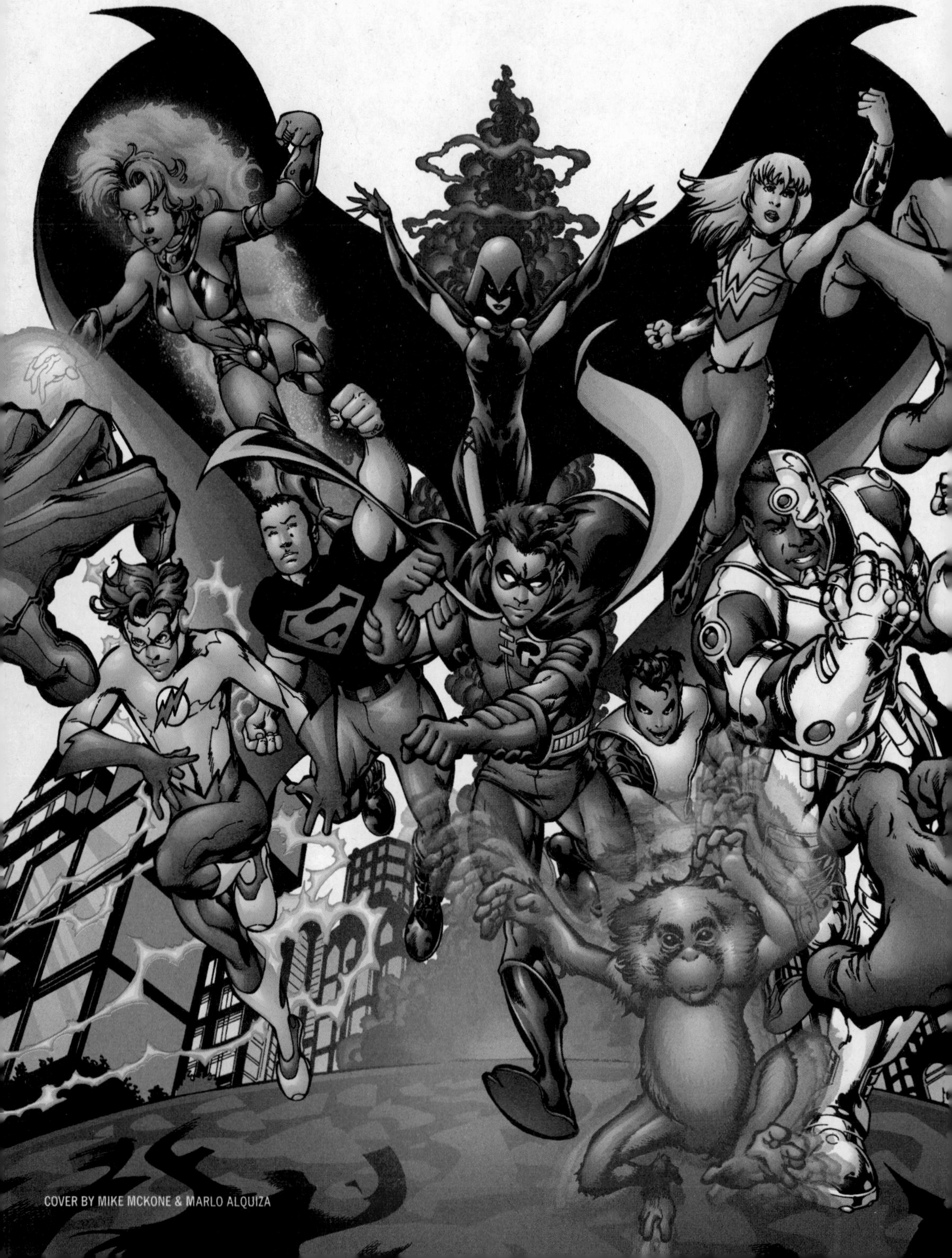

COVER BY MIKE MCKONE & MARLO ALQUIZA

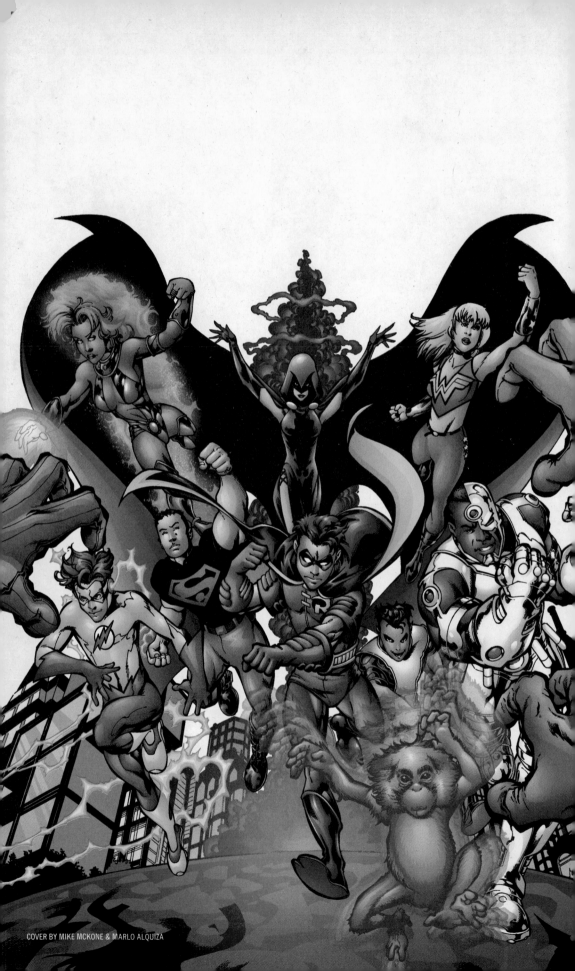

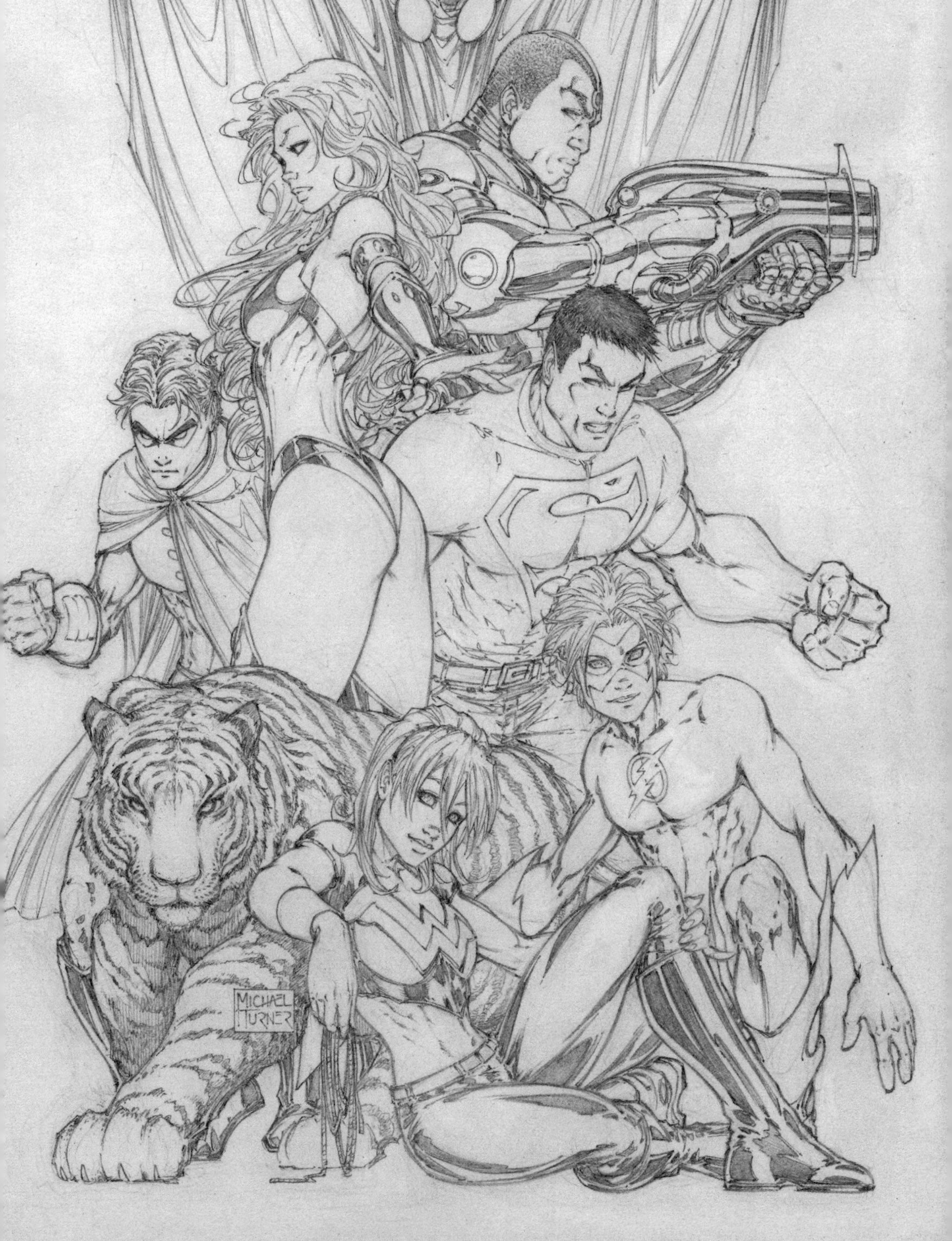
MICHAEL TURNER

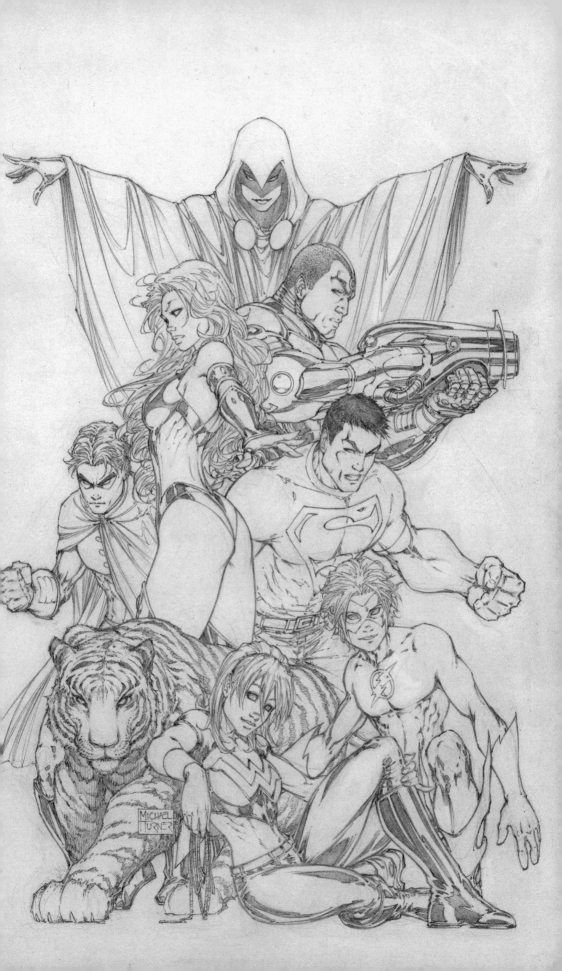

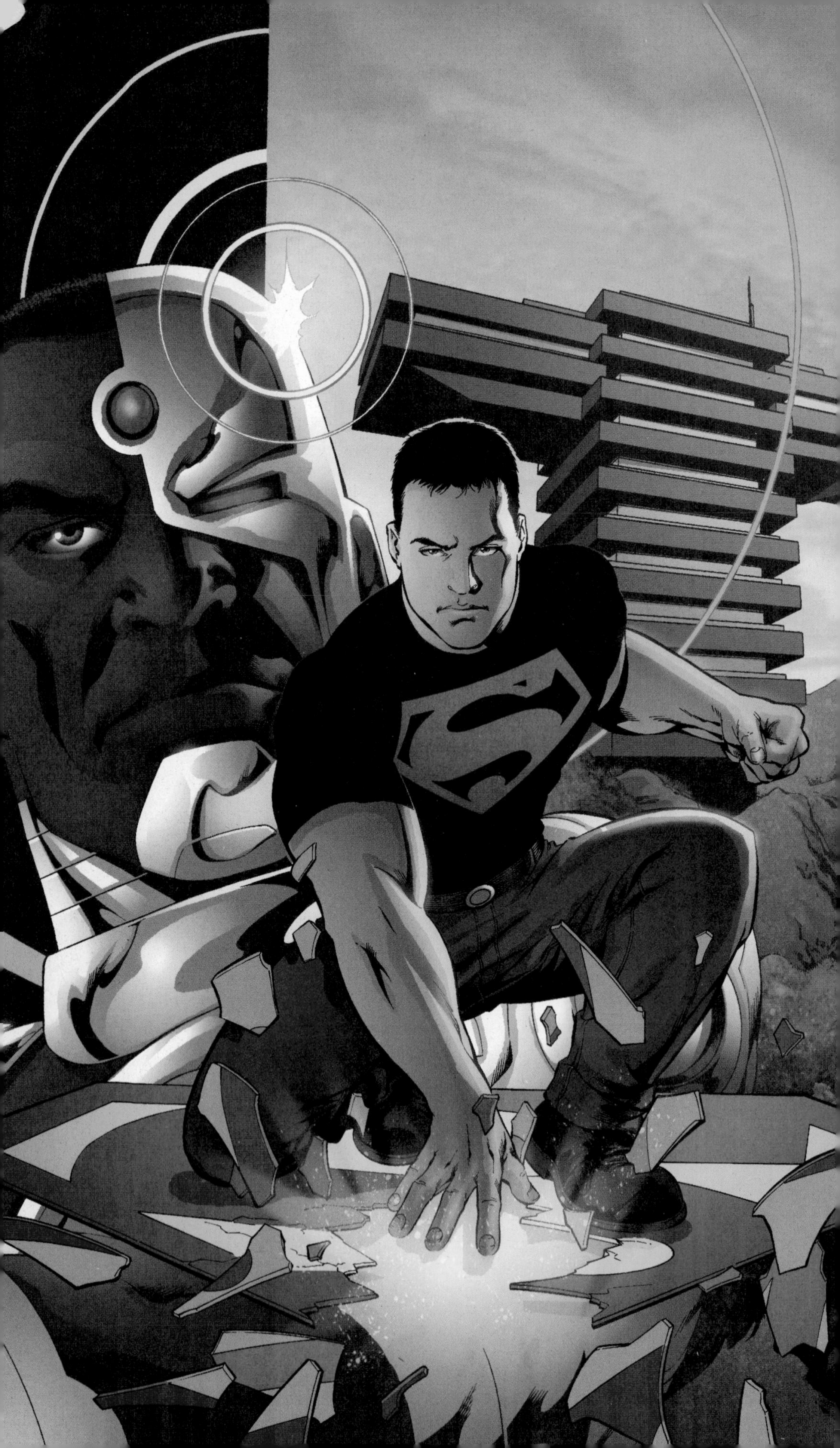

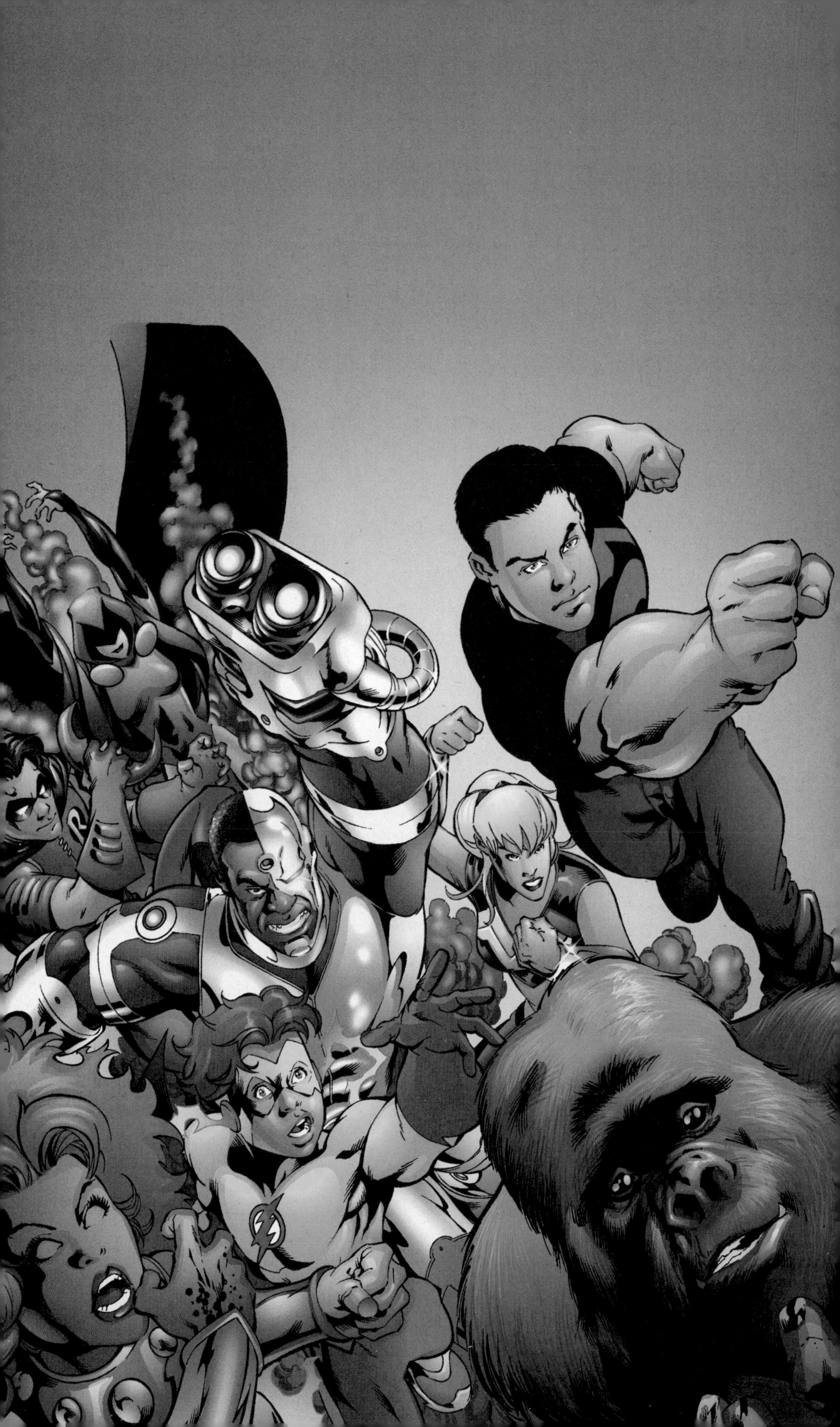

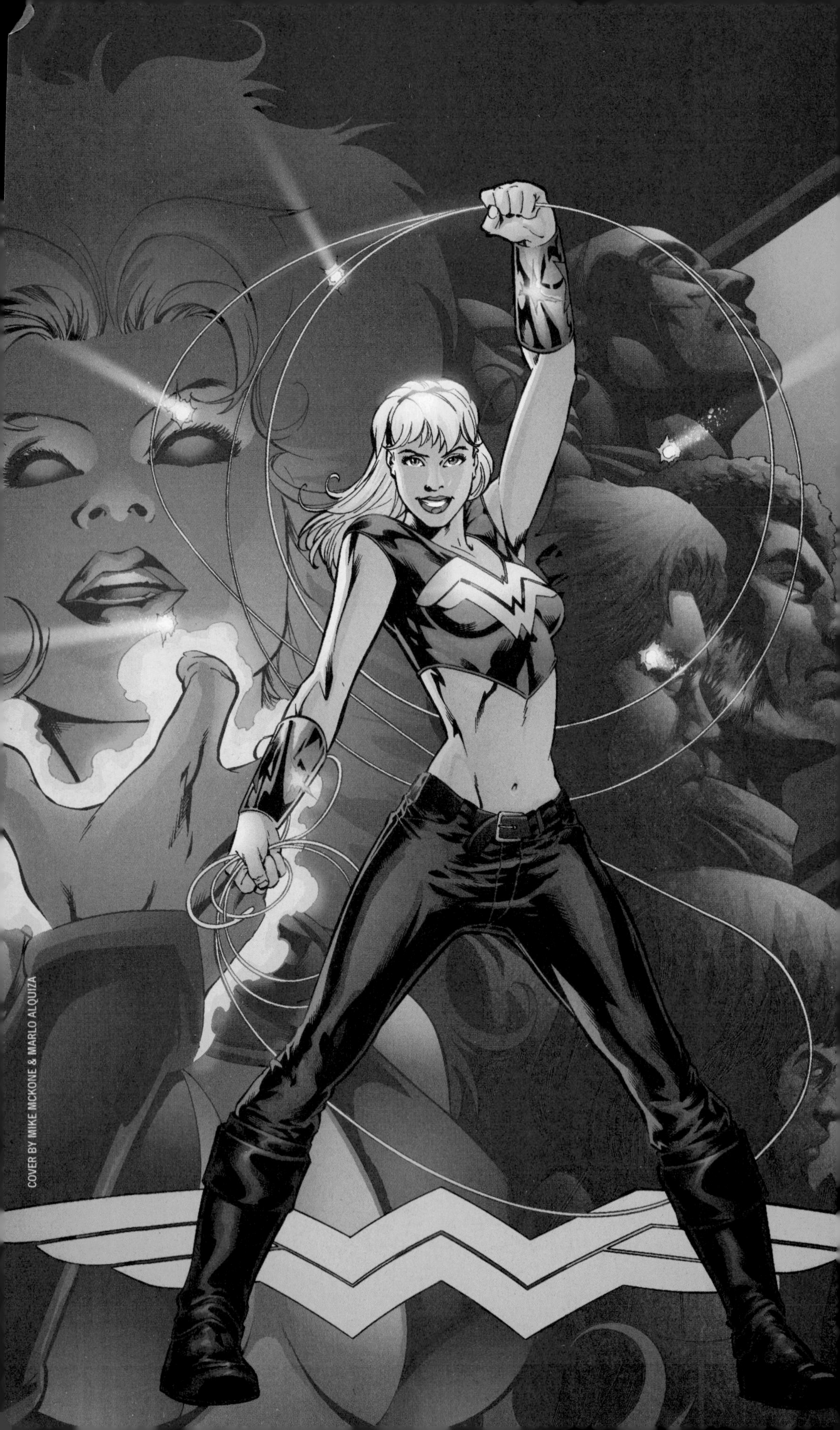
COVER BY MIKE MCKONE & MARLO ALQUIZA

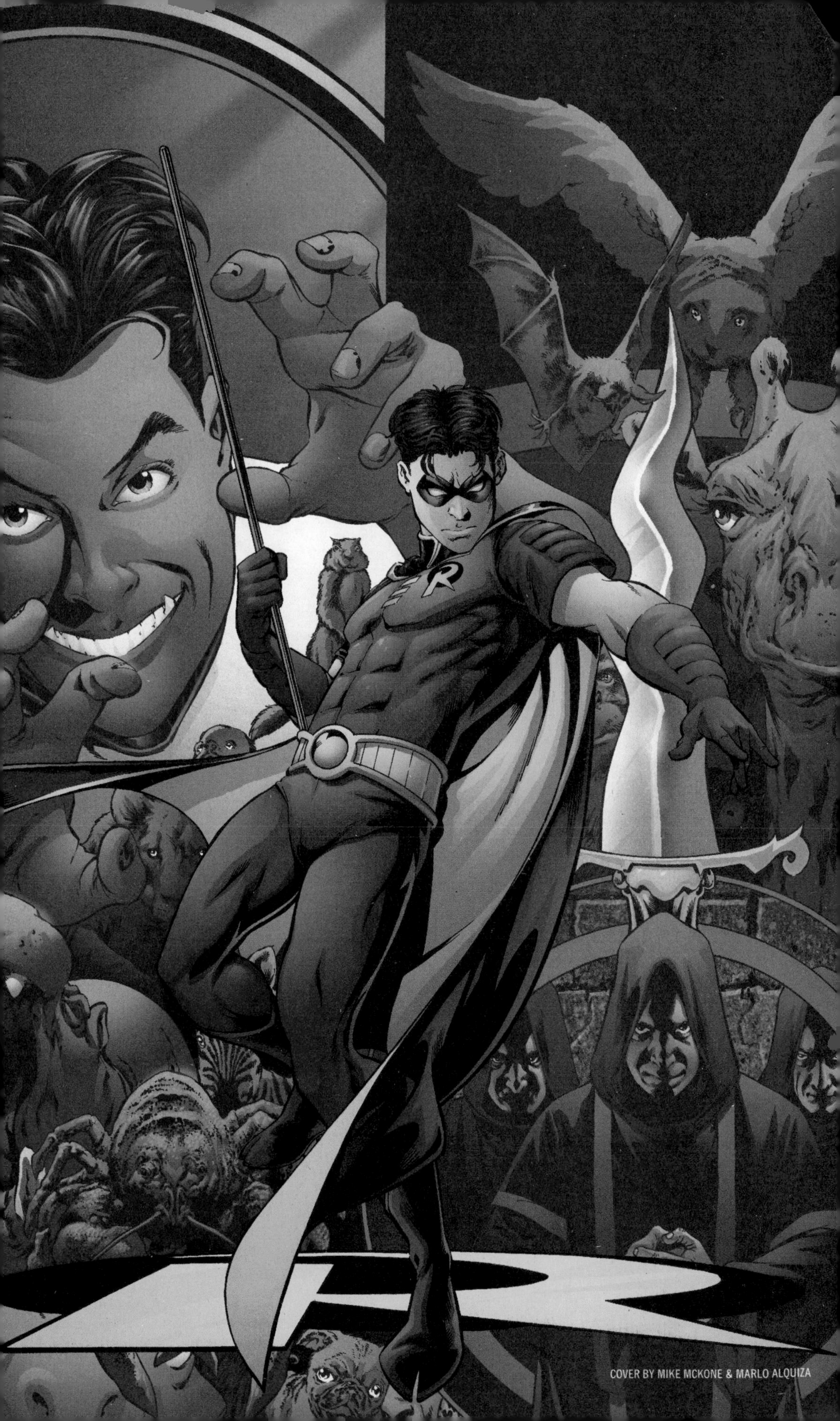

COVER BY MIKE MCKONE & MARLO ALQUIZA

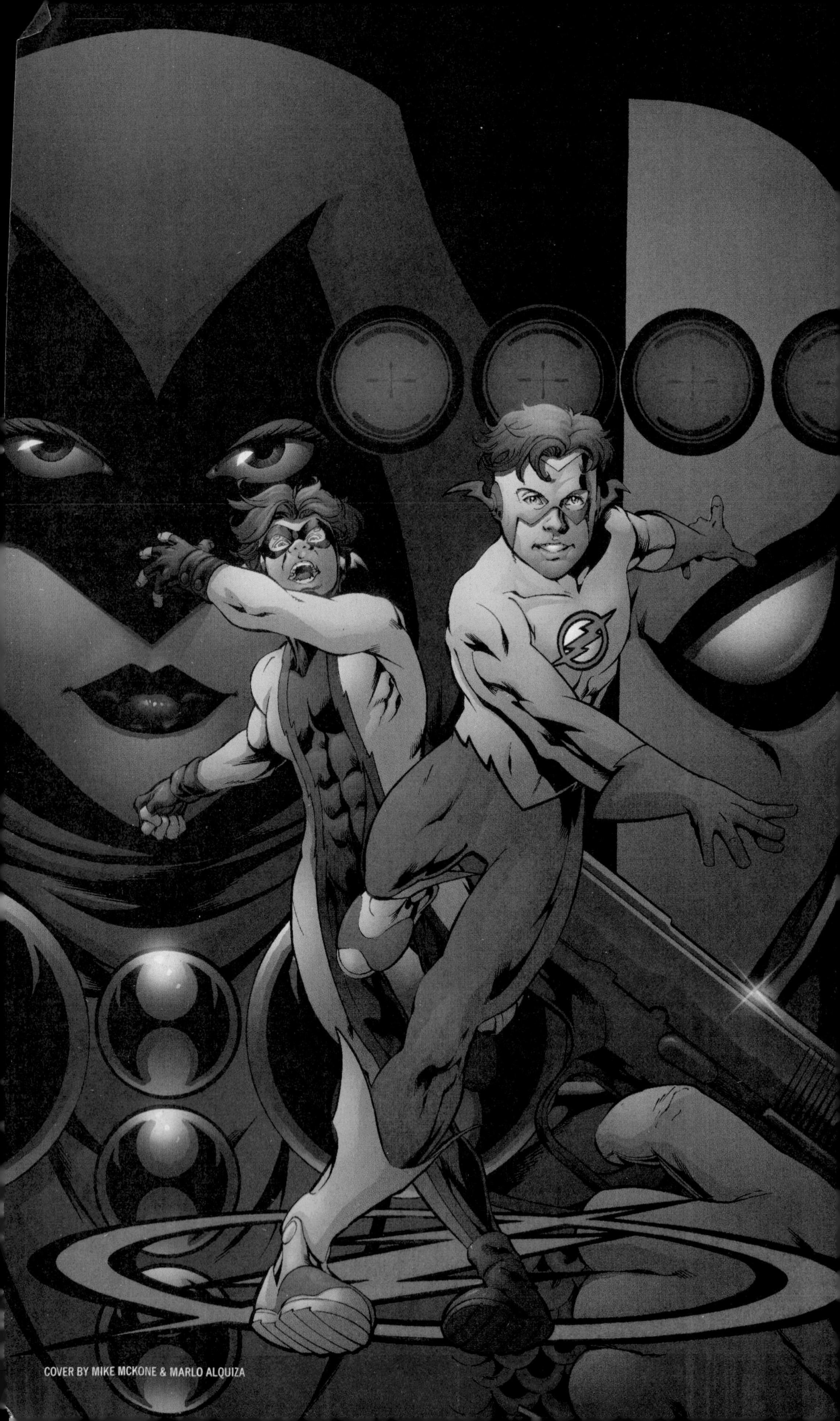

COVER BY MIKE MCKONE & MARLO ALQUIZA

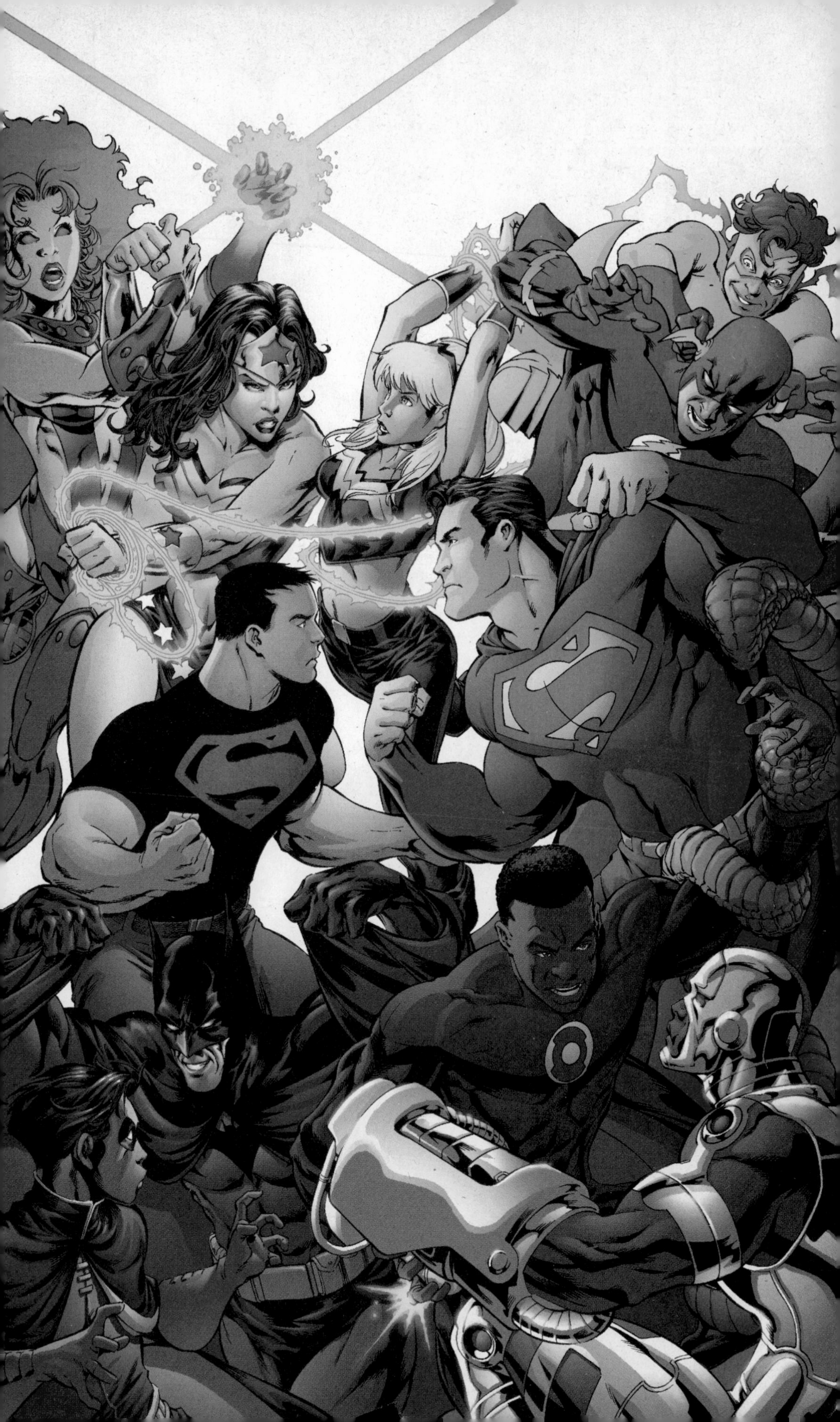

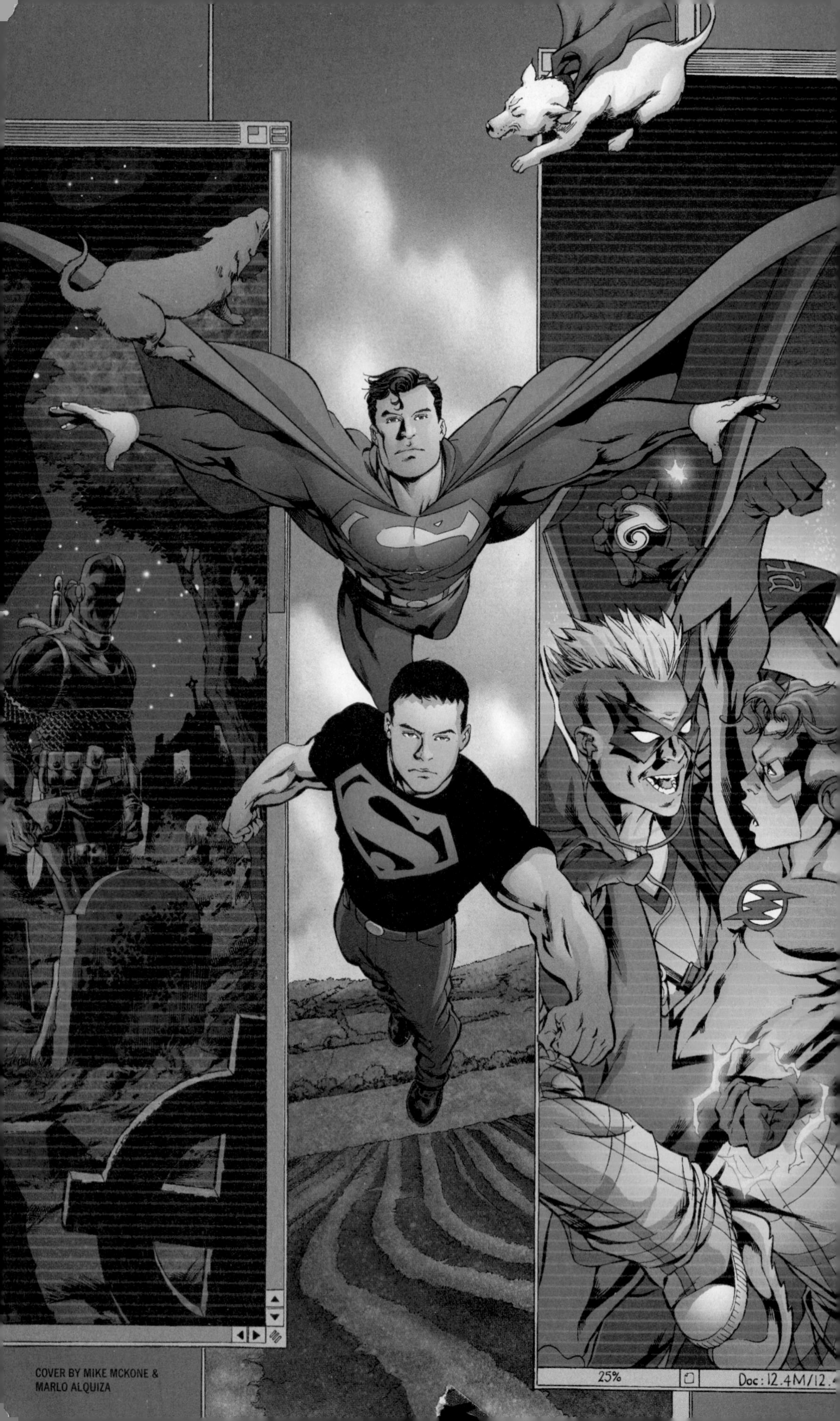
25%
Doc: 12.4M/12.

COVER BY MIKE MCKONE &
MARLO ALQUIZA

Mike McKone's Sketchbook

England's Mike McKone needed to rethink the look of the Titans before embarking on the first issue. Some, like Robin, didn't need any changes at all while Superboy needed some serious attention. Here's a look at the creative process.

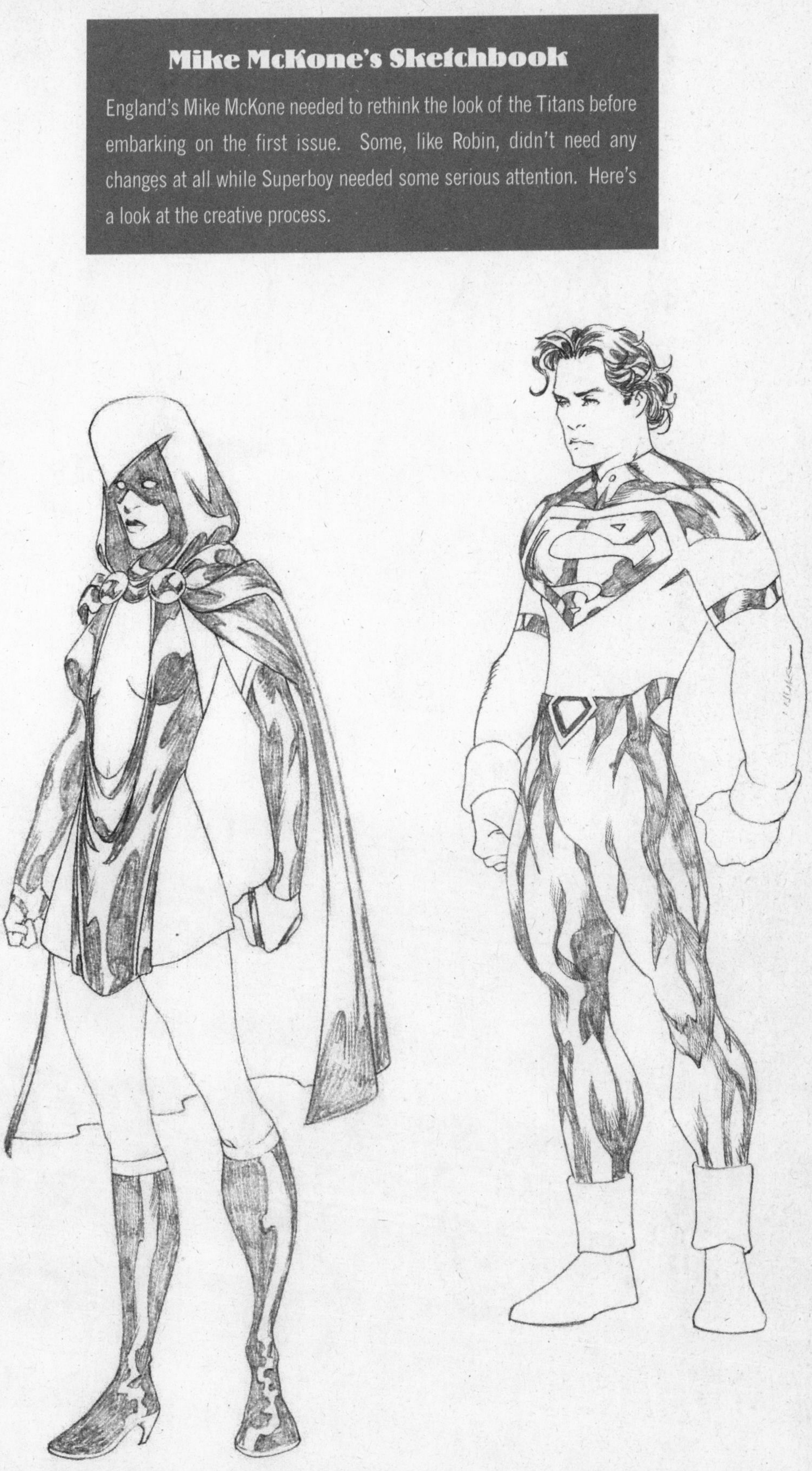

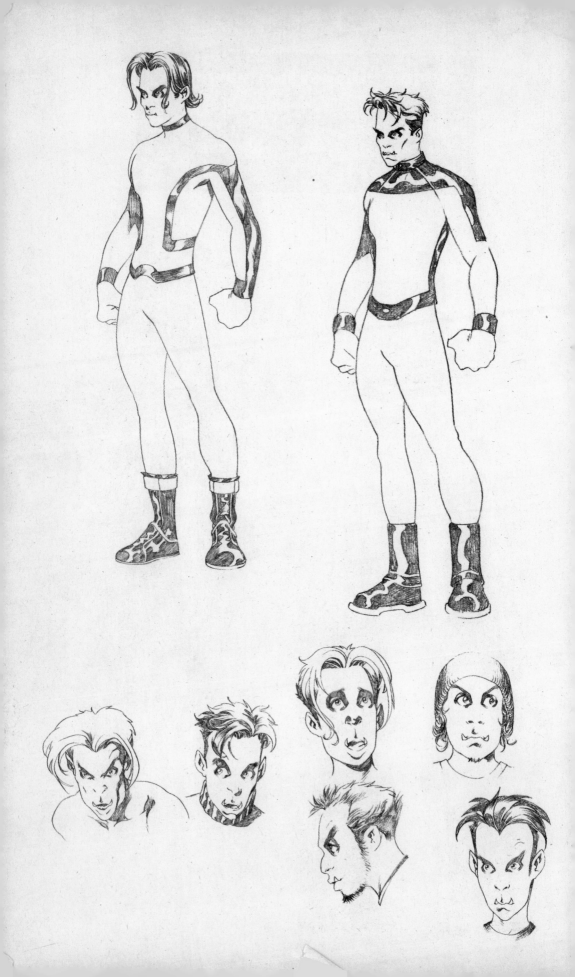

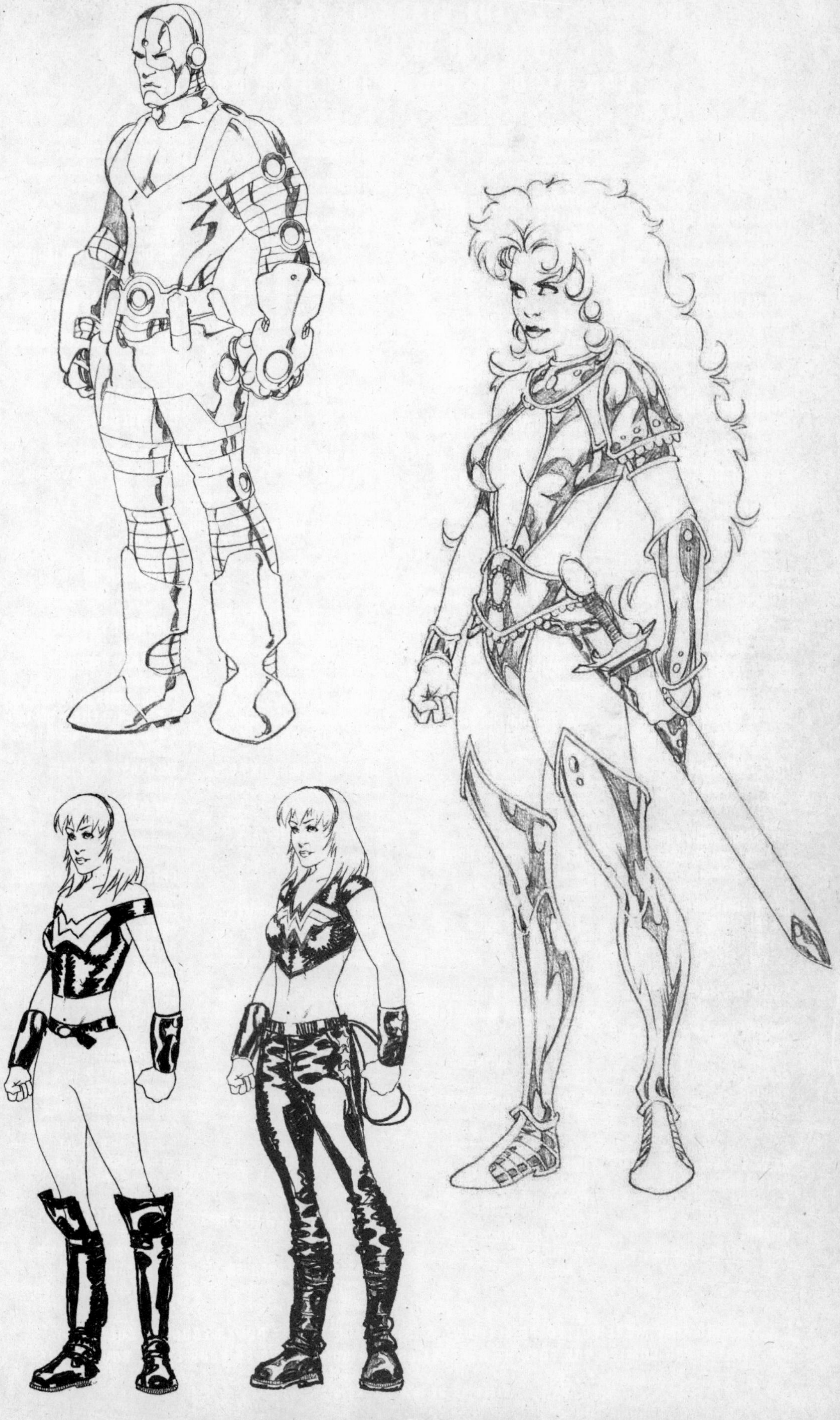

THE STARS OF THE
DC UNIVERSE
CAN ALSO BE FOUND IN THESE BOOKS:

GRAPHIC NOVELS

ENEMY ACE: WAR IDYLL
George Pratt

THE FLASH: LIFE STORY OF THE FLASH
M. Waid/B. Augustyn/G. Kane/
J. Staton/T. Palmer

GREEN LANTERN: FEAR ITSELF
Ron Marz/Brad Parker

THE POWER OF SHAZAM!
Jerry Ordway

WONDER WOMAN: AMAZONIA
William Messner-Loebs/
Phil Winslade

COLLECTIONS

THE GREATEST 1950s STORIES EVER TOLD
Various writers and artists

THE GREATEST TEAM-UP STORIES EVER TOLD
Various writers and artists

AQUAMAN: TIME AND TIDE
Peter David/Kirk Jarvinen/
Brad Vancata

DC ONE MILLION
Various writers and artists

THE FINAL NIGHT
K. Kesel/S. Immonen/
J. Marzan/various

THE FLASH: BORN TO RUN
M. Waid/T. Peyer/G. LaRocque/
H. Ramos/various

GREEN LANTERN: A NEW DAWN
R. Marz/D. Banks/R. Tanghal/
various

GREEN LANTERN: BAPTISM OF FIRE
Ron Marz/Darryl Banks/
various

GREEN LANTERN: EMERALD KNIGHTS
Ron Marz/Darryl Banks/
various

HAWK & DOVE
Karl and Barbara Kesel/
Rob Liefeld

HITMAN
Garth Ennis/John McCrea

HITMAN: LOCAL HEROES
G. Ennis/J. McCrea/
C. Ezquerra/S. Pugh

HITMAN: TEN THOUSAND BULLETS
Garth Ennis/John McCrea

IMPULSE: RECKLESS YOUTH
Mark Waid/various

JACK KIRBY'S FOREVER PEOPLE
Jack Kirby/various

JACK KIRBY'S NEW GODS
Jack Kirby/various

JACK KIRBY'S MISTER MIRACLE
Jack Kirby/various

JUSTICE LEAGUE: A NEW BEGINNING
K. Giffen/J.M. DeMatteis/
K. Maguire/various

JUSTICE LEAGUE: A MIDSUMMER'S NIGHTMARE
M. Waid/F. Nicieza/J. Johnson/
D. Robertson/various

JLA: AMERICAN DREAMS
G. Morrison/H. Porter/J. Dell/
various

JLA: JUSTICE FOR ALL
G. Morrison/M. Waid/H. Porter/
J. Dell/various

JUSTICE LEAGUE OF AMERICA: THE NAIL
Alan Davis/Mark Farmer

JLA: NEW WORLD ORDER
Grant Morrison/
Howard Porter/John Dell

JLA: ROCK OF AGES
G. Morrison/H. Porter/J. Dell/
various

JLA: STRENGTH IN NUMBERS
G. Morrison/M. Waid/H. Porter/
J. Dell/various

JLA: WORLD WITHOUT GROWN-UPS
T. Dezago/T. Nauck/H. Ramos/
M. McKone/various

JLA/TITANS: THE TECHNIS IMPERATIVE
D. Grayson/P. Jimenez/
P. Pelletier/various

JLA: YEAR ONE
M. Waid/B. Augustyn/
B. Kitson/various

KINGDOM COME
Mark Waid/Alex Ross

LEGENDS: THE COLLECTED EDITION
J. Ostrander/L. Wein/J. Byrne/
K. Kesel

LOBO'S GREATEST HITS
Various writers and artists

LOBO: THE LAST CZARNIAN
Keith Giffen/Alan Grant/
Simon Bisley

LOBO'S BACK'S BACK
K. Giffen/A. Grant/S. Bisley/
C. Alamy

MANHUNTER: THE SPECIAL EDITION
Archie Goodwin/Walter Simonson

THE RAY: IN A BLAZE OF POWER
Jack C. Harris/Joe Quesada/
Art Nichols

THE SPECTRE: CRIMES AND PUNISHMENTS
John Ostrander/Tom Mandrake

STARMAN: SINS OF THE FATHER
James Robinson/Tony Harris/
Wade von Grawbadger

STARMAN: NIGHT AND DAY
James Robinson/Tony Harris/
Wade von Grawbadger

STARMAN: TIMES PAST
J. Robinson/O. Jimenez/
L. Weeks/various

STARMAN: A WICKED INCLINATION...
J. Robinson/T. Harris/
W. von Grawbadger/various

UNDERWORLD UNLEASHED
M. Waid/H. Porter/
P. Jimenez/various

WONDER WOMAN: THE CONTEST
William Messner-Loebs/
Mike Deodato, Jr.

WONDER WOMAN: SECOND GENESIS
John Byrne

WONDER WOMAN: LIFELINES
John Byrne

DC/MARVEL: CROSSOVER CLASSICS II
Various writers and artists

DC VERSUS MARVEL/ MARVEL VERSUS DC
R. Marz/P. David/D. Jurgens/
C. Castellini/various

THE AMALGAM AGE OF COMICS: THE DC COMICS COLLECTION
Various writers and artists

RETURN TO THE AMALGAM AGE OF COMICS: THE DC COMICS COLLECTION
Various writers and artists

OTHER COLLECTIONS OF INTEREST

CAMELOT 3000
Mike W. Barr/Brian Bolland/
various

RONIN
Frank Miller

WATCHMEN
Alan Moore/Dave Gibbons

ARCHIVE EDITIONS

THE FLASH ARCHIVES Volume 1
(FLASH COMICS 104, SHOWCASE
4, 8, 13, 14, THE FLASH 105-108)
J. Broome/C. Infantino/J. Giella/
various
THE FLASH ARCHIVES Volume 2
(THE FLASH 109-116)
J.Broome/C. Infantino/J. Giella/
various

GREEN LANTERN ARCHIVES Volume 1
(SHOWCASE 22-23,
GREEN LANTERN 1-5)
GREEN LANTERN ARCHIVES Volume 2
(GREEN LANTERN 6-13)
All by J. Broome/G. Kane/
J. Giella/various

SHAZAM ARCHIVES Volume 1
(WHIZ COMICS 2-15)
SHAZAM ARCHIVES Volume 2
(SPECIAL EDITION COMICS 1,
CAPTAIN MARVEL ADVENTURES 1,
WHIZ COMICS 15-20)
All by B. Parker/C.C. Beck/
J. Simon/J. Kirby/various

THE NEW TEEN TITANS Volume 1
(DC COMICS PRESENTS 26,
THE NEW TITANS 1-8)
Marv Wolfman/George Pérez/
various

TO FIND MORE COLLECTED EDITIONS AND MONTHLY COMIC BOOKS FROM DC COMICS,
CALL 1-888-COMIC BOOK FOR THE NEAREST COMICS SHOP OR GO TO YOUR LOCAL BOOK STORE.

Visit us at www.dccomics.com

DCU0011